The Collected Essays, Journalism
and Letters of George Orwell

---

# MY COUNTRY RIGHT OR LEFT
## 1940–1943

# II

*A BBC Photograph*

George Orwell in 1943

The Collected Essays, Journalism
and Letters of George Orwell

# MY COUNTRY RIGHT
# OR LEFT
## 1940-1943

# II

Edited by
**Sonia Orwell**
and
**Ian Angus**

A HARVEST/HBJ BOOK
HARCOURT BRACE JOVANOVICH
NEW YORK AND LONDON

ISBN 0-15-618621-7

Library of Congress Catalog Card Number: 68–12591

CDEFGHIJ

Printed in the United States of America

# Contents

*War-time Diaries*

# Acknowledgements

The editors wish to express their grateful thanks to the following institutions and libraries, their trustees, curators and staffs for their co-operation and valuable help and for making copies of Orwell material available: Sir Frank Francis, Director and Principal Librarian of the British Museum (for: II: 37; III: 105; IV: 8); Dr John D. Gordan, Curator of the Henry W. and Albert A. Berg Collection of the New York Public Library, Astor, Lenox and Tilden Foundations (for: I: 18, 22, 23, 31, 33, 36, 38, 48, 50–2, 54, 58, 60, 61, 73, 75, 76, 86, 92, 98, 108, 112, 116, 121, 124, 128, 133, 139, 140, 141, 146, 154; III: 53, 97, 106; IV: 29, 59, 92, 95, 100, 106, 107, 110, 115, 121, 126, 136, 137, 142, 144, 159, 164, 165); Dr Warren Roberts, Director of the Humanities Research Center, University of Texas (for: I: 65, 66, 79, 102, 122, 123, 161; II: 4, 6, 10, 50; III: 52); S. C. Sutton, Librarian and Keeper of India Office Records (for: I: 115); Robert L. Collison, Librarian of the BBC Library (for: II: 38, 39, 52); Dr G. Chandler, Librarian of Liverpool City Library (for: I: 94); Wilbur Smith, Head of the Department of Special Collections, Library of the University of California, Los Angeles (for: I: 84); Anne Abley, Librarian of St Antony's College, Oxford (for: IV: 31, 32); and J.W. Scott, Librarian of University College London, for the material in the George Orwell Archive.

We are also deeply indebted to all those recipients of letters from Orwell, or their executors, who have been kind enough to make available the correspondence published in these volumes.

We would like to thank the following publications for permission to reproduce material first published in their pages: *Commentary*; *Encounter*; the *Evening Standard*; *Forward*; *Life*; the *Listener*; the *London Magazine*; the *Manchester Evening News*; the *New Leader* (NY); the *New Statesman and Nation*; the *New Yorker*; the *New York Times Book Review*; the *Observer*; *Partisan Review*; *Peace News*; the

*Socialist Leader*; *Time and Tide*; *The Times*; *Tribune*; *Wiadomosci*.

We would like to thank the following for allowing us to use material whose copyright they own: the executors of the late Frank Richards for his "Reply to George Orwell" in *Horizon*; H.W. Wilson & Co. for Orwell's entry in *Twentieth Century Authors*; George Allen & Unwin Ltd for "The Rediscovery of Europe" from *Talking to India*; Professor George Woodcock and D.S. Savage for their contributions to the controversy "Pacifism and the War" in *Partisan Review*; Dr Alex Comfort for his contribution to the same controversy and for his "Letter to an American Visitor" in *Tribune*; William Collins Sons & Co. Ltd for *The English People*; the executors of the late James Agate for his contribution to the controversy in the *Manchester Evening News*; the executors of Gerard Manley Hopkins and the Oxford University Press for "Felix Randal"; Elek Books Ltd for the Introduction to Jack London's *Love Of Life*; Eyre & Spottiswoode Ltd for the Introduction to Leonard Merrick's *The Position of Peggy Harper* and the executors of the late Konni Zilliacus for his letters to *Tribune*.

We would like to thank the following for their co-operation and invaluable help; Mrs Evelyn Anderson, the Hon. David Astor, Frank D. Barber, Dennis Collings, Dr Alex Comfort, Jack Common, Lettice Cooper, Stafford Cottman, Humphrey Dakin, Mrs John Deiner, Mrs William Dunn, Mrs T.S. Eliot, Dr McDonald Emslie, Faber and Faber Ltd, Mr and Mrs Francis Fierz, Roy Fuller, T.R. Fyvel, Livia Gollancz, Victor Gollancz Ltd, Mrs Arthur Goodman, A.S.F. Gow, James Hanley, Rayner Heppenstall, Inez Holden, Mrs Humphry House, Mrs Lydia Jackson, Frank Jellinek, Dr Shirley E. Jones, Jon Kimche, Denys King-Farlow, Arthur Koestler, Mrs Georges Kopp, James Laughlin, F.A. Lea, John Lehmann, John McNair, Michael Meyer, Henry Miller, Raymond Mortimer, Mrs Middleton Murry, Mrs Rosalind Obermeyer, Laurence O'Shaughnessy, *Partisan Review*, Professor R.S. Peters, Ruth Pitter, Joyce Pritchard, Philip Rahv, Sir Herbert Read, Vernon Richards, the Rev. Herbert Rogers, the Hon. Sir Steven Runciman, Brenda Salkeld, John Sceats, Roger Senhouse, Stephen Spender, Oliver Stallybrass, Professor Gleb Struve, Julian Symons, F.J. Warburg and Professor George Woodcock. We would also like to thank: Angus Calder (for allowing us to consult his unpublished thesis on the Common Wealth Party); Howard Fink (for allowing us to consult his unpublished *Chronology of Orwell's Loci and Activities*); and I.R. Willison (whose *George*

*Orwell: Some Materials for a Bibliography*, School of Librarianship, London University, 1953, was indispensable).

Finally, this edition would not have been possible but for the patient and understanding editorial help of Aubrey Davis and the support and help of the Library staff of University College London, particularly that of J.W. Scott, the Librarian, Margaret Skerl, Karen Bishop, Mrs Michael Kraushaar and Mrs Gordon Leitch.

# A Note on the Editing

The contents are arranged in order of publication except where the time lag between writing and appearance in print is unusually large, when we have chosen the date of writing. There are one or two rare exceptions to this rule, generally made for the sake of illustrating the development in Orwell's thought, but a note at the end of each article or review states when, and in which publication, it appeared first. If it was not published or the date of writing has determined its position the date of writing is given. Where there is no mention of a periodical at the end of an article, it has never been published before. "Why I Write", written in 1946, has been placed at the beginning of Volume I, as it seems a suitable introduction to the whole collection. Where an article was reprinted in the major collections of his writing, this has been indicated and the following abbreviations used for the various books: CE, *Collected Essays*; CrE, *Critical Essays*; DD, *Dickens, Dali and Others*; EYE, *England Your England*; ITW, *Inside the Whale*; OR, *The Orwell Reader*; SE, *Shooting an Elephant*; SJ, *Such, Such Were the Joys*.

Any title in square brackets at the head of an article or review has been supplied by us. All the others are either Orwell's own or those of the editors of the publication in question. He certainly wrote his own titles for his *Tribune* pieces: some of the others read as if he had written them but with most it is hard to tell and there is no way of finally checking.

Only when the article has never been printed before have we had the manuscript to work from and none of these were revised by Orwell as they would have been had he published them. With everything else we have had to use the text as it appeared in print. As anyone who has ever done any journalism or book reviewing knows, this means the text which appears here may well be slightly, if not very, different from the text Orwell originally wrote. Editors cut, printers make errors which are not thought of as very important in journalism, and it is only when the writer wants to reprint his pieces in book form that he bothers to restore the cuts, correct the errors and generally prepare them to survive in more lasting form: the reader therefore should bear in mind that they might well be very different if Orwell himself had revised them for re-publication. Both to these previously printed essays and journalism and to the hitherto unpublished articles and diaries we have given a uniform style in spelling, quotation marks and punctuation.

The letters were written, nearly always in haste, with scant attention to style and hardly any to punctuation; but throughout them we have corrected spelling mistakes, regularised the punctuation and have put book and periodical titles in italics. In a few cases postscripts of an unimportant nature have been omitted without indication. Otherwise cuts in both the letters and the journalism have been indicated by three dots, with a fourth dot to indicate a period. The same method was used by Orwell for indicating omissions when abridging excerpts he was quoting in reviews and essays, but as we have not made cuts in any of these excerpts there should be no confusion between our cuts and Orwell's own.

Orwell's "As I Please" column often consisted of two or more sections each devoted to a specific topic. Whenever one of the self-contained sections has been entirely omitted, this has not been indicated, but any cut made within a section is indicated by the usual three or four dots.

George Orwell never legally changed his name from Eric Blair and all the friends he made when young knew him and addressed him as Eric Blair. Later on new friends and acquaintances knew him and addressed him as George Orwell. In his letters he signs himself by the name his correspondent used. His earlier articles were signed E.A. Blair or Eric Blair and we have indicated these. From the moment this name is dropped in his published writing it is entirely signed George Orwell. Where a footnote deals with a period or a situation in which he would have looked upon himself primarily as Eric Blair we have referred to him by this name.

As this is an Anglo-American edition, many of the footnotes have been provided for the benefit of American readers and contain information we know to be familiar to English readers. We have put in the minimum of footnotes. This is largely because of the great difficulty of annotating the history of the period during which he wrote. It is still too recent for standard histories of it to exist and the events and people he discussed are often still the subjects of fierce polemic making it difficult to give an "objective" footnote. We have only footnoted the text in some detail where he talks about people or events in his personal life or where there is a reference to some topic about which the reader could find nothing in any existing book of reference. The numbers in the cross-references in the footnotes refer to items, not pages.

The Editors

1940

14.3.42. I reopen this diary after an interval of about 6 months, the war being once again in a new phase.

The actual date of Cripps's departure for India was not given out, but presumably he has gone by this time. Ordinary public opinion here seems gloomy about his departure. A frequent comment — "They've done it to get him out of the way" (which is also one of the reasons alleged by the German wireless). This is very silly & reflects the provincialism of English people who can't grasp that India is of any importance. Better-informed people are pessimistic because the non-publication of the government's terms to India indicates almost certainly that they are not good terms. Impossible to discover what powers Cripps has got. Those who may know something will disclose nothing & one can draw hints out of them only by indirect means. Eg. I propose in my newsletters, have been instructed to give Cripps a build-up, to build him up as a political extremist. This draws the warning, "don't go too far in that direction", which raises the presumption that the higher-ups haven't much hope of full independence being offered to India.

Rumours of all descriptions flying round. Many people

# 1. New Words

At present the formation of new words is a slow process (I have
read somewhere that English gains about six and loses about four
words a year) and no new words are deliberately coined except
as names for material objects. Abstract words are never coined at all,
though old words (e.g. "condition", "reflex" etc) are sometimes
twisted into new meanings for scientific purposes. What I am going
to suggest here is that it would be quite feasible to invent a vocabulary, perhaps amounting to several thousands of words, which would
deal with parts of our experience now practically unamenable to
language. There are several obvious objections to the idea, and I will
deal with these as they arise. The first step is to indicate the kind of
purpose for which new words are needed.

Everyone who thinks at all has noticed that our language is
practically useless for describing anything that goes on inside the
brain. This is so generally recognised that writers of high skill (e.g.
Trollope and Mark Twain) will start their autobiographies by saying
that they do not intend to describe their inner life, because it is of
its nature indescribable. So soon as we are dealing with anything
that is not concrete or visible (and even there to a great extent—
look at the difficulty of describing anyone's appearance) we find
that words are no liker to the reality than chessmen to living beings.
To take an obvious case which will not raise side-issues, consider a
dream. How do you describe a dream? Clearly you *never* describe
it, because no words that convey the atmosphere of dreams exist
in our language. Of course, you can give a crude approximation of
some of the major facts in a dream. You can say "I dreamed that
I was walking down Regent Street with a porcupine wearing a
bowler hat" etc, but this is no real description of the dream. And
even if a psychologist interprets your dream in terms of "symbols",
he is still going largely by guesswork; for the *real* quality of the
dream, the quality that gave the porcupine its sole significance, is

outside the world of words. In fact, describing a dream is like translating a poem into the language of one of Bohn's cribs; it is a paraphrase which is meaningless unless one knows the original.

I chose dreams as an instance that would not be disputed, but if it were only dreams that were indescribable, the matter might not be worth bothering about. But, as has been pointed out over and over again, the waking mind is not so different from the dreaming mind as it appears—or as we like to pretend that it appears. It is true that most of our waking thoughts are "reasonable"—that is, there exists in our minds a kind of chessboard upon which thoughts move logically and verbally; we use this part of our minds for any straightforward intellectual problem, and we get into the habit of thinking (i.e. thinking in our chessboard moments) that it is the whole of the mind. But obviously it is not the whole. The disordered, un-verbal world belonging to dreams is never quite absent from our minds, and if any calculation were possible I dare say it would be found that quite half the volume of our waking thoughts were of this order. Certainly the dream-thoughts take a hand even when we are trying to think verbally, they influence the verbal thoughts, and it is largely they that make our inner life valuable. Examine your thought at any casual moment. The main movement in it will be a stream of nameless things—so nameless that one hardly knows whether to call them thoughts, images or feelings. In the first place there are the objects you see and the sounds you hear, which are in themselves describable in words, but which as soon as they enter your mind become something quite different and totally indescribable.[1] And besides this there is the dream-life which your mind unceasingly creates for itself—and though most of this is trivial and soon forgotten, it contains things which are beautiful, funny, etc beyond anything that ever gets into words. In a way this un-verbal part of your mind is even the most important part, for it is the source of nearly all *motives*. All likes and dislikes, all aesthetic feeling, all notions of right and wrong (aesthetic and moral considerations are in any case inextricable) spring from feelings which are generally admitted to be subtler than words. When you are asked "Why do you do, or not do, so and so?" you are invariably aware that your

[1] The mind, that ocean where each kind
Doth straight its own resemblance find,
Yet it creates, transcending these,
Far other worlds and other seas, etc. [Author's footnote.]

*real* reason will not go into words, even when you have no wish to conceal it; consequently you rationalise your conduct, more or less dishonestly. I don't know whether everyone would admit this, and it is a fact that some people seem unaware of being influenced by their inner life, or even of having any inner life. I notice that many people never laugh when they are alone, and I suppose that if a man does not laugh when he is alone his inner life must be relatively barren. Still, every at all individual man has an inner life, and is aware of the practical impossibility of understanding others or being understood—in general, of the star-like isolation in which human beings live. Nearly all literature is an attempt to escape from this isolation by roundabout means, the direct means (words in their primary meanings) being almost useless.

"Imaginative" writing is as it were a flank-attack upon positions that are impregnable from the front. A writer attempting anything that is not coldly "intellectual" can do very little with words in their primary meanings. He gets his effect if at all by using words in a tricky roundabout way, relying on their cadences and so forth, as in speech he would rely upon tone and gesture. In the case of poetry this is too well known to be worth arguing about. No one with the smallest understanding of poetry supposes that

> The mortal moon hath her eclipse endured,
> And the sad augurs mock their own presage

really *means* what the words "mean" in their dictionary-sense. (The couplet is said to refer to Queen Elizabeth having got over her grand climacteric safely.) The dictionary-meaning has, as nearly always, *something* to do with the real meaning, but not more than the "anecdote" of a picture has to do with its design. And it is the same with prose, *mutatis mutandis*. Consider a novel, even a novel which has ostensibly nothing to do with the inner life—what is called a "straight story". Consider *Manon Lescaut*. Why does the author invent this long rigmarole about an unfaithful girl and a runaway abbé? Because he has a certain feeling, vision, whatever you like to call it, and knows, possibly after experiment, that it is no use trying to convey this vision by describing it as one would describe a crayfish for a book of zoology. But by *not* describing it, by inventing something else (in this case a picaresque novel: in another age he would choose another form) he can convey it, or part of it. The art of writing is in fact largely the perversion of words, and I would even say that the less obvious this perversion is, the more thoroughly it has been done. For a writer who *seems* to twist words out of their meanings (e.g. Gerard Manley Hopkins) is really, if one looks closely, making a desperate attempt to use them straightforwardly. Whereas a writer who seems to have no tricks whatever, for instance the old ballad writers, is making an especially subtle flank-attack, though, in the case of the ballad-writers, this is no doubt unconscious. Of course one hears a lot of cant to the effect that all good art is "objective" and every true artist keeps his inner life to himself. But the people who say this do not mean it. All they mean is that they want the inner life to be expressed by an exceptionally roundabout method, as in the ballad or the "straight story".

The weakness of the roundabout method, apart from its difficulty, is that it usually fails. For anyone who is not a considerable artist (possibly for them too) the lumpishness of words results in constant falsification. Is there anyone who has ever written so much as a love letter in which he felt that he had said exactly what he intended? A writer falsifies himself both intentionally and unintentionally. Intentionally, because the accidental qualities of words constantly tempt and frighten him away from his true meaning. He gets an idea, begins trying to express it, and then, in the frightful mess of words that generally results, a pattern begins to form itself more or less accidentally. It is not by any means the pattern he wants, but it is at any rate not vulgar or disagreeable; it is "good art". He takes it, because "good art" is a more or less mysterious gift from heaven, and it seems a pity to waste it when it presents itself. Is not anyone with any degree of mental honesty conscious of telling lies all day long, both in talking and writing, simply because lies will fall into artistic shape when truth will not? Yet if words represented meanings as fully and accurately as height multiplied by base represents the area of a parallelogram, at least the *necessity* for lying would never exist. And in the mind of reader or hearer there are further falsifications, because, words not being a direct channel of thought, he constantly sees meanings which are not there. A good illustration of this is our supposed appreciation of foreign poetry. We know, from the "Vie Amoureuse du Docteur Watson" stuff of foreign critics, that true understanding of foreign literature is almost impossible; yet quite ignorant people profess to get, do get, vast pleasure out of poetry in foreign and even dead languages. Clearly the pleasure they derive may come from something the writer never intended, possibly from something that would make him squirm in his grave if he knew it was attributed to him. I say to myself *Vixi puellis nuper idoneus*, and I repeat this over and over for five minutes for the beauty of the word *idoneus*. Yet, considering the gulf of time and culture, and my ignorance of Latin, and the fact that no one even knows how Latin was pronounced, is it possible that the effect I am enjoying is the effect Horace was trying for? It is as though I were in ecstasies over the beauty of a picture, and all because of some splashes of paint which had accidentally got on to the canvas 200 years after it was painted. Notice, I am not saying that *art* would necessarily improve if words conveyed meaning more reliably. For all I know art thrives on the crudeness and vagueness of language. I am only criticising *words* in their supposed function as vehicles of thought. And it seems to me that from the point of view of exactitude and expressiveness our language has remained in the Stone Age.

The solution I suggest is to invent new words as deliberately as we would invent new parts for a motor-car engine. Suppose that a vocabulary existed which would accurately express the life of the mind, or a great part of it. Suppose that there need be no stultifying feeling that life is inexpressible, no jiggery-pokery with artistic tricks; expressing one's meaning simply [being] a matter of taking the right words and putting them in place, like working out an equation in algebra. I think the advantages of this would be obvious. It is less obvious, though, that to sit down and deliberately coin words is a common-sense proceeding. Before indicating a way in which satisfactory words might be coined, I had better deal with the objections which are bound to arise.

If you say to any thinking person "Let us form a society for the invention of new and subtler words", he will first of all object that it is the idea of a crank, and then probably say that our present words, properly handled, will meet all difficulties. (This last, of course, is only a theoretical objection. In practice everyone recognises the inadequacy of language—consider such expressions as "Words fail", "It wasn't what he said, it was the way he said it", etc.) But finally he will give you an answer something like this: "Things cannot be done in that pedantic way. Languages can only grow slowly, like flowers; you can't patch them up like pieces of machinery. Any *made-up* language must be characterless and lifeless —look at Esperanto, etc. The whole meaning of a word is in its slowly-acquired associations" etc.

In the first place, this argument, like most of the arguments produced when one suggests changing anything, is a long-winded way of saying that what is must be. Hitherto we have never set ourselves to the deliberate creation of words, and all living languages have grown slowly and haphazard; *therefore* language cannot grow otherwise. At present, when we want to say anything above the level of a geometrical definition, we are obliged to do conjuring tricks with sounds, associations etc; *therefore* this necessity is inherent in the nature of words. The *non sequitur* is obvious. And notice that when I suggest coining abstract words I am only suggesting an extension of our present practice. For we do now coin concrete words. Aeroplanes and bicycles are invented, and we invent names for them, which is the natural thing to do. It is only a step to coining names for the now unnamed things that exist in the mind. You say to me "Why do you dislike Mr Smith?" and I say "Because he is a liar, coward, etc" and I am almost certainly giving the wrong reason. In my own mind the answer runs "Because he is a —— kind of man", —— standing for something which I understand, and you would understand if I could tell it you. Why not find a name for ——? The only difficulty is to agree about *what* we are naming. But long before this difficulty arises, the reading, thinking type of man will have recoiled from such an idea as the invention of words. He will produce arguments like the one I indicated above, or others of a more or less sneering, question-begging kind. In reality all these arguments are humbug. The recoil comes from a deep unreasoned instinct, superstitious in origin. It is the feeling that any direct rational approach to one's difficulties, any attempt to solve the problems of life as one would solve an equation, can lead nowhere—more, is definitely *unsafe*. One can see this idea expressed everywhere in a roundabout way. All the bosh that is talked about our national genius for "muddling through", and all the squashy godless mysticism that is urged against any hardness and soundness of intellect, mean *au fond* that it is *safer not to think*. This feeling starts, I am certain, in the common belief of children that the air is full of avenging demons waiting to punish presumption.[1] In adults the belief survives as a fear of too rational

---

[1] The idea is that the demons will come down on you for being too self-confident. Thus children believe that if you hook a fish and say "Got him" before he is landed, he will escape; that if you put your pads on before it is your turn to bat you will be out first ball etc. Such beliefs often survive in adults.

thinking. I the Lord thy God am a jealous God, pride comes before a fall etc—and the most dangerous pride is the false pride of the intellect. David was punished because he numbered the people—i.e. because he used his intellect scientifically. Thus such an idea as, for instance, ectogenesis, apart from its possible effects upon the health of the race, family life etc, is felt to be *in itself* blasphemous. Similarly any attack on such a fundamental thing as language, an attack as it were on the very structure of our own minds, is blasphemy and therefore dangerous. To reform language is practically an interference with the work of God—though I don't say that anyone would put it quite in these words. This objection is important, because it would prevent most people from even considering such an idea as the reform of language. And of course the idea is useless unless undertaken by large numbers. For one man, or a clique, to try and make up a language, as I believe James Joyce is now doing, is as absurd as one man trying to play football alone. What is wanted is several thousands of gifted but normal people who would give themselves to word-invention as seriously as people now give themselves to Shakespearean research. Given these, I believe we could work wonders with language.

Now as to the means. One sees an instance of the successful invention of words, though crude and on a small scale, among the members of large families. All large families have two or three words peculiar to themselves—words which they have made up and which convey subtilised, non-dictionary meanings. They say "Mr Smith is a —— kind of man", using some home-made word, and the others understand perfectly; here then, within the limits of the family, exists an adjective filling one of the many gaps left by the dictionary. What makes it possible for the family to invent these words is the basis of their common experience. Without common experience, of course, no word can mean anything. If you say to me "What does bergamot smell like?" I say "Something like verbena", and so long as you know the smell of verbena you are somewhere near understanding me. The method in inventing words, therefore, is the method of analogy based on unmistakable common knowledge; one must have standards that can be referred to without any chance of misunderstanding, as one can refer to a physical

Adults are only less superstitious than children in proportion as they have more power over their environment. In predicaments where everyone is powerless (e.g. war, gambling) everyone is superstitious. [Author's footnote.]

thing like the smell of verbena. In effect it must come down to
giving words a physical (probably visible) existence. Merely *talking*
about definitions is futile; one can see this whenever it is attempted
to define one of the words used by literary critics (e.g. "sentimental",[1] "vulgar", "morbid" etc). All meaningless—or rather, having
a different meaning for every one who uses them. What is needed
is to *show* a meaning in some unmistakable form, and then, when
various people have identified it in their own minds and recognised
it as worth naming, to give it a name. The question is simply of
finding a way in which one can give thought an objective existence.

The thing that suggests itself immediately is the cinematograph.
Everyone must have noticed the extraordinary powers that are
latent in the film—the powers of distortion, of fantasy, in general
of escaping the restrictions of the physical world. I suppose it is
only from commercial necessity that the film has been used chiefly
for silly imitations of stage plays, instead of concentrating as it ought
on things that are beyond the stage. Properly used, the film is the
one possible medium for conveying mental processes. A dream,
for instance, as I said above, is totally indescribable in words, but it
can quite well be represented on the screen. Years ago I saw a film
of Douglas Fairbanks', part of which was a representation of a
dream. Most of it, of course, was silly joking about the dream
where you have no clothes on in public, but for a few minutes it
really was like a dream, in a manner that would have been impossible in words, or even in a picture, or, I imagine, in music. I
have seen the same kind of thing by flashes in other films. For
instance in *Dr Caligari*—a film, however, which was for the most
part merely silly, the fantastic element being exploited for its own
sake and not to convey any definite meaning. If one thinks of it,
there is very little in the mind that could not *somehow* be represented
by the strange distorting powers of the film. A millionaire with a
private cinematograph, all the necessary props and a troupe of
intelligent actors could, if he wished, make practically all of his
inner life known. He could explain the real reasons of his actions
instead of telling rationalised lies, point out the things that seemed
to him beautiful, pathetic, funny, etc—things that an ordinary

---

[1] I once began making a list of writers whom the critics called "sentimental".
In the end it included nearly every English writer. The word is in fact a meaningless symbol of hatred, like the bronze tripods in Homer which were given to
guests as a symbol of friendship. [Author's footnote.]

man has to keep locked up because there are no words to express them. In general, he could make other people understand him. Of course, it is not desirable that any one man, short of a genius, should make a show of his inner life. What is wanted is to discover the now nameless feelings that men have *in common*. All the powerful motives which will not go into words and which are a cause of constant lying and misunderstanding, could be tracked down, given visible form, agreed upon, and named. I am sure that the film, with its almost limitless powers of representation, could accomplish this in the hands of the right investigators, though putting thoughts into visible shape would not always be easy—in fact, at first it might be as difficult as any other art.

A note on the actual form new words ought to take. Suppose that several thousands of people with the necessary time, talents and money undertook to make additions to language; suppose that they managed to agree upon a number of new and necessary words; they would still have to guard against producing a mere Volapuk which would drop out of use as soon as it was invented. It seems to me probable that a word, even a not yet existing word, has as it were a natural form—or rather, various natural forms in various languages. If language were truly expressive there would be no need to play upon the sounds of words as we do now, but I suppose there must always be *some* correlation between the sound of a word and its meaning. An accepted (I believe) and plausible theory of the origin of language is this. Primitive man, before he had words, would naturally rely upon gesture, and like any other animal he would cry out at the moment of gesticulating, in order to attract attention. Now one instinctively makes the gesture that is appropriate to one's meaning, and all parts of the body follow suit including the tongue. Hence certain tongue-movements—i.e. certain sounds—would come to be associated with certain meanings. In poetry one can point to words which, apart from their direct meanings, regularly convey certain ideas by their sound. Thus: "Deeper than did ever *plummet* sound" (Shakespeare—more than once I think). "Past the *plunge* of *plummet*" (A.E. Housman). "The un*plumbed*, salt, estranging sea" (Matthew Arnold) etc. Clearly, apart from direct meanings, the sound plum- or plun- has something to do with bottomless oceans. Therefore in forming new words one would have to pay attention to appropriateness of sound as well as exactitude of meaning. It would not do, as at present, to clip a new word of any real novelty by making it out of old ones, but it also would not do to make it out of a mere arbitrary collection of letters. One would have to determine the natural form of the word. Like agreeing upon the actual meanings of the words, this would need the co-operation of a large number of people.

I have written all this down hastily, and when I read through it I see that there are weak patches in my argument and much of it is commonplace. To most people in any case the whole idea of re-forming language would seem either dilettantish or crankish. Yet it is worth considering what utter incomprehension exists between human beings—at least, between those who are not deeply intimate. At present, as Samuel Butler said, the best art (i.e. the most perfect thought-transference) must be "lived" from one person to another. It need not be so if our language were more adequate. It is curious that when our knowledge, the complication of our lives and there-fore (I think it must follow) our minds, develop so fast, language, the chief means of communication, should scarcely stir. For this reason I think that the idea of the deliberate invention of words is at least worth thinking over.

Written 1940?

## 2. Review

*Mein Kampf* by Adolf Hitler (unabridged translation)

It is a sign of the speed at which events are moving that Hurst and Blackett's unexpurgated edition of *Mein Kampf*, published only a year ago, is edited from a pro-Hitler angle. The obvious intention of the translator's preface and notes is to tone down the book's ferocity and present Hitler in as kindly a light as possible. For at that date Hitler was still respectable. He had crushed the German labour movement, and for that the property-owning classes were willing to forgive him almost anything. Both Left and Right concurred in the very shallow notion that National Socialism was merely a version of Conservatism.

Then suddenly it turned out that Hitler was not respectable after all. As one result of this, Hurst and Blackett's edition was reissued in a new jacket explaining that all profits would be devoted to the Red Cross. Nevertheless, simply on the internal evidence of *Mein*

*Kampf*, it is difficult to believe that any real change has taken place in Hitler's aims and opinions. When one compares his utterances of a year or so ago with those made fifteen years earlier, a thing that strikes one is the rigidity of his mind, the way in which his world-view *doesn't* develop. It is the fixed vision of a monomaniac and not likely to be much affected by the temporary manoeuvres of power politics. Probably, in Hitler's own mind, the Russo-German Pact represents no more than an alteration of time-table. The plan laid down in *Mein Kampf* was to smash Russia first, with the implied intention of smashing England afterwards. Now, as it has turned out, England has got to be dealt with first, because Russia was the more easily bribed of the two. But Russia's turn will come when England is out of the picture—that, no doubt, is how Hitler sees it. Whether it will turn out that way is of course a different question.

Suppose that Hitler's programme could be put into effect. What he envisages, a hundred years hence, is a continuous state of 250 million Germans with plenty of "living room" (i.e. stretching to Afghanistan or thereabouts), a horrible brainless empire in which, essentially, nothing ever happens except the training of young men for war and the endless breeding of fresh cannon-fodder. How was it that he was able to put this monstrous vision across? It is easy to say that at one stage of his career he was financed by the heavy industrialists, who saw in him the man who would smash the Socialists and Communists. They would not have backed him, however, if he had not talked a great movement into existence already. Again, the situation in Germany, with its seven million unemployed, was obviously favourable for demagogues. But Hitler could not have succeeded against his many rivals if it had not been for the attraction of his own personality, which one can feel even in the clumsy writing of *Mein Kampf*, and which is no doubt overwhelming when one hears his speeches. I should like to put it on record that I have never been able to dislike Hitler. Ever since he came to power—till then, like nearly everyone, I had been deceived into thinking that he did not matter—I have reflected that I would certainly kill him if I could get within reach of him, but that I could feel no personal animosity. The fact is that there is something deeply appealing about him. One feels it again when one sees his photographs—and I recommend especially the photograph at the beginning of Hurst and Blackett's edition, which shows Hitler in his early Brownshirt days. It is a pathetic, dog-like face, the face of a man suffering under intolerable wrongs. In a rather more manly way it reproduces the expression of innumerable pictures of Christ crucified, and there is little doubt that that is how Hitler sees himself. The initial, personal cause of his grievance against the universe can only be guessed at; but at any rate the grievance is there. He is the martyr, the victim, Prometheus chained to the rock, the self-sacrificing hero who fights single-handed against impossible odds. If he were killing a mouse he would know how to make it seem like a dragon. One feels, as with Napoleon, that he is fighting against destiny, that he *can't* win, and yet that he somehow deserves to. The attraction of such a pose is of course enormous; half the films that one sees turn upon some such theme.

Also he has grasped the falsity of the hedonistic attitude to life. Nearly all western thought since the last war, certainly all "progressive" thought, has assumed tacitly that human beings desire nothing beyond ease, security and avoidance of pain. In such a view of life there is no room, for instance, for patriotism and the military virtues. The Socialist who finds his children playing with soldiers is usually upset, but he is never able to think of a substitute for the tin soldiers; tin pacifists somehow won't do. Hitler, because in his own joyless mind he feels it with exceptional strength, knows that human beings *don't* only want comfort, safety, short working-hours, hygiene, birth-control and, in general, common sense; they also, at least intermittently, want struggle and self-sacrifice, not to mention drums, flags and loyalty-parades. However they may be as economic theories, Fascism and Nazism are psychologically far sounder than any hedonistic conception of life. The same is probably true of Stalin's militarised version of Socialism. All three of the great dictators have enhanced their power by imposing intolerable burdens on their peoples. Whereas Socialism, and even capitalism in a more grudging way, have said to people "I offer you a good time," Hitler has said to them "I offer you struggle, danger and death," and as a result a whole nation flings itself at his feet. Perhaps later on they will get sick of it and change their minds, as at the end of the last war. After a few years of slaughter and starvation "Greatest happiness of the greatest number" is a good slogan, but at this moment "Better an end with horror than a horror without end" is a winner. Now that we are fighting against the man who coined it, we ought not to underrate its emotional appeal.

# 3. Notes on the Way

Reading Mr Malcolm Muggeridge's brilliant and depressing book, *The Thirties*, I thought of a rather cruel trick I once played on a wasp. He was sucking jam on my plate, and I cut him in half. He paid no attention, merely went on with his meal, while a tiny stream of jam trickled out of his severed oesophagus. Only when he tried to fly away did he grasp the dreadful thing that had happened to him. It is the same with modern man. The thing that has been cut away is his soul, and there was a period—twenty years, perhaps—during which he did not notice it.

It was absolutely necessary that the soul should be cut away. Religious belief, in the form in which we had known it, had to be abandoned. By the nineteenth century it was already in essence a lie, a semi-conscious device for keeping the rich rich and the poor poor. The poor were to be contented with their poverty, because it would all be made up to them in the world beyond the grave, usually pictured as something mid-way between Kew Gardens and a jeweller's shop. Ten thousand a year for me, two pounds a week for you, but we are all the children of God. And through the whole fabric of capitalist society there ran a similar lie, which it was absolutely necessary to rip out.

Consequently there was a long period during which nearly every thinking man was in some sense a rebel, and usually a quite irresponsible rebel. Literature was largely the literature of revolt or of disintegration. Gibbon, Voltaire, Rousseau, Shelley, Byron, Dickens, Stendhal, Samuel Butler, Ibsen, Zola, Flaubert, Shaw, Joyce—in one way or another they are all of them destroyers, wreckers, saboteurs. For two hundred years we had sawed and sawed and sawed at the branch we were sitting on. And in the end, much more suddenly than anyone had foreseen, our efforts were rewarded, and down we came. But unfortunately there had been a little mistake. The thing at the bottom was not a bed of roses after all, it was a cesspool full of barbed wire.

It is as though in the space of ten years we had slid back into the Stone Age. Human types supposedly extinct for centuries, the dancing dervish, the robber chieftain, the Grand Inquisitor, have suddenly reappeared, not as inmates of lunatic asylums, but as the masters of the world. Mechanisation and a collective economy seemingly aren't enough. By themselves they lead merely to the nightmare we are now enduring: endless war and endless under-feeding for the sake of war, slave populations toiling behind barbed wire, women dragged shrieking to the block, cork-lined cellars where the executioner blows your brains out from behind. So it appears that amputation of the soul *isn't* just a simple surgical job, like having your appendix out. The wound has a tendency to go septic.

The gist of Mr Muggeridge's book is contained in two texts from *Ecclesiastes*: "Vanity of vanities, saith the preacher; all is vanity" and "Fear God, and keep His commandments: for this is the whole duty of man". It is a viewpoint that has gained a lot of ground lately, among people who would have laughed at it only a few years ago. We are living in a nightmare precisely *because* we have tried to set up an earthly paradise. We have believed in "progress", trusted to human leadership, rendered unto Caesar the things that are God's—that approximately is the line of thought.

Unfortunately Mr Muggeridge shows no sign of believing in God himself. Or at least he seems to take it for granted that this belief is vanishing from the human mind. There is not much doubt that he is right there, and if one assumes that no sanction can ever be effective except the supernatural one, it is clear what follows. There is no wisdom except in the fear of God; but nobody fears God; therefore there is no wisdom. Man's history reduces itself to the rise and fall of material civilisations, one Tower of Babel after another. In that case we can be pretty certain what is ahead of us. Wars and yet more wars, revolutions and counter-revolutions, Hitlers and super-Hitlers—and so downwards into abysses which are horrible to contemplate, though I rather suspect Mr Muggeridge of enjoying the prospect.

It must be about thirty years since Mr Hilaire Belloc, in his book *The Servile State*, foretold with astonishing accuracy the things that are happening now. But unfortunately he had no remedy to offer. He could conceive nothing between slavery and a return to small-ownership, which is obviously not going to happen and in fact cannot happen. There is [little] question now of averting a col-lectivist society. The only question is whether it is to be founded on willing co-operation or on the machine-gun. The Kingdom of Heaven, old style, has definitely failed, but on the other hand

"Marxist realism" has also failed, whatever it may achieve materially. Seemingly there is no alternative except the thing that Mr Muggeridge, and Mr F.A. Voigt, and the others who think like them, so earnestly warn us against: the much-derided "Kingdom of Earth", the concept of a society in which men know that they are mortal and are nevertheless willing to act as brothers.

Brotherhood implies a common father. Therefore it is often argued that men can never develop the sense of a community unless they believe in God. The answer is that in a half-conscious way most of them have developed it already. Man is not an individual, he is only a cell in an everlasting body, and he is dimly aware of it. There is no other way of explaining why it is that men will die in battle. It is nonsense to say that they only do it because they are driven. If whole armies had to be coerced, no war could ever be fought. Men die in battle—not gladly, of course, but at any rate voluntarily—because of abstractions called "honour", "duty", "patriotism" and so forth.

All that this really means is that they are aware of some organism greater than themselves, stretching into the future and the past, within which they feel themselves to be immortal. "Who dies if England live?" sounds like a piece of bombast, but if you alter "England" to whatever you prefer, you can see that it expresses one of the main motives of human conduct. People sacrifice themselves for the sake of fragmentary communities—nation, race, creed, class—and only become aware that they are not individuals in the very moment when they are facing bullets. A very slight increase of consciousness, and their sense of loyalty could be transferred to humanity itself, which is not an abstraction.

Mr Aldous Huxley's *Brave New World* was a good caricature of the hedonistic Utopia, the kind of thing that seemed possible and even imminent before Hitler appeared, but it had no relation to the actual future. What we are moving towards at this moment is something more like the Spanish Inquisition, and probably far worse, thanks to the radio and the secret police. There is very little chance of escaping it unless we can reinstate the belief in human brotherhood without the need for a "next world" to give it meaning. It is this that leads innocent people like the Dean of Canterbury to imagine that they have discovered true Christianity in Soviet Russia. No doubt they are only the dupes of propaganda, but what makes them so willing to be deceived is their knowledge that the Kingdom of Heaven has somehow got to be brought on to the surface of the earth. We have got to be the children of God, even though the God of the Prayer Book no longer exists.

The very people who have dynamited our civilisation have sometimes been aware of this. Marx's famous saying that "religion is the opium of the people" is habitually wrenched out of its context and given a meaning subtly but appreciably different from the one he gave it. Marx did not say, at any rate in that place, that religion is merely a dope handed out from above; he said that it is something the people create for themselves to supply a need that he recognised to be a real one. "Religion is the sigh of the soul in a soulless world. Religion is the opium of the people." What is he saying except that man does *not* live by bread alone, that hatred is *not* enough, that a world worth living in cannot be founded on "realism" and machine-guns? If he had foreseen how great his intellectual influence would be, perhaps he would have said it more often and more loudly.

*Time and Tide*, 6 April 1940

# 4. Letter to Rayner Heppenstall

> The Stores
> Wallington
> Nr Baldock, Herts.
> 11 April 1940

Dear Rayner,[1]
Did those photos come to anything? If so, I'd be very obliged if you'd send me any that seemed worth reproducing and let me know what the negatives etc cost. I've just had a thing from some kind of American literary *Who's Who*[2] wanting to put me in, with photo, and I suppose I'd better comply as it's all an advert.

---

[1] Rayner Heppenstall (1911–   ), novelist, poet and critic, whose works include *The Blaze of Noon* and *Four Absentees*, met Orwell in the spring of 1935 through Richard Rees and their friendship continued until Orwell's death.

[2] Stanley J. Kunitz and Howard Haycraft, *Twentieth Century Authors* (New York 1942). See 7.

Hope all goes well with you. I'm here alone, Eileen[1] coming down at weekends when she can. They are working her to death in that office[2] and I want to get her out of it if possible, but at present nothing is transpiring about a job for me. I haven't touched my novel[3] but am kept very busy doing reviews which help to keep the wolf a few paces from the backdoor. Also with the garden, spring sowing being in full swing. I am aiming to raise 6 cwt of potatoes against the famine I foresee next winter. Did you go to the Easter conference at Langham[4] by any chance? They asked me to speak, I couldn't get away, but sent a lecture[5] to be read by someone else, attacking pacifism for all I was worth. I don't know how they liked it and would like to hear from someone who was there. Please give my love to Margaret.[6] I hope she is going on OK.

Yours,
Eric

PS. I had some publications by some BFs who call themselves the Apocalytpic school[7] to review recently and took the opportunity of giving a boost to Dylan,[8] whose stuff I have decided I really like in a way.

## 5. Review

*Personal Record 1928–1939* by Julian Green, translated by Jocelyn Godefroi

Julian Green's diaries, which ten years ago or even five years ago might have seemed comparatively commonplace, are at this moment

[1] Eileen Blair, Orwell's wife.

[2] The Censorship Department.

[3] A projected Saga in three parts which was never begun seriously. See I, 159.

[4] The Adelphi Centre at Langham, Essex, an offshoot of the *Adelphi* magazine, founded in 1936 for Summer Schools, conferences etc to promote Socialist studies. At this time it was dominated by Max Plowman, an ardent pacifist.

[5] This has not been preserved.

[6] Mrs Rayner Heppenstall.

[7] *New Apocalypse, an anthology of criticism, poems and stories*, 1940, representing a neo-Romantic movement centred round the poets Henry Treece and J.F Hendry.

[8] Dylan Thomas.

of the greatest interest. What they really record is the twilight
of the aesthetic age, the last gasp of the cultivated second-generation
*rentier*. With his extreme sensitiveness and his almost effeminate
manner of writing, Mr Green is a figure peculiarly representative
of the nineteen-twenties, of the period when simply to preserve your
aesthetic integrity seemed a sufficient return for living on inherited
money. Although the diary records visits to London, to various
parts of Europe, and to America (Mr Green is of American origin
though he writes in French), one has the feeling of being all the
while in Paris, the Paris of old yellow-faced houses and green plane
trees, and also of first nights, private views and interminable literary
conversations with Gide, Gertrude Stein and Madame de Noailles.
Everything is recorded with the restless sensitiveness of the writer,
who translates his experience into literature almost as automatically
as a cow turns grass into milk:

> *December 19th.* A gas-lamp burning behind the glass door of a
> concierge's room at the end of a winter's day, with darkness
> overhead—what a lovely opening for a novel! Today, for a whole
> hour, I had nothing but this admirable picture in my mind.
> *February 2nd.* At Versailles. . . . As I looked at the ivy-leaves
> with their dainty pale yellow borders, I had a moment of sadness
> at the thought that, till my life's end, things as lovely as they will
> be there for me to see and I shall have no time to describe them.

He writes much of his work, and his difficulties with his work
(like the majority of writers he never feels in the mood for writing,
and yet his books somehow get finished), of his dreams, which
seem to affect his waking life considerably, and of his remembered
childhood in the golden age "before the war". Nearly all his thoughts
have a nostalgic tinge. But what gives them their special interest
is that he is far too intelligent to imagine that his way of life or his
scheme of values will last for ever. Totally uninterested in politics,
he is nevertheless able to see, even as early as the nineteen-twenties,
that the age of liberalism is ending and that wars, revolutions and
dictatorships are just round the corner. Everything is cracking and
collapsing. The shadow of Hitler flits almost constantly across the
pages:

> We are going to see life changing under our very eyes. Every-
> thing that gives us pleasure will be taken from us. . . . I am

growing accustomed to the idea of vanishing from sight, together with all that I love in this world; for it seems reasonable to
suppose that we are approaching the end of a long era. How long
shall we sleep? . . . Paris is living in a sort of latent panic. . . .
In the Europe of 1934 murder inevitably and fatally leads to
other murder. How far can this go without the outbreak of war?
. . . The war rumours continue as before. Everyone's daily life
seems to be saturated with these feelings of apprehension. . . .
The Rhineland has been reoccupied. . . . I was asked to say
something on the wireless about *Minuit*. As if that were of the
slightest importance with things as they are at the moment! But
one has to go on pretending. . . .

The feeling of futility and impermanence, of hanging about in a
draughty room and waiting for the guns to begin to shoot, which
has haunted many of us during the past seven years, is present
everywhere, and it grows stronger and stronger as the diary moves
towards 1939. Perhaps even the possession of this feeling depends
upon being of a certain age (Julian Green is not quite forty), young
enough to expect something from life and old enough to remember
"before the war". It is a fact that the people who are now twenty
do not appear to notice that the world is falling into ruins. But what
is attractive in this diary is its complete impenitence, its refusal to
move with the times. It is the diary of a civilised man who realises
that barbarism is bound to triumph, but who is unable to stop
being civilised. A new world is coming to birth, a world in which
there will be no room for him. He has too much vision to fight
against it; on the other hand, he makes no pretence of liking it. As
it is exactly that pretence that has been the stock-in-trade of the
younger intelligentsia during the last few years, the ghostly sincerity
of this book is deeply appealing. It has the charm of the ineffectual,
which is so out-of-date as to wear an air of novelty.

*Time and Tide*, 13 April 1940

## 6. Letter to Rayner Heppenstall

The Stores
Wallington
Nr Baldock, Herts.
16 April 1940

Dear Rayner,

Thousands of congratulations on the kid. I hope and trust both are doing well. Please give Margaret all the best and my congratulations. What a wonderful thing to have a kid of one's own, I've always wanted one so. But, Rayner, don't afflict the poor little brat with a Celtic sort of name that nobody knows how to spell. She'll grow up psychic or something. People always grow up like their names. It took me nearly thirty years to work off the effects of being called Eric. If I wanted a girl to grow up beautiful I'd call her Elizabeth, and if I wanted her to be honest and a good cook I'd choose something like Mary or Jane. The trouble is that if you called her Elizabeth everyone would think you'd done it after the queen, as she presumably will be some day.

Thanks for the photos but you didn't tell me what the negatives etc cost. I chose the ones marked 3 and 5 to send to the people. I thought the one marked 3 the best likeness, but naturally I know my own face best from the front. Let's hope the photo will have the desired effect. Seeing that it's for people at the other end of the world I don't know why one shouldn't send a photo of some nice-looking boy in the Air Force or something. I am afraid I definitely lack glamour, because I get quite a lot of letters from readers nowadays, but it's always from people snootily pointing out some mistake I've made and never from young women telling me I'm a sheik. I had some wonderful letters once from a midwife, and I wrote back not telling her I was married, but in the end to Eileen's great glee she turned out to be 35 and have 4 children.

I don't know when I'll be in town. I am buried under books I keep reviewing and not getting on with my own book. God knows whether it will ever get written or whether such things as publishing novels will still be happening two years hence. All the best.

Yours
Eric

# 7. [Autobiographical Note]

I was born in 1903 at Motihari, Bengal, the second child of an Anglo-Indian family. I was educated at Eton, 1917–21, as I had been lucky enough to win a scholarship, but I did no work there and learned very little, and I don't feel that Eton has been much of a formative influence in my life.

From 1922 to 1927 I served with the Indian Imperial Police in Burma. I gave it up partly because the climate had ruined my health, partly because I already had vague ideas of writing books, but mainly because I could not go on any longer serving an imperialism which I had come to regard as very largely a racket. When I came back to Europe I lived for about a year and a half in Paris, writing novels and short stories which no one would publish. After my money came to an end I had several years of fairly severe poverty during which I was, among other things, a dishwasher, a private tutor and a teacher in cheap private schools. For a year or more I was also a part-time assistant in a London bookshop, a job which was interesting in itself but had the disadvantage of compelling me to live in London, which I detest. By about 1935 I was able to live on what I earned by writing, and at the end of that year I moved into the country and set up a small general store. It barely paid its way, but it taught me things about the trade which would be useful if I ever made a venture in that direction again. I was married in the summer of 1936. At the end of the year I went to Spain to take part in the civil war, my wife following soon afterwards. I served four months on the Aragon front with the POUM militia and was rather badly wounded, but luckily with no serious after-effects. Since that, except for spending a winter in Morocco, I cannot honestly say that I have done anything except write books and raise hens and vegetables.

What I saw in Spain, and what I have seen since of the inner workings of left-wing political parties, have given me a horror of politics. I was for a while a member of the Independent Labour Party, but left them at the beginning of the present war because I considered that they were talking nonsense and proposing a line of policy that could only make things easier for Hitler. In sentiment I am definitely "left", but I believe that a writer can only remain honest if he keeps free of party labels.

The writers I care most about and never grow tired of are Shakespeare, Swift, Fielding, Dickens, Charles Reade, Samuel Butler, Zola, Flaubert and, among modern writers, James Joyce, T.S. Eliot and D.H. Lawrence. But I believe the modern writer who has influenced me most is Somerset Maugham, whom I admire immensely for his power of telling a story straightforwardly and without frills. Outside my work the thing I care most about is gardening, especially vegetable gardening. I like English cookery and English beer, French red wines, Spanish white wines, Indian tea, strong tobacco, coal fires, candlelight and comfortable chairs. I dislike big towns, noise, motor cars, the radio, tinned food, central heating and "modern" furniture. My wife's tastes fit in almost perfectly with my own. My health is wretched, but it has never prevented me from doing anything that I wanted to, except, so far, fight in the present war. I ought perhaps to mention that though this account that I have given of myself is true, George Orwell is not my real name.

I am not at the moment writing a novel, chiefly owing to upsets caused by the war. But I am projecting a long novel in three parts, to be called either *The Lion and the Unicorn* or *The Quick and the Dead*, and hope to produce the first part by some time in 1941.

*Publications: Down and Out in Paris and London* (1933). *Burmese Days* (Published in America before being published in a slightly bowdlerised form in England) (1934). *A Clergyman's Daughter* (1935). *Keep the Aspidistra Flying* (1936). *The Road to Wigan Pier* (1937). *Homage to Catalonia* (1938). *Coming up for Air* (1939). *Inside the Whale* (1940).

Written 17 April 1940 for *Twentieth Century Authors*, Ed. Stanley J. Kunitz and H. Haycraft, N.Y., W.H. Wilson & Co, 1942

# 8. Review

*The Totalitarian Enemy* by F. Borkenau

Although this is not one of Dr Borkenau's best books, it contains a study of the nature of totalitarianism which deserves and in fact needs to be widely read at this moment. We cannot struggle against Fascism unless we are willing to understand it, a thing which both left-wingers and right-wingers have conspicuously failed to do—basically, of course, because they dared not.

Until the signing of the Russo-German Pact, the assumption made on both sides was that the Nazi régime was in no way revolutionary. National Socialism was simply capitalism with the lid off, Hitler was a dummy with Thyssen pulling the strings—that was the official theory, proved in many a pamphlet by Mr John Strachey and tacitly accepted by *The Times*. Blimps and Left Book Club members alike swallowed it whole, both of them having, so to speak, a vested interest in ignoring the real facts. Quite naturally the propertied classes wanted to believe that Hitler would protect them against Bolshevism, and equally naturally the Socialists hated having to admit that the man who had slaughtered their comrades was a Socialist himself. Hence, on both sides, the frantic efforts to explain away the more and more striking resemblance between the German and Russian régimes. Then came the eye-opener of the Hitler-Stalin pact. Suddenly the scum of the earth and the blood-stained butcher of the workers (for so they had described one another) were marching arm in arm, their friendship "cemented in blood", as Stalin cheerily expressed it. Thereafter the Strachey-Blimp thesis became untenable. National Socialism *is* a form of Socialism, *is* emphatically revolutionary, *does* crush the property owner just as surely as it crushes the worker. The two régimes, having started from opposite ends, are rapidly evolving towards the same system—a form of oligarchical collectivism. And at the moment, as Dr Borkenau points out, it is Germany that is moving towards Russia, rather than the other way about. It is therefore nonsense to talk about Germany "going Bolshevik" if Hitler falls. Germany is going Bolshevik *because* of Hitler and not in spite of him.

The question that really arises is not so much how the Nazis could start out to save the world from Bolshevism and end by becoming Bolshevik, as how they could do it without losing either their power or their self-confidence. Dr Borkenau points to two reasons, one economic, the other psychological. From the first the aim of the Nazis was to turn Germany into a war-machine, and to subordinate everything else to that purpose. But a country, and especially a poor country, which is waging or preparing for "total" war must be in some sense socialistic. When the State has taken complete control of industry, when the so-called capitalist is reduced to the status of a manager, and when consumption goods are so scarce and so strictly rationed that you cannot spend a big income even if you earn one, then the essential structure of Socialism already exists, plus the comfortless equality of war-Communism. Simply in the interest of efficiency the Nazis found themselves expropriating, nationalising, destroying the very people they had set out to save. It did not bother them, because their aim was simply power and not any particular form of society. They would just as soon be Reds as Whites, provided that it left them on top. If the first step is to smash the Socialists to the tune of anti-Marxist slogans—well and good, smash the Socialists. If the next step is to smash the capitalists to the tune of Marxist slogans—well and good, smash the capitalists. It is all-in wrestling, and the only rule is to win. Russia since 1928 shows distinctly similar reversals of policy, always tending to keep the ruling clique in power. As for the hate-campaigns in which totalitarian régimes ceaselessly indulge, they are real enough while they last, but are simply dictated by the needs of the moment. Jews, Poles, Trotskyists, English, French, Czechs, Democrats, Fascists, Marxists—almost anyone can figure as Public Enemy No 1. Hatred can be turned in any direction at a moment's notice, like a plumber's blow-flame.

On the strategic aspects of the war Dr Borkenau is less satisfactory. He is too optimistic about the probable attitude of Italy, about the probable military effects of the Russo-German Pact, about the solidarity of the home front and, above all, about the power of the present Government to win the war and win the peace. Basically, as he sees and points out, what we have got to do is to put our own house in order—to oppose a humaner, freer form of collectivism to the purge-and-censorship variety. We could do it rapidly, almost easily, but it needs the eye of faith to see the present Government doing it.

I hope that Dr Borkenau will write a longer and better book on approximately the same subject. The present one, in spite of some brilliant passages, seems to have been hastily written and has faults of arrangement. Nevertheless Dr Borkenau is one of the most valuable gifts that Hitler has made to England. In a period when nearly all books on current politics have been compounded of lies, or folly, or both, his has been one of the few sane voices heard in the land, and long may it continue.

*Time and Tide*, 4 May 1940

# 9. Letter to the Editor of *Time and Tide*

Sir,
It is almost certain that England will be invaded within the next few days or weeks, and a large-scale invasion by sea-borne troops is quite likely. At such a time our slogan should be ARM THE PEOPLE. I am not competent to deal with the wider questions of repelling the invasion, but I submit that the campaign in France and the recent civil war in Spain have made two facts clear. One is that when the civil population is unarmed, parachutists, motor cyclists and stray tanks can not only work fearful havoc but draw off large bodies of regular troops who should be opposing the main enemy. The other fact (demonstrated by the Spanish war) is that the advantages of arming the population outweigh the danger of putting weapons into the wrong hands. By-elections since the war started have shown that only a tiny minority among the common people of England are disaffected, and most of these are already marked down.

ARM THE PEOPLE is in itself a vague phrase, and I do not, of course, know what weapons are available for immediate distribution. But there are at any rate several things that can and should be done *now*, i.e. within the next three days:

1. Hand-grenades. These are the only modern weapon of war that can be rapidly and easily manufactured, and they are one of the most useful. Hundreds of thousands of men in England are accustomed to using hand-grenades and would be only too ready to instruct others. They are said to be useful against tanks and will be absolutely necessary if enemy parachutists with machine-guns manage to establish themselves in our big towns. I had a front-seat view of the street fighting in Barcelona in May 1937, and it convinced me that a few hundred men with machine-guns can paralyse the life of a large city, because of the fact that a bullet will not penetrate an ordinary brick wall. They can be blasted out with artillery, but it is not always possible to bring a gun to bear. On the other hand, the early street fighting in Spain showed that armed men can be driven out of stone buildings with grenades or even sticks of dynamite if the right tactics are used.

2. Shotguns. There is talk of arming some of the Local Defence Volunteer contingents with shotguns. This may be necessary if all the rifles and Bren guns are needed for the regular troops. But in

that case the distribution should be made *now* and all weapons should be immediately requisitioned from the gunsmiths' shops. There was talk of doing this weeks ago, but in fact many gunsmiths' windows show rows of guns which are not only useless where they are, but actually a danger, as these shops could easily be raided. The powers and limitations of the shotgun (with buckshot, lethal up to about sixty yards) should be explained to the public over the radio.

3. Blocking fields against aircraft landings. There has been much talk of this, but it has only been done sporadically. The reason is that it has been left to voluntary effort, i.e. to people who have insufficient time and no power of requisitioning materials. In a small, thickly populated country like England we could within a very few days make it impossible for an aeroplane to land anywhere except at an aerodrome. All that is needed is the labour. Local authorities should therefore have powers to conscript labour and requisition such materials as they require.

4. Painting out place-names. This has been well done as regards signposts, but there are everywhere shop-fronts, tradesmen's vans etc, bearing the name of their locality. Local authorities should have the power to enforce the painting-out of these immediately. This should include the brewers' names on public houses. Most of these are confined to a fairly small area, and the Germans are probably methodical enough to know this.

5. Radio sets. Every Local Defence Volunteer headquarters should be in possession of a radio receiving set, so that if necessary it can receive its orders over the air. It is fatal to rely on the telephone in a moment of emergency. As with weapons, the Government should not hesitate to requisition what it needs.

All of these are things that could be done within the space of a very few days. Meanwhile, let us go on repeating ARM THE PEOPLE, in the hope that more and more voices will take it up. For the first time in decades we have a Government with imagination,[1] and there is at least a chance that they will listen.

I am, etc

George Orwell

*Time and Tide*, 22 June 1940

[1] On 10 May the Chamberlain Government had fallen and Winston Churchill became Prime Minister at the head of a Coalition Government.

## 10. Letter to John Lehmann

18 Dorset Chambers
Chagford Street
Ivor Place NW1
6 July 1940

Dear Lehmann,[1]

Thanks for your two letters, which arrived in one envelope.[2] I am very sorry I have written nothing for you after promising I would. I began something, then the war started to get serious. I just can't write with this kind of thing going on. I have written nothing except book reviews etc for a long time past, and also my time has been rather filled up with helping with the LDV.[2] What is so terrible about this kind of situation is to be able to do nothing. The govt won't use me in any capacity, not even a clerk, and I have failed to get into the army because of my lungs. It is a terrible thing to feel oneself useless and at the same time on every side to see halfwits and profascists filling important jobs. However, things *are* moving a little. I was informed at the WO[3] that it is no longer held against a man to have fought in the Spanish civil war. Of course you can use the elephant sketch[4] again if you like. Two guineas would be very handsome. As to the photo referred to in your other letter, does it have to be a real portrait or will a snap do? I don't photograph well as a rule. The enclosed was taken for a carte d'identité or something and is a very good likeness, but I don't know whether it would enlarge. In case I have to be properly photographed my address is as above, at any rate for the next week or so. I have been living in London because I am now doing theatre criticism for *Time & Tide*.

Yours
George Orwell

---

[1] John Lehmann (1907–    ), poet, critic and publisher. Founder and editor of *New Writing*, a literary magazine committed to anti-Fascism 1936–46, and later first editor of the *London Magazine*, 1954.

[2] The Local Defence Volunteers, which later became the Home Guard, consisted of civilians formed into military detachments against the possibility of invasion.

[3] War Office.

[4] "Shooting an Elephant". See I, 88.

# 11. Prophecies of Fascism

The reprinting of Jack London's *The Iron Heel* brings within general reach a book which has been much sought after during the years of Fascist aggression. Like others of Jack London's books it has been widely read in Germany, and it has had the reputation of being an accurate forecast of the coming of Hitler. In reality it is not that. It is merely a tale of capitalist oppression, and it was written at a time when various things that have made Fascism possible—for instance, the tremendous revival of nationalism—were not easy to foresee.

Where London did show special insight, however, was in realising that the transition to Socialism was not going to be automatic or even easy. The capitalist class was not going to "perish of its own contradictions" like a flower dying at the end of the season. The capitalist class was quite clever enough to see what was happening, to sink its own differences and counter-attack against the workers; and the resulting struggle would be the most bloody and unscrupulous the world had ever seen.

It is worth comparing *The Iron Heel* with another imaginative novel of the future which was written somewhat earlier and to which it owes something, H.G. Wells's *The Sleeper Wakes*. By doing so one can see both London's limitations and also the advantage he enjoyed in not being, like Wells, a fully civilised man. As a book, *The Iron Heel* is hugely inferior. It is clumsily written, it shows no grasp of scientific possibilities, and the hero is the kind of human gramophone who is now disappearing even from Socialist tracts. But because of his own streak of savagery London could grasp something that Wells apparently could not, and that is that hedonistic societies do not endure.

Everyone who has ever read *The Sleeper Wakes* remembers it. It is a vision of a glittering, sinister world in which society has hardened into a caste-system and the workers are permanently enslaved. It is also a world without purpose, in which the upper castes for whom the workers toil are completely soft, cynical and faithless. There is no consciousness of any object in life, nothing corresponding to the fervour of the revolutionary or the religious martyr.

In Aldous Huxley's *Brave New World*, a sort of post-war parody of the Wellsian Utopia, these tendencies are immensely exaggerated.

Here the hedonistic principle is pushed to its utmost, the whole world has turned into a Riviera hotel. But though *Brave New World* was a brilliant caricature of the present (the present of 1930), it probably casts no light on the future. No society of that kind would last more than a couple of generations, because a ruling class which thought principally in terms of a "good time" would soon lose its vitality. A ruling class has got to have a strict morality, a quasi-religious belief in itself, a mystique. London was aware of this, and though he describes the caste of plutocrats who rule the world for seven centuries as inhuman monsters, he does not describe them as idlers or sensualists. They can only maintain their position while they honestly believe that civilisation depends on themselves alone, and therefore in a different way they are just as brave, able and devoted as the revolutionaries who oppose them.

In an intellectual way London accepted the conclusions of Marxism, and he imagined that the "contradictions" of capitalism, the unconsumable surplus and so forth, would persist even after the capitalist class had organised themselves into a single corporate body. But temperamentally he was very different from the majority of Marxists. With his love of violence and physical strength, his belief in "natural aristocracy", his animal-worship and exaltation of the primitive, he had in him what one might fairly call a Fascist strain. This probably helped him to understand just how the possessing class would behave when once they were seriously menaced.

It is just here that Marxian Socialists have usually fallen short. Their interpretation of history has been so mechanistic that they have failed to foresee dangers that were obvious to people who had never heard the name of Marx. It is sometimes urged against Marx that he failed to predict the rise of Fascism. I do not know whether he predicted it or not—at that date he could only have done so in very general terms—but it is at any rate certain that his followers failed to see any danger in Fascism until they themselves were at the gates of the concentration camp. A year or more *after* Hitler had risen to power official Marxism was still proclaiming that Hitler was of no importance and "Social Fascism" (i.e. democracy) was the real enemy. London would probably not have made this mistake. His instincts would have warned him that Hitler was dangerous. He knew that economic laws do not operate in the same way as the law of gravity, that they can be held up for long periods by people who, like Hitler, believe in their own destiny.

*The Iron Heel* and *The Sleeper Wakes* are both written from the popular standpoint. *Brave New World*, though primarily an attack on hedonism, is also by implication an attack on totalitarianism and caste rule. It is interesting to compare them with a less well-known Utopia which treats the class struggle from the upper or rather the middle-class point of view, Ernest Bramah's *The Secret of the League*.

*The Secret of the League* was written in 1907, when the growth of the labour movement was beginning to terrify the middle class, who wrongly imagined that they were menaced from below and not from above. As a political forecast it is trivial, but it is of great interest for the light it casts on the mentality of the struggling middle class.

The author imagines a Labour government coming into office with so huge a majority that it is impossible to dislodge them. They do not, however, introduce a full Socialist economy. They merely continue to operate capitalism for their own benefit by constantly raising wages, creating a huge army of bureaucrats and taxing the upper classes out of existence. The country is therefore "going to the dogs" in the familiar manner; moreover in their foreign politics the Labour Government behave rather like the National Government between 1931 and 1939. Against this there arises a secret conspiracy of the middle and upper classes. The manner of their revolt is very ingenious, provided that one looks upon capitalism as something internal: it is the method of the consumers' strike. Over a period of two years the upper-class conspirators secretly hoard fuel-oil and convert coal-burning plant to oil-burning; then they suddenly boycott the principal British industry, the coal industry. The miners are faced with a situation in which they will be able to sell no coal for two years. There is vast unemployment and distress, ending in civil war, in which (thirty years before General Franco!) the upper classes receive foreign aid. After their victory they abolish the trade unions and institute a "strong" non-parliamentary régime—in other words a régime that we should now describe as Fascist. The tone of the book is good-natured, as it could afford to be at that date, but the trend of thought is unmistakable.

Why should a decent and kindly writer like Ernest Bramah find the crushing of the proletariat a pleasant vision? It is simply the reaction of a struggling class which felt itself menaced not so much in its economic position as in its code of conduct and way of life.

One can see the same purely social antagonism to the working class in an earlier writer of much greater calibre, George Gissing. Time, and Hitler have taught the middle classes a great deal, and perhaps they will not again side with their oppressors against their natural allies. But whether they do so or not depends partly on how they are handled, and the stupidity of Socialist propaganda, with its constant baiting of the "petty bourgeois", has a lot to answer for.

*Tribune*, 12 July 1940

## 12. Letter to James Laughlin

> 18 Dorset Chambers
> Chagford Street
> Ivor Place
> London NW1 England
> 16 July 1940

Dear Mr Laughlin,[1]

Many thanks for your letter, which I have only just received. Yes, you may certainly reprint the Henry Miller essay.[2] I'm not sure how my contract with my publisher stands, and I have written to him, but I know he won't object. When I've heard from him I'll send you another line confirming this. I trust neither letter will be torpedoed on the way.

I wonder whether by any chance you know where Henry Miller is. I haven't heard from him since about the beginning of 1939. When this book[2] came out he asked me through someone in England to send him a copy at some American address, and I did so, but never heard whether it got there. His friend Alfred Perlès is over here and has joined the British army. As you say, all these projects about books may be blown to pieces by the war. Hitler entered Paris a week or two before a book of mine was due to be reprinted there, and comically enough a few days later I got a demand for income tax which I had been counting on this reprint to pay. I have practically given up writing except for journalism. I can't

---

[1] James Laughlin, American publisher of New Directions books, editor and writer.

[2] "Inside the Whale" from the book of this title. See I, 164.

write with this sort of business going on, and in a few months there is going to be such a severe paper shortage that very few books will be published. In any case I feel that literature as we have known it is coming to an end. Things look rather black at the moment. We are all on our toes waiting for an invasion which quite possibly won't happen. Personally I am much more afraid of Hitler mopping up north Africa and the near East and then making a peace offer. I actually rather hope that the invasion will happen. The local morale is extremely good, and if we are invaded we shall at any rate get rid once and for all of the gang who had got us into this mess. However, I expect you are better informed about European affairs than I am. I will send the confirmation of this letter within a few days. Thanks for writing.

> Yours sincerely
> George Orwell

## 13. Charles Reade

Since Charles Reade's books are published in cheap editions one can assume that he still has his following, but it is unusual to meet anyone who has voluntarily read him. In most people his name seems to evoke, at most, a vague memory of "doing" *The Cloister and the Hearth* as a school holiday task. It is his bad luck to be remembered by this particular book, rather as Mark Twain, thanks to the films, is chiefly remembered by *A Connecticut Yankee in King Arthur's Court*. Reade wrote several dull books, and *The Cloister and the Hearth* is one of them. But he also wrote three novels which I personally would back to outlive the entire works of Meredith and George Eliot, besides some brilliant long-short stories such as *A Jack of All Trades* and *The Autobiography of a Thief*.

What is the attraction of Reade? At bottom it is the same charm as one finds in R. Austin Freeman's detective stories or Lieutenant-Commander Gould's collections of curiosities—the charm of useless knowledge. Reade was a man of what one might call penny-encyclopaedic learning. He possessed vast stocks of disconnected information which a lively narrative gift allowed him to cram into books which would at any rate pass as novels. If you have the sort of mind that takes a pleasure in dates, lists, catalogues, concrete details, descriptions of processes, junk-shop windows and back numbers of the *Exchange and Mart*, the sort of mind that likes knowing exactly how a medieval catapult worked or just what objects a prison cell of the eighteen-forties contained, then you can hardly help enjoying Reade. He himself, of course, did not see his work in quite this light. He prided himself on his accuracy and compiled his books largely from newspaper cuttings, but the strange facts which he collected were subsidiary to what he would have regarded as his "purpose". For he was a social reformer in a fragmentary way, and made vigorous attacks on such diverse evils as blood-letting, the treadmill, private lunatic asylums, clerical celibacy and tight-lacing.

My own favourite has always been *Foul Play*, which as it happens is not an attack on anything in particular. Like most nineteenth-century novels *Foul Play* is too complicated to be summarised, but its central story is that of a young clergyman, Robert Penfold, who is unjustly convicted of forgery, is transported to Australia, absconds in disguise, and is wrecked on a desert island together with the heroine. Here, of course, Reade is in his element. Of all men who ever lived, he was the best fitted to write a desert-island story. Some desert-island stories, of course, are worse than others, but none is altogether bad when it sticks to the actual concrete details of the struggle to keep alive. A list of the objects in a shipwrecked man's possession is probably the surest winner in fiction, surer even than a trial scene. Nearly thirty years after reading the book I can still remember more or less exactly what things the three heroes of Ballantyne's *Coral Island* possessed between them. (A telescope, six yards of whipcord, a penknife, a brass ring and a piece of hoop iron.) Even a dismal book like *Robinson Crusoe*, so unreadable as a whole that few people even know that the second part exists, becomes interesting when it describes Crusoe's efforts to make a table, glaze earthenware and grow a patch of wheat. Reade, however, was an expert on desert islands, or at any rate he was very well up in the geography textbooks of the time. Moreover he was the kind of man who would have been at home on a desert island himself. He would never, like Crusoe, have been stumped by such an easy problem as that of leavening bread and, unlike Ballantyne, he knew that civilised men cannot make fire by rubbing sticks together.

The hero of *Foul Play*, like most of Reade's heroes, is a kind of superman. He is hero, saint, scholar, gentleman, athlete, pugilist,

navigator, physiologist, botanist, blacksmith and carpenter all rolled
into one, the sort of compendium of all the talents that Reade
honestly imagined to be the normal product of an English university.
Needless to say, it is only a month or two before this wonderful
clergyman has got the desert island running like a West End hotel.
Even before reaching the island, when the last survivors of the
wrecked ship are dying of thirst in an open boat, he has shown his
ingenuity by constructing a distilling apparatus with a jar, a hot-
water bottle and a piece of tubing. But his best stroke of all is the
way in which he contrives to leave the island. He himself, with a price
on his head, would be glad enough to remain, but the heroine, Helen
Rollestone, who has no idea that he is a convict, is naturally anxious
to escape. She asks Robert to turn his "great mind" to this problem.
The first difficulty, of course, is to discover exactly where the island
is. Luckily, however, Helen is still wearing her watch, which is still
keeping Sydney time. By fixing a stick in the ground and watching its
shadow Robert notes the exact moment of noon, after which it is a
simple matter to work out the longitude—for naturally a man of his
calibre would know the longitude of Sydney. It is equally natural that
he can determine the latitude within a degree or two by the nature
of the vegetation. But the next difficulty is to send a message to the
outside world. After some thought Robert writes a series of messages
on pieces of parchment made from seals' bladders, with ink obtained
from cochineal insects. He has noticed that migrant birds often use
the island as a stopping-place, and he fixes on ducks as the likeliest
messengers, because every duck is liable to be shot sooner or later.
By a stratagem often used in India he captures a number of ducks,
ties a message to each of their legs and lets them go. Finally, of
course, one of the ducks takes refuge on a ship, and the couple are
rescued, but even then the story is barely half finished. There
follow enormous ramifications, plots and counterplots, intrigues,
triumphs and disasters, ending with the vindication of Robert, and
wedding bells.

In any of Reade's three best books, *Foul Play*, *Hard Cash* and *It
Is Never Too Late to Mend*, it is not fair to say that the sole interest
is in the technical detail. His power of descriptive writing, especially
of describing violent action, is also very striking, and on a serial-
story level he is a wonderful contriver of plots. Simply as a novelist
it is impossible to take him seriously, because he has no sense
whatever of character or of probability, but he himself had the

advantage of believing in even the absurdest details of his own stories. He wrote of life as he saw it, and many Victorians saw it in the same way: that is, as a series of tremendous melodramas, with virtue triumphant every time. Of all the nineteenth-century novelists who have remained readable, he is perhaps the only one who is completely in tune with his own age. For all his unconventionality, his "purpose", his eagerness to expose abuses, he never makes a fundamental criticism. Save for a few surface evils he sees nothing wrong in an acquisitive society, with its equation of money and virtue, its pious millionaires and erastian clergymen. Perhaps nothing gives one his measure better than the fact that in introducing Robert Penfold, at the beginning of *Foul Play*, he mentions that he is a scholar and a cricketer and only thirdly and almost casually adds that he is a priest.

That is not to say that Reade's social conscience was not sound so far as it went, and in several minor ways he probably helped to educate public opinion. His attack on the prison system in *It Is Never Too Late to Mend* is relevant to this day, or was so till very recently, and in his medical theories he is said to have been a long way ahead of his time. What he lacked was any notion that the early railway age, with the special scheme of values appropriate to it, was not going to last for ever. This is a little surprising when one remembers that he was the brother of Winwood Reade. However hasty and unbalanced Winwood Reade's *Martyrdom of Man* may seem now, it is a book that shows an astonishing width of vision, and it is probably the unacknowledged grandparent of the "outlines" so popular today. Charles Reade might have written an "outline" of phrenology, cabinet-making or the habits of whales, but not of human history. He was simply a middle-class gentleman with a little more conscience than most, a scholar who happened to prefer popular science to the classics. Just for that reason he is one of the best "escape" novelists we have. *Foul Play* and *Hard Cash* would be good books to send to a soldier enduring the miseries of trench warfare, for instance. There are no problems in them, no genuine "message", merely the fascination of a gifted mind functioning within very narrow limits, and offering as complete a detachment from real life as a game of chess or a jigsaw puzzle.

*New Statesman and Nation*, 17 August 1940

# 14. The Proletarian Writer
### Discussion between George Orwell and Desmond Hawkins

HAWKINS: I have always doubted if there is such a thing as proletarian literature—or ever could be. The first question is what people mean by it. What do *you* mean by it? You would expect it to mean literature written specifically for the proletariat, and read by them, but does it?

ORWELL: No, obviously not. In that case the most definitely proletarian literature would be some of our morning papers. But you can see by the existence of publications like *New Writing*, or the Unity Theatre, for instance, that the term has a sort of meaning, though unfortunately there are several different ideas mixed up in it. What people mean by it, roughly speaking, is a literature in which the viewpoint of the working class, which is supposed to be completely different from that of the richer classes, gets a hearing. And that, of course, has got mixed up with Socialist propaganda. I don't think the people who throw this expression about mean literature written *by* proletarians. W.H. Davies was a proletarian, but he would not be called a proletarian writer. Paul Potts would be called a proletarian writer, but he is not a proletarian. The reason why I am doubtful of the whole conception is that I don't believe the proletariat can create an independent literature while they are not the dominant class. I believe that their literature is and must be bourgeois literature with a slightly different slant. After all, so much that is supposed to be new is simply the old standing on its head. The poems that were written about the Spanish civil war, for instance, were simply a deflated version of the stuff that Rupert Brooke and Co were writing in 1914.

HAWKINS: Still, I think one must admit that the cult of proletarian literature—whether the theory is right or not—has had some effect. Look at writers like James Hanley, for instance, or Jack Hilton, or Jack Common. They have something new to say—something at any rate that could not quite be said by anyone who had had the ordinary middle-class upbringing. Of course there was a tremendous amount of cant about proletarian literature in the years after the Slump, when Bloomsbury went all Marxist, and Communism became fashionable. But the thing had really started earlier. I should say it started just before the last war, when Ford Madox Ford, the editor of the *English Review*, met D.H. Lawrence and saw in him the portent of a new class finding expression in literature. Lawrence's *Sons and Lovers* really did break new ground. It recorded a kind of experience that simply had not got into print before. And yet it was an experience that had been shared by millions of people. The question is why it had never been recorded earlier. Why would you say there had been no books like *Sons and Lovers* before that time?

ORWELL: I think it is simply a matter of education. After all, though Lawrence was the son of a coal miner he had had an education that was not very different from that of the middle class. He was a university graduate, remember. Before a certain date—roughly speaking, before the 'nineties, when the Education Act began to take effect—very few genuine proletarians could write: that is, write with enough facility to produce a book or a story. On the other hand the professional writers knew nothing about proletarian life. One feels this even with a really radical writer like Dickens. Dickens does not write about the working class; he does not know enough about them. He is *for* the working class, but he feels himself completely different from them—far more different than the average middle-class person would feel nowadays.

HAWKINS: Then, after all, the appearance of the proletariat as a class capable of producing books means a fresh development of literature—completely new subject-matter, and a new slant on life?

ORWELL: Yes, except in so far as the experience of all classes in society tends to become more and more alike. I maintain that the class distinctions in a country like England are now so unreal that they cannot last much longer. Fifty years ago or even twenty years ago a factory worker and a small professional man, for instance, were very different kinds of creature. Nowadays they are very much alike, though they may not realise it. They see the same films and listen to the same radio programmes, and they wear very similar clothes and live in very similar houses. What used to be called a proletarian—what Marx would have meant by a proletarian—only exists now in the heavy industries and on the land. All the same, there's no doubt that it was a big step forward when the *facts* of working-class life were first got on to paper. I think it has done something to push fiction back towards realities and away from the over-civilised stuff that Galsworthy and so forth used to write. I think possibly the first book that did this was *The Ragged-Trousered Philanthropists*, which has always seemed to me a wonderful book, although it is very clumsily written. It recorded things that were every-day experience but which simply had not been noticed before—just as, so it is said, no one before AD 1800 ever noticed that the sea was blue. And Jack London was another pioneer in the same line.

HAWKINS: And how about language and technique? Cyril Connolly, you may remember, said last week that the great innovations in literature have been made in technique rather than in content. As an example, he said that there is nothing new in Joyce except his technique. But surely these revolutionary proletarians have not shown much interest in technique? Some of them seem to be little different in manner from the pious moralising lady novelists of the last century. Their revolt is entirely in content, in theme—is that so?

ORWELL: I think in the main that's true. It's a fact that written English is much more colloquial now than it was twenty years ago, and that's all to the good. But we've borrowed much more from America than from the speech of the English working class. As for technique, one of the things that strikes one about the proletarian writers, or the people who are called proletarian writers, is how conservative they are. We might make an exception of Lionel Brittain's *Hunger and Love*. But if you look through a volume of *New Writing* or the *Left Review* you won't find many experiments.

HAWKINS: Then we come back to this: that what is called proletarian literature stands or falls by its subject-matter. The mystique behind these writers, I suppose, is the class-war, the hope of a better future, the struggle of the working class against miserable living conditions.

ORWELL: Yes, proletarian literature is mainly a literature of revolt. It can't help being so.

HAWKINS: And my quarrel with it has always been that it is too much dominated by political considerations. I believe politicians and artists do not go well together. The goal of a politician is always limited, partial, short-term, over-simplified. It has to be, to have any hope of realisation. As a principle of action, it cannot afford to consider its own imperfections and the possible virtues of its opponents. It cannot afford to dwell on the pathos and the tragedy of all human endeavour. In short, it must exclude the very things that are valuable in art Would you agree therefore that when proletarian literature becomes literature it ceases to be proletarian—in the political sense? Or that when it becomes propaganda it ceases to be literature?

ORWELL: I think that's putting it too crudely. I have always maintained that every artist is a propagandist. I don't mean a political propagandist. If he has any honesty or talent at all he cannot be that. Most political propaganda is a matter of telling lies, not only about the facts but about your own feelings. But every artist is a propagandist in the sense that he is trying, directly or indirectly, to impose a vision of life that seems to him desirable. I think we are broadly agreed about the vision of life that proletarian literature is trying to impose. As you said just now, the mystique behind it is the class-war. That is something real; at any rate, it is something that is believed in. People will die for it as well as write about it. Quite a lot of people died for it in Spain. My point about proletarian literature is that though it has been important and useful so far as it went, it isn't likely to be permanent or to be the beginning of a new age in literature. It is founded on the revolt against capitalism, and capitalism is disappearing. In a Socialist State, a lot of our left-wing writers—people like Edward Upward, Christopher Caudwell, Alec Brown, Arthur Calder-Marshall and all the rest of them—who have specialised in attacking the society they live in, would have nothing to attack. Just to revert for a moment to a book I mentioned above, Lionel Brittain's *Hunger and Love*. This was an outstanding book and I think in a way it is representative of proletarian literature. Well, what is it about? It is about a young proletarian who wishes he wasn't a proletarian. It simply goes on and on about the intolerable conditions of working-class life, the fact that the roof leaks and the sink smells and all the rest of it. Now, you couldn't found a literature on the fact that the sink smells. As a convention it isn't likely to last so long as the siege of Troy. And behind this book, and lots of others like it, you can see what is really the history of a proletarian writer nowadays. Through some accident—very often it is simply due to having a long period on the dole—a young man of the working class gets a chance to educate himself. Then he starts writing books, and naturally he makes use of his early experiences, his sufferings under poverty, his revolt against the existing system, and so forth. But he isn't really creating an independent literature. He writes in the bourgeois manner, in the middle-class dialect. He is simply the black sheep of the bourgeois family, using the old methods for slightly different purposes. Don't mistake me. I'm not saying that he can't be as good a writer as anyone else; but if he is, it won't be because he is a working man but because he is a talented person who has learnt to write well. So long as the bourgeoisie are the dominant class, literature must be bourgeois. But I don't believe that they will be dominant much longer, or any other class either. I believe we are passing into a classless period, and what we call proletarian literature is one of the signs of the change. But I don't deny for an instant the good that it has done—the vitalising effect of getting working-class experience and working-class values on to paper.

HAWKINS: And, of course, as a positive gain, it has left behind quite a lot of good books?

ORWELL: Oh yes, lots. Jack London's book *The Road*, Jack Hilton's *Caliban Shrieks*, Jim Phelan's prison books, George Garrett's sea stories, Private Richards's *Old Soldier Sahib*, James Hanley's *Grey Children*—to name just a few.

HAWKINS: All this time we have said nothing about the literature that the proletariat does read—not so much the daily papers, but the weeklies, the twopennies.

ORWELL: Yes, I should say that the small weekly press is much more representative. Papers like *Home Chat* or the *Exchange and Mart*, and *Cage-Birds*, for instance.

HAWKINS: And the literature that really comes out of the people themselves—we have said nothing about that. Take, for instance, the camp-fire ballads of the men who built the Canadian Pacific Railway; the sea shanties; Negro poems like "Stagolee"; and the old street broadsheets—especially the ones about executions, the sort of thing that must have inspired Kipling's "Danny Deever". And epitaphs, limericks, advertisement jingles—sticking simply to poetry, those are the special literature of the proletariat, aren't they?

ORWELL: Yes, and don't forget the jokes on the comic coloured postcards, especially Donald McGill's. I'm particularly attached to those. And above all the songs that the soldiers made up and sang for themselves in the last war. And the army songs for bugle calls and military marches—those are the real popular poetry of our time, like the ballads in the Middle Ages. It's a pity they are always unprintable.

HAWKINS: Yes, but I'm afraid now we are drifting into folk literature, and it seems to me that we must keep the two things distinct. From what you say I imagine that this word "proletarian" is going to be quite meaningless if you detach it from revolutionary politics.

ORWELL: Yes, the term "proletariat" is a political term belonging solely to the industrial age.

HAWKINS: Well, I think we are completely in agreement that the theory of a separate proletarian literature just doesn't work. For all its apparent difference it comes within the framework of what you call bourgeois writing.

ORWELL: By "bourgeois" and "bourgeoisie" I don't mean merely the people who buy and sell things. I mean the whole dominant culture of our time.

HAWKINS: If we agree about that, we have still got to assess the contribution that these so-called proletarian writers have made. Because it *is* a contribution and it would be absurd to pass that over in disposing of the theory.

ORWELL: I think they have made two kinds of contribution. One is that they have to some extent provided new subject-matter, which has also led other writers who are not of the working class to look at things which were under their noses, but not noticed, before. The other is that they have introduced a note of what you might call crudeness and vitality. They have been a sort of voice in the gallery, preventing people from becoming too toney and too civilised.

HAWKINS: And then there's another contribution, which you yourself mentioned earlier, and that is language. T. S. Eliot stressed the importance of constantly drawing newly minted words into the language, and in recent years it is pre-eminently from the working class that new words and phrases have come. It may be from the film or the street or through any channel, but the proletarian writer deserves credit for giving modern English much of its raciness and colour.

ORWELL: Well, of course, the question is whether it has got much colour! But the thing you can say for the typical prose of the last ten years is that it has not got many frills or unnecessary adjectives. It's plain. It is rather questionable whether the sort of prose that has developed in this way is suitable for expressing very subtle thoughts, but it is excellent for describing action, and it is a good antidote to the over-refined type of prose which used to be fashionable—very good in its way, of course, but tending to emasculate the language altogether.

HAWKINS: Well, to conclude—it looks as if the slogan of proletarian literature has made a nice rallying-point for some work that was well worth having and it has been a focus for working-class writers, whether they were revolutionary or not, either in technique or in politics or in subject. But the phrase itself as a critical term is virtually useless.

ORWELL: It has had a certain use as a label for a rather heterogeneous literature belonging to a transition period, but I do agree with you that for there to be what could really be called a proletarian literature the proletariat would have to be the dominant class.

HAWKINS: Yes, and in assuming that it would certainly have to change its character. And that still leaves open the question we have only just touched on—how far can politics be introduced into art without spoiling the art?

Broadcast in the Home Service of the BBC, 6 December 1940; printed in the *Listener* 19 December 1940.

## 15. Review

*Landfall* by Nevil Shute, *Nailcruncher* by Albert Cohen, translated from the French by Vyvyan Holland

It is commonly said that every human being has in him the material for one good book, which is true in the same sense as it is true that every block of stone contains a statue. What is perhaps more to the point is that anyone able to hold a pen can write a fairly good novel of the unpretentious kind, if only at some period of his life he has managed to escape from literary society. There is no lack nowadays of clever writers; the trouble is that such writers are so cut off from the life of their time as to be unable to write about ordinary people. A "distinguished" modern novel almost always has some kind of artist or near-artist as its hero. There is, however, one experience that happens to nearly all human beings alike, and that is war. The "intellectual" has a chance of seeing war at close quarters as he will never see, for instance, stockbroking or marine insurance, and good war-books are in consequence fairly common. The present war, owing to its peculiar character, has not yet produced a literature of its own, but Mr Nevil Shute's *Landfall* is a beginning. It is a straightforward, convincing story, and I shall keep an eye open for Mr Shute's books in future.

What makes it interesting is that it brings out the essential peculiarity of war, the mixture of heroism and meanness. The whole story turns upon the jealousy between the navy and air force over the control of the Coastal Command. The hero, a young airman, is accused of bombing and sinking a British submarine. He has not in fact done so, but is found guilty by a board of enquiry composed of naval officers who are faintly prejudiced against him. Later in the book he is exonerated by a roundabout but curiously convincing chain of circumstances in which the chief link is a dirty joke about contraceptives. The way in which the author handles him shows what an advantage it is for a thinking man to live sometimes on equal terms with men who are not "thinking". The young airman is completely unintellectual. His hobbies are getting difficult stations on the wireless and fitting together model ships of which he buys the parts ready-made. He is conducting a flirtation with a barmaid, whom he finally marries, and there are whole chapters of the kind of conversation that one hears flung to and fro across saloon bars, full of *doubles entendres* and "Oo, aren't you awful!" But the author treats none of this ironically. He sees the young airman's point of view, because, presumably, he has at some time shared his experiences. He can stand inside him as well as outside him and realise that he is heroic as well as childish, competent as well as silly. The result is a good, simple story, pleasantly free from cleverness, and at times genuinely moving.

*Nailcruncher*, on the other hand, is one of the most pretentious novels I have read for a long time. It is an enormous, deliberately farcical story about some semi-imbecile Jews, first in the Greek island of Cephalonia and later in Switzerland. What is chiefly remarkable in it is the length and disgustingness of its scatological passages. As soon as I came on the first of these I turned back to the blurb on the dust-jacket, well knowing what adjective I should find, and, sure enough, there it was—"Rabelaisian". It is curious that this word is invariably used as a term of praise. We are forever being told that whereas pornography is reprehensible, "hearty Rabelaisian humour" (meaning a preoccupation with the WC) is perfectly all right. This is partly, perhaps, because Rabelais is nowadays seldom read. So far from being "healthy" as is always alleged, he is an exceptionally perverse, morbid writer, a case for psycho-analysis. But people who lead strict lives have dirty minds, and Rabelais had a considerable underground reputation in Victorian times. Archdeacon Grantly read him on the sly, it will be remembered, and the bachelor in Browning's poem possessed "a little

edition of Rabelais". Perhaps the only way of making him respectable was to maintain that there is something "normal" and "hearty"
in coprophilia, and the legend has survived into an age when few
people have glanced at his dirtier passages. At any rate "Rabelaisian"
is a correct description of *Nailcruncher*. If you like scatology, this is
the book for you; if you don't, I should steer clear of it, for long
passages in it are calculated to make any ordinary person physically
sick.

*New Statesman and Nation*, 7 December 1940

1941

# 16. London Letter to *Partisan Review*[1]

[From this date until the summer of 1946 George Orwell wrote a regular London letter for *Partisan Review*.]

London, NW1 England
3 January 1941

Dear Editors,

As I am writing this letter in answer to a privately addressed one of your own, perhaps I had better start by quoting what you said, so as to make clear what questions I am trying to answer:

> There are things the news reports do not tell us. For instance, what's happening under the surface in the way of politics? Among the labour groups? What is the general mood, if there is such a thing, among writers, artists and intellectuals? What transmutations have their lives and their preoccupations suffered?

Well, as to the political situation, I think it is true to say that at the moment we are in the middle of a backwash which is not going to make very much ultimate difference. The reactionaries, which means roughly the people who read *The Times*, had a bad scare in the summer, but they saved themselves by the skin of their teeth, and they are now consolidating their position against the new crisis which is likely to arise in the spring. In the summer what amounted to a revolutionary situation existed in England, though there was no one to take advantage of it. After twenty years of being fed on sugar and water the nation had suddenly realised what its rulers were like, and there was a widespread readiness for sweeping economic and social changes, combined with absolute determination to

---

[1] *Partisan Review*, most influential of American left-wing literary magazines, was started by the Communist "John Reed Club" in NYC in 1934. Publication was suspended for most of 1937, and resumed at the end of that year, becoming more literary and politically more Trotskyist in sympathy. William Phillips and Philip Rahv have edited it since 1934.

prevent invasion. At that moment, I believe, the opportunity existed to isolate the moneyed class and swing the mass of the nation behind a policy in which resistance to Hitler and destruction of class-privilege were combined. Clement Greenberg's remark in his article in *Horizon*, that the working class is the only class in England that seriously means to defeat Hitler, seems to me quite untrue. The bulk of the middle class are just as anti-Hitler as the working class, and their morale is probably more reliable. The fact which Socialists, especially when they are looking at the English scene from the outside, seldom seem to me to grasp, is that the patriotism of the middle classes is a thing to be made use of. The people who stand to attention during "God Save the King" would readily transfer their loyalty to a Socialist régime, if they were handled with the minimum of tact. However, in the summer months no one saw the opportunity, the Labour leaders (with the possible exception of Bevin) allowed themselves to be made the tame cats of the Government, and when the invasion failed to come off and the air raids were less terrible than everyone had expected, the quasi-revolutionary mood ebbed away. At present the Right are counter-attacking. Margesson's entry into the Cabinet—the nearest equivalent possible to bringing Chamberlain out of his grave—was a swift cash-in on Wavell's victory in Egypt. The campaign in the Mediterranean is not finished, but events there have justified the Conservatives as against the Left and they can be expected to take advantage of it. It is not impossible that one or two leftish newspapers will be suppressed before long. Suppression of the *Daily Worker* is said to have been mooted already in the Cabinet. But this swing of the pendulum is not vitally important unless one believes, as I do not—and I doubt whether many people under fifty believe it either—that England can win the war without passing through revolution and go straight back to pre-1939 "normality", with 3 million unemployed etc etc.

But at present there does not effectively exist any policy between being patriotic in the "King and Country" style and being pro-Hitler. If another wave of anti-capitalist feeling arrived it could at the moment only be canalised into defeatism. At the same time there is little sign of this in England, though the morale is probably worse in the industrial towns than elsewhere. In London, after four months of almost ceaseless bombing, morale is far better than a year ago when the war was stagnant. The only people who are overtly defeatist are Mosley's followers, the Communists and the pacifists.

The Communists still possess a footing in the factories and may some time stage a come-back by fomenting grievances about working hours etc. But they have difficulty in getting their working-class followers to accept a definitely pro-Hitler policy, and they had to pipe down during the desperate days in the summer. With the general public their influence is nil, as one can see by the votes in the by-elections, and the powerful hold they had on the press in the years 1935–9 has been completely broken. Mosley's Blackshirts have ceased to exist as a legal organisation, but they probably deserve to be taken more seriously than the Communists, if only because the tone of their propaganda is more acceptable to soldiers, sailors and airmen. No left-wing organisation in England has ever been able to gain a footing in the armed forces. The Fascists have, of course, tried to put the blame for both the war and the discomfort caused by the air raids on to the Jews, and during the worst of the East End bombings they did succeed in raising a mutter of antisemitism, though only a faint one. The most interesting development of the anti-war front has been the interpenetration of the pacifist movement by Fascist ideas, especially antisemitism. After Dick Sheppard's death British pacifism seems to have suffered a moral collapse; it has not produced any significant gesture nor even many martyrs, and only about 15 per cent of the membership of the Peace Pledge Union now appear to be active. But many of the surviving pacifists now spin a line of talk indistinguishable from that of the Blackshirts ("Stop this Jewish war" etc), and the actual membership of the PPU[1] and the British Union[2] overlap to some extent. Put all together, the various pro-Hitler organisations can hardly number 150,000 members, and they are not likely to achieve much by their own efforts, but they might play an important part at a time when a government of the Pétain type was contemplating surrender. There is some reason to think that Hitler does not want Mosley's organisation to grow too strong. Lord Haw-Haw, the most effective of the English-language German broadcasters, has been identified with fair certainty as Joyce, a member of the split-off Fascist party and a very bitter personal enemy of Mosley.

You ask also about the intellectual life of England, the various currents of thought in the literary world etc. I think the dominating factors are these:

[1] Peace Pledge Union.
[2] British Union of Fascists led by Sir Oswald Mosley.

a. The complete destruction, owing to the Russo-German Pact, of the left-wing "anti-Fascist" orthodoxy of the past five years.

b. The fact that physically fit people under 35 are mostly in the army, or expect soon to be so.

c. The increase in book-consumption owing to the boredom of war, together with the unwillingness of publishers to risk money on unknown writers.

d. The bombing (of which more presently—but I should say here that it is less terrifying and more of a nuisance than you perhaps imagine).

The Russo-German Pact not only brought the Stalinists and near-Stalinists into the pro-Hitler position, but it also put an end to the game of "I told you so" which the left-wing writers had been so profitably playing for five years past. "Anti-Fascism" as interpreted by the *News Chronicle*, the *New Statesman* and the Left Book Club had depended on the belief—I think it was also half-consciously a hope—that no British government would ever stand up to Hitler. When the Chamberlain Government finally went to war it took the wind out of the left-wingers' sails by putting into effect the policy which they themselves had been demanding. In the few days before war was declared it was extremely amusing to watch the behaviour of orthodox Popular Front-ers, who were exclaiming dolefully "It's going to be another Munich", although in fact it had been obvious for months past that war was inevitable. These people were in reality *hoping* for another Munich, which would allow them to continue with their Cassandra role without having to face the facts of modern war. I was recently in very severe trouble for saying in print that those who were most "anti-Fascist" during the period 1935–9 were most defeatist now. Nevertheless I believe that this is broadly true, and not only of the Stalinists. It is a fact that as soon as war began all the fire went out of orthodox "anti-Fascism". All the stuff about Fascist atrocities, denunciations of Chamberlain, etc, which it had been completely impossible to get away from in any highbrow magazine in peace time, suddenly came to an end, and far more fuss has been made among the left-wing intelligentsia about the internment of German refugees than about anything done by the enemy. During the Spanish civil war the left-wing intellectuals felt that this was "their" war and that they were influencing events in it to some extent. In so far as they expected the war against Germany to happen they imagined that it would be a sort of enlarged version of the war in Spain, a left-wing war in which poets and novelists could be important figures. Of course, it is nothing of the kind. It is an all-in modern war fought mainly by technical experts (airmen etc) and conducted by people who are patriotic according to their lights but entirely reactionary in outlook. At present there is no function in it for intellectuals. From the start the Government have more or less frankly gone on the principle of "keeping the Reds out of it", and it was not till after the disaster in France that they began to allow men known to have fought in Spain to join the army. Consequently the chief activity among left-wing writers is a rather pettifogging criticism which turns into a kind of dismay when England wins a victory, because this always falsifies their predictions. In the summer the left-wing intelligentsia were completely defeatist, far more so than they allowed to appear in print. At the moment when England seemed likely to be invaded one well-known left-wing writer actually wanted to discourage the idea of mass resistance, on the ground that the Germans would behave more leniently if not opposed. There was also a move on foot, with an eye to the coming Nazi occupation, to get the Scotland Yard Special Branch to destroy the political dossiers which, no doubt, most of us possess. All this was in marked contrast to the attitude of the common people, who either had not woken up to the fact that England was in danger, or were determined to resist to the last ditch. But certain left-wing writers and lecturers who had fought in Spain, notably Tom Wintringham, did a lot to stem the tide of defeatism.

Personally I consider it all to the good that the confident war-mongering mood of the Popular Front period, with its lying propaganda and its horrible atmosphere of orthodoxy, has been destroyed. But it has left a sort of hole. Nobody knows what to think, nothing is being started. It is very difficult to imagine any new "school" of literature arising at a moment when the youngish writers have had their universe punctured and the very young are either in the army or kept out of print by lack of paper. Moreover the economic foundations of literature are shifting, for the highbrow literary magazine, depending ultimately on leisured people who have been brought up in a minority culture, is becoming less and less possible. *Horizon* is a sort of modern democratised version of this (compare its general tone with that of the *Criterion* of ten years ago), and even *Horizon* keeps going only with difficulty. On the other hand the reading public is increasing and the intellectual level of the popular press has taken a tremendous bound upwards since the

outbreak of war. But hardly any good *books* are appearing. Novels
are still being published in great numbers, but they are of a trashi-
ness that passes belief. Only the mentally dead are capable of sitting
down and writing novels while this nightmare is going on. The
conditions that made it possible for Joyce and Lawrence to do their
best work during the war of 1914–18 (i.e. the consciousness that
presently the world would be sane again) no longer exist. There is
such a doubt about the continuity of civilisation as can hardly have
existed for hundreds of years, and meanwhile there are the air raids,
which make continuous intellectual life very difficult. I don't mean
because of physical danger. It is true that by this time everyone in
London has had at least one "providential escape"—these so
common that it is now considered bad form to talk about them—but
the actual casualties are very few and even the damage, though
enormous, is mostly localised to the City of London and the East
End slums. But the disorganisation of transport, communications,
etc causes endless inconvenience. One seems to spend half one's
time trying to buy a sack of coal because the electricity has failed,
or trying to put through telephone calls on a wire that has gone
dead, or wandering about looking for a bus—and this is a miserably
cold, slushy winter. The night life of London has almost ceased, not
because of the bombs but because of the shrapnel, which is often
plentiful enough to make it dangerous to go out after dusk. The
movies close early and theatres have stopped altogether, except for
a few matinées. Only the pubs are much as usual, in spite of the
now enormous price of beer. On nights when the raids are bad the
deafening racket of the guns makes it difficult to work. It is a time
in which it is hard to settle down to anything and even the writing
of a silly newspaper article takes twice as long as usual.

I wonder whether, even in what I have said, I exaggerate the
seriousness of the air raids? It is worth remembering that at the
worst period of the blitz it was calculated that only 15 per cent of
London's population were sleeping in shelters. The number is added
to by those whose homes are destroyed by bombs, but also constantly
decreased by those who grow gradually callous. When all is said and
done one's main impression is the immense stolidity of ordinary
people, the widespread vague consciousness that things can never be
the same again, and yet, together with that, the tendency of life to
slip back into the familiar pattern. On the day in September when the
Germans broke through and set the docks on fire, I think few people

can have watched those enormous fires without feeling that this was the end of an epoch. One seemed to feel that the immense changes through which our society has got to pass were going to happen there and then. But to an astonishing extent things have slipped back to normal. I will end with a few extracts from my diary, to try and give you some idea of the atmosphere:

> The aeroplanes come back and back, every few minutes. It is just like in an eastern country, when you keep thinking you have killed the last mosquito inside your net, and every time, as soon as you have turned the light out, another starts droning. . . . The commotion made by the mere passage of a bomb through the air is astonishing. The whole house shakes, enough to rattle objects on the table. Why it is that the electric lights dip when a bomb passes close by, nobody seems to know. . . . Oxford Street yesterday, from Oxford Circus up to the Marble Arch, completely empty of traffic, and only a few pedestrians, with the late afternoon sun shining straight down the empty roadway and glittering on innumerable fragments of broken glass. Outside John Lewis's, a pile of plaster dress models, very pink and realistic, looking so like a pile of corpses that one could have mistaken them for that at a little distance. Just the same sight in Barcelona, only there it was plaster saints from desecrated churches. . . . Regular features of the time: neatly swept-up piles of glass, litter of stone and splinters of flint, smell of escaping gas, knots of sight-seers waiting at the cordons where there are unexploded bombs. . . . Nondescript people wandering about, having been evacuated from their houses because of delayed-action bombs. Yesterday two girls stopping me in the street, very elegant in appearance except that their faces were filthily dirty: "Please, sir, can you tell us where we are?". . . . Withal, huge areas of London almost normal, and everyone quite happy in the daytime, never seeming to think about the coming night, like animals which are unable to foresee the future so long as they have a bit of food and a place in the sun.

Cyril Connolly and Stephen Spender send all the best. Good luck to America.

Yours sincerely
George Orwell

**The Lion and the Unicorn: Socialism and the English Genius** *was published in London by Secker & Warburg on 19 February 1941. This was the first volume in the series, The Searchlight Books, edited by T.R. Fyvel and George Orwell.*

## 17. The Lion and the Unicorn: Socialism and the English Genius

PART I: ENGLAND YOUR ENGLAND

i

As I write, highly civilised human beings are flying overhead, trying to kill me.

They do not feel any enmity against me as an individual, nor I against them. They are "only doing their duty", as the saying goes. Most of them, I have no doubt, are kind-hearted law-abiding men who would never dream of committing murder in private life. On the other hand, if one of them succeeds in blowing me to pieces with a well-placed bomb, he will never sleep any the worse for it. He is serving his country, which has the power to absolve him from evil.

One cannot see the modern world as it is unless one recognises the overwhelming strength of patriotism, national loyalty. In certain circumstances it can break down, at certain levels of civilisation it does not exist, but as a *positive* force there is nothing to set beside it. Christianity and international Socialism are as weak as straw in comparison with it. Hitler and Mussolini rose to power in their own countries very largely because they could grasp this fact and their opponents could not.

Also, one must admit that the divisions between nation and nation are founded on real differences of outlook. Till recently it was thought proper to pretend that all human beings are very much alike, but in fact anyone able to use his eyes knows that the average of human behaviour differs enormously from country to country. Things that could happen in one country could not happen in another. Hitler's June Purge, for instance, could not have happened in England. And, as western peoples go, the English are very highly differentiated. There is a sort of backhanded admission of this in the dislike which nearly all foreigners feel for our national way of life. Few Europeans can endure living in England, and even Americans often feel more at home in Europe.

When you come back to England from any foreign country, you have immediately the sensation of breathing a different air. Even in the first few minutes dozens of small things conspire to give you this feeling. The beer is bitterer, the coins are heavier, the grass is greener, the advertisements are more blatant. The crowds in the big towns, with their mild knobby faces, their bad teeth and gentle manners, are different from a European crowd. Then the vastness of England swallows you up, and you lose for a while your feeling that the whole nation has a single identifiable character. Are there really such things as nations? Are we not 46 million individuals, all different? And the diversity of it, the chaos! The clatter of clogs in the Lancashire mill towns, the to-and-fro of the lorries on the Great North Road, the queues outside the Labour Exchanges, the rattle of pin-tables in the Soho pubs, the old maids biking to Holy Communion through the mists of the autumn mornings—all these are not only fragments, but *characteristic* fragments, of the English scene. How can one make a pattern out of this muddle?

But talk to foreigners, read foreign books or newspapers, and you are brought back to the same thought. Yes, there *is* something distinctive and recognisable in English civilisation. It is a culture as individual as that of Spain. It is somehow bound up with solid breakfasts and gloomy Sundays, smoky towns and winding roads, green fields and red pillar-boxes. It has a flavour of its own. Moreover it is continuous, it stretches into the future and the past, there is something in it that persists, as in a living creature. What can the England of 1940 have in common with the England of 1840? But then, what have you in common with the child of five whose photograph your mother keeps on the mantelpiece? Nothing, except that you happen to be the same person.

And above all, it is *your* civilisation, it is *you*. However much you hate it or laugh at it, you will never be happy away from it for any length of time. The suet puddings and the red pillar-boxes have entered into your soul. Good or evil, it is yours, you belong to it, and this side the grave you will never get away from the marks that it has given you.

Meanwhile England, together with the rest of the world, is changing. And like everything else it can change only in certain directions, which up to a point can be foreseen. That is not to say that the future is fixed, merely that certain alternatives are possible and others not. A seed may grow or not grow, but at any rate a turnip seed never grows into a parsnip. It is therefore of the deepest

importance to try and determine what England *is*, before guessing
what part England *can play* in the huge events that are happening.

## ii

National characteristics are not easy to pin down, and when
pinned down they often turn out to be trivialities or seem to have
no connection with one another. Spaniards are cruel to animals,
Italians can do nothing without making a deafening noise, the
Chinese are addicted to gambling. Obviously such things don't matter
in themselves. Nevertheless, nothing is causeless, and even the
fact that Englishmen have bad teeth can tell one something about
the realities of English life.

Here are a couple of generalisations about England that would
be accepted by almost all observers. One is that the English are not
gifted artistically. They are not as musical as the Germans or
Italians, painting and sculpture have never flourished in England
as they have in France. Another is that, as Europeans go, the
English are not intellectual. They have a horror of abstract thought,
they feel no need for any philosophy or systematic "world-view".
Nor is this because they are "practical", as they are so fond of
claiming for themselves. One has only to look at their methods of
town planning and water supply, their obstinate clinging to everything that is out of date and a nuisance, a spelling system that defies
analysis and a system of weights and measures that is intelligible
only to the compilers of arithmetic books, to see how little they
care about mere efficiency. But they have a certain power of acting
without taking thought. Their world-famed hypocrisy—their double-
faced attitude towards the Empire, for instance—is bound up with this.
Also, in moments of supreme crisis the whole nation can suddenly
draw together and act upon a species of instinct, really a code of conduct which is understood by almost everyone, though never formulated.
The phrase that Hitler coined for the Germans, "a sleep-walking
people", would have been better applied to the English. Not that
there is anything to be proud of in being called a sleep-walker.

But here it is worth noting a minor English trait which is extremely well marked though not often commented on, and that is a
love of flowers. This is one of the first things that one notices when
one reaches England from abroad, especially if one is coming from
southern Europe. Does it not contradict the English indifference
to the arts? Not really, because it is found in people who have no

aesthetic feelings whatever. What it does link up with, however, is another English characteristic which is so much a part of us that we barely notice it, and that is the addiction to hobbies and spare-time occupations, the *privateness* of English life. We are a nation of flower-lovers, but also a nation of stamp-collectors, pigeon-fanciers, amateur carpenters, coupon-snippers, darts-players, crossword-puzzle fans. All the culture that is most truly native centres round things which even when they are communal are not official—the pub, the football match, the back garden, the fireside and the "nice cup of tea". The liberty of the individual is still believed in, almost as in the nineteenth century. But this has nothing to do with economic liberty, the right to exploit others for profit. It is the liberty to have a home of your own, to do what you like in your spare time, to choose your own amusements instead of having them chosen for you from above. The most hateful of all names in an English ear is Nosey Parker. It is obvious, of course, that even this purely private liberty is a lost cause. Like all other modern peoples, the English are in process of being numbered, labelled, conscripted, "co-ordinated". But the pull of their impulses is in the other direction, and the kind of regimentation that can be imposed on them will be modified in consequence. No party rallies, no Youth Movements, no coloured shirts, no Jew-baiting or "spontaneous" demonstrations. No Gestapo either, in all probability.

But in all societies the common people must live to some extent *against* the existing order. The genuinely popular culture of England is something that goes on beneath the surface, unofficially and more or less frowned on by the authorities. One thing one notices if one looks directly at the common people, especially in the big towns, is that they are not puritanical. They are inveterate gamblers, drink as much beer as their wages will permit, are devoted to bawdy jokes, and use probably the foulest language in the world. They have to satisfy these tastes in the face of astonishing, hypocritical laws (licensing laws, lottery acts, etc etc) which are designed to interfere with everybody but in practice allow everything to happen. Also, the common people are without definite religious belief, and have been so for centuries. The Anglican Church never had a real hold on them, it was simply a preserve of the landed gentry, and the Nonconformist sects only influenced minorities. And yet they have retained a deep tinge of Christian feeling, while almost forgetting the name of Christ. The power-worship which is the new religion of Europe, and which has infected the English intelligentsia, has never touched the common people. They have never caught up with power politics. The "realism" which is preached in Japanese and Italian newspapers would horrify them. One can learn a good deal about the spirit of England from the comic coloured postcards that you see in the windows of cheap stationers' shops. These things are a sort of diary upon which the English people have unconsciously recorded themselves. Their old-fashioned outlook, their graded snobberies, their mixture of bawdiness and hypocrisy, their extreme gentleness, their deeply moral attitude to life, are all mirrored there.

The gentleness of the English civilisation is perhaps its most marked characteristic. You notice it the instant you set foot on English soil. It is a land where the bus conductors are good-tempered and the policemen carry no revolvers. In no country inhabited by white men is it easier to shove people off the pavement. And with this goes something that is always written off by European observers as "decadence" or hypocrisy, the English hatred of war and militarism. It is rooted deep in history, and it is strong in the lower-middle class as well as the working class. Successive wars have shaken it but not destroyed it. Well within living memory it was common for "the redcoats" to be booed at in the streets and for the landlords of respectable public houses to refuse to allow soldiers on the premises. In peace time, even when there are two million unemployed, it is difficult to fill the ranks of the tiny standing army, which is officered by the county gentry and a specialised stratum of the middle class, and manned by farm labourers and slum proletarians. The mass of the people are without military knowledge or tradition, and their attitude towards war is invariably defensive. No politician could rise to power by promising them conquests or military "glory", no Hymn of Hate has ever made any appeal to them. In the last war the songs which the soldiers made up and sang of their own accord were not vengeful but humorous and mock-defeatist.[1] The only enemy they ever named was the sergeant-major.

[1] For example:

> I don't want to join the bloody Army,
> I don't want to go unto the war;
> I want no more to roam,
> I'd rather stay at home,
> Living on the earnings of a whore.

But it was not in that spirit that they fought. [Author's footnote.]

In England all the boasting and flag-wagging, the "Rule Britannia" stuff, is done by small minorities. The patriotism of the common people is not vocal or even conscious. They do not retain among their historical memories the name of a single military victory. English literature, like other literatures, is full of battle-poems, but it is worth noticing that the ones that have won for themselves a kind of popularity are always a tale of disasters and retreats. There is no popular poem about Trafalgar or Waterloo, for instance. Sir John Moore's army at Corunna, fighting a desperate rearguard action before escaping overseas (just like Dunkirk!) has more appeal than a brilliant victory. The most stirring battle-poem in English is about a brigade of cavalry which charged in the wrong direction. And of the last war, the four names which have really engraved themselves on the popular memory are Mons, Ypres, Gallipoli and Passchendaele, every time a disaster. The names of the great battles that finally broke the German armies are simply unknown to the general public.

The reason why the English anti-militarism disgusts foreign observers is that it ignores the existence of the British Empire. It looks like sheer hypocrisy. After all, the English have absorbed a quarter of the earth and held on to it by means of a huge navy. How dare they then turn round and say that war is wicked?

It is quite true that the English are hypocritical about their Empire. In the working class this hypocrisy takes the form of not knowing that the Empire exists. But their dislike of standing armies is a perfect sound instinct. A navy employs comparatively few people, and it is an external weapon which cannot affect home politics directly. Military dictatorships exist everywhere, but there is no such thing as a naval dictatorship. What English people of nearly all classes loathe from the bottom of their hearts is the swaggering officer type, the jingle of spurs and the crash of boots. Decades before Hitler was ever heard of, the word "Prussian" had much the same significance in England as "Nazi" has today. So deep does this feeling go that for a hundred years past the officers of the British army, in peace time, have always worn civilian clothes when off duty.

One rapid but fairly sure guide to the social atmosphere of a country is the parade-step of its army. A military parade is really a kind of ritual dance, something like a ballet, expressing a certain philosophy of life. The goose-step, for instance, is one of the most horrible sights in the world, far more terrifying than a dive-bomber.

It is simply an affirmation of naked power; contained in it, quite consciously and intentionally, is the vision of a boot crashing down on a face. Its ugliness is part of its essence, for what it is saying is "Yes, I *am* ugly, and you daren't laugh at me", like the bully who makes faces at his victim. Why is the goose-step not used in England? There are, heaven knows, plenty of army officers who would be only too glad to introduce some such thing. It is not used because the people in the street would laugh. Beyond a certain point, military display is only possible in countries where the common people dare not laugh at the army. The Italians adopted the goose-step at about the time when Italy passed definitely under German control, and, as one would expect, they do it less well than the Germans. The Vichy government, if it survives, is bound to introduce a stiffer parade-ground discipline into what is left of the French army. In the British army the drill is rigid and complicated, full of memories of the eighteenth century, but without definite swagger; the march is merely a formalised walk. It belongs to a society which is ruled by the sword, no doubt, but a sword which must never be taken out of the scabbard.

And yet the gentleness of English civilisation is mixed up with barbarities and anachronisms. Our criminal law is as out-of-date as the muskets in the Tower. Over against the Nazi Storm Trooper you have got to set that typically English figure, the hanging judge, some gouty old bully with his mind rooted in the nineteenth century, handing out savage sentences. In England people are still hanged by the neck and flogged with the cat o' nine tails. Both of these punishments are obscene as well as cruel, but there has never been any genuinely popular outcry against them. People accept them (and Dartmoor, and Borstal) almost as they accept the weather. They are part of "the law", which is assumed to be unalterable.

Here one comes upon an all-important English trait: the respect for constitutionalism and legality, the belief in "the law" as something above the State and above the individual, something which is cruel and stupid, of course, but at any rate *incorruptible*.

It is not that anyone imagines the law to be just. Everyone knows that there is one law for the rich and another for the poor. But no one accepts the implications of this, everyone takes it for granted that the law, such as it is, will be respected, and feels a sense of outrage when it is not. Remarks like "They can't run me in; I haven't done anything wrong", or "They can't do that; it's against the law", are part of the atmosphere of England. The professed enemies of society have this feeling as strongly as anyone else. One sees it in prison-books like Wilfred Macartney's *Walls Have Mouths* or Jim Phelan's *Jail Journey*, in the solemn idiocies that take place at the trials of conscientious objectors, in letters to the papers from eminent Marxist professors, pointing out that this or that is a "miscarriage of British justice". Everyone believes in his heart that the law can be, ought to be, and, on the whole, will be impartially administered. The totalitarian idea that there is no such thing as law, there is only power, has never taken root. Even the intelligentsia have only accepted it in theory.

An illusion can become a half-truth, a mask can alter the expression of a face. The familiar arguments to the effect that democracy is "just the same as" or "just as bad as" totalitarianism never take account of this fact. All such arguments boil down to saying that half a loaf is the same as no bread. In England such concepts as justice, liberty and objective truth are still believed in. They may be illusions, but they are very powerful illusions. The belief in them influences conduct, national life is different because of them. In proof of which, look about you. Where are the rubber truncheons, where is the castor oil? The sword is still in the scabbard, and while it stays there corruption cannot go beyond a certain point. The English electoral system, for instance, is an all but open fraud. In a dozen obvious ways it is gerrymandered in the interest of the moneyed class. But until some deep change has occurred in the public mind, it cannot become *completely* corrupt. You do not arrive at the polling booth to find men with revolvers telling you which way to vote, nor are the votes miscounted, nor is there any direct bribery. Even hypocrisy is a powerful safeguard. The hanging judge, that evil old man in scarlet robe and horse-hair wig, whom nothing short of dynamite will ever teach what century he is living in, but who will at any rate interpret the law according to the books and will in no circumstances take a money bribe, is one of the symbolic figures of England. He is a symbol of the strange mixture of reality and illusion, democracy and privilege, humbug and decency, the subtle network of compromises, by which the nation keeps itself in its familiar shape.

### iii

I have spoken all the while of "the nation", "England", "Britain", as though 45 million souls could somehow be treated as a unit.

But is not England notoriously two nations, the rich and the poor? Dare one pretend that there is anything in common between people with £100,000 a year and people with £1 a week? And even Welsh and Scottish readers are likely to have been offended because I have used the word "England" oftener than "Britain", as though the whole population dwelt in London and the Home Counties and neither north nor west possessed a culture of its own.

One gets a better view of this question if one considers the minor point first. It is quite true that the so-called races of Britain feel themselves to be very different from one another. A Scotsman, for instance, does not thank you if you call him an Englishman. You can see the hesitation we feel on this point by the fact that we call our islands by no less than six different names, England, Britain, Great Britain, the British Isles, the United Kingdom and, in very exalted moments, Albion. Even the differences between north and south England loom large in our own eyes. But somehow these differences fade away the moment that any two Britons are confronted by a European. It is very rare to meet a foreigner, other than an American, who can distinguish between English and Scots or even English and Irish. To a Frenchman, the Breton and the Auvergnat seem very different beings, and the accent of Marseilles is a stock joke in Paris. Yet we speak of "France" and "the French", recognising France as an entity, a single civilisation, which in fact it is. So also with ourselves. Looked at from the outside, even the cockney and the Yorkshireman have a strong family resemblance.

And even the distinction between rich and poor dwindles somewhat when one regards the nation from the outside. There is no question about the inequality of wealth in England. It is grosser than in any European country, and you have only to look down the nearest street to see it. Economically, England is certainly two nations, if not three or four. But at the same time the vast majority of the people *feel* themselves to be a single nation and are conscious of resembling one another more than they resemble foreigners. Patriotism is usually stronger than class-hatred, and always stronger than any kind of internationalism. Except for a brief moment in 1920 (the "Hands off Russia" movement) the British working class have never thought or acted internationally. For two and a half years they watched their comrades in Spain slowly strangled, and never aided them by even a single strike.[1] But when their own country (the country of Lord Nuffield and Mr Montagu Norman) was in danger, their attitude was very different. At the moment when it seemed likely that England might be invaded, Anthony Eden appealed over the radio for Local Defence Volunteers. He got a quarter of a million men in the first twenty-four hours, and another million in the subsequent month. One has only to compare these figures with, for instance, the number of conscientious objectors to see how vast is the strength of traditional loyalties compared with new ones.

In England patriotism takes different forms in different classes, but it runs like a connecting thread through nearly all of them. Only the Europeanised intelligentsia are really immune to it. As a positive emotion it is stronger in the middle class than in the upper class—the cheap public schools, for instance, are more given to patriotic demonstrations than the expensive ones—but the number of definitely treacherous rich men, the Laval-Quisling type, is probably very small. In the working class patriotism is profound, but it is unconscious. The working man's heart does not leap when he sees a Union Jack. But the famous "insularity" and "xenophobia" of the English is far stronger in the working class than in the bourgeoisie. In all countries the poor are more national than the rich, but the English working class are outstanding in their abhorrence of foreign habits. Even when they are obliged to live abroad for years they refuse either to accustom themselves to foreign food or to learn foreign languages. Nearly every Englishman of working-class origin considers it effeminate to pronounce a foreign word correctly. During the war of 1914–18 the English working class were in contact with foreigners to an extent that is rarely possible. The sole result was that they brought back a hatred of all Europeans, except the Germans, whose courage they admired. In four years on French soil they did not even acquire a liking for wine. The insularity of the English, their refusal to take foreigners seriously, is a folly that has to be paid for very heavily from time to time. But it plays its part in the English mystique, and the intellectuals who have tried to break it down have generally done more harm than good. At bottom it is the same quality in the English character that repels the tourist and keeps out the invader.

Here one comes back to two English characteristics that I pointed

---

[1] It is true that they aided them to a certain extent with money. Still, the sums raised for the various aid-Spain funds would not equal five per cent of the turn-over of the Football Pools during the same period. [Author's footnote.]

out, seemingly rather at random, at the beginning of the last chapter. One is the lack of artistic ability. This is perhaps another way of saying that the English are outside the European culture. For there is one art in which they have shown plenty of talent, namely literature. But this is also the only art that cannot cross frontiers. Literature, especially poetry, and lyric poetry most of all, is a kind of family joke, with little or no value outside its own language-group. Except for Shakespeare, the best English poets are barely known in Europe, even as names. The only poets who are widely read are Byron, who is admired for the wrong reasons, and Oscar Wilde, who is pitied as a victim of English hypocrisy. And linked up with this, though not very obviously, is the lack of philosophical faculty, the absence in nearly all Englishmen of any need for an ordered system of thought or even for the use of logic.

Up to a point, the sense of national unity is a substitute for a "world-view". Just because patriotism is all but universal and not even the rich are uninfluenced by it, there can be moments when the whole nation suddenly swings together and does the same thing, like a herd of cattle facing a wolf. There was such a moment, unmistakably, at the time of the disaster in France. After eight months of vaguely wondering what the war was about, the people suddenly knew what they had got to do: first, to get the army away from Dunkirk, and secondly to prevent invasion. It was like the awakening of a giant. Quick! Danger! The Philistines be upon thee, Samson! And then the swift unanimous action—and then, alas, the prompt relapse into sleep. In a divided nation that would have been exactly the moment for a big peace movement to arise. But does this mean that the instinct of the English will always tell them to do the right thing? Not at all, merely that it will tell them to do the same thing. In the 1931 General Election, for instance, we all did the wrong thing in perfect unison. We were as single-minded as the Gadarene swine. But I honestly doubt whether we can say that we were shoved down the slope against our will.

It follows that British democracy is less of a fraud than it sometimes appears. A foreign observer sees only the huge inequality of wealth, the unfair electoral system, the governing-class control over the press, the radio and education, and concludes that democracy is simply a polite name for dictatorship. But this ignores the considerable agreement that does unfortunately exist between the leaders and the led. However much one may hate to admit it, it is almost certain that between 1931 and 1940 the National Government represented the will of the mass of the people. It tolerated slums, unemployment and a cowardly foreign policy. Yes, but so did public opinion. It was a stagnant period, and its natural leaders were mediocrities.

In spite of the campaigns of a few thousand left-wingers, it is fairly certain that the bulk of the English people were behind Chamberlain's foreign policy. More, it is fairly certain that the same struggle was going on in Chamberlain's mind as in the minds of ordinary people. His opponents professed to see in him a dark and wily schemer, plotting to sell England to Hitler, but it is far likelier that he was merely a stupid old man doing his best according to his very dim lights. It is difficult otherwise to explain the contradictions of his policy, his failure to grasp any of the courses that were open to him. Like the mass of the people, he did not want to pay the price either of peace or of war. And public opinion was behind him all the while, in policies that were completely incompatible with one another. It was behind him when he went to Munich, when he tried to come to an understanding with Russia, when he gave the guarantee to Poland, when he honoured it, and when he prosecuted the war half-heartedly. Only when the results of his policy became apparent did it turn against him; which is to say that it turned against its own lethargy of the past seven years. Thereupon the people picked a leader nearer to their mood, Churchill, who was at any rate able to grasp that wars are not won without fighting. Later, perhaps, they will pick another leader who can grasp that only Socialist nations can fight effectively.

Do I mean by all this that England is a genuine democracy? No, not even a reader of the *Daily Telegraph* could quite swallow that.

England is the most class-ridden country under the sun. It is a land of snobbery and privilege, ruled largely by the old and silly. But in any calculation about it one has got to take into account its emotional unity, the tendency of nearly all its inhabitants to feel alike and act together in moments of supreme crisis. It is the only great country in Europe that is not obliged to drive hundreds of thousands of its nationals into exile or the concentration camp. At this moment, after a year of war, newspapers and pamphlets abusing the Government, praising the enemy and clamouring for surrender are being sold on the streets, almost without interference. And this is less from a respect for freedom of speech than from a simple perception that these things don't matter. It is safe to let a paper like *Peace News* be sold, because it is certain that ninety-five per cent of the population will never want to read it. The nation is bound together by an invisible chain. At any normal time the ruling class will rob, mismanage, sabotage, lead us into the muck; but let popular opinion really make itself heard, let them get a tug from below that they cannot avoid feeling, and it is difficult for them not to respond. The left-wing writers who denounce the whole of the ruling class as "pro-Fascist" are grossly over-simplifying. Even among the inner clique of politicians who brought us to our present pass, it is doubtful whether there were any *conscious* traitors. The corruption that happens in England is seldom of that kind. Nearly always it is more in the nature of self-deception, of the right hand not knowing what the left hand doeth. And being unconscious, it is limited. One sees this at its most obvious in the English press. Is the English press honest or dishonest? At normal times it is deeply dishonest. All the papers that matter live off their advertisements, and the advertisers exercise an indirect censorship over news. Yet I do not suppose there is one paper in England that can be straight-forwardly bribed with hard cash. In the France of the Third Republic all but a very few of the newspapers could notoriously be bought over the counter like so many pounds of cheese. Public life in England has never been *openly* scandalous. It has not reached the pitch of disintegration at which humbug can be dropped.

England is not the jewelled isle of Shakespeare's much-quoted passage, nor is it the inferno depicted by Dr Goebbels. More than either it resembles a family, a rather stuffy Victorian family, with not many black sheep in it but with all its cupboards bursting with skeletons. It has rich relations who have to be kow-towed to and poor relations who are horribly sat upon, and there is a deep con-spiracy of silence about the source of the family income. It is a family in which the young are generally thwarted and most of the power is in the hands of irresponsible uncles and bedridden aunts. Still, it is a family. It has its private language and its common memories, and at the approach of an enemy it closes its ranks. A family with the wrong members in control—that, perhaps, is as near as one can come to describing England in a phrase.

## iv

Probably the battle of Waterloo *was* won on the playing-fields of Eton, but the opening battles of all subsequent wars have been lost there. One of the dominant facts in English life during the past three-quarters of a century has been the decay of ability in the ruling class.

In the years between 1920 and 1940 it was happening with the speed of a chemical reaction. Yet at the moment of writing it is still possible to speak of a ruling class. Like the knife which has had two new blades and three new handles, the upper fringe of English society is still almost what it was in the mid-nineteenth century. After 1832 the old land-owning aristocracy steadily lost power, but instead of disappearing or becoming a fossil they simply intermarried with the merchants, manufacturers and financiers who had replaced them, and soon turned them into accurate copies of themselves. The wealthy ship-owner or cotton-miller set up for himself an alibi as a country gentleman, while his sons learned the right mannerisms at public schools which had been designed for just that purpose. England was ruled by an aristocracy constantly recruited from parvenus. And considering what energy the self-made men possessed, and considering that they were buying their way into a class which at any rate had a tradition of public service, one might have expected that able rulers could be produced in some such way.

And yet somehow the ruling class decayed, lost its ability, its daring, finally even its ruthlessness, until a time came when stuffed shirts like Eden or Halifax could stand out as men of exceptional talent. As for Baldwin, one could not even dignify him with the name of stuffed shirt. He was simply a hole in the air. The mishandling of England's domestic problems during the nineteen-twenties had been bad enough, but British foreign policy between 1931 and 1939 is one of the wonders of the world. Why? What had happened? What was it that at every decisive moment made every British statesman do the wrong thing with so unerring an instinct?

The underlying fact was that the whole position of the moneyed class had long ceased to be justifiable. There they sat, at the centre of a vast empire and a world-wide financial network, drawing interest and profits and spending them—on what? It was fair to say that life within the British Empire was in many ways better than life outside it. Still, the Empire was undeveloped, India slept in the Middle Ages, the Dominions lay empty, with foreigners jealously barred out, and even England was full of slums and unemployment. Only half a million people, the people in the country houses, definitely benefited from the existing system. Moreover, the tendency of small businesses to merge together into large ones robbed more and more of the moneyed class of their function and turned them into mere *owners*, their work being done for them by salaried managers and technicians. For long past there had been in England an entirely functionless class, living on money that was invested they hardly knew where, the "idle rich", the people whose photographs you can look at in the *Tatler* and the *Bystander*, always supposing that you want to. The existence of these people was by any standard unjustifiable. They were simply parasites, less useful to society than his fleas are to a dog.

By 1920 there were many people who were aware of all this. By 1930 millions were aware of it. But the British ruling class obviously could not admit to themselves that their usefulness was at an end. Had they done that they would have had to abdicate. For it was not possible for them to turn themselves into mere bandits, like the American millionaires, consciously clinging to unjust privileges and beating down opposition by bribery and tear-gas bombs. After all, they belonged to a class with a certain tradition, they had been to public schools where the duty of dying for your country, if necessary, is laid down as the first and greatest of the Commandments. They had to *feel* themselves true patriots, even while they plundered their countrymen. Clearly there was only one escape for them—into stupidity. They could keep society in its existing shape only by being *unable* to grasp that any improvement was possible. Difficult though this was, they achieved it, largely by fixing their eyes on the past and refusing to notice the changes that were going on round them.

There is much in England that this explains. It explains the decay of country life, due to the keeping-up of a sham feudalism which drives the more spirited workers off the land. It explains the immobility of the public schools, which have barely altered since the 'eighties of the last century. It explains the military incompetence which has again and again startled the world. Since the 'fifties every war in which England has engaged has started off with a series of disasters, after which the situation has been saved by people comparatively low in the social scale. The higher commanders, drawn from the aristocracy, could never prepare for modern war, because in order to do so they would have had to admit to themselves that the world was changing. They have always clung to obsolete methods and weapons, because they inevitably saw each war as a repetition of the last. Before the Boer War they prepared for the Zulu War, before the 1914 for the Boer War, and before the present war for 1914. Even at this moment hundreds of thousands of men in England are being trained with the bayonet, a weapon entirely useless except for opening tins. It is worth noticing that the navy and, latterly, the air force, have always been more efficient than the regular army. But the navy is only partially, and the air force hardly at all, within the ruling-class orbit.

It must be admitted that so long as things were peaceful the methods of the British ruling class served them well enough. Their own people manifestly tolerated them. However unjustly England might be organised, it was at any rate not torn by class warfare or haunted by secret police. The Empire was peaceful as no area of comparable size has ever been. Throughout its vast extent, nearly a quarter of the earth, there were fewer armed men than would be found necessary by a minor Balkan state. As people to live under, and looking at them merely from a liberal, *negative* standpoint, the British ruling class had their points. They were preferable to the truly modern men, the Nazis and Fascists. But it had long been obvious that they would be helpless against any serious attack from the outside.

They could not struggle against Nazism or Fascism, because they could not understand them. Neither could they have struggled against Communism, if Communism had been a serious force in western Europe. To understand Fascism they would have had to study the theory of Socialism, which would have forced them to realise that the economic system by which they lived was unjust, inefficient and out-of-date. But it was exactly this fact that they had trained themselves never to face. They dealt with Fascism as the cavalry generals of 1914 dealt with the machine-gun—by ignoring it. After years of aggression and massacres, they had grasped only one fact, that Hitler and Mussolini were hostile to Communism. Therefore, it was argued, they *must* be friendly to the British dividend-drawer. Hence the truly frightening spectacle of Conservative MPs wildly cheering the news that British ships, bringing food to the Spanish Republican government, had been bombed by Italian aeroplanes. Even when they had begun to grasp that Fascism was dangerous, its essentially revolutionary nature, the huge military effort it was capable of making, the sort of tactics it would use, were

quite beyond their comprehension. At the time of the Spanish
civil war, anyone with as much political knowledge as can be
acquired from a sixpenny pamphlet on Socialism knew that, if Franco
won, the result would be strategically disastrous for England; and
yet generals and admirals who had given their lives to the study
of war were unable to grasp this fact. This vein of political ignorance
runs right through English official life, through Cabinet ministers,
ambassadors, consuls, judges, magistrates, policemen. The policeman who arrests the "red" does not understand the theories the
"red" is preaching; if he did, his own position as bodyguard of
the moneyed class might seem less pleasant to him. There is reason
to think that even military espionage is hopelessly hampered by
ignorance of the new economic doctrines and the ramifications of
the underground parties.

The British ruling class were not altogether wrong in thinking
that Fascism was on their side. It is a fact that any rich man, unless
he is a Jew, has less to fear from Fascism than from either Communism or democratic Socialism. One ought never to forget this, for
nearly the whole of German and Italian propaganda is designed to
cover it up. The natural instinct of men like Simon, Hoare, Chamberlain etc was to come to an agreement with Hitler. But—and
here the peculiar feature of English life that I have spoken of, the
deep sense of national solidarity, comes in—they could only do
so by breaking up the Empire and selling their own people into semi-
slavery. A truly corrupt class would have done this without hesitation, as in France. But things had not gone that distance in England.
Politicians who would make cringing speeches about "the duty of
loyalty to our conquerors" are hardly to be found in English public
life. Tossed to and fro between their incomes and their principles, it
was impossible that men like Chamberlain should do anything but
make the worst of both worlds.

One thing that has always shown that the English ruling class are
*morally* fairly sound, is that in time of war they are ready enough
to get themselves killed. Several dukes, earls and what nots were
killed in the recent campaign in Flanders. That could not happen if
these people were the cynical scoundrels that they are sometimes
declared to be. It is important not to misunderstand their motives,
or one cannot predict their actions. What is to be expected of them is
not treachery or physical cowardice, but stupidity, unconscious
sabotage, an infallible instinct for doing the wrong thing. They are

not wicked, or not altogether wicked; they are merely unteachable. Only when their money and power are gone will the younger among them begin to grasp what century they are living in.

v

The stagnation of the Empire in the between-war years affected everyone in England, but it had an especially direct effect upon two important sub-sections of the middle class. One was the military and imperialist middle class, generally nicknamed the Blimps, and the other the left-wing intelligentsia. These two seemingly hostile types, symbolic opposites—the half-pay colonel with his bull neck and diminutive brain, like a dinosaur, the highbrow with his domed forehead and stalk-like neck—are mentally linked together and constantly interact upon one another; in any case they are born to a considerable extent into the same families.

Thirty years ago the Blimp class was already losing its vitality. The middle-class families celebrated by Kipling, the prolific lowbrow families whose sons officered the army and navy and swarmed over all the waste places of the earth from the Yukon to the Irrawaddy, were dwindling before 1914. The thing that had killed them was the telegraph. In a narrowing world, more and more governed from Whitehall, there was every year less room for individual initiative. Men like Clive, Nelson, Nicholson, Gordon would find no place for themselves in the modern British Empire. By 1920 nearly every inch of the colonial empire was in the grip of Whitehall. Well-meaning, over-civilised men, in dark suits and black felt hats, with neatly-rolled umbrellas crooked over the left forearm, were imposing their constipated view of life on Malaya and Nigeria, Mombasa and Mandalay. The one-time empire builders were reduced to the status of clerks, buried deeper and deeper under mounds of paper and red tape. In the early 'twenties one could see, all over the Empire, the older officials, who had known more spacious days, writhing impotently under the changes that were happening. From that time onwards it has been next door to impossible to induce young men of spirit to take any part in imperial administration. And what was true of the official world was true also of the commercial. The great monopoly companies swallowed up hosts of petty traders. Instead of going out to trade adventurously in the Indies one went to an office stool in Bombay or Singapore. And life in Bombay or Singapore was actually duller and safer than life in London.

Imperialist sentiment remained strong in the middle class, chiefly owing to family tradition, but the job of administering the Empire had ceased to appeal. Few able men went east of Suez if there was any way of avoiding it.

But the general weakening of imperialism, and to some extent of the whole British morale, that took place during the nineteen-thirties, was partly the work of the left-wing intelligentsia, itself a kind of growth that had sprouted from the stagnation of the Empire.

It should be noted that there is now no intelligentsia that is not in some sense "left". Perhaps the last right-wing intellectual was T.E. Lawrence. Since about 1930 everyone describable as an "intellectual" has lived in a state of chronic discontent with the existing order. Necessarily so, because society as it was constituted had no room for him. In an Empire that was simply stagnant, neither being developed nor falling to pieces, and in an England ruled by people whose chief asset was their stupidity, to be "clever" was to be suspect. If you had the kind of brain that could understand the poems of T.S. Eliot or the theories of Karl Marx, the higher-ups would see to it that you were kept out of any important job. The intellectuals could find a function for themselves only in the literary reviews and the left-wing political parties.

The mentality of the English left-wing intelligentsia can be studied in half a dozen weekly and monthly papers. The immediately striking thing about all these papers is their generally negative, querulous attitude, their complete lack at all times of any constructive suggestion. There is little in them except the irresponsible carping of people who have never been and never expect to be in a position of power. Another marked characteristic is the emotional shallowness of people who live in a world of ideas and have little contact with physical reality. Many intellectuals of the Left were flabbily pacifist up to 1935, shrieked for war against Germany in the years 1935-9, and then promptly cooled off when the war started. It is broadly though not precisely true that the people who were most "anti-Fascist" during the Spanish civil war are most defeatist now. And underlying this is the really important fact about so many of the English intelligentsia—their severance from the common culture of the country.

In intention, at any rate, the English intelligentsia are European-ised. They take their cookery from Paris and their opinions from Moscow. In the general patriotism of the country they form a sort of island of dissident thought. England is perhaps the only great country whose intellectuals are ashamed of their own nationality. In left-wing circles it is always felt that there is something slightly disgraceful in being an Englishman and that it is a duty to snigger at every English institution, from horse racing to suet puddings. It is a strange fact, but it is unquestionably true, that almost any English intellectual would feel more ashamed of standing to attention during "God save the King" than of stealing from a poor box. All through the critical years many left-wingers were chipping away at English morale, trying to spread an outlook that was sometimes squashily pacifist, sometimes violently pro-Russian, but always anti-British. It is questionable how much effect this had, but it certainly had some. If the English people suffered for several years a real weakening of morale, so that the Fascist nations judged that they were "decadent" and that it was safe to plunge into war, the intellectual sabotage from the Left was partly responsible. Both the *New Statesman* and the *News Chronicle* cried out against the Munich settlement, but even they had done something to make it possible. Ten years of systematic Blimp-baiting affected even the Blimps themselves and made it harder than it had been before to get intelligent young men to enter the armed forces. Given the stagnation of the Empire the military middle class must have decayed in any case, but the spread of a shallow Leftism hastened the process.

It is clear that the special position of the English intellectuals during the past ten years, as purely *negative* creatures, mere anti-Blimps, was a by-product of ruling-class stupidity. Society could not use them, and they had not got it in them to see that devotion to one's country implies "for better, for worse". Both Blimps and highbrows took for granted, as though it were a law of nature, the divorce between patriotism and intelligence. If you were a patriot you read *Blackwood's Magazine* and publicly thanked God that you were "not brainy". If you were an intellectual you sniggered at the Union Jack and regarded physical courage as barbarous. It is obvious that this preposterous convention cannot continue. The Bloomsbury highbrow, with his mechanical snigger, is as out-of-date as the cavalry colonel. A modern nation cannot afford either of them. Patriotism and intelligence will have to come together again. It is the fact that we are fighting a war, and a very peculiar kind of war, that may make this possible.

## vi

One of the most important developments in England during the past twenty years has been the upward and downward extension of the middle class. It has happened on such a scale as to make the old classification of society into capitalists, proletarians and petit-bourgeois (small property-owners) almost obsolete.

England is a country in which property and financial power are concentrated in very few hands. Few people in modern England *own* anything at all, except clothes, furniture and possibly a house. The peasantry have long since disappeared, the independent shop-keeper is being destroyed, the small businessman is diminishing in numbers. But at the same time modern industry is so complicated that it cannot get along without great numbers of managers, sales-men, engineers, chemists and technicians of all kinds, drawing fairly large salaries. And these in turn call into being a professional class of doctors, lawyers, teachers, artists, etc etc. The tendency of advanced capitalism has therefore been to enlarge the middle class and not to wipe it out as it once seemed likely to do.

But much more important than this is the spread of middle-class ideas and habits among the working class. The British working class are now better off in almost all ways than they were thirty years ago. This is partly due to the efforts of the trade unions, but partly to the mere advance of physical science. It is not always realised that within rather narrow limits the standard of life of a country can rise without a corresponding rise in real-wages. Up to a point, civilisation can lift itself up by its boot-tags. However unjustly society is organised, certain technical advances are bound to benefit the whole com-munity, because certain kinds of goods are necessarily held in common. A millionaire cannot, for example, light the streets for himself while darkening them for other people. Nearly all citizens of civilised countries now enjoy the use of good roads, germ-free water, police protection, free libraries and probably free education of a kind. Public education in England has been meanly starved of money, but it has nevertheless improved, largely owing to the devoted efforts of the teachers, and the habit of reading has become enormously more widespread. To an increasing extent the rich and the poor read the same books, and they also see the same films and listen to the same radio programmes. And the differences in their way of life have been diminished by the mass-production of cheap clothes and improvements in housing. So far as outward appearance goes, the clothes of rich and poor, especially in the case of women, differ far less than they did thirty or even fifteen years ago. As to housing, England still has slums which are a blot on civilisation, but much building has been done during the past ten years, largely by the local authorities. The modern council house, with its bathroom and electric light, is smaller than the stockbroker's villa, but it is recognisably the same kind of house, which the farm labourer's cottage is not. A person who has grown up in a council housing estate is likely to be—indeed, visibly *is*—more middle-class in outlook than a person who has grown up in a slum.

The effect of all this is a general softening of manners. It is enhanced by the fact that modern industrial methods tend always to demand less muscular effort and therefore to leave people with more energy when their day's work is done. Many workers in the light industries are less truly manual labourers than is a doctor or a grocer. In tastes, habits, manners and outlook the working class and the middle class are drawing together. The unjust distinctions remain, but the real differences diminish. The old-style "proletarian" —collarless, unshaven and with muscles warped by heavy labour— still exists, but he is constantly decreasing in numbers; he only predominates in the heavy-industry areas of the north of England.

After 1918 there began to appear something that had never existed in England before: people of indeterminate social class. In 1910 every human being in these islands could be "placed" in an instant by his clothes, manners and accent. That is no longer the case. Above all, it is not the case in the new townships that have developed as a result of cheap motor cars and the southward shift of industry. The place to look for the germs of the future England is in light-industry areas and along the arterial roads. In Slough, Dagenham, Barnet, Letchworth, Hayes—everywhere, indeed, on the outskirts of great towns—the old pattern is gradually changing into something new. In those vast new wildernesses of glass and brick the sharp distinctions of the older kind of town, with its slums and mansions, or of the country, with its manor-houses and squalid cottages, no longer exist. There are wide gradations of income, but it is the same kind of life that is being lived at different levels, in labour-saving flats or council houses, along the concrete roads and in the naked democracy of the swimming-pools. It is a rather restless, cultureless life, centring round tinned food, *Picture Post*, the radio and the internal combustion engine. It is a civilisation in which children grow up with an intimate knowledge of magnetoes and in complete ignorance of the Bible. To that civilisation belong the people who are most at home in and most definitely *of* the modern world, the technicians and the higher-paid skilled workers, the airmen and their mechanics, the radio experts, film producers, popular journalists and industrial chemists. They are the indeterminate stratum at which the older class distinctions are beginning to break down.

This war, unless we are defeated, will wipe out most of the existing class privileges. There are every day fewer people who wish them to continue. Nor need we fear that as the pattern changes life in England will lose its peculiar flavour. The new red cities of Greater London are crude enough, but these things are only the rash that accompanies a change. In whatever shape England emerges from the war, it will be deeply tinged with the characteristics that I have spoken of earlier. The intellectuals who hope to see it Russianised or Germanised will be disappointed. The gentleness, the hypocrisy, the thoughtlessness, the reverence for law and the hatred of uniforms will remain, along with the suet puddings and the misty skies. It needs some very great disaster, such as prolonged subjugation by a foreign enemy, to destroy a national culture. The Stock Exchange will be pulled down, the horse plough will give way to the tractor, the country houses will be turned into children's holiday camps, the Eton and Harrow match will be forgotten, but England will still be England, an everlasting animal stretching into the future and the past, and, like all living things, having the power to change out of recognition and yet remain the same.

PART II: SHOPKEEPERS AT WAR

i

I began this book to the tune of German bombs, and I begin this second chapter in the added racket of the barrage. The yellow gun-flashes are lighting the sky, the splinters are rattling on the house-tops, and London Bridge is falling down, falling down, falling down. Anyone able to read a map knows that we are in deadly danger. I do not mean that we are beaten or need be beaten. Almost certainly the outcome depends on our own will. But at this moment we are in the soup, full fathom five, and we have been brought there by follies which we are still committing and which will drown us altogether if we do not mend our ways quickly.

What this war has demonstrated is that private capitalism—that is, an economic system in which land, factories, mines and transport are owned privately and operated solely for profit—*does not work*. It cannot deliver the goods. This fact had been known to millions of people for years past, but nothing ever came of it, because there was no real urge from below to alter the system, and those at the top had trained themselves to be impenetrably stupid on just this point. Argument and propaganda got one nowhere. The lords of property simply sat on their bottoms and proclaimed that all was for the best. Hitler's conquest of Europe, however, was a *physical* debunking of capitalism. War, for all its evil, is at any rate an unanswerable test of strength, like a try-your-grip machine. Great strength returns the penny, and there is no way of faking the result.

When the nautical screw was first invented, there was a controversy that lasted for years as to whether screw-steamers or paddle-steamers were better. The paddle-steamers, like all obsolete things, had their champions, who supported them by ingenious arguments. Finally, however, a distinguished admiral tied a screw-steamer and a paddle-steamer of equal horse-power stern to stern and set their engines running. That settled the question once and for all. And it was something similar that happened on the fields of Norway and of Flanders. Once and for all it was proved that a planned economy is stronger than a planless one. But it is necessary here to give some kind of definition to those much-abused words, Socialism and Fascism.

Socialism is usually defined as "common ownership of the means of production". Crudely: the State, representing the whole nation, owns everything, and everyone is a State employee. This does *not* mean that people are stripped of private possessions such as clothes and furniture, but it *does* mean that all productive goods, such as land, mines, ships and machinery, are the property of the State. The State is the sole large-scale producer. It is not certain that Socialism is in all ways superior to capitalism, but it is certain that, unlike capitalism, it can solve the problems of production and consumption. At normal times a capitalist economy can never consume all that it produces, so that there is always a wasted surplus (wheat burned in furnaces, herrings dumped back into the sea etc etc) and always unemployment. In time of war, on the other hand, it has difficulty in producing all that it needs, because nothing is produced unless someone sees his way to making a profit out of it.

In a Socialist economy these problems do not exist. The State simply calculates what goods will be needed and does its best to produce them. Production is only limited by the amount of labour and raw materials. Money, for internal purposes, ceases to be a mysterious all-powerful thing and becomes a sort of coupon or ration-ticket, issued in sufficient quantities to buy up such consumption goods as may be available at the moment.

However, it has become clear in the last few years that "common ownership of the means of production" is not in itself a sufficient definition of Socialism. One must also add the following: approximate equality of incomes (it need be no more than approximate), political democracy, and abolition of all hereditary privilege, especially in education. These are simply the necessary safeguards against the reappearance of a class-system. Centralised ownership has very little meaning unless the mass of the people are living roughly upon an equal level, and have some kind of control over the government. "The State" may come to mean no more than a self-elected political party, and oligarchy and privilege can return, based on power rather than on money.

But what then is Fascism?

Fascism, at any rate the German version, is a form of capitalism that borrows from Socialism just such features as will make it efficient for war purposes. Internally, Germany has a good deal in common with a Socialist state. Ownership has never been abolished, there are still capitalists and workers, and—this is the important point, and the real reason why rich men all over the world tend to sympathise with Fascism—generally speaking the same people are capitalists and the same people workers as before the Nazi revolution. But at the same time the State, which is simply the Nazi Party, is in control of everything. It controls investment, raw materials, rates of interest, working hours, wages. The factory owner still owns his factory, but he is for practical purposes reduced to the status of a manager. Everyone is in effect a State employee, though the salaries vary very greatly. The mere *efficiency* of such a system, the elimination of waste and obstruction, is obvious. In seven years it has built up the most powerful war machine the world has ever seen.

But the idea underlying Fascism is irreconcilably different from that which underlies Socialism. Socialism aims, ultimately, at a world-state of free and equal human beings. It takes the equality of human rights for granted. Nazism assumes just the opposite. The driving force behind the Nazi movement is the belief in human *inequality*, the superiority of Germans to all other races, the right of Germany to rule the world. Outside the German Reich it does not recognise any obligations. Eminent Nazi professors have "proved" over and over again that only nordic man is fully human, have even mooted the idea that non-nordic peoples (such as ourselves) can interbreed with gorillas! Therefore, while a species of war-Socialism exists within the German state, its attitude towards conquered nations is frankly that of an exploiter. The function of the Czechs, Poles, French, etc is simply to produce such goods as Germany may need, and get in return just as little as will keep them from open rebellion. If we are conquered, our job will probably be to manufacture weapons for Hitler's forthcoming wars with Russia and America. The Nazis aim, in effect, at setting up a kind of caste system, with four main castes corresponding rather closely to those of the Hindu religion. At the top comes the Nazi party, second come the mass of the German people, third come the conquered European populations. Fourth and last are to come the coloured peoples, the "semi-apes" as Hitler calls them, who are to be reduced quite openly to slavery.

However horrible this system may seem to us, *it works*. It works because it is a planned system geared to a definite purpose, world-conquest, and not allowing any private interest, either of capitalist or worker, to stand in its way. British capitalism does not work, because it is a competitive system in which private profit is and must be the main objective. It is a system in which all the forces are pulling in opposite directions and the interests of the individual are as often as not totally opposed to those of the State.

All through the critical years British capitalism, with its immense industrial plant and its unrivalled supply of skilled labour, was unequal to the strain of preparing for war. To prepare for war on the modern scale you have got to divert the greater part of your national income to armaments, which means cutting down on consumption goods. A bombing plane, for instance, is equivalent in price to fifty small motor cars, or eighty thousand pairs of silk stockings, or a million loaves of bread. Clearly you can't have *many* bombing planes without lowering the national standard of life. It is guns or butter, as Marshal Goering remarked. But in Chamberlain's England the transition could not be made. The rich would not face the necessary taxation, and while the rich are still visibly rich it is not possible to tax the poor very heavily either. Moreover, so long as *profit* was the main object the manufacturer had no incentive to change over from consumption goods to armaments. A businessman's first duty is to his shareholders. Perhaps England needs tanks, but perhaps it pays better to manufacture motor cars. To prevent war material from reaching the enemy is common sense, but to sell in the highest market is a business duty. Right at the end of August 1939 the British dealers were tumbling over one another in their eagerness to sell Germany tin, rubber, copper and shellac—and this in the clear, certain knowledge that war was going to break out in a week or two. It was about as sensible as selling somebody a razor to cut your throat with. But it was "good business".

And now look at the results. After 1934 it was known that Germany was rearming. After 1936 everyone with eyes in his head knew that war was coming. After Munich it was merely a question of how soon the war would begin. In September 1939 war broke out. *Eight months later* it was discovered that, so far as equipment went, the British army was barely beyond the standard of 1918. We saw our soldiers fighting their way desperately to the coast, with one aeroplane against three, with rifles against tanks, with bayonets against tommy-guns. There were not even enough revolvers to supply all the officers. After a year of war the regular army was still short of 300,000 tin hats. There had even, previously, been a shortage of uniforms—this in one of the greatest woollen-goods producing countries in the world!

What had happened was that the whole moneyed class, unwilling to face a change in their way of life, had shut their eyes to the nature of Fascism and modern war. And false optimism was fed to the general public by the gutter press, which lives on its advertisements and is therefore interested in keeping trade conditions normal. Year after year the Beaverbrook press assured us in huge headlines that THERE WILL BE NO WAR, and as late as the beginning of 1939 Lord Rothermere was describing Hitler as "a great gentleman". And while England in the moment of disaster proved to be short of every war material except ships, it is not recorded that there was any shortage of motor cars, fur coats, gramophones, lipstick, chocolates or silk stockings. And dare anyone pretend that the same tug-of-war between private profit and public necessity is not still continuing? England fights for her life, but business must fight for profits. You can hardly open a newspaper without seeing the two contradictory processes happening side by side. On the very same page you will find the Government urging you to save and the seller of some useless luxury urging you to spend. Lend to Defend, but Guinness is Good for You. Buy a Spitfire, but also buy Haig and Haig, Pond's Face Cream and Black Magic Chocolates.

But one thing gives hope—the visible swing in public opinion. If we can survive this war, the defeat in Flanders will turn out to have been one of the great turning-points in English history. In that spectacular disaster the working class, the middle class and even a section of the business community could see the utter rottenness of private capitalism. Before that the case against capitalism had never been *proved*. Russia, the only definitely Socialist country, was backward and far away. All criticism broke itself against the rat-trap faces of bankers and the brassy laughter of stockbrokers. Socialism? Ha! ha! ha! Where's the money to come from? Ha! ha! ha! The lords of property were firm in their seats, and they knew it. But after the French collapse there came something that could not be laughed away, something that neither cheque-books nor policemen were any use against—the bombing. Zweee—BOOM! What's that? Oh, only a bomb on the Stock Exchange. Zweee—BOOM! Another acre of somebody's valuable slum-property gone west. Hitler will at any rate go down in history as the man who made the City of London laugh on the wrong side of its face. For the first time in their lives the comfortable were uncomfortable, the professional optimists had to admit that there was something wrong. It was a great step forward. From that time onwards the ghastly job of trying to convince artificially stupefied people that a planned economy might be better than a free-for-all in which the worst man wins—that job will never be quite so ghastly again.

## ii

The difference between Socialism and capitalism is not primarily a difference of technique. One cannot simply change from one system to the other as one might install a new piece of machinery in a factory, and then carry on as before, with the same people in positions of control. Obviously there is also needed a complete shift of power. New blood, new men, new ideas—in the true sense of the word, a revolution.

I have spoken earlier of the soundness and homogeneity of

England, the patriotism that runs like a connecting thread through almost all classes. After Dunkirk anyone who had eyes in his head could see this. But it is absurd to pretend that the promise of that moment has been fulfilled. Almost certainly the mass of the people are now ready for the vast changes that are necessary; but those changes have not even begun to happen.

England is a family with the wrong members in control. Almost entirely we are governed by the rich, and by people who step into positions of command by right of birth. Few if any of these people are consciously treacherous, some of them are not even fools, but as a class they are quite incapable of leading us to victory. They could not do it, even if their material interests did not constantly trip them up. As I pointed out earlier, they have been artificially stupefied. Quite apart from anything else, the rule of money sees to it that we shall be governed largely by the old—that is, by people utterly unable to grasp what age they are living in or what enemy they are fighting. Nothing was more desolating at the beginning of this war than the way in which the whole of the older generation conspired to pretend that it was the war of 1914–18 over again. All the old duds were back on the job, twenty years older, with the skull plainer in their faces. Ian Hay was cheering up the troops, Belloc was writing articles on strategy, Maurois doing broadcasts, Bairnsfather drawing cartoons. It was like a tea-party of ghosts. And that state of affairs has barely altered. The shock of disaster brought a few able men like Bevin to the front, but in general we are still commanded by people who managed to live through the years 1931–9 without even discovering that Hitler was dangerous. A generation of the unteachable is hanging upon us like a necklace of corpses.

As soon as one considers any problem of this war—and it does not matter whether it is the widest aspect of strategy or the tiniest detail of home organisation—one sees that the necessary moves cannot be made while the social structure of England remains what it is. Inevitably, because of their position and upbringing, the ruling class are fighting for their own privileges, which cannot possibly be reconciled with the public interest. It is a mistake to imagine that war aims, strategy, propaganda and industrial organisation exist in watertight compartments. All are interconnected. Every strategic plan, every tactical method, even every weapon will bear the stamp of the social system that produced it. The British ruling class are fighting against Hitler, whom they have always regarded and whom some of them still regard as their protector against Bolshevism. That does not mean that they will deliberately sell out; but it does mean that at every decisive moment they are likely to falter, pull their punches, do the wrong thing.

Until the Churchill Government called some sort of halt to the process, they have done the wrong thing with an unerring instinct ever since 1931. They helped Franco to overthrow the Spanish Government, although anyone not an imbecile could have told them that a Fascist Spain would be hostile to England. They fed Italy with war materials all through the winter of 1939–40, although it was obvious to the whole world that the Italians were going to attack us in the spring. For the sake of a few hundred thousand dividend-drawers they are turning India from an ally into an enemy. Moreover, so long as the moneyed classes remain in control, we cannot develop any but a *defensive* strategy. Every victory means a change in the *status quo*. How can we drive the Italians out of Abyssinia without rousing echoes among the coloured peoples of our own Empire? How can we even smash Hitler without the risk of bringing the German Socialists and Communists into power? The left-wingers who wail that "this is a capitalist war" and that "British Imperialism" is fighting for loot have got their heads screwed on backwards. The last thing the British moneyed class wish for is to acquire fresh territory. It would simply be an embarrassment. Their war aim (both unattainable and unmentionable) is simply to hang on to what they have got.

Internally, England is still the rich man's Paradise. All talk of "equality of sacrifice" is nonsense. At the same time as factory-workers are asked to put up with longer hours, advertisements for "Butler. One in family, eight in staff" are appearing in the press. The bombed-out populations of the East End go hungry and homeless while wealthier victims simply step into their cars and flee to comfortable country houses. The Home Guard swells to a million men in a few weeks, and is deliberately organised from above in such a way that only people with private incomes can hold positions of command. Even the rationing system is so arranged that it hits the poor all the time, while people with over £2,000 a year are practically unaffected by it. Everywhere privilege is squandering good will. In such circumstances even propaganda becomes almost impossible. As attempts to stir up patriotic feeling, the red posters issued by the Chamberlain Government at the beginning of the war broke all depth-records. Yet they could not have been much other than they were, for how could Chamberlain and his followers take the risk of rousing strong popular feeling *against Fascism*? Anyone who was genuinely hostile to Fascism must also be opposed to Chamberlain himself and to all the others who had helped Hitler into power. So also with external propaganda. In all Lord Halifax's speeches there is not one concrete proposal for which a single inhabitant of Europe would risk the top joint of his little finger. For what war-aim can Halifax, or anyone like him, conceivably have, except to put the clock back to 1933?

It is only by revolution that the native genius of the English people can be set free. Revolution does not mean red flags and street fighting, it means a fundamental shift of power. Whether it happens with or without bloodshed is largely an accident of time and place. Nor does it mean the dictatorship of a single class. The people in England who grasp what changes are needed and are capable of carrying them through are not confined to any one class, though it is true that very few people with over £2,000 a year are among them. What is wanted is a conscious open revolt by ordinary people against inefficiency, class privilege and the rule of the old. It is not primarily a question of change of government. British governments do, broadly speaking, represent the will of the people, and if we alter our structure from below we shall get the government we need. Ambassadors, generals, officials and colonial administrators who are senile or pro-Fascist are more dangerous than Cabinet ministers whose follies have to be committed in public. Right through our national life we have got to fight against privilege, against the notion that a half-witted public-schoolboy is better fitted for command than an intelligent mechanic. Although there are gifted and honest *individuals* among them, we have got to break the grip of the moneyed class as a whole. England has got to assume its real shape. The England that is only just beneath the surface, in the factories and the newspaper offices, in the aeroplanes and the submarines, has got to take charge of its own destiny.

In the short run, equality of sacrifice, "war-Communism", is even more important than radical economic changes. It is very necessary that industry should be nationalised, but it is more urgently necessary that such monstrosities as butlers and "private incomes" should disappear forthwith. Almost certainly the main reason why the Spanish Republic could keep up the fight for two and a half years against impossible odds was that there were no gross contrasts of wealth. The people suffered horribly, but they all suffered alike. When the private soldier had not a cigarette, the general had not one either. Given equality of sacrifice, the morale of a country like England would probably be unbreakable. But at present we have nothing to appeal to except traditional patriotism, which is deeper here than elsewhere, but is not necessarily bottomless. At some point or another you have got to deal with the man who says "I should be no worse off under Hitler". But what answer can you give him—that is, what answer that you can expect him to listen to— while common soldiers risk their lives for two and sixpence a day, and fat women ride about in Rolls-Royce cars, nursing pekineses?

It is quite likely that this war will last three years. It will mean cruel overwork, cold dull winters, uninteresting food, lack of amusements, prolonged bombing. It cannot but lower the general standard of living, because the essential act of war is to manufacture armaments instead of consumable goods. The working class will have to suffer terrible things. And they *will* suffer them, almost indefinitely, provided that they know what they are fighting for. They are not cowards, and they are not even internationally minded. They can stand all that the Spanish workers stood, and more. But they will want some kind of proof that a better life is ahead for themselves and their children. The one sure earnest of that is that when they are taxed and overworked they shall see that the rich are being hit even harder. And if the rich squeal audibly, so much the better.

We can bring these things about, if we really want to. It is not true that public opinion has no power in England. It never makes itself heard without achieving something; it has been responsible for most of the changes for the better during the past six months. But we have moved with glacier-like slowness, and we have learned only from disasters. It took the fall of Paris to get rid of Chamberlain and the unnecessary suffering of scores of thousands of people in the East End to get rid or partially rid of Sir John Anderson. It is not worth losing a battle in order to bury a corpse. For we are fighting against swift evil intelligences, and time presses, and

history to the defeated
May say Alas! but cannot alter or pardon.

iii

During the last six months there has been much talk of "the Fifth Column". From time to time obscure lunatics have been jailed for making speeches in favour of Hitler, and large numbers of German refugees have been interned, a thing which has almost certainly done us great harm in Europe. It is of course obvious that the idea of a large, organised army of Fifth Columnists suddenly appearing on the streets with weapons in their hands, as in Holland and Belgium, is ridiculous. Nevertheless a Fifth Column danger does exist. One can only consider it if one also considers in what way England might be defeated.

It does not seem probable that air bombing can settle a major war. England might well be invaded and conquered, but the invasion would be a dangerous gamble, and if it happened and failed it would probably leave us more united and less Blimp-ridden than before. Moreover, if England were overrun by foreign troops the English people would know that they had been beaten and would continue the struggle. It is doubtful whether they could be held down permanently, or whether Hitler wishes to keep an army of a million men stationed in these islands. A government of ——, —— and —— (you can fill in the names) would suit him better. The English can probably not be bullied into surrender, but they might quite easily be bored, cajoled or cheated into it, provided that, as at Munich, they did not know that they were surrendering. It could happen most easily when the war seemed to be going well rather than badly. The threatening tone of so much of the German and Italian propaganda is a psychological mistake. It only gets home on intellectuals. With the general public the proper approach would be "Let's call it a draw". It is when a peace-offer along *those* lines is made that the pro-Fascists will raise their voices.

But who are the pro-Fascists? The idea of a Hitler victory appeals to the very rich, to the Communists, to Mosley's followers, to the pacifists, and to certain sections among the Catholics. Also, if things went badly enough on the Home Front, the whole of the poorer section of the working class might swing round to a position that was defeatist though not actively pro-Hitler.

In this motley list one can see the daring of German propaganda, its willingness to offer everything to everybody. But the various pro-Fascist forces are not consciously acting together, and they operate in different ways.

The Communists must certainly be regarded as pro-Hitler, and are bound to remain so unless Russian policy changes, but they have not very much influence. Mosley's Blackshirts, though now lying very low, are a more serious danger, because of the footing they probably possess in the armed forces. Still, even in its palmiest days Mosley's following can hardly have numbered 50,000. Pacifism is a psychological curiosity rather than a political movement. Some of the extremer pacifists, starting out with a complete renunciation of violence, have ended by warmly championing Hitler and even toying with antisemitism. This is interesting, but it is not important. "Pure" pacifism, which is a by-product of naval power, can only appeal to people in very sheltered positions. Moreover, being negative and irresponsible, it does not inspire much devotion. Of the membership of the Peace Pledge Union, less than 15 per cent even pay their annual subscriptions. None of these bodies of people, pacifists, Communists or Blackshirts, could bring a large-scale stop-the-war movement into being by their own efforts. But they might help to make things very much easier for a treacherous government negotiating surrender. Like the French Communists, they might become the half-conscious agents of millionaires.

The real danger is from above. One ought not to pay any attention to Hitler's recent line of talk about being the friend of the poor man, the enemy of plutocracy, etc etc. Hitler's real self is in *Mein Kampf*, and in his actions. He has never persecuted the rich, except when they were Jews or when they tried actively to oppose him. He stands for a centralised economy which robs the capitalist of most of his power but leaves the structure of society much as before. The State controls industry, but there are still rich and poor, masters and men. Therefore, as against genuine Socialism, the moneyed class have always been on his side. This was crystal clear at the time of the Spanish civil war, and clear again at the time when France surrendered. Hitler's puppet government are not working men, but a gang of bankers, gaga generals and corrupt right-wing politicians.

That kind of spectacular, *conscious* treachery is less likely to succeed in England, indeed is far less likely even to be tried. Nevertheless, to many payers of supertax this war is simply an insane family squabble which ought to be stopped at all costs. One need not doubt that a "peace" movement is on foot somewhere in high places; probably a shadow Cabinet has already been formed. These people will get their chance not in the moment of defeat but in some stagnant period when boredom is reinforced by discontent. They will not talk about surrender, only about peace; and doubtless they will persuade themselves, and perhaps other people, that they are acting for the best. An army of unemployed led by millionaires quoting the Sermon on the Mount—that is our danger. But it cannot arise when we have once introduced a reasonable degree of social justice. The lady in the Rolls-Royce car is more damaging to morale than a fleet of Goering's bombing planes.

PART III: THE ENGLISH REVOLUTION

i

The English revolution started several years ago, and it began to gather momentum when the troops came back from Dunkirk. Like all else in England, it happens in a sleepy, unwilling way, but it is happening. The war has speeded it up, but it has also increased, and desperately, the necessity for speed.

Progress and reaction are ceasing to have anything to do with party labels. If one wishes to name a particular moment, one can say that the old distinction between Right and Left broke down when *Picture Post* was first published. What are the politics of *Picture Post*? Or of *Cavalcade*, or Priestley's broadcasts, or the leading articles in the *Evening Standard*? None of the old classifications will fit them. They merely point to the existence of multitudes of unlabelled people who have grasped within the last year or two that something is wrong. But since a classless, ownerless society is generally spoken of as "Socialism", we can give that name to the society towards which we are now moving. The war and the revolution are inseparable. We cannot establish anything that a western nation would regard as Socialism without defeating Hitler; on the other hand we cannot defeat Hitler while we remain economically and socially in the nineteenth century. The past is fighting the future and we have two years, a year, possibly only a few months, to see to it that the future wins.

We cannot look to this or to any similar government to put through the necessary changes of its own accord. The initiative will have to come from below. That means that there will have to arise something that has never existed in England, a Socialist movement that actually has the mass of the people behind it. But one must start by recognising why it is that English Socialism has failed.

In England there is only one Socialist party that has ever seriously mattered, the Labour Party. It has never been able to achieve any major change, because except in purely domestic matters it has never possessed a genuinely independent policy. It was and is primarily a party of the trade unions, devoted to raising wages and improving working conditions. This meant that all through the critical years it was directly interested in the prosperity of British capitalism. In particular it was interested in the maintenance of the British Empire, for the wealth of England was drawn largely from Asia and Africa. The standard of living of the trade union workers, whom the Labour Party represented, depended indirectly on the sweating of Indian coolies. At the same time the Labour Party was a Socialist party, using Socialist phraseology, thinking in terms of an old-fashioned anti-imperialism and more or less pledged to make restitution to the coloured races. It had to stand for the "independence" of India, just as it had to stand for disarmament and "progress" generally. Nevertheless everyone was aware that this was nonsense. In the age of the tank and the bombing plane, backward agricultural countries like India and the African colonies can no more be independent than can a cat or a dog. Had any Labour government come into office with a clear majority and then proceeded to grant India anything that could truly be called independence, India would simply have been absorbed by Japan, or divided between Japan and Russia.

To a Labour government in power, three imperial policies would have been open. One was to continue administering the Empire exactly as before, which meant dropping all pretensions to Socialism. Another was to set the subject peoples "free", which meant in practice handing them over to Japan, Italy and other predatory powers, and incidentally causing a catastrophic drop in the British standard of living. The third was to develop a *positive* imperial policy, and aim at transforming the Empire into a federation of Socialist states, like a looser and freer version of the Union of Soviet Republics. But the Labour Party's history and background made this impossible. It was a party of the trade unions, hopelessly parochial in outlook, with little interest in imperial affairs and no contacts among the men who actually held the Empire together. It would have had to hand the administration of India and Africa and the whole job of imperial defence to men drawn from a different class and traditionally hostile to Socialism. Overshadowing everything was the doubt whether a Labour government which meant business could make itself obeyed. For all the size of its following, the Labour Party had no footing in the navy, little or none in the army or air force, none whatever in the Colonial Services, and not even a sure footing in the Home Civil Service. In England its position was strong but not unchallengeable, and outside England all the key points were in the hands of its enemies. Once in power, the same dilemma would always have faced it: carry out your promises, and risk revolt, or continue with the same policy as the Conservatives, and stop talking about Socialism. The Labour leaders never found a solution, and from 1935 onwards it was very doubtful whether they had any wish to take office. They had degenerated into a Permanent Opposition.

Outside the Labour Party there existed several extremist parties, of whom the Communists were the strongest. The Communists had considerable influence in the Labour Party in the years 1920–6 and 1935–9. Their chief importance, and that of the whole left wing of the Labour movement, was the part they played in alienating the middle classes from Socialism.

The history of the past seven years has made it perfectly clear that Communism has no chance in western Europe. The appeal of Fascism is enormously greater. In one country after another the Communists have been rooted out by their more up-to-date enemies, the Nazis. In the English-speaking countries they never had a serious footing. The creed they were spreading could appeal only to a rather rare type of person, found chiefly in the middle-class intelligentsia, the type who has ceased to love his own country but still feels the need of patriotism, and therefore develops patriotic sentiments towards Russia. By 1940, after working for twenty years and spending a great deal of money, the British Communists had barely 20,000 members, actually a smaller number than they had started out with in 1920. The other Marxist parties were of even less importance. They had not the Russian money and prestige behind them, and even more than the Communists they were tied to the nineteenth-century doctrine of the class war. They continued year after year to preach this out-of-date gospel, and never drew any inference from the fact that it got them no followers.

Nor did any strong native Fascist movement grow up. Material conditions were not bad enough, and no leader who could be taken seriously was forthcoming. One would have had to look a long time to find a man more barren of ideas than Sir Oswald Mosley. He was as hollow as a jug. Even the elementary fact that Fascism must not offend national sentiment had escaped him. His entire movement was imitated slavishly from abroad, the uniform and the party programme from Italy and the salute from Germany, with the Jew-baiting tacked on as an afterthought, Mosley having actually started his movement with Jews among his most prominent followers. A man of the stamp of Bottomley or Lloyd George could perhaps have brought a real British Fascist movement into existence. But such leaders only appear when the psychological need for them exists.

After twenty years of stagnation and unemployment, the entire English Socialist movement was unable to produce a version of Socialism which the mass of the people could even find desirable. The Labour Party stood for a timid reformism, the Marxists were looking at the modern world through nineteenth-century spectacles. Both ignored agriculture and imperial problems, and both antagonised the middle classes. The suffocating stupidity of left-wing propaganda had frightened away whole classes of necessary people, factory managers, airmen, naval officers, farmers, white-collar workers, shopkeepers, policemen. All of these people had been taught to think of Socialism as something which menaced their livelihood, or as something seditious, alien, "anti-British" as they would have called it. Only the intellectuals, the least useful section of the middle class, gravitated towards the movement.

A Socialist Party which genuinely wished to achieve anything would have started by facing several facts which to this day are considered unmentionable in left-wing circles. It would have recognised that England is more united than most countries, that the British workers have a great deal to lose besides their chains, and that the differences in outlook and habits between class and class are rapidly diminishing. In general, it would have recognised that the old-fashioned "proletarian revolution" is an impossibility. But all through the between-war years no Socialist programme that was both revolutionary and workable ever appeared; basically, no doubt, because no one genuinely wanted any major change to happen. The Labour leaders wanted to go on and on, drawing their salaries and periodically swapping jobs with the Conservatives. The Communists wanted to go on and on, suffering a comfortable martyrdom, meeting with endless defeats and afterwards putting the blame on other people. The left-wing intelligentsia wanted to go on and on, sniggering at the Blimps, sapping away at middle-class morale, but still keeping their favoured position as hangers-on of the dividend-drawers. Labour Party politics had become a variant of Conservatism, "revolutionary" politics had become a game of make-believe.

Now, however, the circumstances have changed, the drowsy years have ended. Being a Socialist no longer means kicking theoretically against a system which in practice you are fairly well satisfied with. This time our predicament is real. It is "the Philistines be upon thee, Samson". We have got to make our words take physical shape, or perish. We know very well that with its present social structure England cannot survive, and we have got to make other people see that fact and act upon it. We cannot win the war without introducing Socialism, nor establish Socialism without winning the war. At such a time it is possible, as it was not in the peaceful years, to be both revolutionary and realistic. A Socialist movement which can swing the mass of the people behind it, drive the pro-Fascists out of positions of control, wipe out the grosser injustices and let the working class see that they have something to fight for, win over the middle classes instead of antagonising them, produce a workable imperial policy instead of a mixture of humbug and Utopianism, bring patriotism and intelligence into partnership —for the first time, a movement of such a kind becomes possible.

ii

The fact that we are at war has turned Socialism from a textbook word into a realisable policy.

The inefficiency of private capitalism has been proved all over Europe. Its injustice has been proved in the East End of London. Patriotism, against which the Socialists fought so long, has become a tremendous lever in their hands. People who at any other time would cling like glue to their miserable scraps of privilege, will surrender them fast enough when their country is in danger. War is the greatest of all agents of change. It speeds up all processes, wipes out minor distinctions, brings realities to the surface. Above all, war brings it home to the individual that he is *not* altogether an individual. It is only because they are aware of this that men will die on the field of battle. At this moment it is not so much a question of surrendering life as of surrendering leisure, comfort, economic liberty, social prestige. There are very few people in England who really want to see their country conquered by

Germany. If it can be made clear that defeating Hitler means wiping out class privilege, the great mass of middling people, the £6 a week to £2,000 a year class, will probably be on our side. These people are quite indispensable, because they include most of the technical experts. Obviously the snobbishness and political ignorance of people like airmen and naval officers will be a very great difficulty. But without those airmen, destroyer commanders, etc etc we could not survive for a week. The only approach to them is through their patriotism. An intelligent Socialist movement will *use* their patriotism, instead of merely insulting it, as hitherto.

But do I mean that there will be no opposition? Of course not. It would be childish to expect anything of the kind.

There will be a bitter political struggle, and there will be unconscious and half-conscious sabotage everywhere. At some point or other it may be necessary to use violence. It is easy to imagine a pro-Fascist rebellion breaking out in, for instance, India. We shall have to fight against bribery, ignorance and snobbery. The bankers and the larger businessmen, the landowners and dividend-drawers, the officials with their prehensile bottoms, will obstruct for all they are worth. Even the middle classes will writhe when their accustomed way of life is menaced. But just because the English sense of national unity has never disintegrated, because patriotism is finally stronger than class-hatred, the chances are that the will of the majority will prevail. It is no use imagining that one can make fundamental changes without causing a split in the nation; but the treacherous minority will be far smaller in time of war than it would be at any other time.

The swing of opinion is visibly happening, but it cannot be counted on to happen fast enough of its own accord. This war is a race between the consolidation of Hitler's empire and the growth of democratic consciousness. Everywhere in England you can see a ding-dong battle ranging to and fro—in Parliament and in the Government, in the factories and the armed forces, in the pubs and the air-raid shelters, in the newspapers and on the radio. Every day there are tiny defeats, tiny victories. Morrison for Home Security—a few yards forward. Priestley shoved off the air—a few yards back. It is a struggle between the groping and the unteachable, between the young and the old, between the living and the dead. But it is very necessary that the discontent which undoubtedly exists should take a purposeful and not merely obstructive form. It is time for *the people* to define their war-aims. What is wanted is a simple, concrete programme of action, which can be given all possible publicity, and round which public opinion can group itself.

I suggest that the following six-point programme is the kind of thing we need. The first three points deal with England's internal policy, the other three with the Empire and the world:

1. Nationalisation of land, mines, railways, banks and major industries.

2. Limitation of incomes, on such a scale that the highest tax-free income in Britain does not exceed the lowest by more than ten to one.

3. Reform of the educational system along democratic lines.

4. Immediate Dominion status for India, with power to secede when the war is over.

5. Formation of an Imperial General Council, in which the coloured peoples are to be represented.

6. Declaration of formal alliance with China, Abyssinia and all other victims of the Fascist powers.

The general tendency of this programme is unmistakable. It aims quite frankly at turning this war into a revolutionary war and England into a Socialist democracy. I have deliberately included in it nothing that the simplest person could not understand and see the reason for. In the form in which I have put it, it could be printed on the front page of the *Daily Mirror*. But for the purposes of this book a certain amount of amplification is needed.

1. *Nationalisation.* One can "nationalise" industry by the stroke of a pen, but the actual process is slow and complicated. What is needed is that the ownership of all major industry shall be formally vested in the State, representing the common people. Once that is done it becomes possible to eliminate the class of mere *owners* who live not by virtue of anything they produce but by the possession of title-deeds and share certificates. State-ownership implies, therefore, that nobody shall live without working. How sudden a change in the conduct of industry it implies is less certain. In a country like England we cannot rip down the whole structure and build again from the bottom, least of all in time of war. Inevitably the majority of industrial concerns will continue with much the same personnel as before, the one-time owners or managing directors carrying on with their jobs as State employees. There is reason to think that many of the smaller capitalists would actually welcome some such arrangement. The resistance will come from the big

capitalists, the bankers, the landlords and the idle rich, roughly speaking the class with over £2,000 a year—and even if one counts in all their dependants there are not more than half a million of these people in England. Nationalisation of agricultural land implies cutting out the landlord and the tithe drawer, but not necessarily interfering with the farmer. It is difficult to imagine any reorganisation of English agriculture that would not retain most of the existing farms as units, at any rate at the beginning. The farmer, when he is competent, will continue as a salaried manager. He is virtually that already, with the added disadvantage of having to make a profit and being permanently in debt to the bank. With certain kinds of petty trading, and even the small-scale ownership of land, the State will probably not interfere at all. It would be a great mistake to start by victimising the smallholder class, for instance. These people are necessary, on the whole they are competent, and the amount of work they do depends on the feeling that they are "their own masters". But the State will certainly impose an upward limit to the ownership of land (probably fifteen acres at the very most), and will never permit any ownership of land in town areas.

From the moment that all productive goods have been declared the property of the State, the common people will feel, as they cannot feel now, that the State *is themselves*. They will be ready then to endure the sacrifices that are ahead of us, war or no war. And even if the face of England hardly seems to change, on the day that our main industries are formally nationalised the dominance of a single class will have been broken. From then onwards the emphasis will be shifted from ownership to management, from privilege to competence. It is quite possible that State-ownership will in itself bring about less social change than will be forced upon us by the common hardships of war. But it is the necessary first step without which any *real* reconstruction is impossible.

2. *Incomes.* Limitation of incomes implies the fixing of a minimum wage, which implies a managed internal currency based simply on the amount of consumption goods available. And this again implies a stricter rationing scheme than is now in operation. It is no use at this stage of the world's history to suggest that all human beings should have *exactly* equal incomes. It has been shown over and over again that without some kind of money reward there is no incentive to undertake certain jobs. On the other hand the money

reward need not be very large. In practice it is impossible that
earnings should be limited quite as rigidly as I have suggested. There
will always be anomalies and evasions. But there is no reason why
ten to one should not be the maximum normal variation. And within
those limits some sense of equality is possible. A man with £3 a week
and a man with £1,500 a year can feel themselves fellow creatures,
which the Duke of Westminster and the sleepers on the Embankment benches cannot.

3. *Education.* In wartime, educational reform must necessarily
be promise rather than performance. At the moment we are not in
a position to raise the school-leaving age or increase the teaching
staffs of the elementary schools. But there are certain immediate
steps that we could take towards a democratic educational system.
We could start by abolishing the autonomy of the public schools
and the older universities and flooding them with State-aided pupils
chosen simply on grounds of ability. At present, public-school
education is partly a training in class prejudice and partly a sort of
tax that the middle classes pay to the upper class in return for the
right to enter certain professions. It is true that that state of affairs
is altering. The middle classes have begun to rebel against the
expensiveness of education, and the war will bankrupt the majority of
the public schools if it continues for another year or two. The evacuation is also producing certain minor changes. But there is a danger
that some of the older schools, which will be able to weather the
financial storm longest, will survive in some form or another as
festering centres of snobbery. As for the 10,000 "private" schools
that England possesses, the vast majority of them deserve nothing
except suppression. They are simply commercial undertakings, and
in many cases their educational level is actually lower than that of
the elementary schools. They merely exist because of a widespread
idea that there is something disgraceful in being educated by the
public authorities. The State could quell this idea by declaring itself
responsible for *all* education, even if at the start this were no more
than a gesture. We need gestures as well as actions. It is all too
obvious that our talk of "defending democracy" is nonsense while
it is a mere accident of birth that decides whether a gifted child
shall or shall not get the education it deserves.

4. *India.* What we must offer India is not "freedom", which,
as I have said earlier, is impossible, but alliance, partnership—in a
word, equality. But we must also tell the Indians that they are free

to secede, if they want to. Without that there can be no equality of partnership, and our claim to be defending the coloured peoples against Fascism will never be believed. But it is a mistake to imagine that if the Indians were free to cut themselves adrift they would immediately do so. When a British government *offers* them unconditional independence, they will refuse it. For as soon as they have the power to secede the chief reasons for doing so will have disappeared.

A complete severance of the two countries would be a disaster for India no less than for England. Intelligent Indians know this. As things are at present, India not only cannot defend itself, it is hardly even capable of feeding itself. The whole administration of the country depends on a framework of experts (engineers, forest officers, railwaymen, soldiers, doctors) who are predominantly English and could not be replaced within five or ten years. Moreover, English is the chief lingua franca and nearly the whole of the Indian intelligentsia is deeply anglicised. Any transference to foreign rule —for if the British marched out of India the Japanese and other powers would immediately march in—would mean an immense dislocation. Neither the Japanese, the Russians, the Germans nor the Italians would be capable of administering India even at the low level of efficiency that is attained by the British. They do not possess the necessary supplies of technical experts or the knowledge of languages and local conditions, and they probably could not win the confidence of indispensable go-betweens such as the Eurasians. If India were simply "liberated", i.e. deprived of British military protection, the first result would be a fresh foreign conquest, and the second a series of enormous famines which would kill millions of people within a few years.

What India needs is the power to work out its own constitution without British interference, but in some kind of partnership that ensures its military protection and technical advice. This is unthinkable until there is a Socialist government in England. For at least eighty years England has artificially prevented the development of India, partly from fear of trade competition if Indian industries were too highly developed, partly because backward peoples are more easily governed than civilised ones. It is a commonplace that the average Indian suffers far more from his own countrymen than from the British. The petty Indian capitalist exploits the town worker with the utmost ruthlessness, the peasant lives from birth to death in the grip of the money-lender. But all this is an indirect result of the British rule, which aims half-consciously at keeping India as backward as possible. The classes most loyal to Britain are the princes, the landowners and the business community —in general, the reactionary classes who are doing fairly well out of the *status quo*. The moment that England ceased to stand towards India in the relation of an exploiter, the balance of forces would be altered. No need then for the British to flatter the ridiculous Indian princes, with their gilded elephants and cardboard armies, to prevent the growth of the Indian trade unions, to play off Moslem against Hindu, to protect the worthless life of the money-lender, to receive the salaams of toadying minor officials, to prefer the half-barbarous Gurkha to the educated Bengali. Once check that stream of dividends that flows from the bodies of Indian coolies to the banking accounts of old ladies in Cheltenham, and the whole sahib-native nexus, with its haughty ignorance on one side and envy and servility on the other, can come to an end. Englishmen and Indians can work side by side for the development of India, and for the training of Indians in all the arts which, so far, they have been systematically prevented from learning. How many of the existing British personnel in India, commercial or official, would fall in with such an arrangement— which would mean ceasing once and for all to be "sahibs"—is a different question. But, broadly speaking, more is to be hoped from the younger men and from those officials (civil engineers, forestry and agricultural experts, doctors, educationists) who have been scientifically educated. The higher officials, the provincial governors, commissioners, judges, etc are hopeless; but they are also the most easily replaceable.

That, roughly, is what would be meant by Dominion status if it were offered to India by a Socialist government. It is an offer of partnership on equal terms until such time as the world has ceased to be ruled by bombing planes. But we must add to it the unconditional right to secede. It is the only way of proving that we mean what we say. And what applies to India applies, *mutatis mutandis*, to Burma, Malaya and most of our African possessions.

5 and 6 explain themselves. They are the necessary preliminary to any claim that we are fighting this war for the protection of peaceful peoples against Fascist aggression.

Is it impossibly hopeful to think that such a policy as this could get a following in England? A year ago, even six months ago, it would have been, but not now. Moreover—and this is the peculiar opportunity of this moment—it could be given the necessary publicity. There is now a considerable weekly press, with a circulation of millions, which would be ready to popularise—if not *exactly* the programme I have sketched above, at any rate *some* policy along those lines. There are even three or four daily papers which would be prepared to give it a sympathetic hearing. That is the distance we have travelled in the last six months.

But is such a policy realisable? That depends entirely on ourselves.

Some of the points I have suggested are of the kind that could be carried out immediately, others would take years or decades and even then would not be perfectly achieved. No political programme is ever carried out in its entirety. But what matters is that that or something like it should be our declared policy. It is always the *direction* that counts. It is of course quite hopeless to expect the present Government to pledge itself to any policy that implies turning this war into a revolutionary war. It is at best a government of compromise, with Churchill riding two horses like a circus acrobat. Before such measures as limitation of incomes become even thinkable, there will have to be a complete shift of power away from the old ruling class. If during this winter the war settles into another stagnant period, we ought in my opinion to agitate for a General Election, a thing which the Tory Party machine will make frantic efforts to prevent. But even without an election we can get the government we want, provided that we want it urgently enough. A real shove from below will accomplish it. As to who will be in that government when it comes, I make no guess. I only know that the right men will be there when the people really want them, for it is movements that make leaders and not leaders movements.

Within a year, perhaps even within six months, if we are still unconquered, we shall see the rise of something that has never existed before, a specifically *English* Socialist movement. Hitherto there has been only the Labour Party, which was the creation of the working class but did not aim at any fundamental change, and Marxism, which was a German theory interpreted by Russians and unsuccessfully transplanted to England. There was nothing that really touched the heart of the English people. Throughout its entire history the English Socialist movement has never produced a song with a catchy tune—nothing like *La Marseillaise* or *La Cucuracha*, for instance. When a Socialist movement native to England appears, the Marxists, like all others with a vested interest in the past, will be its bitter enemies. Inevitably they will denounce it as "Fascism". Already it is customary among the more soft-boiled intellectuals of the Left to declare that if we fight against the Nazis we shall "go Nazi" ourselves. They might almost equally well say that if we fight against Negroes we shall turn black. To "go Nazi" we should have to have the history of Germany behind us. Nations do not escape from their past merely by making a revolution. An English Socialist government will transform the nation from top to bottom, but it will still bear all over it the unmistakable marks of our own civilisation, the peculiar civilisation which I discussed earlier in this book.

It will not be doctrinaire, nor even logical. It will abolish the House of Lords, but quite probably will not abolish the Monarchy. It will leave anachronisms and loose ends everywhere, the judge in his ridiculous horsehair wig and the lion and the unicorn on the soldier's cap-buttons. It will not set up any explicit class dictatorship. It will group itself round the old Labour Party and its mass following will be in the trade unions, but it will draw into it most of the middle class and many of the younger sons of the bourgeoisie. Most of its directing brains will come from the new indeterminate class of skilled workers, technical experts, airmen, scientists, architects and journalists, the people who feel at home in the radio and ferro-concrete age. But it will never lose touch with the tradition of compromise and the belief in a law that is above the State. It will shoot traitors, but it will give them a solemn trial beforehand and occasionally it will acquit them. It will crush any open revolt promptly and cruelly, but it will interfere very little with the spoken and written word. Political parties with different names will still exist, revolutionary sects will still be publishing their newspapers and making as little impression as ever. It will disestablish the Church, but will not persecute religion. It will retain a vague reverence for the Christian moral code, and from time to time will refer to England as "a Christian country". The Catholic Church will war against it, but the Nonconformist sects and the bulk of the Anglican Church will be able to come to terms with it. It will show a power of assimilating the past which will shock foreign observers and sometimes make them doubt whether any revolution has happened.

But all the same it will have done the essential thing. It will have nationalised industry, scaled down incomes, set up a classless educational system. Its real nature will be apparent from the hatred which the surviving rich men of the world will feel for it. It will aim not at disintegrating the Empire but at turning it into a federation of Socialist states, freed not so much from the British flag as from the money-lender, the dividend-drawer and the wooden-headed British official. Its war strategy will be totally different from that of any property-ruled state, because it will not be afraid of the revolutionary after-effects when any existing régime is brought down. It will not have the smallest scruple about attacking hostile neutrals or stirring up native rebellion in enemy colonies. It will fight in such a way that even if it is beaten its memory will be dangerous to the victor, as the memory of the French Revolution was dangerous to Metternich's Europe. The dictators will fear it as they could not fear the existing British régime, even if its military strength were ten times what it is.

But at this moment, when the drowsy life of England has barely altered, and the offensive contrast of wealth and poverty still exists everywhere, even amid the bombs, why do I dare to say that all these things "will" happen?

Because the time has come when one can predict the future in terms of an "either—or". Either we turn this war into a revolutionary war (I do not say that our policy will be *exactly* what I have indicated above—merely that it will be along those general lines) or we lose it, and much more besides. Quite soon it will be possible to say definitely that our feet are set upon one path or the other. But at any rate it is certain that with our present social structure we cannot win. Our real forces, physical, moral or intellectual, cannot be mobilised.

### iii

Patriotism has nothing to do with Conservatism. It is actually the opposite of Conservatism, since it is a devotion to something that is always changing and yet is felt to be mystically the same. It is the bridge between the future and the past. No real revolutionary has ever been an internationalist.

During the past twenty years the negative, *fainéant* outlook which has been fashionable among English left-wingers, the sniggering of the intellectuals at patriotism and physical courage, the persistent effort to chip away English morale and spread a hedonistic, what-do-I-get-out-of-it attitude to life, has done nothing but harm. It would have been harmful even if we had been living in the squashy League of Nations universe that these people imagined. In an age of Fuehrers and bombing planes it was a disaster. However little we may like it, toughness is the price of survival. A nation trained to think hedonistically cannot survive amid peoples who work like slaves and breed like rabbits, and whose chief national industry is war. English Socialists of nearly all colours have wanted to make a stand against Fascism, but at the same time they have aimed at making their own countrymen unwarlike. They have failed, because in England traditional loyalties are stronger than new ones. But in spite of all the "anti-Fascist" heroics of the left-wing press, what chance should we have stood when the real struggle with Fascism came, if the average Englishman had been the kind of creature that the *New Statesman*, the *Daily Worker* or even the *News Chronicle* wished to make him?

Up to 1935 virtually all English left-wingers were vaguely pacifist. After 1935 the more vocal of them flung themselves eagerly into the Popular Front movement, which was simply an evasion of the whole problem posed by Fascism. It set out to be "anti-Fascist" in a purely negative way—"against" Fascism without being "for" any discoverable policy—and underneath it lay the flabby idea that when the time came the Russians would do our fighting for us. It is astonishing how this illusion fails to die. Every week sees its spate of letters to the press, pointing out that if we had a government with no Tories in it the Russians could hardly avoid coming round to our side. Or we are to publish high-sounding war-aims (*vide* books like *Unser Kampf*, *A Hundred Million Allies—If We Choose*, etc), whereupon the European populations will infallibly rise on our behalf. It is the same idea all the time—look abroad for your inspiration, get someone else to do your fighting for you. Underneath it lies the frightful inferiority complex of the English intellectual, the belief that the English are no longer a martial race, no longer capable of enduring.

In truth there is no reason to think that anyone will do our fighting for us yet awhile, except the Chinese, who have been doing it for three years already.[1] The Russians may be driven to fight on our side by the fact of a direct attack, but they have made it clear enough that they will not stand up to the German army if there is any way of avoiding it. In any case they are not likely to be attracted

[1] Written before the outbreak of the war in Greece. [Author's footnote.]

by the spectacle of a left-wing government in England. The present Russian régime must almost certainly be hostile to any revolution in the West. The subject peoples of Europe will rebel when Hitler begins to totter, but not earlier. Our potential allies are not the Europeans but on the one hand the Americans, who will need a year to mobilise their resources even if Big Business can be brought to heel, and on the other hand the coloured peoples, who cannot be even sentimentally on our side till our own revolution has started. For a long time, a year, two years, possibly three years, England has got to be the shock-absorber of the world. We have got to face bombing, hunger, overwork, influenza, boredom and treacherous peace offers. Manifestly it is a time to stiffen morale, not to weaken it. Instead of taking the mechanically anti-British attitude which is usual on the Left, it is better to consider what the world would really be like if the English-speaking culture perished. For it is childish to suppose that the other English-speaking countries, even the USA, will be unaffected if Britain is conquered.

Lord Halifax, and all his tribe, believe that when the war is over things will be exactly as they were before. Back to the crazy pavement of Versailles, back to "democracy", i.e. capitalism, back to dole queues and the Rolls-Royce cars, back to the grey top hats and the sponge-bag trousers, *in saecula saeculorum*. It is of course obvious that nothing of the kind is going to happen. A feeble imitation of it might just possibly happen in the case of a negotiated peace, but only for a short while. *Laissez-faire* capitalism is dead.[1] The choice lies between the kind of collective society that Hitler will set up and the kind that can arise if he is defeated.

If Hitler wins this war he will consolidate his rule over Europe, Africa and the Middle East, and if his armies have not been too greatly exhausted beforehand, he will wrench vast territories from Soviet Russia. He will set up a graded caste-society in which the German *Herrenvolk* ("master race" or "aristocratic race") will rule over Slavs and other lesser peoples whose job it will be to produce low-priced agricultural products. He will reduce the coloured peoples once and for all to outright slavery. The real quarrel of the Fascist powers with British imperialism is that they

---

[1] It is interesting to notice that Mr Kennedy, USA Ambassador in London, remarked on his return to New York in October 1940 that as a result of the war "democracy is finished". By "democracy", of course, he meant private capitalism. [Author's footnote.]

know that it is disintegrating. Another twenty years along the present line of development, and India will be a peasant republic linked with England only by voluntary alliance. The "semi-apes" of whom Hitler speaks with such loathing will be flying aeroplanes and manufacturing machine-guns. The Fascist dream of a slave empire will be at an end. On the other hand, if we are defeated we simply hand over our own victims to new masters who come fresh to the job and have not developed any scruples.

But more is involved than the fate of the coloured peoples. Two incompatible visions of life are fighting one another. "Between democracy and totalitarianism," says Mussolini, "there can be no compromise." The two creeds cannot even, for any length of time, live side by side. So long as democracy exists, even in its very imperfect English form, totalitarianism is in deadly danger. The whole English-speaking world is haunted by the idea of human equality, and though it would be simply a lie to say that either we or the Americans have ever acted up to our professions, still, the *idea* is there, and it is capable of one day becoming a reality. From the English-speaking culture, if it does not perish, a society of free and equal human beings will ultimately arise. But it is precisely the idea of human equality—the "Jewish" or "Judaeo-Christian" idea of equality—that Hitler came into the world to destroy. He has, heaven knows, said so often enough. The thought of a world in which black men would be as good as white men and Jews treated as human beings brings him the same horror and despair as the thought of endless slavery brings to us.

It is important to keep in mind how irreconcilable these two viewpoints are. Some time within the next year a pro-Hitler reaction within the left-wing intelligentsia is likely enough. There are premonitory signs of it already. Hitler's positive achievement appeals to the emptiness of these people, and, in the case of those with pacifist leanings, to their masochism. One knows in advance more or less what they will say. They will start by refusing to admit that British capitalism is evolving into something different, or that the defeat of Hitler can mean any more than a victory for the British and American millionaires. And from that they will proceed to argue that, after all, democracy is "just the same as" or "just as bad as" totalitarianism. There is *not much* freedom of speech in England; therefore there is *no more* than exists in Germany. To be on the dole is a horrible experience; therefore it is *no worse* to be in the torture-chambers of the Gestapo. In general, two blacks make a white, half a loaf is the same as no bread.

But in reality, whatever may be true about democracy and totalitarianism, it is not true that they are the same. It would not be true, even if British democracy were incapable of evolving beyond its present stage. The whole conception of the militarised continental state, with its secret police, its censored literature and its conscript labour, is utterly different from that of the loose maritime democracy, with its slums and unemployment, its strikes and party politics. It is the difference between land power and sea power, between cruelty and inefficiency, between lying and self-deception, between the SS man and the rent-collector. And in choosing between them one chooses not so much on the strength of what they now are as of what they are capable of becoming. But in a sense it is irrelevant whether democracy, at its higher or at its lowest, is "better" than totalitarianism. To decide that one would have to have access to absolute standards. The only question that matters is where one's real sympathies will lie when the pinch comes. The intellectuals who are so fond of balancing democracy against totalitarianism and "proving" that one is as bad as the other are simply frivolous people who have never been shoved up against realities. They show the same shallow misunderstanding of Fascism now, when they are beginning to flirt with it, as a year or two ago, when they were squealing against it. The question is not, "Can you make out a debating-society 'case' in favour of Hitler?" The question is, "Do you genuinely accept that case? Are you willing to submit to Hitler's rule? Do you want to see England conquered, or don't you?" It would be better to be sure on that point before frivolously siding with the enemy. For there is no such thing as neutrality in war; in practice one must help one side or the other.

When the pinch comes, no one bred in the western tradition can accept the Fascist vision of life. It is important to realise that *now*, and to grasp what it entails. With all its sloth, hypocrisy and injustice, the English-speaking civilisation is the only large obstacle in Hitler's path. It is a living contradiction of all the "infallible" dogmas of Fascism. That is why all Fascist writers for years past have agreed that England's power must be destroyed. England must be "exterminated", must be "annihilated", must "cease to exist". Strategically it would be possible for this war to end with Hitler in secure possession of Europe, and with the British Empire intact and British sea-power barely affected. But ideologically it is not possible; were Hitler to make an offer along those lines, it could only be treacherously, with a view to conquering England indirectly or renewing the attack at some more favourable moment. England cannot possibly be allowed to remain as a sort of funnel through which deadly ideas from beyond the Atlantic flow into the police states of Europe. And turning it round to our own point of view, we see the vastness of the issue before us, the all-importance of preserving our democracy more or less as we have known it. But to *preserve* is always to *extend*. The choice before us is not so much between victory and defeat as between revolution and apathy. If the thing we are fighting for is altogether destroyed, it will have been destroyed partly by our own act.

It could happen that England could introduce the beginnings of Socialism, turn this war into a revolutionary war, and still be defeated. That is at any rate thinkable. But, terrible as it would be for anyone who is now adult, it would be far less deadly than the "compromise peace" which a few rich men and their hired liars are hoping for. The final ruin of England could only be accomplished by an English government acting under orders from Berlin. But that cannot happen if England has awakened beforehand. For in that case the defeat would be unmistakable, the struggle would continue, the *idea* would survive. The difference between going down fighting, and surrendering without a fight, is by no means a question of "honour" and schoolboy heroics. Hitler said once that to *accept* defeat destroys the soul of a nation. This sounds like a piece of claptrap, but it is strictly true. The defeat of 1870 did not lessen the world-influence of France. The Third Republic had more influence, intellectually, than the France of Napoleon III. But the sort of peace that Pétain, Laval and Co have accepted can only be purchased by deliberately wiping out the national culture. The Vichy Government will enjoy a spurious independence only on condition that it destroys the distinctive marks of French culture: republicanism, secularism, respect for the intellect, absence of colour prejudice. We cannot be *utterly* defeated if we have made our revolution beforehand. We may see German troops marching down Whitehall, but another process, ultimately deadly to the German power-dream, will have been started. The Spanish people were defeated, but the things they learned during those two and a half memorable years will one day come back upon the Spanish Fascists like a boomerang.

A piece of Shakespearean bombast was much quoted at the beginning of the war. Even Mr Chamberlain quoted it once, if my memory does not deceive me:

> Come the four corners of the world in arms
> And we shall shock them: naught shall make us rue
> If England to herself do rest but true.

It is right enough, if you interpret it rightly. But England has got to be true to herself. She is not being true to herself while the refugees who have sought our shores are penned up in concentration camps, and company directors work out subtle schemes to dodge their Excess Profits Tax. It is goodbye to the *Tatler* and the *Bystander*, and farewell to the lady in the Rolls-Royce car. The heirs of Nelson and of Cromwell are not in the House of Lords. They are in the fields and the streets, in the factories and the armed forces, in the four-ale bar and the suburban back garden; and at present they are still kept under by a generation of ghosts. Compared with the task of bringing the real England to the surface, even the winning of the war, necessary though it is, is secondary. By revolution we become more ourselves, not less. There is no question of stopping short, striking a compromise, salvaging "democracy", standing still. Nothing ever stands still. We must add to our heritage or lose it, we must grow greater or grow less, we must go forward or backward. I believe in England, and I believe that we shall go forward.

Part of *England Your England* with the title *The Ruling Class* appeared in *Horizon*, December 1940. *England Your England* was reprinted in *SJ; EYE; OR*.

# 18. Letter to the Reverend Iorwerth Jones

111 Langford Court
Abbey Road
London NW8
8 April 1941

Dear Mr Jones,[1]
Many thanks for your letter.[2] Perhaps in one or two cases I expressed myself rather ambiguously and can make things clearer by answering some of your queries.

[1] A Congregationalist minister.

[2] In his letter the Rev. Iorwerth Jones had asked for the amplification of certain points Orwell had made in *The Lion and the Unicorn*.

1. "The USA will need a year to mobilise its resources even
if Big Business can be brought to heel." You comment that it is
the strikers who are holding up production. That is so, of course,
but I was trying to look deeper than the immediate obstruction.
The sort of effort that a nation at war now needs can only be made
if *both labour and capital* are conscripted. Ultimately what is needed
is that labour should be as much under discipline as the armed forces.
This condition practically obtains in the USSR and the totalitarian
countries. But it is only practicable if *all* classes are disciplined alike,
otherwise there is constant resentment and social friction, showing
itself in strikes and sabotage. In the long run I think the hardest
people to bring to heel will be the business men, who have most to
lose by the passing of the present system and in some cases are
consciously pro-Hitler. Beyond a certain point they will struggle
against the loss of their economic freedom, and as long as they do so
the causes of labour unrest will exist.

2. War aims. Of course I am in favour of declaring our war aims,
though there is a danger in proclaiming any very detailed scheme for
post-war reconstruction, in that Hitler, who is not troubled by any
intention of keeping his promises, will make a higher bid as soon as
our war aims are declared. All I protested against in the book was
the idea that propaganda *without* a display of military strength can
achieve anything. Acland's book *Unser Kampf*,[1] which I referred to,
seemed to assume that if we told the Germans we wanted a just peace
they would stop fighting. The same idea is being put about, though in
this case not in good faith, by the People's Convention[2] crowd
(Pritt[3] and Co.)

3. A pro-Fascist rebellion in India. I wasn't thinking of a rebellion
primarily by Indians, I was thinking of the British community in
India. A British general attempting a Fascist coup d'état would

[1] See 35.
[2] The People's Convention, organised in January 1941 by the Communists, was
ostensibly founded to fight for public rights, higher wages, better air-raid precautions etc and friendship with the USSR, but some historians say its true
purpose was to agitate against the war effort. In July 1941, after Russia's entry
into the war, it immediately called for a Second Front. By 1942 it had suspended
active work.
[3] D.N. Pritt (1887–    ), QC, Labour MP 1935–40, then, on his expulsion from
the Party for policy disagreements, Independent Socialist MP until 1950. Well
known as a barrister and fervent supporter of left-wing causes and the Soviet
Union.

probably use India as his jumping-off place, as Franco used Morocco. Of course it isn't a likelihood at this stage of the war, but one has got to think of the future. If an attempt to impose open naked Fascism upon Britain is ever made, I think coloured troops are almost certain to be used.

4. Gandhi and pacifism. Perhaps I ought not to have implied that pacifists are always people who *as individuals* have led sheltered lives, though it is a fact that "pure" pacifists usually belong to the middle classes and have grown up in somewhat exceptional circumstances. But it is a fact that pacifism as a movement barely exists except in communities where people don't feel foreign invasion and conquest to be likely. That is why pacifist movements are always found in maritime countries (there is even I believe a fairly considerable pacifist movement in Japan). Government cannot be conducted on "pure" pacifist lines, because any government which refused in all circumstances to use force could be overthrown by anyone, even any individual, who *was* willing to use force. Pacifism refuses to face the problem of government and pacifists think always as people who will never be in a position of control, which is why I call them irresponsible.

Gandhi has been regarded for twenty years by the Government of India as one of its right-hand men. I know what I am talking about—I used to be an officer in the Indian police. It was always admitted in the most cynical way that Gandhi made it easier for the British to rule India, because his influence was always against taking any action that would make any difference. The reason why Gandhi when in prison is always treated with such lenience, and small concessions sometimes made when he has prolonged one of his fasts to a dangerous extent, is that the British officials are in terror that he may die and be replaced by someone who believes less in "soul force" and more in bombs. Gandhi is of course personally quite honest and unaware of the way in which he is made use of, and his personal integrity makes him all the more useful. I won't undertake to say that his methods will not succeed in the long run. One can at any rate say that by preventing violence and therefore preventing relations being embittered beyond a certain point, he has made it more likely that the problem of India will ultimately be settled in a peaceful way. But it is hard to believe that the British will ever be got out of India by those means, and certainly the British on the spot don't think so. As to the conquest of England,

Gandhi would certainly advise us to let the Germans rule here rather than fight against them—in fact he did advocate just that. And if Hitler conquered England he would, I imagine, try to bring into being a nation-wide pacifist movement, which would prevent serious resistance and therefore make it easier for him to rule.

Thank you for writing.

Yours sincerely
George Orwell

## 19. London Letter to *Partisan Review*

London NW8
15 April 1941

Dear Editors,

As you see by the above date, I only received your letter a month after it was sent, so there is not much hope of my getting a reply to you by 20 April. I expect this will reach you before June, however. I will try to make some sort of answer to all your questions, but I should go over the allotted space if I answered them all in full, so I will concentrate on the ones I know most about. You don't mention anything in my previous letter having been blacked out by the censor, so I presume I can speak fairly freely.[1]

1. *What is the level and tone of the popular press these days? How much real information about the war effort comes out? How fully are strikes and labour troubles reported? Debates in Parliament? How dominant is the propaganda note? Is this propaganda mostly anti-Hun and jingoistic flag-waving as in the last war, or is it more anti-Fascist? What about the radio? Cinema?*

The tone of the popular press has improved out of recognition during the last year. This is especially notable in the *Daily Mirror* and *Sunday Pictorial* ("tabloid" papers of vast circulation, read largely by the army), and the Beaverbrook papers, the *Daily Express*, *Sunday Express* and *Evening Standard*. Except for the *Daily Mail* and certain Sunday papers these used to be the most lowbrow section of the press, but they have all grown politically serious, while preserving their "stunt" make-up, with screaming headlines, etc.

[1] Neither in this nor in Mr Orwell's last letter did the British censor make any deletions. [Editors of *Partisan Review*.]

All of them print articles which would have been considered hopelessly above their readers' heads a couple of years ago, and the *Mirror* and the *Standard* are noticeably "left". The *Standard* is the least important of Beaverbrook's three papers, and he has apparently taken his eye off it and left its direction almost entirely to young journalists of left-wing views who are allowed to say what they like so long as they don't attack the boss directly. Nearly the whole of the press is now "left" compared with what it was before Dunkirk—even *The Times* mumbles about the need for centralised ownership and greater social equality—and to find any straightforward expression of reactionary opinions, i.e. reactionary in the old pre-Fascist sense, you now have to go to obscure weekly and monthly papers, mostly Catholic papers. There is an element of eyewash in all this, but it is partly due to the fact that the decline in the trade in consumption goods has robbed the advertisers of much of their power over editorial policy. Ultimately this will bankrupt the newspapers and compel the State to take them over, but at the moment they are in an interim period when they are controlled by journalists rather than advertisers, which is all to the good for the short time it will last.

As to accuracy of news, I believe this is the most truthful war that has been fought in modern times. Of course one only sees enemy newspapers very rarely, but in our own papers there is certainly nothing to compare with the frightful lies that were told on both sides in 1914–18 or in the Spanish civil war. I believe that the radio, especially in countries where listening-in to foreign broadcasts is not forbidden, is making large-scale lying more and more difficult. The Germans have now sunk the British navy several times over in their published pronouncements, but don't otherwise seem to have lied much about major events. When things are going badly our own Government lies in a rather stupid way, withholding information and being vaguely optimistic, but generally has to come out with the truth within a few days. I have it on very good authority that reports of air-battles etc issued by the Air Ministry are substantially truthful, though of course favourably coloured. As to the other two fighting services I can't speak. I doubt whether labour troubles are really fully reported. News of a large-scale strike would probably never be suppressed, but I think you can take it that there is a strong tendency to pipe down on labour friction, and also on the discontent caused by billeting, evacuation, separation allowances for soldiers' wives etc

etc. Debates in Parliament are probably not misrepresented in the press, but with a House full of deadheads they are growing less and less interesting and only about four newspapers now give them prominence.

Propaganda enters into our lives more than it did a year ago, but not so grossly as it might. The flag-waving and Hun-hating is absolutely nothing to what it was in 1914–18, but it is growing. I think the majority opinion would now be that we are fighting the German people and not merely the Nazis. Vansittart's hate-Germany pamphlet, *Black Record,* sold like hot cakes. It is idle to pretend that this is simply something peculiar to the bourgeoisie. There have been very ugly manifestations of it among the common people. Still, as wars go, there has been remarkably little hatred so far, at any rate in this country. Nor is "anti-Fascism", of the kind that was fashionable during the Popular Front period, a strong force yet. The English people have never caught up with that. Their war morale depends more on old-fashioned patriotism, unwillingness to be governed by foreigners, and simple inability to grasp when they are in danger.

I believe that the BBC, in spite of the stupidity of its foreign propaganda and the unbearable voices of its announcers, is very truthful. It is generally regarded here as more reliable than the press. The movies seem almost unaffected by the war, i.e. in technique and subject-matter. They go on and on with the same treacly rubbish, and when they do touch on politics they are years behind the popular press and decades behind the average book.

2. *Is there any serious writing being done? Is there any anti-war literature like Barbusse etc in the last war? Over here we hear there is a tendency towards romanticism and escapism in current British writing. Is this true?*

So far as I know, nothing of consequence is being written, except in fragmentary form, diaries and short sketches for instance. The best novels I have read during the past year were either American or translations of foreign books written several years earlier. There is much production of anti-war literature, but of a one-eyed irresponsible kind. There is nothing corresponding to the characteristic war books of 1914–18. All of those in their different ways depended on a belief in the unity of European civilisation, and generally on a belief in international working-class solidarity. That doesn't exist any longer—Fascism has killed it. No one believes any longer that a war can be stopped by the workers on both sides simultaneously refusing to fight. To be effectively anti-war in England now one has to be pro-Hitler, and few people have the intellectual courage to be that, at any rate wholeheartedly. I don't see why good books shouldn't be written from the pro-Hitler angle, but none are appearing as yet.

I don't see any tendency to escapism in current literature, but I believe that if any major work were now produced it *would* be escapist, or at any rate subjective. I infer this from looking into my own mind. If I could get the time and mental peace to write a novel now, I should want to write about the past, the pre-1914 period, which I suppose comes under the heading of "escapism".

3. *What is the morale of the regular army like? Is there any tendency towards more democracy? Is it, so to speak, a* British *army primarily, or an* anti-Fascist *army—like the Loyalist army in Spain?*

I believe that the morale of the army is very good in a fighting sense but that there is much discontent about low separation allowances and class-privilege in the matter of promotion, and that the troops in England are horribly bored by the long inaction, the dull, muddy camps where they have spent the winter while their families were being bombed in the big towns, and the stupidity of a military system which was designed for illiterate mercenaries and is now being applied to fairly well-educated conscripts. It is still primarily a "non-political" British army. But there are now regular classes in political instruction, and subject to local variation, depending on the commander of the unit, there seems to be a good deal of freedom of discussion. As to "tendency towards democracy", I should say that there is probably less than there was a year ago, but that if one looks back five years the advance is enormous. On active service the officers now wear almost the same uniform as the men (battledress), and some of them habitually wear this on home service. The practice of saluting officers in the street has largely lapsed. New drafts of recruits all have to pass through the ranks and promotion is theoretically on merit alone, but the official claim, based on this, that the army is now entirely democratic should not be taken seriously. The framework of regular officers is still there and newcomers tend to be promoted on social grounds, with, no doubt, an eye to political reliability. But all this will gradually change if the war goes on. The need for able men will be too great, and the difference between the middle class and the better-paid working class is now too small, for at any rate the lower ranks of the army to remain on a class basis. The disasters now probably ahead of us may push the process of democratisation forward, as the disaster in Flanders did a year ago.

4. *We read your interesting article in a recent* Tribune *on the Home Guards. Could you tell us something of the present status of the movement? Is Wintringham the moving force behind it still? Is it mostly a middle-class or a working-class army? How democratic is it today?*

The Home Guard is the most anti-Fascist body existing in England at this moment, and at the same time is an astonishing phenomenon, a sort of People's Army officered by Blimps. The rank and file are predominantly working-class, with a strong middle-class seasoning, but practically all the commands are held by wealthy elderly men, a lot of whom are utterly incompetent. The Home Guard is a part-time force, practically unpaid, and at the beginning it was organised, I think consciously and intentionally, in such a way that a working-class person would never have enough spare time to hold any post above that of sergeant. Just recently the higher positions have been stuffed with retired generals, admirals and titled dugouts of all kinds. Principal age-groups of the rank and file are between 35 and 50 or under 20. Officers from Company Commander (Captain) upwards are much older on average, sometimes as old as seventy.

Given this set-up you can imagine the struggle that has gone on between the blimpocracy, wanting a parade-ground army of pre-1914 type, and the rank and file wanting, though less articulately, a more democratic type of force specialising in guerilla methods and weapons. The controversy has never been overtly political but has turned upon technical points of organisation, discipline and tactics, all of which, of course, have political implications which are half-consciously grasped on both sides. The War Office has been fairly open-minded and helpful, but I think it is true to say that the higher ranks within the Home Guard have fought steadily against a realistic view of war and that all experimentation and attempts at serious training have been due to proddings from below. Wintringham and some of his associates are still at the Home Guard training school (started unofficially by the weekly *Picture Post* and afterwards taken over by the War Office), but the Wintringham ("People's Army") school of thought has lost ground during the past six months. It or something like it will probably gain ground again during the coming months, and Wintringham has had very great influence, as thousands of men from all parts of the country have passed through his hands in three-day training courses. Although the Home Guard is now more similar to the regular army, or rather to the pre-war Territorials, than it was when it began, it is much more democratic and consciously anti-Fascist than some of its commanders would wish. It has several times been rumoured that the Government was growing nervous about it and contemplated disbanding it, but no move has been made to do this. A very important point, technically necessary to a force of this kind but only obtained after a struggle, is that the men keep their rifles and usually some ammunition in their own homes. The officers wear practically the same uniform as the men and there is no saluting off parade. Although the class nature of the command is widely grasped there has not been much friction. Within the lower ranks the spirit is extremely democratic and comradely, with an absence of snobbishness and class-uneasiness that would have been unthinkable ten years ago. I speak from experience here as I serve in a mixed residential area where factory-workers and quite rich men march in the ranks together. In general the political outlook of the men is old-fashioned patriotism mixed up with ill-defined but genuine hatred of the Nazis. Jews are numerous in the London units. In general, I think the danger of the Home Guard being turned into a reactionary middle-class militia still exists, but that this is not now likely to happen.

5. *How aggressive and articulate is big-business reaction today (not Mosley's Blackshirts, but the more solid and serious forces of big capital)? You mention a political swing to the right in the Churchill Government of late months. Does this mean the forces of organised business are climbing back into the saddle?*

I don't know what is going on behind the scenes and can only answer this question very generally, thus: *laissez-faire* capitalism is dead in England and can't revive unless the war ends within the next few months. Centralised ownership and planned production are bound to come. The whole question is who is to be in control. The recent rightward swing means that we are being regimented by wealthy men and aristocrats rather than by representatives of the common people. They will use their power to keep the structure of government on a class basis, manipulate taxation and rationing in their own favour, and avoid a revolutionary war strategy; but not to return to capitalism of the old chaotic kind. The swing of the past six months hasn't meant more economic freedom or profits for the individual businessman—quite the contrary; but it has meant that you are less likely to get an important job unless you have been to one of the right schools. I have given elsewhere my reasons for thinking that this tendency will change, but that *has* been the tendency since last autumn.

6. *Would you say that Bevin and Morrison still command the support of the British working class? Are there any other Labour Party politicians who have taken on new dimensions in the course of the war—assuming those two have? Is the shop-steward movement still growing?*

I know very little of industrial matters. I should say that Bevin does command working-class support and Morrison probably not. There is a widespread feeling that the Labour Party as a whole has simply abdicated. The only other Labour man whose reputation has grown is Cripps. If Churchill should go, Cripps and Bevin are tipped as the likeliest men for the premiership, with Bevin evidently favourite.

7. *How do you explain what, over here, seems to be the remarkable amount of democracy and civil liberties preserved during the war? Labour pressure? British tradition? Weakness of the upper classes?*

"British tradition" is a vague phrase, but I think it is the nearest answer. I suppose I shall seem to be giving myself a free advert, but may I draw attention to a recent book of mine, *The Lion and the Unicorn* (I believe copies have reached the USA)? In it I pointed out that there is in England a certain feeling of family loyalty which cuts across the class system (also makes it easier for the class system to survive, I am afraid) and checks the growth of political hatred. There *could*, I suppose, be a civil war in England, but I have never met any English person able to imagine one. At the same time one ought not to overrate the amount of freedom of the intellect existing here. The position is that in England there is a great respect for freedom of speech but very little for freedom of the press. During the past twenty years there has been much tampering, direct and indirect, with the freedom of the press, and this has never raised a flicker of popular protest. This is a lowbrow country and it is felt that the printed word doesn't matter greatly and that writers and such people don't deserve much sympathy. On the other hand the sort of atmosphere in which you daren't talk politics for fear that the Gestapo may be listening isn't thinkable in England. Any attempt to produce it would be broken not so much by conscious resistance as by the inability of ordinary people to grasp what was wanted of them. With the working classes, in particular, grumbling is so habitual that they don't know when they are grumbling. Where unemployment can be used as a screw, men are often afraid of expressing "red" opinions which might get round to the overseer or the boss, but hardly anyone would bother, for instance, about being overheard by a policeman. I believe that an organisation now exists for political espionage in factories, pubs, etc, and of course in the army, but I doubt whether it can do more than report on the state of public opinion and occasionally victimise some individual held to be dangerous. A foolish law was passed some time back making it a punishable offence to say anything "likely to cause alarm and despondency" (or words to that effect). There have been prosecutions under it, a few score I should say, but it is practically a dead letter and probably the majority of people don't know of its existence. You can hardly go into a pub or railway carriage without hearing it technically infringed, for obviously one can't discuss the war seriously without making statements which *might* cause alarm. Possibly at some time a law will be passed forbidding people to listen-in to foreign radio stations, but it will never be enforceable.

The British ruling class believe in democracy and civil liberty in a narrow and partly hypocritical way. At any rate they believe in the *letter* of the law and will sometimes keep to it when it is not to their advantage. They show no sign of developing a genuinely Fascist mentality. Liberty of every kind must obviously decline as a result of war, but given the present structure of society and social atmosphere there is a point beyond which the decline cannot go. Britain may be fascised from without or as a result of some internal revolution, but the old ruling class can't, in my opinion, produce a genuine totalitarianism of their own. Not to put it on any other grounds, they are too stupid. It is largely because they have been unable to grasp the first thing about the nature of Fascism that we are in this mess at all.

8. *From over here, it looks as though there had been a very rapid advance towards a totalitarian war economy in the last few months—rationing spreading wider, Bevin's conscription of certain classes of workers, extension of government controls over business. Is this impression correct? Is the tempo growing more or less rapid? How does the man in the street feel about the efficiency of the war effort? How much does he feel in his daily life the effect of these measures?*

Yes, the thing is already happening at great speed and will accelerate enormously in the coming months. In a very little while we shall all be in uniform or doing some kind of compulsory labour, and probably eating communally. I don't believe it will meet with much opposition so long as it hits all classes equally. The rich will squeal, of course—at present they are manifestly evading taxation, and the rationing barely affects them—but they will be brought to heel if the predicament is really desperate. I don't believe that the ordinary man cares a damn about the totalitarianisation of our economy, as such. People like small manufacturers, farmers and shopkeepers seem to accept their transition from small capitalists to State employees without much protest, provided that their livelihood is safeguarded. People in England hate the idea of a Gestapo, and there has been a lot of opposition, some of it successful, to official snooping and persecution of political dissidents, but I don't believe economic liberty has much appeal any longer. The changeover to a centralised economy doesn't seem to be altering people's way of life nearly so much as the shift of population, and mingling of classes, consequent on conscription and the bombing. But this may be less true in the industrial North, where on the whole people are working much harder in more trying conditions, and unemployment has practically ceased. What the reaction will be when we begin to experience hunger, as we may within the next few months, I don't prophesy. Apart from the bombing, and the overworking of certain categories of workers, one cannot honestly say that this war has caused much hardship as yet. The people still have more to eat than most European peoples would have in peacetime.

9. *What war aims does the left-and-labour movement now agree on? How sanguine are you about these aims being carried out? How much pressure is there now on the Government to proclaim Socialist war aims? On the question of war aims, of policy towards Europe and Germany in the event of victory, does there seem to be any radical difference between the Labour and Tory members of the Churchill Government? How definite are the plans for the "social rebuilding" of England after the war?*

I haven't space to answer this question properly, but I think you can take it that the Labour Party, as such, has now no policy genuinely independent of the Government. Some people even think that the Left Conservatives (Eden, and possibly Churchill) are more likely to adopt a Socialist policy than the Labour men. There are constant appeals to the Government to declare its war aims, but these come from individuals and are not the official act of the Labour Party. There is no sign that the Government has any detailed or even general post-war plan. Nevertheless the feeling that after the the war "things will be different" is so widespread that though, of course, the future England may be *worse* than that of the past, a return to Chamberlain's England is not thinkable even if it is technically possible.

10. *Would you say that the masses, working-class and middle-class, are more or less enthusiastically behind the present Government than in May 1940? Are they more or less behind the war effort in general?*

So far as the Government goes, less enthusiastically, but not very greatly so. This Government came in with a degree of popular support which is quite unusual. In its home policy it has disappointed expectations, but not so grossly as governments usually do. Churchill's personal popularity will have waned somewhat, but he still has a bigger following than any premier of the last twenty years. As to the war, I don't believe there is much variation. People are fed up, but nothing to what one might expect. But one can't speak with certainty of this till after the coming crisis, which will be of a different nature, less intelligible, perhaps harder to bear, than that of a year ago.

I hope that answers your questions. It is a bit over the length you allowed me, I am afraid. All well here, or fairly well. We had hell's own bombing last night, huge fires raging all over the place and a racket of guns that kept one awake half the night. But it doesn't matter, the hits were chiefly on theatres and fashionable shops, and this morning it is a beautiful spring day, the almond trees are in blossom, postmen and milk carts wandering to and fro as usual, and down at the corner the inevitable pair of fat women gossiping beside the pillar-box. The best of luck to you all.

POSTSCRIPT (15 May 1941)
The chief events since I wrote on April 15th have been the British defeats in Libya and Greece, and the general worsening of the situation in the Middle East, with Iraq in revolt, Stalin evidently preparing to go into closer partnership with Hitler, and Darlan getting ready to let German troops into Syria. There has also, within the last two days, been the mysterious arrival of Hess, which has

caused much amusement and speculation but which it is too early to comment on.

The question that matters is whether the disastrous turn the war has taken will lead to a further growth of democratic sentiment, as happened last year. I am afraid one must say that the chances are against this. The reason why the Dunkirk campaign and the collapse of France impressed public opinion, and did a great deal of good, was that these things were happening close at hand. There was the immediate threat of invasion, and there were the soldiers coming home in hundreds of thousands to tell their families how they had been let down. This time the thing is happening far away, in countries that the average person neither knows nor cares anything about— the ordinary British working man hasn't the faintest notion that the Suez Canal has anything to do with his own standard of living— and if the troops who got away from Greece have tales to tell they are telling them in Egypt and Palestine. Also, no one expected the Greek campaign to be anything but a disaster. Long before any official announcement was made it was known that we had troops in Greece, and I could find no one of whatever kind who believed that the expedition would be successful; on the other hand, nearly every-one felt that it was our duty to intervene. It is generally recognised that as yet, i.e. until we have an up-to-date army, we can't fight the Germans on the continent of Europe, but at the same time "we couldn't let the Greeks down". The English people have never been infected with power-worship and don't feel the futility of this sort of gesture as a continental people probably would. I can see no sign anywhere of any big swing of opinion. In the parliamentary debate on the Greek campaign the attack on the Government was led by envious throw-outs like Lloyd George, and instead of being a proper discussion the debate was easily twisted into a demand for a vote of confidence, which on the whole the Government deserves—at any rate it deserves it in the sense that no alternative government is at present possible. The repercussions which are probably happening in Australia, however, may do something towards democratising the conduct of the war. People here are beginning to say that the next leftward push must come from America. It is suggested, for instance, that Roosevelt might make it a condition of further help that the British Government do something about India. You are better able than I am to judge whether this is likely.

The air raids continue. To the ordinary people this is the part of the war that matters, in fact it *is* the war, but their stolidity is surprising. There was a sidelight on the popular mind which probably did not get into the American press, and which may interest you, in a recent by-election in Birmingham. A dissident Conservative who called himself a "reprisals candidate" ran against the Government's nominee. His claim was that we should concentrate on bombing German civilians to avenge what has been done here. Canon Stuart Morris, one of the leading lights in the Peace Pledge Union, also ran on a pacifist ticket. The respective slogans of the three candidates were "Bomb Berlin", "Stop the War" and "Back Churchill". The government man got about 15,000 votes and the other two about 1500 each. The whole poll was probably low, but considering the times we live in I think these figures are encouraging.

George Orwell

*Partisan Review*, July–August 1941

## 20. The Frontiers of Art and Propaganda

I am speaking on literary criticism, and in the world in which we are actually living that is almost as unpromising as speaking about peace. This is not a peaceful age, and it is not a critical age. In the Europe of the last ten years literary criticism of the older kind—criticism that is really judicious, scrupulous, fair-minded, treating a work of art as a thing of value in itself—has been next door to impossible.

If we look back at the English literature of the last ten years, not so much at the literature as at the prevailing literary attitude, the thing that strikes us is that it has almost ceased to be aesthetic. Literature has been swamped by propaganda. I do not mean that all the books written during that period have been bad. But the characteristic writers of the time, people like Auden and Spender and MacNeice, have been didactic, political writers, aesthetically conscious, of course, but more interested in subject-matter than in technique. And the most lively criticism has nearly all of it been the work of Marxist writers, people like Christopher Caudwell and Philip Henderson and Edward Upward, who look on every book virtually as a political pamphlet and are far more interested in digging out its political and social implications than in its literary qualities in the narrow sense.

This is all the more striking because it makes a very sharp and sudden contrast with the period immediately before it. The characteristic writers of the nineteen-twenties—T.S. Eliot, for instance, Ezra Pound, Virginia Woolf—were writers who put the main emphasis on technique. They had their beliefs and prejudices, of course, but they were far more interested in technical innovations than in any moral or meaning or political implication that their work might contain. The best of them all, James Joyce, was a technician and very little else, about as near to being a "pure" artist as a writer can be. Even D.H. Lawrence, though he was more of a "writer with a purpose" than most of the others of his time, had not much of what we should now call social consciousness. And though I have narrowed this down to the nineteen-twenties, it had really been the same from about 1890 onwards. Throughout the whole of that period, the notion that form is more important than subject-matter, the notion of "art for art's sake", had been taken for granted. There were writers who disagreed, of course—Bernard Shaw was one—but that was the prevailing outlook. The most important critic of the period, George Saintsbury, was a very old man in the nineteen-twenties, but he had a powerful influence up to about 1930, and Saintsbury had always firmly upheld the technical attitude to art. He claimed that he himself could and did judge any book solely on its execution, its *manner*, and was very nearly indifferent to the author's opinions.

Now, how is one to account for this very sudden change of outlook? About the end of the nineteen-twenties you get a book like Edith Sitwell's book on Pope, with a completely frivolous emphasis on technique, treating literature as a sort of embroidery, almost as though words did not have meanings: and only a few years later you get a Marxist critic like Edward Upward asserting that books can be "good" only when they are Marxist in tendency. In a sense both Edith Sitwell and Edward Upward were representative of their period. The question is, why should their outlook be so different?

I think one has got to look for the reason in external circumstances. Both the aesthetic and the political attitude to literature were produced, or at any rate conditioned, by the social atmosphere of a certain period. And now that another period has ended—for

Hitler's attack on Poland in 1939 ended one epoch as surely as the great slump of 1931 ended another—one can look back and see more clearly than was possible a few years ago the way in which literary attitudes are affected by external events. A thing that strikes anyone who looks back over the last hundred years is that literary criticism worth bothering about, and the critical attitude towards literature, barely existed in England between roughly 1830 and 1890. It is not that good books were not produced in that period. Several of the writers of that time, Dickens, Thackeray, Trollope and others, will probably be remembered longer than any that have come after them. But there are no literary figures in Victorian England corresponding to Flaubert, Baudelaire, Gautier and a host of others. What now appears to us as aesthetic scrupulousness hardly existed. To a mid-Victorian English writer, a book was partly something that brought him money and partly a vehicle for preaching sermons. England was changing very rapidly, a new moneyed class had come up on the ruins of the old aristocracy, contact with Europe had been severed, and a long artistic tradition had been broken. The mid-nineteenth-century English writers were barbarians, even when they happened to be gifted artists, like Dickens.

But in the later part of the century contact with Europe was re-established through Matthew Arnold, Pater, Oscar Wilde and various others, and the respect for form and technique in literature came back. It is from then that the notion of "art for art's sake"—a phrase very much out of fashion, but still, I think, the best available —really dates. And the reason why it could flourish so long, and be so much taken for granted, was that the whole period between 1890 and 1930 was one of exceptional comfort and security. It was what we might call the golden afternoon of the capitalist age. Even the Great War did not really disturb it. The Great War killed ten million men, but it did not shake the world as this war will shake it and has shaken it already. Almost every European between 1890 and 1930 lived in the tacit belief that civilisation would last for ever. You might be individually fortunate or unfortunate, but you had inside you the feeling that nothing would ever fundamentally change. And in that kind of atmosphere intellectual detachment, and also dilettantism, are possible. It is that feeling of continuity, of security, that could make it possible for a critic like Saintsbury, a real old crusted Tory and High Churchman, to be scrupulously fair to books written by men whose political and moral outlook he detested.

But since 1930 that sense of security has never existed. Hitler and the slump shattered it as the Great War and even the Russian Revolution had failed to shatter it. The writers who have come up since 1930 have been living in a world in which not only one's life but one's whole scheme of values is constantly menaced. In such circumstances detachment is not possible. You cannot take a purely aesthetic interest in a disease you are dying from; you cannot feel dispassionately about a man who is about to cut your throat. In a world in which Fascism and Socialism were fighting one another, any thinking person had to take sides, and his feelings had to find their way not only into his writing but into his judgements on literature. Literature had to become political, because anything else would have entailed mental dishonesty. One's attachments and hatreds were too near the surface of consciousness to be ignored. What books were *about* seemed so urgently important that the way they were written seemed almost insignificant.

And this period of ten years or so in which literature, even poetry, was mixed up with pamphleteering, did a great service to literary criticism, because it destroyed the illusion of pure aestheticism. It reminded us that propaganda in some form or other lurks in every book, that every work of art has a meaning and a purpose—a political, social and religious purpose—and that our aesthetic judgements are always coloured by our prejudices and beliefs. It debunked art for art's sake. But it also led for the time being into a blind alley, because it caused countless young writers to try to tie their minds to a political discipline which, if they had stuck to it, would have made mental honesty impossible. The only system of thought open to them at that time was official Marxism, which demanded a nationalistic loyalty towards Russia and forced the writer who called himself a Marxist to be mixed up in the dishonesties of power politics. And even if that was desirable, the assumptions that these writers built upon were suddenly shattered by the Russo-German Pact. Just as many writers about 1930 had discovered that you cannot really be detached from contemporary events, so many writers about 1939 were discovering that you cannot really sacrifice your intellectual integrity for the sake of a political creed—or at least you cannot do so and remain a writer. Aesthetic scrupulousness is not enough, but political rectitude is not enough either. The events of the last ten years have left us rather in the air, they have left England for the time being without any discoverable literary trend, but they have helped us to define, better than was possible before, the frontiers of art and propaganda.

A broadcast talk in the BBC Overseas Service, 30 April 1941; printed in the *Listener*, 29 May 1941.


# 21. Tolstoy and Shakespeare

Last week I pointed out that art and propaganda are never quite separable, and that what are supposed to be purely aesthetic judgements are always corrupted to some extent by moral or political or religious loyalties. And I added that in times of trouble, like the last ten years, in which no thinking person can ignore what is happening round him or avoid taking sides, these underlying loyalties are pushed nearer to the surface of consciousness. Criticism becomes more and more openly partisan, and even the pretence of detachment becomes very difficult. But one cannot infer from that that there is no such thing as an aesthetic judgement, that every work of art is simply and solely a political pamphlet and can be judged only as such. If we reason like that we lead our minds into a blind alley in which certain large and obvious facts become inexplicable. And in illustration of this I want to examine one of the greatest pieces of moral, non-aesthetic criticism—*anti*-aesthetic criticism, one might say—that have ever been written: Tolstoy's essay on Shakespeare.

Towards the end of his life Tolstoy wrote a terrific attack on Shakespeare, purporting to show not only that Shakespeare was not the great man he was claimed to be, but that he was a writer entirely without merit, one of the worst and most contemptible writers the world has ever seen. This essay caused tremendous indignation at the time, but I doubt whether it was ever satisfactorily answered. What is more, I shall point out that in the main it was unanswerable. Part of what Tolstoy says is strictly true, and parts of it are too much a matter of personal opinion to be worth arguing about. I do not mean, of course, that there is no detail in the essay which could not be answered. Tolstoy contradicts himself several times; the fact that he is dealing with a foreign language makes him misunderstand a great deal, and I think there is little doubt that his hatred and jealousy of Shakespeare make him resort to a certain amount of falsification, or at least wilful blindness. But all that is beside the point. In the main what Tolstoy says is justified after its fashion, and at the time it probably acted as a useful corrective to the silly adulation of Shakespeare that was then fashionable. The answer to it is less in anything I can say than in certain things that Tolstoy is forced to say himself.

Tolstoy's main contention is that Shakespeare is a trivial, shallow writer, with no coherent philosophy, no thoughts or ideas worth bothering about, no interest in social or religious problems, no grasp of character or probability, and, in so far as he could be said to have a definable attitude at all, with a cynical, immoral, worldly outlook on life. He accuses him of patching his plays together without caring twopence for credibility, of dealing in fantastic fables and impossible situations, of making all his characters talk in an artificial flowery language completely unlike that of real life. He also accuses him of thrusting anything and everything into his plays— soliloquies, scraps of ballads, discussions, vulgar jokes and so forth —without stopping to think whether they had anything to do with the plot, and also of taking for granted the immoral power politics and unjust social distinctions of the times he lived in. Briefly, he accuses him of being a hasty, slovenly writer, a man of doubtful morals, and, above all, of not being a *thinker*.

Now, a good deal of this could be contradicted. It is not true, in the sense implied by Tolstoy, that Shakespeare is an immoral writer. His moral code might be different from Tolstoy's, but he very definitely *has* a moral code, which is apparent all through his work. He is much more of a moralist than, for instance, Chaucer or Boccaccio. He also is not such a fool as Tolstoy tries to make out. At moments, incidentally, one might say, he shows a vision which goes far beyond his time. In this connection I would like to draw attention to the piece of criticism which Karl Marx—who, unlike Tolstoy, admired Shakespeare—wrote on *Timon of Athens*. But once again, what Tolstoy says is true on the whole. Shakespeare is not a thinker, and the critics who claimed that he was one of the great philosophers of the world were talking nonsense. His thoughts are simply a jumble, a rag-bag. He was like most Englishmen in having a code of conduct but no world-view, no philosophical faculty. Again, it is quite true that Shakespeare cares very little about probability and seldom bothers to make his characters coherent. As we know, he usually stole his plots from other people and hastily made them up into plays, often introducing absurdities and inconsistencies that were not present in the original. Now and again, when he happens to have got hold of a foolproof plot—*Macbeth*, for instance—his characters are reasonably consistent, but in many cases they are forced into actions which are completely incredible by any ordinary standard. Many of his plays have not even the sort of credibility that belongs to a fairy story. In any case we have no evidence that he himself took them seriously, except as a means of livelihood. In his sonnets he never even refers to his plays as part of his literary achievement, and only once mentions in a rather shame-faced way that he has been an actor. So far Tolstoy is justified. The claim that Shakespeare was a profound thinker, setting forth a coherent philosophy in plays that were technically perfect and full of subtle psychological observation, is ridiculous.

Only, what has Tolstoy achieved? By this furious attack he ought to have demolished Shakespeare altogether, and he evidently believes that he has done so. From the time when Tolstoy's essay was written, or at any rate from the time when it began to be widely read, Shakespeare's reputation ought to have withered away. The lovers of Shakespeare ought to have seen that their idol had been debunked, that in fact he had no merits, and they ought to have ceased forthwith to take any pleasure in him. But that did not happen. Shakespeare is demolished, and yet somehow he remains standing. So far from his being forgotten as the result of Tolstoy's attack, it is the attack itself that has been almost forgotten. Although Tolstoy is a popular writer in England, both the translations of this essay are out of print, and I had to search all over London before running one to earth in a museum.

It appears, therefore, that though Tolstoy can explain away nearly everything about Shakespeare, there is one thing that he cannot explain away, and that is his popularity. He himself is aware of this, and greatly puzzled by it. I said earlier that the answer to Tolstoy really lies in something he himself is obliged to say. He asks himself how it is that this bad, stupid and immoral writer Shakespeare is everywhere admired, and finally he can only explain it as a sort of worldwide conspiracy to pervert the truth. Or it is a sort of collective hallucination—a hypnosis, he calls it—by which everyone except Tolstoy himself is taken in. As to how this conspiracy or delusion began, he is obliged to set it down to the machinations of certain German critics at the beginning of the nineteenth century. They started telling the wicked lie that Shakespeare is a good writer, and no one since has had the courage to contradict them. Now, one need not spend very long over a theory of this kind. It is nonsense. The enormous majority of the people who have enjoyed watching Shakespeare's plays have never been influenced by any German critics, directly or indirectly. For Shakespeare's popularity is real enough, and it is a popularity that extends to ordinary, by no means bookish people. From his lifetime onwards he has been a stage favourite in England, and he is popular not only in the English-speaking countries but in most of Europe and parts of Asia. Almost as I speak the Soviet Government are celebrating the three hundred and twenty-fifth anniversary of his death, and in Ceylon I once saw a play of his being performed in some language of which I did not know a single word. One must conclude that there is something good—something durable—in Shakespeare which millions of ordinary people can appreciate, though Tolstoy happened to be unable to do so. He can survive exposure of the fact that he is a confused thinker whose plays are full of improbabilities. He can no more be debunked by such methods than you can destroy a flower by preaching a sermon at it.

And that, I think, tells one a little more about something I referred to last week: the frontiers of art and propaganda. It shows one the limitation of any criticism that is solely a criticism of subject and of meaning. Tolstoy criticises Shakespeare not as a poet, but as a thinker and a teacher, and along those lines he has no difficulty in demolishing him. And yet all that he says is irrelevant; Shakespeare is completely unaffected. Not only his reputation but the pleasure we take in him remain just the same as before. Evidently a poet is more than a thinker and a teacher, though he has to be that as well. Every piece of writing has its propaganda aspect, and yet in any book or play or poem or what not that is to endure there has to be a residuum of something that simply is not affected by its moral or meaning—a residuum of something we can only call art. Within certain limits, bad thought and bad morals can be good literature. If so great a man as Tolstoy could not demonstrate the contrary, I doubt whether anyone else can either.

A broadcast talk in the BBC Overseas Service, 7 May 1941; printed in the *Listener*, 5 June 1941.

## 22. The Meaning of a Poem

I shall start by quoting the poem called "Felix Randal", by Gerard Manley Hopkins, the well-known English poet—he was a Roman Catholic priest—who died in 1893:

Felix Randal the farrier, O is he dead then? my duty all ended,
Who have watched his mould of man, big-boned and hardy-handsome
Pining, pining, till time when reason rambled in it and some
Fatal four disorders, fleshed there, all contended?

Sickness broke him. Impatient he cursed at first, but mended
Being anointed and all; though a heavenlier heart began some
Months earlier, since I had our sweet reprieve and ransom
Tendered to him. Ah well, God rest him all road ever he offended!

This seeing the sick endears them to us, us too it endears.
My tongue had taught thee comfort, touch had quenched thy tears,
Thy tears that touched my heart, child, Felix, poor Felix Randal;

How far from then forethought of, all thy more boisterous years,
When thou at the random grim forge, powerful amidst peers,
Didst fettle for the great grey drayhorse his bright and battering
sandal!

It is what people call a "difficult" poem—I have a reason for choosing a difficult poem, which I will come back to in a moment—but no doubt the general drift of its meaning is clear enough. Felix Randal is a blacksmith—a farrier. The poet, who is also his priest, has known him in the prime of life as a big powerful man, and then he has seen him dying, worn out by disease and weeping on his bed like a child. That is all there is to it, so far as the "story" of the poem goes.

But now to come back to the reason why I deliberately chose such an obscure and one might say mannered poem. Hopkins is what people call a writer's writer. He writes in a very strange, twisted style—perhaps it is a bad style, really: at any rate, it would be a bad one to imitate—which is not at all easy to understand but which appeals to people who are professionally interested in points of technique. In criticisms of Hopkins, therefore, you will usually find all the emphasis laid on his use of language and his subject-matter very lightly touched on. And in any criticism of poetry, of course, it seems natural to judge primarily by the ear. For in verse the words—the sounds of words, their associations, and the harmonies of sound and association that two or three words together can set up—obviously matter more than they do in prose. Otherwise there would be no reason for writing in metrical form. And with Hopkins, in particular, the strangeness of his language and the astonishing beauty of some of the sound-effects he manages to bring off seem to overshadow everything else.

The best touch, one might say the especial touch, in this poem is due to a verbal coincidence. For the word that pins the whole poem together and gives it finally an air of majesty, a feeling of being tragic instead of merely pathetic, is that final word "sandal", which no doubt only came into Hopkins's mind because it happened to rhyme with Randal. I ought perhaps to add that the word "sandal" is more impressive to an English reader than it would be to an oriental, who sees sandals every day and perhaps wears them himself. To us a sandal is an exotic thing, chiefly associated with the ancient Greeks and Romans. When Hopkins describes the cart-horse's shoe as a sandal, he suddenly converts the cart-horse into a magnificent mythical beast, something like a heraldic animal. And he reinforces that effect by the splendid rhythm of the last line— "Didst fettle for the great grey drayhorse his bright and battering sandal"—which is actually a hexameter, the same metre in which Homer and Vergil wrote. By a combination of sound and association he manages to lift an ordinary village death on to the plane of tragedy.

But that tragic effect cannot simply exist in the void, on the strength of a certain combination of syllables. One cannot regard a poem as simply a pattern of words on paper, like a sort of mosaic. This poem is moving because of its sound, its musical qualities, but it is also moving because of an emotional content which could not be there if Hopkins's philosophy and beliefs were different from what they were. It is the poem, first of all, of a Catholic, and secondly of a man living at a particular moment of time, the latter part of the nineteenth century, when the old English agricultural way of life—the old Saxon village community—was finally passing away. The whole feeling of the poem is Christian. It is about death, and the attitude towards death varies in the great religions of the world. The Christian attitude towards death is not that it is something to be welcomed, or that it is something to be met with stoical indifference, or that it is something to be avoided as long as possible; but that it is something profoundly tragic which has to be gone through with. A Christian, I suppose, if he were offered the chance of everlasting life on this earth would refuse it, but he would still feel that death is profoundly sad. Now this feeling conditions Hopkins's use of words. If it were not for his special relationship as priest it would not, probably, occur to him to address the dead blacksmith as "child". And he could not, probably, have evolved that phrase I have quoted, "all thy more boisterous years", if he had not the special Christian vision of the necessity and the sadness of death. But, as I have said, the poem is also conditioned by the fact that Hopkins lived at the latter end of the nineteenth century. He had lived in rural communities when they were still distinctly similar to what they had been in Saxon times, but when they were just beginning to break up under the impact of the railway. Therefore he can see a type like Felix Randal, the small independent village craftsman, in perspective, as one can only see something when it is passing away. He can admire him, for instance, as an earlier writer probably could not have done. And that is why in speaking of his work he can evolve phrases like "the random grim forge" and "powerful amidst peers".

But one comes back to the technical consideration that a subject of this kind is very much helped by Hopkins's own peculiar style. English is a mixture of several languages, but mainly Saxon and Norman French, and to this day, in the country districts, there is a class distinction between the two. Many agricultural labourers speak almost pure Saxon. Now, Hopkins's own language is very Saxon, he tends to string several English words together instead of using a single long Latin one, as most people do when they want to express a complicated thought, and he deliberately derived from the early English poets, the ones who come before Chaucer. In this poem, he even uses several dialect words, "road" for way, and "fettle" for fix. The special power he has of re-creating the atmosphere of an English village would not belong to him if it were not for the purely technical studies he had made, earlier in his life, of the old Saxon poets. It will be seen that the poem is a synthesis—but more than a synthesis, a sort of growing together—of a special

vocabulary and a special religious and social outlook. The two fuse
together, inseparably, and the whole is greater than the parts.

I have tried to analyse this poem as well as I can in a short
period, but nothing I have said can explain, or explain away, the
pleasure I take in it. That is finally inexplicable, and it is just because
it *is* inexplicable that detailed criticism is worth while. Men of
science can study the life-process of a flower, or they can split it
up into its component elements, but any scientist will tell you that a
flower does not become less wonderful, it becomes more wonderful,
if you know all about it.

A broadcast talk in the BBC Overseas Service, 14 May 1941; printed in
the *Listener*, 12 June 1941

# 23. Literature and Totalitarianism

I said at the beginning of my first talk that this is not a critical age.
It is an age of partisanship and not of detachment, an age in which
it is especially difficult to see literary merit in a book with whose
conclusions you disagree. Politics—politics in the most general sense
—have invaded literature, to an extent that does not normally
happen, and this has brought to the surface of our consciousness the
struggle that always goes on between the individual and the community. It is when one considers the difficulty of writing honest un-
biased criticism in a time like ours that one begins to grasp the nature
of the threat that hangs over the whole of literature in the coming
age.

We live in an age in which the autonomous individual is ceasing to
exist—or perhaps one ought to say, in which the individual is ceasing
to have the illusion of being autonomous. Now, in all that we say
about literature, and (above all) in all that we say about criticism, we
instinctively take the autonomous individual for granted. The whole
of modern European literature—I am speaking of the literature of
the past four hundred years—is built on the concept of intellectual
honesty, or, if you like to put it that way, on Shakespeare's maxim,
"To thine own self be true". The first thing that we ask of a writer
is that he shall not tell lies, that he shall say what he really thinks,
what he really feels. The worst thing we can say about a work of art
is that it is insincere. And this is even truer of criticism than of

creative literature, in which a certain amount of posing and manner-ism, and even a certain amount of downright humbug, doesn't matter so long as the writer is fundamentally sincere. Modern literature is essentially an individual thing. It is either the truthful expression of what one man thinks and feels, or it is nothing.

As I say, we take this notion for granted, and yet as soon as one puts it into words one realises how literature is menaced. For this is the age of the totalitarian state, which does not and probably cannot allow the individual any freedom whatever. When one mentions totalitarianism one thinks immediately of Germany, Russia, Italy, but I think one must face the risk that this phenomenon is going to be world-wide. It is obvious that the period of free capitalism is coming to an end and that one country after another is adopting a centralised economy that one can call Socialism or state capitalism according as one prefers. With that the economic liberty of the individual, and to a great extent his liberty to do what he likes, to choose his own work, to move to and fro across the surface of the earth, comes to an end. Now, till recently the implications of this were not foreseen. It was never fully realised that the disappearance of economic liberty would have any effect on intellectual liberty. Socialism was usually thought of as a sort of moralised liberalism. The state would take charge of your economic life and set you free from the fear of poverty, unemployment and so forth, but it would have no need to interfere with your private intellectual life. Art could flourish just as it had done in the liberal-capitalist age, only a little more so, because the artist would not any longer be under economic compulsions.

Now, on the existing evidence, one must admit that these ideas have been falsified. Totalitarianism has abolished freedom of thought to an extent unheard of in any previous age. And it is im-portant to realise that its control of thought is not only negative, but positive. It not only forbids you to express—even to think—certain thoughts, but it dictates what you *shall* think, it creates an ideology for you, it tries to govern your emotional life as well as setting up a code of conduct. And as far as possible it isolates you from the outside world, it shuts you up in an artificial universe in which you have no standards of comparison. The totalitarian state tries, at any rate, to control the thoughts and emotions of its sub-jects at least as completely as it controls their actions.

The question that is important for us is: can literature survive in such an atmosphere? I think one must answer shortly that it cannot. If totalitarianism becomes world-wide and permanent, what we have known as literature must come to an end. And it will not do— as may appear plausible at first—to say that what will come to an end is merely the literature of post-Renaissance Europe.

There are several vital differences between totalitarianism and all the orthodoxies of the past, either in Europe or in the East. The most important is that the orthodoxies of the past did not change, or at least did not change rapidly. In medieval Europe the Church dictated what you should believe, but at least it allowed you to retain the same beliefs from birth to death. It did not tell you to believe one thing on Monday and another on Tuesday. And the same is more or less true of any orthodox Christian, Hindu, Buddhist or Muslim today. In a sense his thoughts are circumscribed, but he passes his whole life within the same framework of thought. His emotions are not tampered with.

Now, with totalitarianism, exactly the opposite is true. The peculiarity of the totalitarian state is that though it controls thought, it does not fix it. It sets up unquestionable dogmas, and it alters them from day to day. It needs the dogmas, because it needs absolute obedience from its subjects, but it cannot avoid the changes, which are dictated by the needs of power politics. It declares itself infallible, and at the same time it attacks the very concept of objective truth. To take a crude, obvious example, every German up to September, 1939, had to regard Russian Bolshevism with horror and aversion, and since September, 1939, he has had to regard it with admiration and affection. If Russia and Germany go to war, as they may well do within the next few years, another equally violent change will have to take place. The German's emotional life, his loves and hatreds, are expected, when necessary, to reverse themselves overnight. I hardly need to point out the effect of this kind of thing upon literature. For writing is largely a matter of feeling, which cannot always be controlled from outside. It is easy to pay lip-service to the orthodoxy of the moment, but writing of any consequence can only be produced when a man *feels* the truth of what he is saying; without that, the creative impulse is lacking. All the evidence we have suggests that the sudden emotional changes which totalitarianism demands of its followers are psychologically impossible. And that is the chief reason why I suggest that if totalitarianism triumphs throughout the world, literature, as we have known it, is at an end. And, in fact, totalitarianism does seem to have had that effect so far. In Italy literature has been crippled, and in Germany it seems almost to have ceased. The most characteristic activity of the Nazis is burning books. And even in Russia the literary renaissance we once expected has not happened, and the most promising Russian writers show a marked tendency to commit suicide or disappear into prison.

I said earlier that liberal capitalism is obviously coming to an end, and therefore I may have seemed to suggest that freedom of thought is also inevitably doomed. But I do not believe this to be so, and I will simply say in conclusion that I believe the hope of literature's survival lies in those countries in which liberalism has struck its deepest roots, the non-military countries, western Europe and the Americas, India and China. I believe—it may be no more than a pious hope—that though a collectivised economy is bound to come, those countries will know how to evolve a form of Socialism which is not totalitarian, in which freedom of thought can survive the disappearance of economic individualism. That, at any rate, is the only hope to which anyone who cares for literature can cling. Whoever feels the value of literature, whoever sees the central part it plays in the development of human history, must also see the life and death necessity of resisting totalitarianism, whether it is imposed on us from without or from within.

A broadcast talk in the BBC Overseas Service; printed in the *Listener*, 19 June 1941

## 24. Letter to Dorothy Plowman

111 Langford Court
Abbey Road
London NW8
20 June 1941

Dear Dorothy,[1]

I can't say much about Max's[2] death. You know how it is, the seeming uselessness of trying to offer any consolation when somebody is dead. My chief sorrow is that he should have died while this beastly war is still going on. I had not seen him for nearly two years, I deeply disagreed with him over the issue of pacifism, but though I am sorry about that you will perhaps understand when I say that I feel that at bottom it didn't matter. I always felt that with Max the most fundamental disagreement didn't alter one's personal relationship in any way, not only because he was incapable of any pettiness but also because one never seems able to feel any resentment against an opinion which is sincerely held. I felt that though Max and I held different opinions on nearly all specific subjects, there was a sense in which I could agree with his vision of life. I was very fond of him, and he was always very good to me. If I remember rightly, he was the first English editor to print any writing of mine, twelve years ago or more.

There is still the £300 which I borrowed through you from my anonymous benefactor.[3] I hope this doesn't embarrass you personally in any way. I can't possibly repay it at this moment, though I hope you understand that I haven't abandoned the intention of doing so. It is hard to make much more than a living nowadays.

[1] Dorothy Plowman (1887–1967), widow of Max Plowman.

[2] Max Plowman (1883–1941), journalist and author; worked on the *Adelphi*, 1929–41; Warden of the Adelphi Centre 1938–41; ardent supporter of Peace Pledge Union from its foundation in 1934, and its General Secretary 1937–8. Publications include *Introduction to the Study of Blake*, *A Subaltern on the Somme*, and *The Faith Called Pacifism*. He encouraged Orwell in his early writing and was one of the first to publish him. Plowman and his wife, Dorothy, always remained friends of Orwell's.

[3] L.H. Myers, the novelist. An admirer of Orwell's work, he first met Orwell with Max and Dorothy Plowman in the Sanatorium at Aylesford in the summer of 1938. Realising that Orwell needed to recuperate in a warm climate he lent him, anonymously, £300 through Dorothy Plowman. Orwell always regarded this as a loan and as late as 1946 was still unaware of the source of the money. See IV, 27.

One can't write books with this nightmare going on, and though I can get plenty of journalistic and broadcasting work, it is rather a hand-to-mouth existence. We have been in London almost from the outbreak of the war. We have kept on our cottage, but we let it furnished and only manage to go down there very occasionally. For more than a year Eileen was working in the Censorship Department, but I have induced her to drop it for a while, as it was upsetting her health. She is going to have a good rest and then perhaps get some less futile and exasperating work to do. I can't join the army because I am medically graded as class D, but I am in the Home Guard (a sergeant!) I haven't heard from Richard Rees[1] for some time, but last time I heard from him he was a gunner on a coal boat.

Eileen sends her best love. Please remember me also to Piers[2] and everyone. I gather from your card that Piers is now in England. I hope you succeed in keeping him out of danger. This is a rotten time to be alive, but I think anyone of Piers's age has a chance of seeing something better.

Yours
Eric Blair

## 25. Wells, Hitler and the World State

"In March or April, say the wiseacres, there is to be a stupendous knockout blow at Britain. . . . What Hitler has to do it with, I cannot imagine. His ebbing and dispersed military resources are now probably not so very much greater than the Italians' before they were put to the test in Greece and Africa."

"The German air power has been largely spent. It is behind the times and its first-rate men are mostly dead or disheartened or worn out."

"In 1914 the Hohenzollern army was the best in the world. Behind that screaming little defective in Berlin there is nothing of

---

[1] Sir Richard Rees, Bt. (1900–    ), painter, author and critic, whose writings include *George Orwell: Fugitive from the Camp of Victory*, *Simone Weil* and *A Theory of my Time*. From 1930–36 he edited the *Adelphi* and met Orwell as a young contributor. They remained close friends until Orwell's death. Rees was constant in his devotion, help and encouragement throughout the years.

[2] The Plowmans' son.

the sort. . . . Yet our military 'experts' discuss the waiting phantom. In their imaginations it is perfect in its equipment and invincible in discipline. Sometimes it is to strike a decisive 'blow' through Spain and North Africa and on, or march through the Balkans, march from the Danube to Ankara, to Persia, to India, or 'crush Russia', or 'pour' over the Brenner into Italy. The weeks pass and the phantom does none of these things—for one excellent reason. It does not exist to that extent. Most of such inadequate guns and munitions as it possessed must have been taken away from it and fooled away in Hitler's silly feints to invade Britain. And its raw jerry-built discipline is wilting under the creeping realisation that the Blitzkrieg is spent, and the war is coming home to roost."

These quotations are not taken from the *Cavalry Quarterly* but from a series of newspaper articles by Mr H.G. Wells, written at the beginning of this year and now reprinted in a book entitled *Guide to the New World*. Since they were written, the German army has overrun the Balkans and reconquered Cyrenaica, it can march through Turkey or Spain at such time as may suit it, and it has undertaken the invasion of Russia. How that campaign will turn out I do not know, but it is worth noticing that the German general staff, whose opinion is probably worth something, would not have begun it if they had not felt fairly certain of finishing it within three months. So much for the idea that the German army is a bogey, its equipment inadequate, its morale breaking down, etc etc.

What has Wells to set against the "screaming little defective in Berlin"? The usual rigmarole about a World State, plus the Sankey Declaration, which is an attempted definition of fundamental human rights, of anti-totalitarian tendency. Except that he is now especially concerned with federal world control of air power, it is the same gospel as he has been preaching almost without interruption for the past forty years, always with an air of angry surprise at the human beings who can fail to grasp anything so obvious.

What is the use of saying that we need federal world control of the air? The whole question is how we are to get it. What is the use of pointing out that a World State is desirable? What matters is that not one of the five great military powers would think of submitting to such a thing. All sensible men for decades past have been substantially in agreement with what Mr Wells says; but the sensible men have no power and, in too many cases, no disposition to sacrifice themselves. Hitler is a criminal lunatic, and Hitler has an army of millions of men, aeroplanes in thousands, tanks in tens of thousands. For his sake a great nation has been willing to over-work itself for six years and then to fight for two years more, whereas for the common-sense, essentially hedonistic world-view which Mr Wells puts forward, hardly a human creature is willing to shed a pint of blood. Before you can even talk of world recon-struction, or even of peace, you have got to eliminate Hitler, which means bringing into being a dynamic not necessarily the same as that of the Nazis, but probably quite as unacceptable to "en-lightened" and hedonistic people. What has kept England on its feet during the past year? In part, no doubt, some vague idea about a better future, but chiefly the atavistic emotion of patriotism, the ingrained feeling of the English-speaking peoples that they are superior to foreigners. For the last twenty years the main object of English left-wing intellectuals has been to break this feeling down, and if they had succeeded, we might be watching the SS men patrolling the London streets at this moment. Similarly, why are the Russians fighting like tigers against the German invasion? In part, perhaps, for some half-remembered ideal of Utopian Socialism, but chiefly in defence of Holy Russia (the "sacred soil of the Father-land", etc etc), which Stalin has revived in an only slightly altered form. The energy that actually shapes the world springs from emotions—racial pride, leader-worship, religious belief, love of war—which liberal intellectuals mechanically write off as anachron-isms, and which they have usually destroyed so completely in them-selves as to have lost all power of action.

The people who say that Hitler is Antichrist, or alternatively, the Holy Ghost, are nearer an understanding of the truth than the intellectuals who for ten dreadful years have kept it up that he is merely a figure out of comic opera, not worth taking seriously. All that this idea really reflects is the sheltered conditions of Eng-lish life. The Left Book Club was at bottom a product of Scotland Yard, just as the Peace Pledge Union is a product of the navy. One development of the last ten years has been the appearance of the "political book", a sort of enlarged pamphlet combining history with political criticism, as an important literary form. But the best writers in this line—Trotsky, Rauschning, Rosenberg, Silone,

Borkenau, Koestler and others—have none of them been Englishmen, and nearly all of them have been renegades from one or other extremist party, who have seen totalitarianism at close quarters and known the meaning of exile and persecution. Only in the English-speaking countries was it fashionable to believe, right up to the outbreak of war, that Hitler was an unimportant lunatic and the German tanks made of cardboard. Mr Wells, it will be seen from the quotations I have given above, believes something of the kind still. I do not suppose that either the bombs or the German campaign in Greece have altered his opinion. A lifelong habit of thought stands between him and an understanding of Hitler's power.

Mr Wells, like Dickens, belongs to the non-military middle class. The thunder of guns, the jingle of spurs, the catch in the throat when the old flag goes by, leave him manifestly cold. He has an invincible hatred of the fighting, hunting, swashbuckling side of life, symbolised in all his early books by a violent propaganda against horses. The principal villain of his *Outline of History* is the military adventurer, Napoleon. If one looks through nearly any book that he has written in the last forty years one finds the same idea constantly recurring: the supposed antithesis between the man of science who is working towards a planned World State and the reactionary who is trying to restore a disorderly past. In novels, Utopias, essays, films, pamphlets, the antithesis crops up, always more or less the same. On the one side science, order, progress, internationalism, aeroplanes, steel, concrete, hygiene: on the other side war, nationalism, religion, monarchy, peasants, Greek professors, poets, horses. History as he sees it is a series of victories won by the scientific man over the romantic man. Now, he is probably right in assuming that a "reasonable", planned form of society, with scientists rather than witch-doctors in control, will prevail sooner or later, but that is a different matter from assuming that it is just round the corner. There survives somewhere or other an interesting controversy which took place between Wells and Churchill at the time of the Russian Revolution. Wells accuses Churchill of not really believing his own propaganda about the Bolsheviks being monsters dripping with blood etc, but of merely fearing that they were going to introduce an era of common sense and scientific control, in which flag-wavers like Churchill himself would have no place. Churchill's estimate of the Bolsheviks, however, was nearer the mark than Wells's. The early Bolsheviks may have been angels or demons, according as one chooses to regard them, but at any rate they were not sensible men. They were not introducing a Wellsian Utopia but a Rule of the Saints, which, like the English Rule of the Saints, was a military despotism enlivened by witch-craft trials. The same misconception reappears in an inverted form in Wells's attitude to the Nazis. Hitler is all the war-lords and witch-doctors in history rolled into one. Therefore, argues Wells, he is an absurdity, a ghost from the past, a creature doomed to disappear almost immediately. But unfortunately the equation of science with common sense does not really hold good. The aeroplane, which was looked forward to as a civilising influence but in practice has hardly been used except for dropping bombs, is the symbol of that fact. Modern Germany is far more scientific than England, and far more barbarous. Much of what Wells has imagined and worked for is physically there in Nazi Germany. The order, the planning, the State encouragement of science, the steel, the con-crete, the aeroplanes, are all there, but all in the service of ideas appropriate to the Stone Age. Science is fighting on the side of superstition. But obviously it is impossible for Wells to accept this. It would contradict the world-view on which his own works are based. The war-lords and the witch-doctors *must* fail, the common-sense World State, as seen by a nineteenth-century liberal whose heart does not leap at the sound of bugles, *must* triumph. Treachery and defeatism apart, Hitler *cannot* be a danger. That he should finally win would be an impossible reversal of history, like a Jacobite restoration.

But is it not a sort of parricide for a person of my age (thirty-eight) to find fault with H.G. Wells? Thinking people who were born about the beginning of this century are in some sense Wells's own creation. How much influence any mere writer has, and es-pecially a "popular" writer whose work takes effect quickly, is questionable, but I doubt whether anyone who was writing books between 1900 and 1920, at any rate in the English language, in-fluenced the young so much. The minds of all of us, and therefore the physical world, would be perceptibly different if Wells had never existed. Only, just the singleness of mind, the one-sided imagination that made him seem like an inspired prophet in the Edwardian age, make him a shallow, inadequate thinker now. When Wells was young, the antithesis between science and reaction was not false. Society was ruled by narrow-minded, profoundly incurious people,

predatory businessmen, dull squires, bishops, politicians who could
quote Horace but had never heard of algebra. Science was faintly
disreputable and religious belief obligatory. Traditionalism, stupidity, snobbishness, patriotism, superstition and love of war seemed to
be all on the same side; there was need of someone who could
state the opposite point of view. Back in the nineteen-hundreds
it was a wonderful experience for a boy to discover H.G. Wells.
There you were, in a world of pedants, clergymen and golfers, with
your future employers exhorting you to "get on or get out", your
parents systematically warping your sexual life, and your dull-witted
schoolmasters sniggering over their Latin tags; and here was this
wonderful man who could tell you about the inhabitants of the
planets and the bottom of the sea, and who *knew* that the future was
not going to be what respectable people imagined. A decade or so
before aeroplanes were technically feasible Wells knew that within a
little while men would be able to fly. He knew that because he himself
*wanted* to be able to fly, and therefore felt sure that research in that
direction would continue. On the other hand, even when I was a
little boy, at a time when the Wright brothers had actually lifted
their machine off the ground for fifty-nine seconds, the generally
accepted opinion was that if God had meant us to fly He would have
given us wings. Up to 1914 Wells was in the main a true prophet. In
physical details his vision of the new world has been fulfilled to a
surprising extent.

But because he belonged to the nineteenth century and to a
non-military nation and class, he could not grasp the tremendous
strength of the old world which was symbolised in his mind by fox-
hunting Tories. He was, and still is, quite incapable of understanding
that nationalism, religious bigotry and feudal loyalty are far more
powerful forces than what he himself would describe as sanity.
Creatures out of the Dark Ages have come marching into the
present, and if they are ghosts they are at any rate ghosts which need
a strong magic to lay them. The people who have shown the best
understanding of Fascism are either those who have suffered under
it or those who have a Fascist streak in themselves. A crude book
like *The Iron Heel*, written nearly thirty years ago, is a truer prophecy
of the future than either *Brave New World* or *The Shape of Things
to Come*. If one had to choose among Wells's own contemporaries a
writer who could stand towards him as a corrective, one might choose
Kipling, who was not deaf to the evil voices of power and military

"glory". Kipling would have understood the appeal of Hitler, or for that matter of Stalin, whatever his attitude towards them might be. Wells is too sane to understand the modern world. The succession of lower-middle-class novels which are his greatest achievement stopped short at the other war and never really began again, and since 1920 he has squandered his talents in slaying paper dragons. But how much it is, after all, to have any talents to squander.

*Horizon,* August 1941; CTE; DD; CE.

## 26. London Letter to *Partisan Review*

London
17 August 1941

Dear Editors,

You asked me to send you another London letter, and though you left me free to choose what I should write about you added that your readers might be interested to hear some more about the Home Guard. I will give you some notes on the Home Guard, as much as I have space for, but I think my main subject this time ought to be the USSR's entry into the war. It has overshadowed everything in the last seven weeks, and I think it is now possible to make some sort of rough analysis of the state of British opinion.

### THE ANGLO-SOVIET ALLIANCE

The most striking thing about the Anglo-Soviet alliance has been its failure to cause any split in the country or any serious political repercussion whatever. It is true that Hitler's invasion of the USSR took everyone here very much by surprise. If the alliance had come about in 1938 or 1939, as it might have done, after long and bitter controversies, with the Popular Fronters shouting on one side and the Tory press playing Red Russia for all it was worth on the other, there would have been a first-rate political crisis, probably a General Election and certainly the growth of an openly pro-Nazi party in Parliament, the army, etc. But by June 1941 Stalin had come to appear as a very small bogey compared with Hitler, the pro-Fascists had mostly discredited themselves, and the attack happened so suddenly that the advantages and disadvantages of a Russian alliance had not even had time to be discussed.

One fact that this new turn of the war has brought out is that there are now great numbers of English people who have no special reaction towards the USSR. Russia, like China or Mexico, is simply a mysterious country a long way away, which once had a revolution, the nature of which has been forgotten. All the hideous controversies about the purges, the Five Year Plans, the Ukraine famine, etc have simply passed over the average newspaper-reader's head. But as for the rest, the people who have some definite pro-Russian or anti-Russian slant, they are split up into several sharply-defined blocks, of which the following are the ones that matter:

*The rich.* The real bourgeoisie are subjectively anti-Russian, and cannot possibly become otherwise. The existence of large numbers of wealthy parlour Bolsheviks does not alter this fact, because these people invariably belong to the decadent third-generation *rentier* class. Those who are *of* the capitalist class would regard the destruction of the Soviet Union by Hitler with, at best, mixed feelings. But it is an error to suppose that they are plotting direct treachery or that the handful capable of doing so are likely to gain control of the State. Churchill's continuance in office is a guarantee against that.

*The working class.* All the more thoughtful members of the British working class are mildly and vaguely pro-Russian. The shock caused by the Russian war against Finland was real enough, but it depended on the fact that nothing was happening at that time in the major war, and it has been completely forgotten. But it would probably be a mistake to imagine that the fact of Russia being in the war will in itself stimulate the British working class to greater efforts and greater sacrifices. In so far as strikes and wage disputes during the past two years have been due to deliberate troublemaking by the Communists, they will of course cease, but it is doubtful whether the Communists have ever been able to do more than magnify legitimate grievances. The grievances will still be there, and fraternal messages from *Pravda* will not make much difference to the feelings of the dock-worker unloading during an airraid or the tired munition-worker who has missed the last tram home. At one point or another the question of working-class loyalty to Russia is likely to come up in some such form as this: if the Government show signs of letting the Russians down, will the working class take steps to force a more active policy upon them? In that moment I believe it will be found that though a sort of loyalty to the Soviet Union still exists—must exist, so long as Russia is the only country even *pretending* to be a workers' state—it is no longer a positive force. The very fact that Hitler dares to make war on Russia is proof of this. Fifteen years ago such a war would have been impossible for any country except perhaps Japan, because the common soldiers could not have been trusted to use their weapons against the Socialist Fatherland. But that kind of loyalty has been gradually wasted by the nationalistic selfishness of Russian policy. Old-fashioned patriotism is now a far stronger force than any kind of internationalism, or any ideas about the Socialist Fatherland, and this fact also will be reflected in the strategy of the war.

*The Communists.* I do not need to tell you anything about the shifts of official Communist policy during the past two years, but I am not certain whether the mentality of the Communist intelligentsia is quite the same in the USA as here. In England the Communists whom it is possible to respect are factory workers, but they are not very numerous, and precisely because they are usually skilled workmen and loyal comrades they cannot always be rigidly faithful to the "line". Between September 1939 and June 1941 they do not seem to have attempted any definite sabotage of arms production, although the logic of Communist policy demanded this. The middle-class Communists, however, are a different proposition. They include most of the official and unofficial leaders of the party, and with them must be lumped the greater part of the younger literary intelligentsia, especially in the universities. As I have pointed out elsewhere, the "Communism" of these people amounts simply to nationalism and leader-worship in their most vulgar forms, transferred to the USSR. Their importance at this moment is that with the entry of Russia into the war they may regain the influence in the press which they had between 1935 and 1939 and lost during the last two years. The *News Chronicle*, after the *Daily Herald* the leading left-wing daily (circulation about 1,400,000), is already busy whitewashing the men whom it was denouncing as traitors a little while back. The so-called People's Convention, led by D.N. Pritt (Pritt is a Labour MP but is always claimed by Communists as an "underground" member of their party, evidently with truth) is still in existence but has abruptly reversed its policy. If the Communists are allowed the kind of publicity that they were getting in 1938, they will both consciously and unconsciously sow discord between Britain and the USSR. What they wish for is not the destruction of Hitler and the re-settlement of Europe, but a vulgar military triumph for their adopted Fatherland, and they will do their best to insult public opinion here by transferring as much as possible of the prestige of the war to Russia, and by constantly casting doubts on Britain's good faith. The danger of this kind of thing ought not to be underrated. The Russians themselves, however, probably grasp how the land lies and will act accordingly. If we have a long war ahead of us it is not to their advantage that there should be disaffection in this country. But in so far as they can get a hearing, the British Communists must be regarded as one of the forces acting against Anglo-Russian unity.

*The Catholics.* There are supposed to be some two million Catholics in this country, the bulk of them very poor Irish labourers. They vote Labour and act as a sort of silent drag on Labour Party policy, but are not sufficiently under the thumb of their priests to be Fascist in sympathy. The importance of the middle- and upper-class Catholics is that they are extremely numerous in the Foreign Office and the Consular Service, and also have a good deal of influence in the press, though less than formerly. The "born" Catholics of the old Catholic families are less ultramontane and more ordinarily patriotic than the converted intellectuals (Ronald Knox, Arnold Lunn, etc etc), who have very much the same mentality, *mutatis mutandis*, as the British Communists. I suppose I need not repeat the history of their pro-Fascist activities in the past. Since the outbreak of war they have not dared to be openly pro-Hitler, but have done their propaganda indirectly by fulsome praises of Pétain and Franco. Cardinal Hinsley, founder of the Sword of the Spirit Movement (Catholic democracy), seems to be sincerely anti-Nazi according to his lights, but represents only one section of Catholic opinion. As soon as Hitler invaded the USSR, the Catholic press announced that we must take advantage of the respite that this gave us, but "no alliance with godless Russia". Significantly, the Catholic papers became much more anti-Russian when it became apparent that the Russians were resisting successfully. No one who has studied Catholic literature during the past ten years can doubt that the bulk of the hierarchy and the intelligentsia would side with Germany as against Russia if they had a quarter of a chance. Their hatred of

Russia is really venomous, enough even to disgust an anti-Stalinist like myself, though their propaganda is necessarily old-fashioned (Bolshevik atrocities, nationalisation of women, etc) and does not make much impression on working-class people. When the Russian campaign is settled one way or the other, i.e. when Hitler is in Moscow or the Russians show signs of invading Europe, they will come out openly on Hitler's side, and they will certainly be to the fore if any plausible terms are suggested for a compromise peace. If anything corresponding to a Pétain government were established here, it would have to lean largely on the Catholics. They are the only really conscious, logical, intelligent enemies that democracy has got in England, and it is a mistake to despise them.

So much for the various currents of opinion. I began this letter some days ago, and since then the feeling that we are not doing enough to help the Russians has noticeably intensified. The favourite quip now is that what we are giving Russia is "all aid short of war". Even the Beaverbrook press repeats this. Also, since Russia entered the war there has been a cooling-off in people's feelings towards the USA. The Churchill-Roosevelt declaration caused, I believe, a good deal of disappointment. Where Churchill had gone was an official secret but seems to have been widely known, and most people expected the outcome to be America's entry into the war, or at least the occupation of some more strategic points on the Atlantic. People are saying now that the Russians are fighting and the Americans are talking, and the saying that was current last year, "sympathy to China, oil to Japan", begins to be repeated.

### THE HOME GUARD

This force, then known as the Local Defence Volunteers, was raised last spring in response to a radio appeal by Anthony Eden, following on the success of the German parachute troops in Holland. It got a quarter of a million recruits in the first twenty-four hours. The numbers are now somewhere between a million and a half and two millions; they have fluctuated during the past year, but with a tendency to increase. Except for a small nucleus of administrative officers and NCO instructors attached from the regular army, it is entirely part-time and unpaid. Apart from training, the Home Guard relieves the army of some of its routine patrols, pickets on buildings, etc and does a certain amount of ARP[1] work. The amount of

[1] Air Raid Precautions.

time given up to the Home Guard by ordinary members would vary between five and twenty-five hours a week. Since the whole thing is voluntary there is no way of enforcing attendance, but the habitual absentees are usually asked to resign, and the inactive membership at any one time would not be more than ten per cent. In the case of invasion the Home Guard will be put on the same disciplinary basis as the regular army and members will be paid for their services, all ranks receiving the same rate of payment. In the beginning the Home Guard was a heterogeneous force and structurally rather similar to the early Spanish militias, but it has been gradually brigaded on the lines of the regular army, and all the ordinary contingents are affiliated to the regiments belonging to their locality. But factories, railways and government offices have their own separate units, which are responsible only for the defence of their own premises.

The strategic idea of the Home Guard is static defence in *complete* depth, i.e. from one coast of England to the other. The tactical idea is not so much to defeat an invader as to hold him up till the regular troops can get at him. It is not intended that the Home Guard shall manoeuvre in large numbers or over large areas. In practice it probably could not be operated in any larger unit than the company, and no one contingent could advance or retreat more than a few miles. The intention is that any invader who crosses any section of the country will always, until he reaches the sea coast, have innumerable small bands of enemies both behind and in front of him. As to *how* the invader can best be resisted, theories have varied, chiefly as a result of observation of the different campaigns abroad. At the beginning the intention was simply to deal with parachutists, but the events in France and the Low Countries had caused an exaggerated fear of Fifth Columnists, and the authorities had evidently some notion of turning the Home Guard into a sort of auxiliary police force. This idea came to nothing because the men who had joined only wanted to fight the Germans (in June 1940 the invasion was expected to happen almost immediately), and in the chaotic conditions of the time they had to do their organising for themselves. When enough weapons and uniforms had been distributed to make the Home Guard look something like soldiers, the tendency was to turn them into ordinary infantry of the pre-blitzkrieg type. Then the success of the Germans in getting their armoured divisions across the sea to Libya shifted the emphasis to anti-tank fighting. Somewhat later the loss of Crete showed what can be done by parachutists and airborne troops, and tactics for dealing with them were worked out. Finally the struggle of the Russian guerillas behind the German lines led to a renewed emphasis on guerilla tactics and sabotage. All of these successive tendencies are reflected in the voluminous literature, official and unofficial, which has already grown up round the Home Guard.

The Home Guard can by now be regarded as a serious force, capable of strong resistance for at any rate a short period. No invader could travel more than a few miles through open country or more than a few hundred yards in the big towns without coming upon a knot of armed men. Morale can be relied on absolutely, though willingness to commit sabotage and go on fighting in theoretically occupied territory will probably vary according to the political complexion of different units. There are great and obvious difficulties in the way of keeping a force of this kind in the field for more than a week or two at a time, and if there should be prolonged fighting in England the Home Guard would probably be merged by degrees in the regular army and lose its local and voluntary character. The other great difficulty is in the supply of officers. Although there is in theory no class discrimination, the Home Guard is in practice officered on a class basis more completely than is the case in the regular army. Nor is it easy to see how this could have been avoided, even if the wish to avoid it had been there. In any sort of army people from the upper and middle classes will tend to get the positions of command—this happened in the early Spanish militias and had also happened in the Russian civil war—and in a spare-time force the average working man cannot possibly find enough time to do the administrative routine of a platoon-commander or company-commander. Also, the Government makes no financial contribution, except for a token payment when men are on duty all night, and the provision of weapons and uniforms. One cannot command troops without constantly incurring small expenses, and £50 a year would be the very minimum that any commissioned officer spends on his unit. What all this has meant in practice is that nearly all commands are held by retired colonels, people with "private" incomes or, at best, wealthy businessmen. A respectable proportion of the officers are too old to have caught up with the 1914 war, let alone anything subsequent. In the case of prolonged fighting it might be necessary to get rid of as many as half the officers. The rank and file know how matters stand and would probably devise some method of electing their own officers if need be. The election of officers is sometimes discussed among the lower ranks, but it has never been practised except, I think, in some of the factory units.

The personnel of the Home Guard is not quite the same now as it was at the beginning. The men who flocked into the ranks in the first few days were almost all of them men who had fought in the last war and were too old for this one. The weapons that were distributed, therefore, went into the hands of people who were more or less anti-Fascist but politically uneducated. The only leavening was a few class-conscious factory-workers and a handful of men who had fought in the Spanish civil war. The Left as usual had failed to see its opportunity—the Labour Party could have made the Home Guard into its own organisation if it had acted vigorously in the first few days—and in left-wing circles it was fashionable to describe the Home Guard as a Fascist organisation. Later the idea that when weapons are being distributed it is as well to get hold of some of them began to sink in, and a certain number of left-wing intellectuals found their way into the ranks. It has never been possible to get a big influx from the Labour Party, however; the most willing recruits have always been the people whose political ideal would be Churchill. The chief educative force within the movement has been the training school which was started by Tom Wintringham, Hugh Slater and others, especially in the first few months, before they were taken over by the War Office. Their teaching was purely military, but with its insistence on guerilla methods it had revolutionary implications which were perfectly well grasped by many of the men who listened to it. The Communist Party from the first forbade its members to join the Home Guard and conducted a vicious campaign of libel against Wintringham and Co. During recent months the military call-up has almost stripped the Home Guard of men between 20 and 40, but at the same time there has been an influx of working-class boys of about 17. Most of them are quite unpolitical in outlook and when asked their reason for joining say that they want to get some military training against the time when they are called up, three years hence. This reflects the fact that many English people can now hardly imagine a time when there will be no war. There is also a fair number of foreigners in the Home Guard. In the panic period last year they were rigidly excluded. One of my own first jobs was to go round pacifying would-be members who had been rejected because they were not of British extraction on both sides. One man had been turned down because one of his parents was a foreigner and had not been naturalised till 1902. Now these ideas have been dropped and the London units contain Russians, Czechs, Poles, Indians, Negroes and Americans; no Germans or Italians, however. I will not swear that the prevailing outlook in the Home Guard is more "left" than it was a year ago. It reflects the general outlook of the country, which for a year past has turned this way and that like a door on its hinges. But the political discussions that one hears in canteens and guard rooms are much more intelligent than they were, and the social shake-up among men of all classes who have now been forced into close intimacy for a considerable time has done a lot of good.

Up to a point one can foresee the future of the Home Guard. Even should it become clear that no invasion is likely it will not be disbanded before the end of the war, and probably not then. It will play an important part if there is any attempt at a Pétain peace, or in any internal fighting after the war. It already exerts a slight political influence on the regular army, and would exert more under active service conditions. It first came into being precisely because England is a conservative country where the law-abidingness of ordinary people can be relied upon, but once in being it introduces a political factor which has never existed here before. Somewhere near a million British working men now have rifles in their bedrooms and don't in the least wish to give them up. The possibilities contained in that fact hardly need pointing out.

I see that I have written a lot more than I intended. I began this letter on the 17th August, and I end it on the 25th. The Russians and the British have marched into Iran, and everyone is delighted. We have had a goodish summer and the people have got some sunlight in their bones to help them through the winter. London has not had a real air raid for nearly four months. Parts of the East End are simply flattened out, and the City is a mass of ruins with St Paul's almost untouched, standing out of it like an enormous rock, but the less-bombed parts of London have been so completely cleaned up that you would hardly know they had ever been damaged. Standing on the roof of this tall block of flats I live in and looking all round, I can see no bomb damage anywhere, except for a few churches whose spires have broken off in the middle, making them look like lizards that have lost their tails. There is no real food shortage, but the lack of concentrated foods (meat, bacon, cheese and eggs) causes serious underfeeding among heavy labourers, such as miners, who have to eat their midday meal away from home. There is a chronic scarcity of cigarettes and local shortages of beer. Some tobacconists consider that the amount of tobacco smoked has increased by 40 per cent since the war. Wages have not kept up with prices, but on the other hand there is no unemployment, so that though the individual wage is lower than it was, the family income tends to be higher. Clothes are fairly strictly rationed, but the crowds in the streets are not noticeably shabbier as yet. I often wonder how much we are all deteriorating under the influence of war—how much of a shock one would get if one could suddenly see the London of three years ago side by side with this one. But it is a gradual process and we do not notice any change. I can hardly imagine the London skies without the barrage balloons, and should be sorry to see them go.

Arthur Koestler, whose work is probably known to you, is a private in the Pioneers. Franz Borkenau, author of *The Spanish Cockpit* and *The Communist International*, who was deported to Australia during the panic last year, is back in England. Louis MacNeice and William Empson are working for the BBC. Dylan Thomas is in the army. Arthur Calder-Marshall has been made an officer. Tom Wintringham is once again an instructor in the Home Guard, after resigning for a period. Meanwhile the Russians acknowledge seven hundred thousand casualties, and the armies are converging on Leningrad by the same roads as they followed twenty-two years ago. I never thought I should live to say "Good luck to Comrade Stalin", but so I do.

Yours ever,
George Orwell

PS. I must add a word about that appalling "message" to British writers from the Soviet novelist, Alexei Tolstoy, with the old atrocity stories dug up from 1914, which appeared in the September *Horizon*. That is the feature of war that frightens me, much worse than air raids. But I hope people in the USA won't imagine that people here take that kind of stuff seriously. Everyone I know laughs when they hear that old one about the Germans being chained to their machine-guns.

# 27. The Art of Donald McGill

Who does not know the "comics" of the cheap stationers' windows, the penny or twopenny coloured postcards with their endless succession of fat women in tight bathing-dresses and their crude drawing and unbearable colours, chiefly hedge-sparrow's egg tint and Post Office red?

This question ought to be rhetorical, but it is a curious fact that many people seem to be unaware of the existence of these things, or else to have a vague notion that they are something to be found only at the seaside, like nigger minstrels or peppermint rock. Actually they are on sale everywhere—they can be bought at nearly any Woolworth's, for example—and they are evidently produced in enormous numbers, new series constantly appearing. They are not to be confused with the various other types of comic illustrated post-card, such as the sentimental ones dealing with puppies and kittens or the Wendyish, sub-pornographic ones which exploit the love-affairs of children. They are a genre of their own, specialising in very "low" humour, the mother-in-law, baby's nappy, policemen's boots type of joke, and distinguishable from all the other kinds by having no artistic pretensions. Some half-dozen publishing houses issue them, though the people who draw them seem not to be numerous at any one time.

I have associated them especially with the name of Donald McGill because he is not only the most prolific and by far the best of contemporary postcard artists, but also the most representative, the most perfect in the tradition. Who Donald McGill is, I do not know. He is apparently a trade name, for at least one series of post-cards is issued simply as "The Donald McGill Comics", but he is also unquestionably a real person with a style of drawing which is recognisable at a glance. Anyone who examines his postcards in bulk will notice that many of them are not despicable even as draw-ings, but it would be mere dilettantism to pretend that they have any direct aesthetic value. A comic postcard is simply an illustration to a joke, invariably a "low" joke, and it stands or falls by its ability to raise a laugh. Beyond that it has only "ideological" interest. McGill is a clever draughtsman with a real caricaturist's touch in the drawing of faces, but the special value of his postcards is that they are so completely typical. They represent, as it were, the norm of the comic postcard. Without being in the least imitative, they are exactly what comic postcards have been any time these last forty years, and from them the meaning and purpose of the whole genre can be inferred.

Get hold of a dozen of these things, preferably McGill's—if you pick out from a pile the ones that seem to you funniest, you will probably find that most of them are McGill's—and spread them out on a table. What do you see?

Your first impression is of overpowering vulgarity. This is quite apart from the ever-present obscenity, and apart also from the hideousness of the colours. They have an utter lowness of mental atmosphere which comes out not only in the nature of the jokes but, even more, in the grotesque, staring, blatant quality of the drawings. The designs, like those of a child, are full of heavy lines and empty spaces, and all the figures in them, every gesture and attitude, are deliberately ugly, the faces grinning and vacuous, the women monstrously parodied, with bottoms like Hottentots. Your second impression, however, is of indefinable familiarity. What do these things remind you of? What are they so like? In the first place, of course, they remind you of the barely different postcards which you probably gazed at in your childhood. But more than this, what you are really looking at is something as traditional as Greek tragedy, a sort of sub-world of smacked bottoms and scrawny mothers-in-law which is a part of western European consciousness. Not that the jokes, taken one by one, are necessarily stale. Not being debarred from smuttiness, comic postcards repeat themselves less often than the joke columns in reputable magazines, but their basic subject-matter, the *kind* of joke they are aiming at, never varies. A few are genuinely witty, in a Max Millerish style. Examples:

> "I like seeing experienced girls home."
> "But I'm not experienced!"
> "You're not home yet!"

> "I've been struggling for years to get a fur coat. How did you get yours?"
> "I left off struggling."

> Judge: "You are prevaricating, sir. Did you or did you not sleep with this woman?"
> Co-respondent: "Not a wink, my lord!"

In general, however, they are not witty but humorous, and it must be said for McGill's postcards, in particular, that the drawing is often a good deal funnier than the joke beneath it. Obviously the outstanding characteristic of comic postcards is their obscenity, and I must discuss that more fully later. But I give here a rough analysis of their habitual subject-matter, with such explanatory remarks as seem to be needed:

*Sex.* More than half, perhaps three-quarters, of the jokes are sex jokes, ranging from the harmless to the all but unprintable. First favourite is probably the illegitimate baby. Typical captions: "Could you exchange this lucky charm for a baby's feeding-bottle?" "She didn't ask me to the christening, so I'm not going to the wedding." Also newlyweds, old maids, nude statues and women in bathing-dresses. All of these are *ipso facto* funny, mere mention of them being enough to raise a laugh. The cuckoldry joke is very seldom exploited, and there are no references to homosexuality.

Conventions of the sex joke:

 a. Marriage only benefits the woman. Every man is plotting seduction and every woman is plotting marriage. No woman ever remains unmarried voluntarily.

 b. Sex-appeal vanishes at about the age of twenty-five. Well-preserved and good-looking people beyond their first youth are never represented. The amorous honeymooning couple reappear as the grim-visaged wife and shapeless, mustachioed, red-nosed husband, no intermediate stage being allowed for.

*Home life.* Next to sex, the henpecked husband is the favourite joke. Typical caption: "Did they get an X-ray of your wife's jaw at the hospital?"—"No, they got a moving picture instead."

Conventions:

 a. There is no such thing as a happy marriage.

 b. No man ever gets the better of a woman in argument.

*Drunkenness.* Both drunkenness and teetotalism are *ipso facto* funny.

Conventions:

 a. All drunken men have optical illusions.

 b. Drunkenness is something peculiar to middle-aged men. Drunken youths or women are never represented.

*WC jokes.* There is not a large number of these. Chamber-pots are *ipso facto* funny, and so are public lavatories. A typical postcard, captioned "A Friend in Need", shows a man's hat blown off his head and disappearing down the steps of a ladies' lavatory.

*Inter-working-class snobbery.* Much in these postcards suggests that they are aimed at the better-off working class and poorer middle class. There are many jokes turning on malaproprisms, illiteracy, dropped aitches and the rough manners of slum-dwellers. Countless postcards show draggled hags of the stage-charwoman type exchanging "unladylike" abuse. Typical repartee: "I wish you were a statue and I was a pigeon!" A certain number produced since the war treat evacuation from the anti-evacuee angle. There are the usual jokes about tramps, beggars and criminals, and the comic maidservant appears fairly frequently. Also the comic navvy, bargee, etc; but there are no anti-trade-union jokes. Broadly speaking, everyone with much over or much under £5 a week is regarded as laughable. The "swell" is almost as automatically a figure of fun as the slum-dweller.

*Stock figures.* Foreigners seldom or never appear. The chief locality joke is the Scotsman, who is almost inexhaustible. The lawyer is always a swindler, the clergyman always a nervous idiot who says the wrong thing. The "knut" or "masher" still appears, almost as in Edwardian days, in out-of-date-looking evening clothes and an opera hat, or even with spats and a knobby cane. Another survival is the Suffragette, one of the big jokes of the pre-1914 period and too valuable to be relinquished. She has reappeared, unchanged in physical appearance, as the Feminist lecturer or Temperance fanatic. A feature of the last few years is the complete absence of anti-Jew postcards. The "Jew joke", always somewhat more ill-natured than the "Scotch joke", disappeared abruptly soon after the rise of Hitler.

*Politics.* Any contemporary event, cult or activity which has comic possibilities (for example, "free love", feminism, ARP, nudism) rapidly finds its way into the picture postcards, but their general atmosphere is extremely old-fashioned. The implied political outlook is a radicalism appropriate to about the year 1900. At normal times they are not only not patriotic, but go in for a mild guying of patriotism, with jokes about "God save the King", the Union Jack etc. The European situation only began to reflect itself in them at some time in 1939, and first did so through the comic aspects of ARP. Even at this date few postcards mention the war except in ARP jokes (fat woman stuck in the mouth of Anderson shelter: wardens neglecting their duty while young woman undresses at window she had forgotten to black out, etc etc). A few express anti-Hitler sentiments of a not very vindictive kind. One, not McGill's, shows Hitler, with the usual hypertrophied backside, bending down to pick a flower. Caption: "What would *you* do, chums?" This is about as high a flight of patriotism as any postcard is likely to attain. Unlike the twopenny weekly papers, comic postcards are not the product of any great monopoly company, and evidently they are not regarded as having any importance in forming public opinion. There is no sign in them of any attempt to induce an outlook acceptable to the ruling class.

Here one comes back to the outstanding, all-important feature of comic postcards—their obscenity. It is by this that everyone remembers them, and it is also central to their purpose, though not in a way that is immediately obvious.

A recurrent, almost dominant motif in comic postcards is the woman with the stuck-out behind. In perhaps half of them, or more than half, even when the point of the joke has nothing to do with sex, the same female figure appears, a plump "voluptuous" figure with the dress clinging to it as tightly as another skin and with breasts or buttocks grossly over-emphasised, according to which way it is turned. There can be no doubt that these pictures lift the lid off a very widespread repression, natural enough in a country whose women when young tend to be slim to the point of skimpiness. But at the same time the McGill postcard—and this applies to all other postcards in this genre—is not intended as pornography but, a subtler thing, as a skit on pornography. The Hottentot figures of the women are caricatures of the Englishman's secret ideal, not portraits of it. When one examines McGill's postcards more closely, one notices that his brand of humour only has meaning in relation to a fairly strict moral code. Whereas in papers like *Esquire*, for instance, or *La Vie Parisienne*, the imaginary background of the jokes is always promiscuity, the utter breakdown of all standards, the background of the McGill postcard is marriage. The four leading jokes are nakedness, illegitimate babies, old maids and newly married couples, none of which would seem funny in a really dissolute or even "sophisticated" society. The postcards dealing with honeymoon couples always have the enthusiastic indecency of those village weddings where it is still considered screamingly funny to sew bells to the bridal bed. In one, for example, a young bridegroom is shown getting out of bed the morning after his wedding night. "The first morning in our own little home, darling!" he is saying; "I'll go and get the milk and paper and bring you a cup of tea." Inset is a picture of the front doorstep; on it are four newspapers and four bottles of milk. This is obscene, if you like, but it is not immoral. Its implication—and this is just the implication that *Esquire* or the *New Yorker* would avoid at all costs—is that marriage is something profoundly exciting and important, the biggest event in the average human being's life. So also with jokes about nagging wives and tyrannous mothers-in-law. They do at least imply a stable society in which marriage is indissoluble and family loyalty taken for granted. And bound up with this is something I noted earlier, the fact that there are no pictures, or hardly any, of good-looking people beyond their first youth. There is the "spooning" couple and the middle-aged, cat-and-dog couple, but nothing in between. The liaison, the illicit but more or less decorous love-affair which used to be the stock joke of French comic papers, is not a postcard subject. And this reflects, on a comic level, the working-class outlook which takes it as a matter of course that youth and adventure—almost, indeed, individual life—end with marriage. One of the few authentic class-differences, as opposed to class-distinctions, still existing in England is that the working classes age very much earlier. They do not live less long, provided that they survive their childhood, nor do they lose their physical activity earlier, but they do lose very early their youthful appearance. This fact is observable everywhere, but can be most easily verified by watching one of the higher age groups registering for military service; the middle- and upper-class members look, on average, ten years younger than the others. It is usual to attribute this to the harder lives that the working classes have to live, but it is doubtful whether any such difference now exists as would account for it. More probably the truth is that the working classes reach middle age earlier because they accept it earlier. For to look young after, say, thirty is largely a matter of wanting to do so. This generalisation is less true of the better-paid workers, especially those who live in council houses and labour-saving flats, but it is true enough even of them to point to a difference of outlook. And in this, as usual,

they are more traditional, more in accord with the Christian past
than the well-to-do women who try to stay young at forty by means
of physical jerks, cosmetics and avoidance of child-bearing. The
impulse to cling to youth at all costs, to attempt to preserve your
sexual attraction, to see even in middle age a future for yourself
and not merely for your children, is a thing of recent growth and
has only precariously established itself. It will probably disappear
again when our standard of living drops and our birth-rate rises.
"Youth's a stuff will not endure" expresses the normal, traditional
attitude. It is this ancient wisdom that McGill and his colleagues are
reflecting, no doubt unconsciously, when they allow for no transition stage between the honeymoon couple and those glamourless
figures, Mum and Dad.

I have said that at least half McGill's postcards are sex jokes,
and a proportion, perhaps ten per cent, are far more obscene than
anything else that is now printed in England. Newsagents are
occasionally prosecuted for selling them, and there would be many
more prosecutions if the broadest jokes were not invariably protected
by double meanings. A single example will be enough to show how
this is done. In one postcard, captioned "They didn't believe her",
a young woman is demonstrating, with her hands held apart, something about two feet long to a couple of open-mouthed acquaintances. Behind her on the wall is a stuffed fish in a glass case, and
beside that is a photograph of a nearly naked athlete. Obviously it is
not the fish that she is referring to, but this could never be proved.
Now, it is doubtful whether there is any paper in England that
would print a joke of this kind, and certainly there is no paper that
does so habitually. There is an immense amount of pornography of a
mild sort, countless illustrated papers cashing in on women's legs,
but there is no popular literature specialising in the "vulgar",
farcical aspect of sex. On the other hand, jokes exactly like McGill's
are the ordinary small change of the revue and music-hall stage, and
are also to be heard on the radio, at moments when the censor
happens to be nodding. In England the gap between what can be
said and what can be printed is rather exceptionally wide. Remarks
and gestures which hardly anyone objects to on the stage would raise
a public outcry if any attempt were made to reproduce them on
paper. (Compare Max Miller's[1] stage patter with his weekly column

[1] Reviewing *Applesauce*, a variety show, in *Time and Tide*, 7 September 1940,
Orwell wrote: "Anyone wanting to see something really vulgar should visit the

in the *Sunday Dispatch*.) The comic postcards are the only existing exception to this rule, the only medium in which really "low" humour is considered to be printable. Only in postcards and on the variety stage can the stuck-out behind, dog and lamp-post, baby's nappy type of joke be freely exploited. Remembering that, one sees what function these postcards, in their humble way, are performing.

What they are doing is to give expression to the Sancho Panza view of life, the attitude to life that Miss Rebecca West once summed up as "extracting as much fun as possible from smacking behinds in basement kitchens". The Don Quixote-Sancho Panza combination, which of course is simply the ancient dualism of body and soul in fiction form, recurs more frequently in the literature of the last four hundred years than can be explained by mere imitation. It comes up

---

Holborn Empire, where you can get quite a good matinée seat for three shillings. Max Miller, of course, is the main attraction.

Max Miller, who looks more like a Middlesex Street hawker than ever when he is wearing a tail coat and a shiny top hat, is one of a long line of English comedians who have specialised in the Sancho Panza side of life, in real *lowness*. To do this probably needs more talent than to express nobility. Little Tich was a master at it. There was a music-hall farce which Little Tich used to act in, in which he was supposed to be factotum to a crook solicitor. The solicitor is giving him his instructions:

'Now, our client who's coming this morning is a widow with a good figure. Are you following me?'

*Little Tich:* 'I'm ahead of you.'

As it happens, I have seen this farce acted several times with other people in the same part, but I have never seen anyone who could approach the utter baseness that Little Tich could get into these simple words. There is a touch of the same quality in Max Miller. Quite apart from the laughs they give one, it is important that such comedians should exist. They express something which is valuable in our civilisation and which might drop out of it in certain circumstances. To begin with, their genius is entirely masculine. A woman cannot be low without being disgusting, whereas a good male comedian can give the impression of something irredeemable and yet innocent, like a sparrow. Again, they are intensely national. They remind one how closely-knit the civilisation of England is, and how much it resembles a family, in spite of its out-of-date class distinctions. The startling obscenities which occur in *Applesauce* are only possible because they are expressed in *doubles entendres* which imply a common background in the audience. Anyone who had not been brought up on the *Pink 'Un* would miss the point of them. So long as comedians like Max Miller are on the stage and the comic coloured postcards which express approximately the same view of life are in the stationers' windows, one knows that the popular culture of England is surviving. . . ."

again and again, in endless variations, Bouvard and Pécuchet, Jeeves and Wooster, Bloom and Dedalus, Holmes and Watson (the Holmes-Watson variant is an exceptionally subtle one, because the usual physical characteristics of two partners have been transposed). Evidently it corresponds to something enduring in our civilisation, not in the sense that either character is to be found in a "pure" state in real life, but in the sense that the two principles, noble folly and base wisdom, exist side by side in nearly every human being. If you look into your own mind, which are you, Don Quixote or Sancho Panza? Almost certainly you are both. There is one part of you that wishes to be a hero or a saint, but another part of you is a little fat man who sees very clearly the advantages of staying alive with a whole skin. He is your unofficial self, the voice of the belly protesting against the soul. His tastes lie towards safety, soft beds, no work, pots of beer and women with "voluptuous" figures. He it is who punctures your fine attitudes and urges you to look after Number One, to be unfaithful to your wife, to bilk your debts, and so on and so forth. Whether you allow yourself to be influenced by him is a different question. But it is simply a lie to say that he is not part of you, just as it is a lie to say that Don Quixote is not part of you either, though most of what is said and written consists of one lie or the other, usually the first.

But though in varying forms he is one of the stock figures of literature, in real life, especially in the way society is ordered, his point of view never gets a fair hearing. There is a constant world-wide conspiracy to pretend that he is not there, or at least that he doesn't matter. Codes of law and morals, or religious systems, never have much room in them for a humorous view of life. Whatever is funny is subversive, every joke is ultimately a custard pie, and the reason why so large a proportion of jokes centre round obscenity is simply that all societies, as the price of survival, have to insist on a fairly high standard of sexual morality. A dirty joke is not, of course, a serious attack upon morality, but it is a sort of mental rebellion, a momentary wish that things were otherwise. So also with all other jokes, which always centre round cowardice, laziness, dishonesty or some other quality which society cannot afford to encourage. Society has always to demand a little more from human beings than it will get in practice. It has to demand faultless discipline and self-sacrifice, it must expect its subjects to work hard, pay their taxes, and be faithful to their wives, it must assume that men think it glorious to die on the battlefield and women want to wear themselves out with child-bearing. The whole of what one may call official literature is founded on such assumptions: I never read the proclamations of generals before battle, the speeches of Fuehrers and prime ministers, the solidarity songs of public schools and left-wing political parties, national anthems, Temperance tracts, Papal encyclicals and sermons against gambling and contraception, without seeming to hear in the background a chorus of raspberries from all the millions of common men to whom these high sentiments make no appeal. Nevertheless the high sentiments always win in the end, leaders who offer blood, toil, tears and sweat always get more out of their followers than those who offer safety and a good time. When it comes to the pinch, human beings are heroic. Women face childbed and the scrubbing brush, revolutionaries keep their mouths shut in the torture chamber, battleships go down with their guns still firing when their decks are awash. It is only that the other element in man, the lazy, cowardly, debt-bilking adulterer who is inside all of us, can never be suppressed altogether and needs a hearing occasionally.

The comic postcards are one expression of his point of view, a humble one, less important than the music halls, but still worthy of attention. In a society which is still basically Christian they naturally concentrate on sex jokes; in a totalitarian society, if they had any freedom of expression at all, they would probably concentrate on laziness or cowardice, but at any rate on the unheroic in one form or another. It will not do to condemn them on the ground that they are vulgar and ugly. That is exactly what they are meant to be. Their whole meaning and virtue is in their unredeemed lowness, not only in the sense of obscenity, but lowness of outlook in every direction whatever. The slightest hint of "higher" influences would ruin them utterly. They stand for the worm's-eye view of life, for the music-hall world where marriage is a dirty joke or a comic disaster, where the rent is always behind and the clothes are always up the spout, where the lawyer is always a crook and the Scotsman always a miser, where the newlyweds make fools of themselves on the hideous beds of seaside lodging houses and the drunken, red-nosed husbands roll home at four in the morning to meet the linen-nightgowned wives who wait for them behind the front door, poker in hand. Their existence, the fact that people want them, is symptomatically important. Like the music halls, they are a sort of saturnalia, a harmless rebellion against virtue. They express only one tendency in the human mind, but a tendency which is always there and will find its own outlet, like water. On the whole, human beings want to be good, but not too good, and not quite all the time. For:

> there is a just man that perisheth in his righteousness, and there is a wicked man that prolongeth his life in his wickedness. Be not righteous over much; neither make thyself over wise; why shouldest thou destroy thyself? Be not over much wicked, neither be thou foolish: why shouldest thou die before thy time?

In the past the mood of the comic postcard could enter into the central stream of literature, and jokes barely different from McGill's could casually be uttered between the murders in Shakespeare's tragedies. That is no longer possible, and a whole category of humour, integral to our literature till 1800 or thereabouts, has dwindled down to these ill-drawn postcards, leading a barely legal existence in cheap stationers' windows. The corner of the human heart that they speak for might easily manifest itself in worse forms, and I for one should be sorry to see them vanish.

*Horizon*, September 1941; CrE; DD; CE.

## 28. No, Not One

Mr Murry[1] said years ago that the works of the best modern writers, Joyce, Eliot and the like, simply demonstrated the *impossibility* of great art in a time like the present, and since then we have moved onwards into a period in which any sort of *joy* in writing, any such notion as telling a story for the purpose of pure entertainment, has also become impossible. All writing nowadays is propaganda. If, therefore, I treat Mr Comfort's novel[2] as a tract, I am only doing what he himself has done already. It is a good novel as novels go at this moment, but the motive for writing

---

[1] John Middleton Murry (1889–1957), prolific writer, critic and polemicist; founded the *Adelphi*, 1923, and controlled it for the next 25 years. Successively a fervent disciple of D.H. Lawrence, unorthodox Marxist, unorthodox Christian, pacifist and "back to the land" farmer. From July 1940 to April 1946 he was editor of *Peace News*.

[2] *No Such Liberty*, by Alex Comfort.

it was not what Trollope or Balzac, or even Tolstoy, would have recognised as a novelist's impulse. It was written in order to put forward the "message" of pacifism, and it was to fit that "message" that the main incidents in it were devised. I think I am also justified in assuming that it is autobiographical, not in the sense that the events described in it have actually happened, but in the sense that the author identifies himself with the hero, thinks him worthy of sympathy and agrees with the sentiments that he expresses.

Here is the outline of the story. A young German doctor who has been convalescent for two years in Switzerland returns to Cologne a little before Munich to find that his wife has been helping war-resisters to escape from the country and is in imminent danger of arrest. He and she flee to Holland just in time to escape the massacre which followed on Von Rath's assassination. Partly by accident they reach England, he having been seriously wounded on the way. After his recovery he manages to get a hospital appointment, but at the outbreak of war he is brought before a tribunal and put in the B class of aliens. The reason for this is that he has declared that he will not fight against the Nazis, thinking it better to "overcome Hitler by love". Asked why he did not stay in Germany and overcome Hitler by love there, he admits that there is no answer. In the panic following on the invasion of the Low Countries he is arrested a few minutes after his wife has given birth to a baby and kept for a long time in a concentration camp where he cannot communicate with her and where the conditions of dirt, overcrowding, etc are as bad as anything in Germany. Finally he is packed on to the *Arandora Star* (it is given another name, of course), sunk at sea, rescued, and put in another somewhat better camp. When he is at last released and makes contact with his wife, it is to find that she has been confined in another camp in which the baby has died of neglect and underfeeding. The book ends with the couple looking forward to sailing for America and hoping that the war fever will not by this time have spread there as well.

Now, before considering the implications of this story, just consider one or two facts which underlie the structure of modern society and which it is necessary to ignore if the pacifist "message" is to be accepted uncritically.

1. Civilisation rests ultimately on coercion. What holds society together is not the policeman but the goodwill of common men, and yet that goodwill is powerless unless the policeman is there

to back it up. Any government which refused to use violence in its own defence would cease almost immediately to exist, because it could be overthrown by any body of men, or even any individual, that was less scrupulous. Objectively, whoever is not on the side of the policeman is on the side of the criminal, and vice versa. In so far as it hampers the British war effort, British pacifism is on the side of the Nazis, and German pacifism, if it exists, is on the side of Britain and the USSR. Since pacifists have more freedom of action in countries where traces of democracy survive, pacifism can act more effectively against democracy than for it. Objectively the pacifist is pro-Nazi.

2. Since coercion can never be altogether dispensed with, the only difference is between degrees of violence. During the last twenty years there has been less violence and less militarism inside the English-speaking world than outside it, because there has been more money and more security. The hatred of war which undoubtedly characterises the English-speaking peoples is a reflection of their favoured position. Pacifism is only a considerable force in places where people feel themselves very safe, chiefly maritime states. Even in such places, turn-the-other-cheek pacifism only flourishes among the more prosperous classes, or among workers who have in some way escaped from their own class. The real working class, though they hate war and are immune to jingoism, are never really pacifist, because their life teaches them something different. To abjure violence it is necessary to have no experience of it.

If one keeps the above facts in mind one can, I think, see the events in Mr Comfort's novel in truer perspective. It is a question of putting aside subjective feelings and trying to see whither one's actions will lead in practice and where one's motives ultimately spring from. The hero is a research worker—a pathologist. He has not been especially fortunate, he has a defective lung, thanks to the carrying-on of the British blockade into 1919, but in so far as he is a member of the middle class, doing work which he has chosen for himself, he is one of a few million favoured human beings who live ultimately on the degradation of the rest. He wants to get on with his work, wants to be out of reach of Nazi tyranny and regimentation, but he will not *act* against the Nazis in any other way than by running away from them. Arrived in England, he is in terror of being sent back to Germany, but refuses to take part in any physical effort to keep the Nazis out of England. His greatest hope is to get to America, with another three thousand miles of water between himself and the Nazis. He will only get there, you note, if British ships and planes protect him on the way, and having got there he will simply be living under the protection of American ships and planes instead of British ones. If he is lucky he will be able to continue with his work as a pathologist, at the same time keeping up his attitude of moral superiority towards the men who make his work possible. And underlying everything there will still be his position as a research-worker, a favoured person living ultimately on dividends which would cease forthwith if not extorted by the threat of violence.

I do not think this is an unfair summary of Mr Comfort's book. And I think the relevant fact is that this story of a German doctor is written by an Englishman. The argument which is implied all the way through, and sometimes explicitly stated, that there is next to no difference between Britain and Germany, political persecution is as bad in one as in the other, those who fight against the Nazis always go Nazi themselves, would be more convincing if it came from a German. There are probably sixty thousand German refugees in this country, and there would be hundreds of thousands more if we had not meanly kept them out. Why did they come here if there is virtually no difference between the social atmosphere of the two countries? And how many of them have asked to go back? They have "voted with their feet", as Lenin put it. As I pointed out above, the comparative gentleness of the English-speaking civilisation is due to money and security, but that is not to say that no difference exists. Once let it be admitted, however, that there *is* a certain difference, that it matters quite a lot who wins, and the usual short-term case for pacifism falls to the ground. You can be explicitly pro-Nazi without claiming to be a pacifist—and there is a very strong case for the Nazis, though not many people in this country have the courage to utter it—but you can only pretend that Nazism and capitalist democracy are Tweedledum and Tweedledee if you also pretend that every horror from the June purge onwards has been cancelled by an exactly similar horror in England. In practice this has to be done by means of selection and exaggeration. Mr Comfort is in effect claiming that a "hard case" is typical. The sufferings of this German doctor in a so-called democratic country are so terrible, he implies, as to wipe out every shred of moral justification for the struggle against Fascism. One must, however, keep a sense of proportion. Before raising a squeal because two thousand internees have only eighteen latrine buckets between them, one might as well remember what has happened these last few years in Poland, in Spain, in Czechoslovakia, etc etc. If one clings too closely to the "those who fight against Fascism become Fascist themselves" formula, one is simply led into falsification. It is not true, for instance, as Mr Comfort implies, that there is widespread spy-mania and that the prejudice against foreigners increases as the war gathers in momentum. The feeling against foreigners, which was one of the factors that made the internment of the refugees possible, has greatly died away, and Germans and Italians are now allowed into jobs that they would have been debarred from in peace-time. It is not true, as he explicitly says, that the only difference between political persecution in England and in Germany is that in England nobody hears about it. Nor is it true that all the evil in our life is traceable to war or war preparation. "I knew," he says, "that the English people, like the Germans, had never been happy since they put their trust in rearmament." Were they so conspicuously happy before? Is it not the truth, on the contrary, that rearmament, by reducing unemployment, made the English people somewhat happier, if anything? From my own observation I should say that, by and large, the war itself has made England happier; and this is not an argument in favour of war, but simply tells one something about the nature of so-called peace.

The fact is that the ordinary short-term case for pacifism, the claim that you can best frustrate the Nazis by not resisting them, cannot be sustained. If you don't resist the Nazis you are helping them, and ought to admit it. For then the long-term case for pacifism can be made out. You can say: "Yes, I know I am helping Hitler, and I want to help him. Let him conquer Britain, the USSR and America. Let the Nazis rule the world; in the end they will grow into something different." That is at any rate a tenable position. It looks forward into human history, beyond the term of our own lives. What is not tenable is the idea that everything in the garden would be lovely *now* if only we stopped the wicked fighting, and that to fight back is exactly what the Nazis want us to do. Which does Hitler fear more, the PPU or the RAF? Which has he made greater efforts to sabotage? Is he trying to bring America into the war, or to keep America out of it? Would he be deeply distressed if the Russians stopped fighting tomorrow? And after all, the history of the last ten years suggests that Hitler has a pretty shrewd idea of his own interests.

The notion that you can somehow defeat violence by submitting to it is simply a flight from fact. As I have said, it is only possible to people who have money and guns between themselves and reality. But why should they want to make this flight, in any case? Because, rightly hating violence, they do not wish to recognise that it is integral to modern society and that their own fine feelings and noble attitudes are all the fruit of injustice backed up by force. They do not want to learn where their incomes come from. Underneath this lies the hard fact, so difficult for many people to face, that individual salvation is not possible, that the choice before human beings is not, as a rule, between good and evil but between two evils. You can let the Nazis rule the world; that is evil; or you can over-throw them by war, which is also evil. There is no other choice before you, and whichever you choose you will not come out with clean hands. It seems to me that the text for our time is not "Woe to him through whom the evil cometh" but the one from which I took the title of this article, "There is not one that is righteous, no, not one". We have all touched pitch, we are all perishing by the sword. We do not have the chance, in a time like this, to say "To-morrow we can all start being good". That is moonshine. We only have the chance of choosing the lesser evil and of working for the establishment of a new kind of society in which common decency will again be possible. There is no such thing as neutrality in this war. The whole population of the world is involved in it, from the Eskimos to the Andamanese, and since one must inevitably help one side or the other, it is better to know what one is doing and count the cost. Men like Darlan and Laval have at any rate had the courage to make their choice and proclaim it openly. The New Order, they say, must be established at all costs, and "il faut écra-bouiller l'Angleterre". Mr Murry appears, at any rate at moments, to think likewise. The Nazis, he says, are "doing the dirty work of the Lord" (they certainly did an exceptionally dirty job when they attacked Russia), and we must be careful "lest in fighting against Hitler we are fighting against God". Those are not pacifist sentiments, since if carried to their logical conclusion they involve not only surrendering to Hitler but helping him in his various forthcoming wars, but they are at least straightforward and courageous. I do not myself see Hitler as the saviour, even the unconscious saviour, of humanity, but there is a strong case for thinking him so, far stronger than most people in England imagine. What there is no case for is to denounce Hitler and at the same time look down your nose at the people who actually keep you out of his clutches. That is simply a highbrow variant of British hypocrisy, a product of capitalism in decay, and the sort of thing for which Europeans, who at any rate understand the nature of a policeman and a dividend, justifiably despise us.

*Adelphi*, October 1941

1942

## 29. London Letter to *Partisan Review*

London, England
1 January 1942

Dear Editors,

At this moment nothing is happening politically in England, and since we probably have ahead of us a long exhausting war in which morale will be all-important, I want to use most of this letter in discussing certain currents of thought which are moving to and fro just under the surface. Some of the tendencies I mention may seem to matter very little at present, but they do I think tell one something about possible future developments.

### WHOM ARE WE FIGHTING AGAINST?

This question, which obviously had to be answered sooner or later, began to agitate the big public some time in 1941, following on Vansittart's pamphlets and the starting of a German daily paper for the refugees (*Die Zeitung*, mildly Left, circulation about 60,000). Vansittart's thesis is that the Germans are *all* wicked, and not merely the Nazis. I don't need to tell you how gleefully the Blimps have seized upon this as a way of escaping from the notion that we are fighting against Fascism. But of late the "only good German is a dead one" line has taken the rather sinister form of a fresh drive against the refugees. The Austrian monarchists have fallen foul of the German left-wingers, whom they accuse of being pan-Germans in disguise, and this delights the Blimps, who are always trying to manoeuvre their two enemies, Germany and Socialism, into the same place. The point has now been reached where anyone who describes himself as "anti-Fascist" is suspected of being pro-German. But the question is much complicated by the fact that the Blimps have a certain amount of right on their side. Vansittart, badly though he writes, is an able man with more background than most of his opponents, and he has insisted on two facts which the pinks have done their best to obscure. One is that much of the Nazi philosophy is not new but is merely a continuation of pan-Germanism, and the other is that Britain cannot have a European policy without having an army. The pinks cannot admit that the German masses are behind Hitler any more than the Blimps can admit that their class must be levered out of control if we are to win the war. The controversy has raged for four months or more in the correspondence columns of several papers, and one paper in particular is obviously keeping it going as a way of baiting the refugees and the "reds" generally. No one, however, airs any racial theories about Germany, which is a great advance on the war propaganda of 1914–18.

Ordinary working people do not seem either to hate the Germans or to distinguish between Germans and Nazis. Here and there there was violent anti-German feeling at the time of the bad air raids, but it has worn off. The term "Hun" has not caught on with the working classes this time. They call the Germans Jerries, which may have a mildly obscene meaning but is not unfriendly. All the blame for everything is placed on Hitler, even more than on the Kaiser during the last war. After an air raid one often used to hear people say "He was over again last night"—"he" being Hitler. The Italians are generally called Eyeties, which is less offensive than Wops, and there is no popular feeling against them whatever, nor against the Japanese as yet. To judge from photos in the newspapers, the Land Girls are quite ready to get off with Italian prisoners working on the farms. As to the smaller nations who are supposed to be at war with us, no one remembers which is which. The women who a year ago were busy knitting stockings for the Finns are now busy knitting them for the Russians, but there is no ill feeling. The chief impression one derives from all this chaos of opinions is how little the lack of a positive war aim, or even of any definite mental picture of the enemy, matters to people who are at any rate at one in not wanting to be governed by foreigners.

### OUR ALLIES

Whatever may be happening among the higher-ups, the effect of the Russian alliance has been a tremendous net increase of pro-Russian sentiment. It is impossible to discuss the war with ordinary working-class and middle-class people without being struck by this. But the enthusiasm that ordinary people feel for Russia is not coupled with the faintest interest in the Russian political system.

All that has happened is that Russia has become respectable. An enormous hammer and sickle flag flies daily over Selfridge's, the biggest shop in London. The Communists have not caused so much friction as I expected. They have been tactful in their posters and public pronouncements, and have gone to unheard-of lengths in supporting Churchill. But though they may have gained in numbers as a result of the Russian alliance, they do not seem to have gained in political influence. To a surprising extent ordinary people fail to grasp that there is any connection between Moscow and the Communist Party, or even that Communist policy has changed as a result of Russia's entry into the war. Everyone is delighted that the Germans have failed to take Moscow, but no one sees in this any reason for paying any attention to what Palme Dutt and Co may say. In practice this attitude is sensible, but at the bottom of it there lies a profound lack of interest in doctrinaire politics. The ban has not been taken off the *Daily Worker*. Immediately after it was suppressed it reappeared as a factory sheet which was illegally printed, but was winked at. Now, under the title of the *British Worker*, it is sold on the streets without interference. But it has ceased to be a daily and has lost most of its circulation. In the more important parts of the press the Communist influence has not been regained.

There is no corresponding increase in pro-American sentiment—the contrary, if anything. It is true that the entry of Japan and America into the war was expected by everyone, whereas the German invasion of Russia came as a surprise. But our new alliance has simply brought out the immense amount of anti-American feeling that exists in the ordinary lowbrow middle class. English cultural feelings towards America are complicated but can be defined fairly accurately. In the middle class, the people who are *not* anti-American are the declassed technician type (people like radio engineers) and the younger intelligentsia. Up till about 1930 nearly all "cultivated" people loathed the USA, which was regarded as the vulgariser of England and Europe. The disappearance of this attitude was probably connected with the fall of Latin and Greek from their dominant position as school subjects. The younger intellectuals have no objection to the American language and tend to have a masochistic attitude towards the USA, which they believe to be richer and more powerful than Britain. Of course it is exactly this that excites the jealousy of the ordinary patriotic middle class.

I know people who automatically switch off the radio as soon as any American news comes on, and the most banal English film will always get middle-class support because "it's such a relief to get away from those American voices". Americans are supposed to be boastful, bad-mannered and worshippers of money, and are also suspected of plotting to inherit the British Empire. There is also business jealousy, which is very strong in the trades which have been hit by the Lend-Lease agreement. The working-class attitude is quite different. English working-class people nearly always dislike Americans when in actual contact with them, but they have no preconceived cultural hostility. In the big towns they are being more and more Americanised in speech through the medium of the cinema.

It is uncertain whether English xenophobia is being broken down by the presence in England of large numbers of foreigners. I think it is, but plenty of people disagree with me. There is no doubt that in the summer of 1940 working-class suspicion of foreigners helped to make possible the internment of the refugees. At the time I talked with countless people, and except for left intellectuals I could find no one who saw anything wrong in it. The Blimps were after the refugees because they were largely Socialists, and the working-class line was "What did they want to come here for?" Underlying this, a hangover from an earlier period, was a resentment against these foreigners who were supposedly taking Englishmen's jobs. In the years before the war it was largely trade union opposition that prevented a big influx of German Jewish refugees. Of late feelings have grown more friendly, partly because there is no longer a scramble for jobs, but partly also, I think, owing to personal contacts. The foreign troops who are quartered here in large numbers seem to get on unexpectedly well with the population, the Poles in particular being a great success with the girls. On the other hand there is a certain amount of antisemitism. One is constantly coming on pockets of it, not violent but pronounced enough to be disquieting. The Jews are supposed to dodge military service, to be the worst offenders on the Black Market etc etc. I have heard this kind of talk even from country people who had probably never seen a Jew in their lives. But no one wants actually to *do* anything to the Jews, and the idea that the Jews are responsible for the war never seems to have caught on with the big public, in spite of the efforts of the German radio.

DEFEATISM AND GERMAN PROPAGANDA

Appeasement of the Chamberlain type is not "dead", as the newspapers are constantly assuring us, but is lying very low. But there exists another school of right-wing defeatism which can be conveniently studied in the weekly paper *Truth*. *Truth* has had a curious history and is a distinctly influential paper. At one time it was a non-political factual paper specialising in a genteel form of muck-raking (exposure of patent medicine frauds, etc), and was taken in as a matter of course in every club and regimental mess throughout the Empire. So far as I know it still has the same circulation, but latterly it has taken a definite political and economic line and become a stronghold of the worst kind of right-wing Toryism. Sir Ernest Benn, for instance, writes in it every week. It is not only anti-Labour, but in a discreet way anti-Churchill, anti-Russian and, more markedly, anti-American. It opposed the exchange of naval bases for American destroyers, the only other opposers being the Blackshirts and Communists. The strategy it advocates is to avoid entangling alliances, keep out of Europe and concentrate on self-defence on sea and in the air. The obvious logic of this is to make a compromise peace at the earliest possible moment. The quantity of advertisements for banks and insurance companies which *Truth* contains shows how well it is thought of in those quarters, and recently questions in Parliament brought out the fact that it is partly owned by the Conservative Party machine.

Left-wing defeatism is quite different and much more interesting. One or two of the minor political parties (for instance the British Anarchists, who followed up the German invasion of Russia with a terrific and very able anti-Soviet pamphlet, *The Truth about Russia*) follow a line which by implication is "revolutionary defeatist". The ILP[1] is preaching what amounts to a watered version of the "Ten Propositions" set forth in the *Partisan Review*, but in very indefinite terms, never clearly stating whether or not it "supports" the war. But the really interesting development is the increasing overlap between Fascism and pacifism, both of which overlap to some extent with "left" extremism. The attitude of the very young is more significant than that of the *New Statesman* pinks who warmongered between 1935 and 1939 and then sulked when the war started. So far as I know, the greater part of the very young intelligentsia are anti-war—this doesn't stop them from serving in the

[1] Independent Labour Party.

armed forces, of course—don't believe in any "defence of democracy", are inclined to prefer Germany to Britain, and don't feel the
horror of Fascism that we who are somewhat older feel. The entry of
Russia into the war didn't alter this, though most of these people pay
lip-service to Russia. With the out-and-out, turn-the-other-cheek
pacifists you come upon the much stranger phenomenon of people
who have started by renouncing violence ending by championing
Hitler. The antisemitic motif is very strong, though usually soft-
pedalled in print. But not many English pacifists have the intellectual
courage to think their thoughts down to the roots, and since there is
no real answer to the charge that pacifism is objectively pro-Fascist,
nearly all pacifist literature is forensic—i.e. specialises in avoiding
awkward questions. To take one example, during the earlier period of
the war the pacifist monthly the *Adelphi*, edited by Middleton Murry,
accepted at its face value the German claim to be a "Socialist" state
fighting against "plutocratic" Britain, and more or less equated
Germany with Russia. Hitler's invasion of Russia made nonsense of
this line of thought, and in the five or six issues that have followed the
*Adelphi* has performed the surprising feat of not mentioning the
Russo-German war. The *Adelphi* has once or twice engaged in Jew-
baiting of a mild kind. *Peace News*, now also edited by Middleton
Murry, follows its old tradition of opposing war for different and
incompatible reasons, at one moment because violence is wicked, at
another because peace will "preserve the British Empire", etc.

For some years past there has been a tendency for Fascists and
currency reformers to write in the same papers, and it is only
recently that they have been joined by the pacifists. I have in front
of me a copy of the little anti-war paper *Now* which contains contributions from, among others, the Duke of Bedford, Alexander
Comfort, Julian Symons and Hugh Ross Williamson. Alexander
Comfort is a "pure" pacifist of the other-cheek school. The Duke
of Bedford has for years been one of the main props of the Douglas
Credit[1] movement, and is also a devout Anglican, a pacifist or near-

---

[1] The Social Credit movement, which was based on the ideas of Major C.H.
Douglas, claimed that prosperity could be achieved through a reform of the
monetary system. To a letter to *Partisan Review*, September–October 1942, from
Gorham Munson correcting Orwell about Social Credit and Fascism, Orwell
replied: "I am sorry if I gave the impression that Social Creditors, as such, are
pro-Fascist. Certainly Hargrave and the group now running the *New English
Weekly* aren't. I am very glad to hear that they have dropped the Duke of
Bedford, and apologise for not having known this, which I ought to have done."

pacifist, and a landowner upon an enormous scale. In the early months of the war (then Marquis of Tavistock) he went to Dublin on his own initiative and obtained or tried to obtain a draft of peace terms from the German Embassy. Recently he has published pamphlets urging the impossibility of winning the war and describing Hitler as a misunderstood man whose good faith has never really been tested. Julian Symons writes in a vaguely Fascist strain but is also given to quoting Lenin. Hugh Ross Williamson has been mixed up in the Fascist movement for some time, but in the split-off section of it to which William Joyce ("Lord Haw Haw") also belongs. Just before the war he and others formed a fresh Fascist party calling itself the People's Party, of which the Duke of Bedford was a member. The People's Party apparently came to nothing, and in the first period of the war Williamson devoted himself to trying to bring about a get-together between the Communists and Mosley's followers. You see here an example of what I mean by the overlap between Fascism and pacifism.

What is interesting is that every section of anti-war opinion has one section of German radio propaganda, as it were, assigned to it. Since the outbreak of war the Germans have done hardly any direct propaganda in England otherwise than by wireless. The best known of their broadcasts, indeed the only ones that can be said to have been listened to to any appreciable extent, are those of William Joyce. No doubt these are often extravagantly untruthful, but they are a more or less responsible type of broadcast, well delivered and giving news rather than straight propaganda. But in addition the Germans maintain four spurious "freedom" stations, actually operating on the continent but pretending to be operating illegally in England. The best known of these is the New British Broadcasting Station, which earlier in the war the Blackshirts used to advertise by means of stickybacks. The general line of these broadcasts is "uncensored news", or "what the Government is hiding from you". They affect a pessimistic, well-informed manner, as of someone who is on the inside of the inside, and go in for enormous figures of shipping losses, etc. They urge the dismissal of Churchill, talk apprehensively about "the Communist danger", and are anti-American. The anti-American strain is even stronger in Joyce's broadcasts. The Americans are swindling us over the Lend-Lease agreement, are gradually absorbing the Empire, etc etc. More interesting than the New British is the Workers' Challenge Station. This goes in for a line of red-hot revolutionary talks under such titles as "Kick Churchill Out", delivered by an authentic British working man who uses plenty of unprintable words. We are to overthrow the corrupt capitalist government which is selling us to the enemy, and set up a real Socialist government which will come to the rescue of our heroic comrades of the Red Army and give us victory over Fascism. (This German station does not hesitate to talk about "the menace of Nazism", "the horrors of the Gestapo" etc.) The Workers' Challenge is not overtly defeatist. The line is always that it is probably too late, the Red army is done for, but that we *may* be able to save ourselves if only we can "overthrow capitalism", which is to be done by means of strikes, mutinies, sabotage in the armament factories, and so forth. The other two "freedom" stations are the Christian Peace Movement (pacifism) and Radio Caledonia (Scottish nationalism).

You can see how each strain of German propaganda corresponds to one existing, or at any rate potential, defeatist faction. Lord Haw-Haw and the New British are aimed at the anti-American middle class, roughly speaking the people who read *Truth*, and the business interests that have suffered from the war. The Workers' Challenge is aimed at the Communists and the Left extremists generally. The Christian Peace Movement is aimed at the PPU. I don't want to give the impression, however, that German propaganda has much effect at this moment. There is little doubt that it has been an almost complete flop, especially during the last eighteen months. Various things that have happened have suggested that since the outbreak of war the Germans have not been well informed about internal conditions in England, and much of their propaganda, even if listened to, would fail because of simple psychological errors on which anyone with a real knowledge of England could put them right. But the various strains of defeatist feeling are there, and at some time they may grow. In some of what I have said above I may have seemed to mention people and factions too insignificant to be worth noticing, but in this bloodstained harlequinade in which we are living one never knows what obscure individual or half-lunatic theory may not become important. I do seem to notice a tendency in intellectuals, especially the younger ones, to come to terms with Fascism, and it is a thing to keep one's eye on. The quisling intellectual is a phenomenon of the last two years. Previously we all used to assume that Fascism was so self-evidently horrible that no thinking person would have anything to do with it, and also that the Fascists always wiped out the intelligentsia when they had the opportunity. Neither assumption was true, as we can see from what happened in France. Both Vichy and the Germans have found it quite easy to keep a façade of "French culture" in existence. Plenty of intellectuals were ready to go over, and the Germans were quite ready to make use of them, even when they were "decadent". At this moment Drieu la Rochelle is editing the *Nouvelle Revue Française*, Pound is bellowing against the Jews on the Rome radio, and Céline is a valued exhibit in Paris, or at least his books are. All of these would come under the heading of *Kulturbolschewismus*, but they are also useful cards to play against the intelligentsia in Britain and the USA. If the Germans got to England, similar things would happen, and I think I could make out at least a preliminary list of the people who would go over.

Not much news here. All is very quiet on the literary front. The paper shortage seems to be favouring the appearance of very short books, which may be all to the good and may possibly bring back the "long-short story", a form which has never had a fair deal in England. I wrongly told you in an earlier letter that Dylan Thomas was in the army. He is physically unfit and is doing jobs for the BBC and the MOI.[1] So is nearly everybody that used to be a writer, and most of us are rapidly going native.

The food situation is much as before. We had our puddings on Christmas Day, but they were a little paler than usual. The tobacco situation has righted itself, but matches are very short. They are watering the beer again, the third time since rearmament. The black-out is gradually relaxing in the absence of air raids. There are still people sleeping in the Tube stations, but only a handful at each station. The basements of demolished houses have been bricked up and turned into water tanks for use in case of fire. They look just like Roman baths and give the ruins an even more Pompeian look than they had before. The stopping of the air raids has had some queer results. During the worst of the blitz they set in hand huge schemes for levelling waste pieces of ground to make playgrounds, using bomb debris as a subsoil. All these have had to stop in the middle, no more bomb debris being available.

All the best,
Yours ever,
George Orwell

[1] Ministry of Information.

# 30. Rudyard Kipling

It was a pity that Mr Eliot should be so much on the defensive in the long essay with which he prefaces this selection of Kipling's poetry,[1] but it was not to be avoided, because before one can even speak about Kipling one has to clear away a legend that has been created by two sets of people who have not read his works. Kipling is in the peculiar position of having been a by-word for fifty years. During five literary generations every enlightened person has despised him, and at the end of that time nine-tenths of those enlightened persons are forgotten and Kipling is in some sense still there. Mr Eliot never satisfactorily explains this fact, because in answering the shallow and familiar charge that Kipling is a "Fascist", he falls into the opposite error of defending him where he is not defensible. It is no use pretending that Kipling's view of life, as a whole, can be accepted or even forgiven by any civilised person. It is no use claiming, for instance, that when Kipling describes a British soldier beating a "nigger" with a cleaning rod in order to get money out of him, he is acting merely as a reporter and does not necessarily approve what he describes. There is not the slightest sign anywhere in Kipling's work that he disapproves of that kind of conduct—on the contrary, there is a definite strain of sadism in him, over and above the brutality which a writer of that type has to have. Kipling *is* a jingo imperialist, he *is* morally insensitive and aesthetically disgusting. It is better to start by admitting that, and then to try to find out why it is that he survives while the refined people who have sniggered at him seem to wear so badly.

And yet the "Fascist" charge has to be answered, because the first clue to any understanding of Kipling, morally or politically, is the fact that he was *not* a Fascist. He was further from being one than the most humane or the most "progressive" person is able to be nowadays. An interesting instance of the way in which quotations are parroted to and fro without any attempt to look up their context or discover their meaning is the line from "Recessional", "Lesser breeds without the Law". This line is always good for a snigger in pansy-left circles. It is assumed as a matter of course that the "lesser breeds" are "natives", and a mental picture is called up of some pukka sahib in a pith helmet kicking a coolie. In its

[1] *A Choice of Kipling's Verse* made by T.S. Eliot.

context the sense of the line is almost the exact opposite of this. The phrase "lesser breeds" refers almost certainly to the Germans, and especially the pan-German writers, who are "without the Law" in the sense of being lawless, not in the sense of being powerless. The whole poem, conventionally thought of as an orgy of boasting, is a denunciation of power politics, British as well as German. Two stanzas are worth quoting (I am quoting this as politics, not as poetry):

> If, drunk with sight of power, we loose
> Wild tongues that have not Thee in awe,
> Such boastings as the Gentiles use,
> Or lesser breeds without the Law—
> Lord God of hosts, be with us yet,
> Lest we forget—lest we forget!

> For heathen heart that puts her trust
> In reeking tube and iron shard,
> All valiant dust that builds on dust,
> And guarding, calls not Thee to guard,
> For frantic boast and foolish word—
> Thy mercy on Thy People, Lord!

Much of Kipling's phraseology is taken from the Bible, and no doubt in the second stanza he had in mind the text from Psalm 127: "Except the Lord build the house, they labour in vain that build it; except the Lord keep the city, the watchman waketh but in vain." It is not a text that makes much impression on the post-Hitler mind. No one, in our time, believes in any sanction greater than military power; no one believes that it is possible to overcome force except by greater force. There is no "law", there is only power. I am not saying that that is a true belief, merely that it is the belief which all modern men do actually hold. Those who pretend otherwise are either intellectual cowards, or power-worshippers under a thin disguise, or have simply not caught up with the age they are living in. Kipling's outlook is pre-Fascist. He still believes that pride comes before a fall and that the gods punish *hubris*. He does not foresee the tank, the bombing plane, the radio and the secret police, or their psychological results.

But in saying this, does not one unsay what I said above about Kipling's jingoism and brutality? No, one is merely saying that the nineteenth-century imperialist outlook and the modern gangster outlook are two different things. Kipling belongs very definitely to the period 1885–1902. The Great War and its aftermath embittered him, but he shows little sign of having learned anything from any event later than the Boer War. He was the prophet of British imperialism in its expansionist phase (even more than his poems, his solitary novel, *The Light that Failed,* gives you the atmosphere of that time) and also the unofficial historian of the British army, the old mercenary army which began to change its shape in 1914. All his confidence, his bouncing vulgar vitality, sprang out of limitations which no Fascist or near-Fascist shares.

Kipling spent the later part of his life in sulking, and no doubt it was political disappointment rather than literary vanity that accounted for this. Somehow history had not gone according to plan. After the greatest victory she had ever known, Britain was a lesser world power than before, and Kipling was quite acute enough to see this. The virtue had gone out of the classes he idealised, the young were hedonistic or disaffected, the desire to paint the map red had evaporated. He could not understand what was happening, because he had never had any grasp of the economic forces underlying imperial expansion. It is notable that Kipling does not seem to realise, any more than the average soldier or colonial administrator, that an empire is primarily a money-making concern. Imperialism as he sees it is a sort of forcible evangelising. You turn a Gatling gun on a mob of unarmed "natives", and then you establish "the Law", which includes roads, railways and a court-house. He could not foresee, therefore, that the same motives which brought the Empire into existence would end by destroying it. It was the same motive, for example, that caused the Malayan jungles to be cleared for rubber estates, and which now causes those estates to be handed over intact to the Japanese. The modern totalitarians know what they are doing, and the nineteenth-century English did not know what they were doing. Both attitudes have their advantages, but Kipling was never able to move forward from one into the other. His outlook, allowing for the fact that after all he was an artist, was that of the salaried bureaucrat who despises the "box-wallah" and often lives a lifetime without realising that the "box-wallah" calls the tune.

But because he identifies himself with the official class, he does possess one thing which "enlightened" people seldom or never possess, and that is a sense of responsibility. The middle-class Left hate him for this quite as much as for his cruelty and vulgarity. All left-wing parties in the highly industrialised countries are at bottom a sham, because they make it their business to fight against something which they do not really wish to destroy. They have internationalist aims, and at the same time they struggle to keep up a standard of life with which those aims are incompatible. We all live by robbing Asiatic coolies, and those of us who are "enlightened" all maintain that those coolies ought to be set free; but our standard of living, and hence our "enlightenment", demands that the robbery shall continue. A humanitarian is always a hypocrite, and Kipling's understanding of this is perhaps the central secret of his power to create telling phrases. It would be difficult to hit off the one-eyed pacifism of the English in fewer words than in the phrase, "making mock of uniforms that guard you while you sleep". It is true that Kipling does not understand the economic aspect of the relationship between the highbrow and the Blimp. He does not see that the map is painted red chiefly in order that the coolie may be exploited. Instead of the coolie he sees the Indian Civil Servant; but even on that plane his grasp of function, of who protects whom, is very sound. He sees clearly that men can only be highly civilised while other men, inevitably less civilised, are there to guard and feed them.

How far does Kipling really identify himself with the administrators, soldiers and engineers whose praises he sings? Not so completely as is sometimes assumed. He had travelled very widely while he was still a young man, he had grown up with a brilliant mind in mainly philistine surroundings, and some streak in him that may have been partly neurotic led him to prefer the active man to the sensitive man. The nineteenth-century Anglo-Indians, to name the least sympathetic of his idols, were at any rate people who did things. It may be that all that they did was evil, but they changed the face of the earth (it is instructive to look at a map of Asia and compare the railway system of India with that of the surrounding countries), whereas they could have achieved nothing, could not have maintained themselves in power for a single week, if the normal Anglo-Indian outlook had been that of, say, E.M. Forster. Tawdry and shallow though it is, Kipling's is the only literary picture that we possess of nineteenth-century Anglo-India, and he could only make it because he was just coarse enough to be able to exist and keep his mouth shut in clubs and regimental messes. But he did not greatly resemble the people he admired. I know from several private sources that many of the Anglo-Indians who were Kipling's contemporaries did not like or approve of him. They said, no doubt truly, that he knew nothing about India, and on the other hand, he was from their point of view too much of a highbrow. While in India he tended to mix with "the wrong" people, and because of his dark complexion he was wrongly suspected of having a streak of Asiatic blood. Much in his development is traceable to his having been born in India and having left school early. With a slightly different background he might have been a good novelist or a superlative writer of music-hall songs. But how true is it that he was a vulgar flag-waver, a sort of publicity agent for Cecil Rhodes? It is true, but it is not true that he was a yes-man or a time-server. After his early days, if then, he never courted public opinion. Mr Eliot says that what is held against him is that he expressed unpopular views in a popular style. This narrows the issue by assuming that "unpopular" means unpopular with the intelligentsia, but it is a fact that Kipling's "message" was one that the big public did not want, and, indeed, has never accepted. The mass of the people, in the 'nineties as now, were anti-militarist, bored by the Empire, and only unconsciously patriotic. Kipling's official admirers are and were the "service" middle class, the people who read *Blackwood's*. In the stupid early years of this century, the Blimps, having at last discovered someone who could be called a poet and who was on their side, set Kipling on a pedestal, and some of his more sententious poems, such as "If", were given almost Biblical status. But it is doubtful whether the Blimps have ever read him with attention, any more than they have read the Bible. Much of what he says they could not possibly approve. Few people who have criticised England from the inside have said bitterer things about her than this gutter patriot. As a rule it is the British working class that he is attacking, but not always. That phrase about "the flannelled fools at the wicket and the muddied oafs at the goal" sticks like an arrow to this day, and it is aimed at the Eton and Harrow match as well as the Cup-Tie Final. Some of the verses he wrote about the Boer War have a curiously modern ring, so far as their subject-matter goes. "Stellenbosch", which must have been written about 1902, sums up what every intelligent infantry officer was saying in 1918, or is saying now, for that matter.

Kipling's romantic ideas about England and the Empire might not have mattered if he could have held them without having the class prejudices which at that time went with them. If one examines his best and most representative work, his soldier poems, especially *Barrack-Room Ballads*, one notices that what more than anything else spoils them is an underlying air of patronage. Kipling idealises the army officer, especially the junior officer, and that to an idiotic extent, but the private soldier, though lovable and romantic, has to be a comic. He is always made to speak in a sort of stylised cockney, not very broad but with all the aitches and final "g's" carefully omitted. Very often the result is as embarrassing as the humorous recitation at a church social. And this accounts for the curious fact that one can often improve Kipling's poems, make them less facetious and less blatant, by simply going through them and transplanting them from cockney into standard speech. This is especially true of his refrains, which often have a truly lyrical quality. Two examples will do (one is about a funeral and the other about a wedding):

> So it's knock out your pipes and follow me!
> And it's finish up your swipes and follow me!
> Oh, hark to the big drum calling.
> Follow me—follow me home!

and again:

> Cheer for the Sergeant's wedding—
> Give them one cheer more!
> Grey gun-horses in the lando,
> And a rogue is married to a whore!

Here I have restored the aitches etc. Kipling ought to have known better. He ought to have seen that the two closing lines of the first of these stanzas are very beautiful lines, and that ought to have overridden his impulse to make fun of a working-man's accent. In the ancient ballads the lord and the peasant speak the same language. This is impossible to Kipling, who is looking down a distorting class perspective, and by a piece of poetic justice one of his best lines is spoiled—for "follow me 'ome" is much uglier than "follow me home". But even where it makes no difference musically the facetiousness of his stage cockney dialect is irritating. However, he is more often quoted aloud than read on the printed page, and most people instinctively make the necessary alterations when they quote him.

Can one imagine any private soldier, in the 'nineties or now, reading *Barrack-Room Ballads* and feeling that here was a writer who spoke for him? It is very hard to do so. Any soldier capable of reading a book of verse would notice at once that Kipling is almost unconscious of the class war that goes on in an army as much as elsewhere. It is not only that he thinks the soldier comic, but that he thinks him patriotic, feudal, a ready admirer of his officers and proud to be a soldier of the Queen. Of course that is partly true, or battles could not be fought, but "What have I done for thee, England, my England?" is essentially a middle-class query. Almost any working man would follow it up immediately with "What has England done for me?" In so far as Kipling grasps this, he simply sets it down to "the intense selfishness of the lower classes" (his own phrase). When he is writing not of British but of "loyal" Indians he carries the "Salaam, sahib" motif to sometimes disgusting lengths. Yet it remains true that he has far more interest in the common soldier, far more anxiety that he shall get a fair deal, than most of the "liberals" of his day or our own. He sees that the soldier is neglected, meanly underpaid and hypocritically despised by the people whose incomes he safeguards. "I came to realise," he says in his posthumous memoirs, "the bare horrors of the private's life, and the unnecessary torments he endured." He is accused of glorifying war, and perhaps he does so, but not in the usual manner, by pretending that war is a sort of football match. Like most people capable of writing battle poetry, Kipling had never been in battle, but his vision of war is realistic. He knows that bullets hurt, that under fire everyone is terrified, that the ordinary soldier never knows what the war is about or what is happening except in his own corner of the battlefield, and that British troops, like other troops, frequently run away:

> I 'eard the knives be'ind me, but I dursn't face my man,
> Nor I don't know where I went to, 'cause I didn't stop to see,
> Till I 'eard a beggar squealin' out for quarter as 'e ran,
> An' I thought I knew the voice an'—it was me!

Modernise the style of this, and it might have come out of one of the debunking war books of the nineteen-twenties. Or again:

> An' now the hugly bullets come peckin' through the dust,
> An' no one wants to face 'em, but every beggar must;
> So, like a man in irons, which isn't glad to go,
> They moves 'em off by companies uncommon stiff an' slow.

Compare this with:

> "Forward the Light Brigade!"
> Was there a man dismayed?
> No! though the soldier knew
> Someone had blundered.

If anything, Kipling overdoes the horrors, for the wars of his youth were hardly wars at all by our standards. Perhaps that is due to the neurotic strain in him, the hunger for cruelty. But at least he knows that men ordered to attack impossible objectives *are* dismayed, and also that fourpence a day is not a generous pension.

How complete or truthful a picture has Kipling left us of the long-service, mercenary army of the late nineteenth century? One must say of this, as of what Kipling wrote about nineteenth-century Anglo-India, that it is not only the best but almost the only literary picture we have. He has put on record an immense amount of stuff that one could otherwise only gather from verbal tradition or from unreadable regimental histories. Perhaps his picture of army life seems fuller and more accurate than it is because any middle-class English person is likely to know enough to fill up the gaps. At any rate, reading the essay on Kipling that Mr Edmund Wilson has just published or is just about to publish,[1] I was struck by the number of things that are boringly familiar to us and seem to be barely intelligible to an American. But from the body of Kipling's early work there does seem to emerge a vivid and not seriously misleading picture of the old pre-machine-gun army—the sweltering barracks in Gibraltar or Lucknow, the red coats, the pipeclayed belts and the pillbox hats, the beer, the fights, the floggings, hangings and crucifixions, the bugle-calls, the smell of oats and horse-piss, the bellowing sergeants with foot-long moustaches, the bloody skirmishes, invariably mismanaged, the crowded troopships, the cholera-stricken camps, the "native" concubines, the ultimate death in the workhouse. It is a crude, vulgar picture, in which a patriotic music-hall turn seems to have got mixed up with one of Zola's gorier passages, but from it future generations will be able to gather some idea of what a long-term volunteer army was like. On about the same level they will be able to learn something of British India in the days when motor cars and refrigerators were unheard of. It is an error to

[1] Published in a volume of collected essays, *The Wound and the Bow*. [Author's footnote 1945.]

imagine that we might have had better books on these subjects if, for example, George Moore, or Gissing, or Thomas Hardy, had had Kipling's opportunities. That is the kind of accident that cannot happen. It was not possible that nineteenth-century England should produce a book like *War and Peace*, or like Tolstoy's minor stories of army life, such as *Sebastopol* or *The Cossacks*, not because the talent was necessarily lacking but because no one with sufficient sensitiveness to write such books would ever have made the appropriate contacts. Tolstoy lived in a great military empire in which it seemed natural for almost any young man of family to spend a few years in the army, whereas the British Empire was and still is demilitarised to a degree which continental observers find almost incredible. Civilised men do not readily move away from the centres of civilisation, and in most languages there is a great dearth of what one might call colonial literature. It took a very improbable combination of circumstances to produce Kipling's gaudy tableau, in which Private Ortheris and Mrs Hauksbee pose against a background of palm trees to the sound of temple bells, and one necessary circumstance was that Kipling himself was only half civilised.

Kipling is the only English writer of our time who has added phrases to the language. The phrases and neologisms which we take over and use without remembering their origin do not always come from writers we admire. It is strange, for instance, to hear the Nazi broadcasters referring to the Russian soldiers as "robots", thus unconsciously borrowing a word from a Czech democrat whom they would have killed if they could have laid hands on him. Here are half a dozen phrases coined by Kipling which one sees quoted in leaderettes in the gutter press or overhears in saloon bars from people who have barely heard his name. It will be seen that they all have a certain characteristic in common:

> East is East, and West is West.
> The white man's burden.
> What do they know of England who only England know?
> The female of the species is more deadly than the male.
> Somewhere East of Suez.
> Paying the Dane-geld.

There are various others, including some that have outlived their context by many years. The phrase "killing Kruger with your mouth", for instance, was current till very recently. It is also possible that it was Kipling who first let loose the use of the word "Huns" for Germans; at any rate he began using it as soon as the guns opened fire in 1914. But what the phrases I have listed above have in common is that they are all of them phrases which one utters semi-derisively (as it might be "For I'm to be Queen o' the May, mother, I'm to be Queen o' the May"), but which one is bound to make use of sooner or later. Nothing could exceed the contempt of the *New Statesman*, for instance, for Kipling, but how many times during the Munich period did the *New Statesman* find itself quoting that phrase about paying the Dane-geld?[1] The fact is that Kipling, apart from his snack-bar wisdom and his gift for packing much cheap pictures-queness into a few words ("Palm and Pine"—"East of Suez"—"The Road to Mandalay"), is generally talking about things that are of urgent interest. It does not matter, from this point of view, that thinking and decent people generally find themselves on the other side of the fence from him. "White man's burden" instantly con-jures up a real problem, even if one feels that it ought to be altered to "black man's burden". One may disagree to the middle of one's bones with the political attitude implied in "The Islanders", but one cannot say that it is a frivolous attitude. Kipling deals in thoughts which are both vulgar and permanent. This raises the question of his special status as a poet, or verse-writer.

Mr Eliot describes Kipling's metrical work as "verse" and not "poetry", but adds that it is "*great* verse", and further qualifies this by saying that a writer can only be described as a "great verse-writer" if there is some of his work "of which we cannot say whether it is verse or poetry". Apparently Kipling was a versifier who occasionally wrote poems, in which case it was a pity that Mr Eliot did not specify these poems by name. The trouble is that whenever an aesthetic judgement on Kipling's work seems to be called for, Mr Eliot is too much on the defensive to be able to speak plainly. What

---

[1] On the first page of his recent book, *Adam and Eve*, Mr Middleton Murry quotes the well-known lines:

> There are nine and sixty ways
> Of constructing tribal lays,
>     And every single one of them is right.

He attributes these lines to Thackeray. This is probably what is known as a "Freudian error". A civilised person would prefer not to quote Kipling—i.e. would prefer not to feel that it was Kipling who had expressed his thought for him. [Author's footnote 1945.]

he does not say, and what I think one ought to start by saying in any discussion of Kipling, is that most of Kipling's verse is so horribly vulgar that it gives one the same sensation as one gets from watching a third-rate music-hall performer recite "The Pigtail of Wu Fang Fu" with the purple limelight on his face, *and yet* there is much of it that is capable of giving pleasure to people who know what poetry means. At his worst, and also his most vital, in poems like "Gunga Din" or "Danny Deever", Kipling is almost a shameful pleasure, like the taste for cheap sweets that some people secretly carry into middle life. But even with his best passages one has the same sense of being seduced by something spurious, and yet unquestionably seduced. Unless one is merely a snob and a liar it is impossible to say that no one who cares for poetry could not get any pleasure out of such lines as:

> For the wind is in the palm trees, and the temple bells they say,
> "Come you back, you British soldier, come you back to Mandalay!"

and yet those lines are not poetry in the same sense as "Felix Randal" or "When icicles hang by the wall" are poetry. One can, perhaps, place Kipling more satisfactorily than by juggling with the words "verse" and "poetry", if one describes him simply as a good bad poet. He is as a poet what Harriet Beecher Stowe was as a novelist. And the mere existence of work of this kind, which is perceived by generation after generation to be vulgar and yet goes on being read, tells one something about the age we live in.

There is a great deal of good bad poetry in English, all of it, I should say, subsequent to 1790. Examples of good bad poems—I am deliberately choosing diverse ones—are "The Bridge of Sighs", "When all the World is Young, Lad", "The Charge of the Light Brigade", Bret Harte's "Dickens in Camp", "The Burial of Sir John Moore", "Jenny Kissed Me", "Keith of Ravelston", "Casabianca". All of these reek of sentimentality, and yet—not these particular poems, perhaps, but poems of this kind, are capable of giving true pleasure to people who can see clearly what is wrong with them. One could fill a fair-sized anthology with good bad poems, if it were not for the significant fact that good bad poetry is usually too well known to be worth reprinting. It is no use pretending that in an age like our own, "good" poetry can have any genuine popularity. It is, and must be, the cult of a very few people, the least tolerated of

the arts. Perhaps that statement needs a certain amount of quali-
fication. True poetry can sometimes be acceptable to the mass
of the people when it disguises itself as something else. One can
see an example of this in the folk-poetry that England still possesses,
certain nursery rhymes and mnemonic rhymes, for instance, and the
songs that soldiers make up, including the words that go to some
of the bugle-calls. But in general ours is a civilisation in which the
very word "poetry" evokes a hostile snigger or, at best, the sort of
frozen disgust that most people feel when they hear the word "God".
If you are good at playing the concertina you could probably go
into the nearest public bar and get yourself an appreciative audience
within five minutes. But what would be the attitude of that same
audience if you suggested reading them Shakespeare's sonnets, for
instance? Good bad poetry, however, can get across to the most
unpromising audiences if the right atmosphere has been worked up
beforehand. Some months back Churchill produced a great effect by
quoting Clough's "Endeavour" in one of his broadcast speeches. I
listened to this speech among people who could certainly not be
accused of caring for poetry, and I am convinced that the lapse into
verse impressed them and did not embarrass them. But not even
Churchill could have got away with it if he had quoted anything
much better than this.

In so far as a writer of verse can be popular, Kipling has been
and probably still is popular. In his own lifetime some of his poems
travelled far beyond the bounds of the reading public, beyond the
world of school prize-days, Boy Scout sing-songs, limp-leather
editions, poker-work and calendars, and out into the yet vaster world
of the music halls. Nevertheless, Mr Eliot thinks it worth while to
edit him, thus confessing to a taste which others share but are not
always honest enough to mention. The fact that such a thing as good
bad poetry can exist is a sign of the emotional overlap between the
intellectual and the ordinary man. The intellectual *is* different from
the ordinary man, but only in certain sections of his personality, and
even then not all the time. But what is the peculiarity of a good bad
poem? A good bad poem is a graceful monument to the obvious. It
records in memorable form—for verse is a mnemonic device, among
other things—some emotion which very nearly every human being
can share. The merit of a poem like "When all the World is Young,
Lad" is that, however sentimental it may be, its sentiment is "true"
sentiment in the sense that you are bound to find yourself thinking

the thought it expresses sooner or later; and then, if you happen to know the poem, it will come back into your mind and seem better than it did before. Such poems are a kind of rhyming proverb, and it is a fact that definitely popular poetry is usually gnomic or sententious. One example from Kipling will do:

> White hands cling to the bridle rein,
> Slipping the spur from the booted heel;
> Tenderest voices cry "Turn again!"
> Red lips tarnish the scabbarded steel:
> Down to Gehenna or up to the Throne,
> He travels the fastest who travels alone.

There is a vulgar thought vigorously expressed. It may not be true, but at any rate it is a thought that everyone thinks. Sooner or later you will have occasion to feel that he travels the fastest who travels alone, and there the thought is, ready made and, as it were, waiting for you. So the chances are that, having once heard this line, you will remember it.

One reason for Kipling's power as a good bad poet I have already suggested—his sense of responsibility, which made it possible for him to have a world-view, even though it happened to be a false one. Although he had no direct connection with any political party, Kipling was a Conservative, a thing that does not exist nowadays. Those who now call themselves Conservatives are either Liberals, Fascists or the accomplices of Fascists. He identified himself with the ruling power and not with the opposition. In a gifted writer this seems to us strange and even disgusting, but it did have the advantage of giving Kipling a certain grip on reality. The ruling power is always faced with the question, "In such and such circumstances, what would you *do*?", whereas the opposition is not obliged to take responsibility or make any real decisions. Where it is a permanent and pensioned opposition, as in England, the quality of its thought deteriorates accordingly. Moreover, anyone who starts out with a pessimistic, reactionary view of life tends to be justified by events, for Utopia never arrives and "the gods of the copybook headings", as Kipling himself put it, always return. Kipling sold out to the British governing class, not financially but emotionally. This warped his political judgement, for the British ruling class were not what he imagined, and it led him into abysses of folly and snobbery, but he gained a corresponding advantage from having at least tried to imagine what action and responsibility are like. It is a great thing in his favour that he is not witty, not "daring", has no wish to *épater les bourgeois*. He dealt largely in platitudes, and since we live in a world of platitudes, much of what he said sticks. Even his worst follies seem less shallow and less irritating than the "enlightened" utterances of the same period, such as Wilde's epigrams or the collection of cracker-mottoes at the end of *Man and Superman*.

*Horizon*, February 1942; CrE; DD; OR; CE.

# 31. The Rediscovery of Europe

When I was a small boy and was taught history—very badly, of course, as nearly everyone in England is—I used to think of history as a sort of long scroll with thick black lines ruled across it at intervals. Each of these lines marked the end of what was called a "period", and you were given to understand that what came afterwards was completely different from what had gone before. It was almost like a clock striking. For instance, in 1499 you were still in the Middle Ages, with knights in plate armour riding at one another with long lances, and then suddenly the clock struck 1500, and you were in something called the Renaissance, and everyone wore ruffs and doublets and was busy robbing treasure ships on the Spanish Main. There was another very thick black line drawn at the year 1700. After that it was the Eighteenth Century, and people suddenly stopped being Cavaliers and Roundheads and became extraordinarily elegant gentlemen in knee breeches and three-cornered hats. They all powdered their hair, took snuff and talked in exactly balanced sentences, which seemed all the more stilted because for some reason I didn't understand they pronounced most of their S's as F's. The whole of history was like that in my mind—a series of completely different periods changing abruptly at the end of a century, or at any rate at some sharply defined date.

Now in fact these abrupt transitions don't happen, either in politics, manners or literature. Each age lives on into the next—it must do so, because there are innumerable human lives spanning every gap. And yet there are such things as periods. We feel our own age to be deeply different from, for instance, the early Victorian period, and an eighteenth-century sceptic like Gibbon would have felt himself to be among savages if you had suddenly thrust him into the Middle Ages. Every now and again something happens—no doubt it's ultimately traceable to changes in industrial technique, though the connection isn't always obvious—and the whole spirit and tempo of life changes, and people acquire a new outlook which reflects itself in their political behaviour, their manners, their architecture, their literature and everything else. No one could write a poem like Gray's "Elegy in a Country Churchyard" today, for instance, and no one could have written Shakespeare's lyrics in the age of Gray. These things belong in different periods. And though, of course, those black lines across the page of history are an illusion, there are times when the transition is quite rapid, sometimes rapid enough for it to be possible to give it a fairly accurate date. One can say without grossly over-simplifying, "About such and such a year, such and such a style of literature began". If I were asked for the starting-point of modern literature—and the fact that we still call it "modern" shows that this particular period isn't finished yet— I should put it at 1917, the year in which T.S. Eliot published his poem "Prufrock". At any rate that date isn't more than five years out. It is certain that about the end of the last war the literary climate changed, the typical writer came to be quite a different person, and the best books of the subsequent period seemed to exist in a different world from the best books of only four or five years before.

To illustrate what I mean, I ask you to compare in your mind two poems which haven't any connection with one another, but which will do for purposes of comparison because each is entirely typical of its period. Compare, for instance, one of Eliot's characteristic earlier poems with a poem of Rupert Brooke, who was, I should say, the most admired English poet in the years before 1914. Perhaps the most representative of Brooke's poems are his patriotic ones, written in the early days of the war. A good one is the sonnet beginning "If I should die, think only this of me: That there's some corner of a foreign field That is for ever England". Now read side by side with this one of Eliot's Sweeney poems; for example, "Sweeney among the Nightingales"—you know, "The circles of the stormy moon Slide westward toward the River Plate". As I say, these poems have no connection in theme or anything else, but it's possible in a way to compare them, because each is representative of its own time and each seemed a good poem when it was written. The second still seems a good poem now.

Not only the technique but the whole spirit, the implied outlook on life, the intellectual paraphernalia of these poems are abysmally different. Between the young Englishman with a public-school and university background, going out enthusiastically to die for his country with his head full of English lanes, wild roses and what not, and the rather jaded cosmopolitan American, getting glimpses of eternity in some slightly squalid restaurant in the Latin Quarter of Paris, there is a huge gulf. That might be only an individual difference, but the point is that you come upon rather the same kind of difference, a difference that raises the same comparisons, if you read side by side almost any two characteristic writers of the two periods. It's the same with the novelists as with the poets—Joyce, Lawrence, Huxley and Wyndham Lewis on the one side, and Wells, Bennett and Galsworthy on the other, for instance. The newer writers are immensely less prolific than the older ones, more scrupulous, more interested in technique, less optimistic and, in general, less confident in their attitude to life. But more than that, you have all the time the feeling that their intellectual and aesthetic background is different, rather as you do when you compare a nineteenth-century French writer such as, say, Flaubert with a nineteenth-century English writer like Dickens. The Frenchman seems enormously more sophisticated than the Englishman, though he isn't necessarily a better writer because of that. But let me go back a bit and consider what English literature was like in the days before 1914.

The giants of that time were Thomas Hardy—who, however, had stopped writing novels some time earlier—Shaw, Wells, Kipling, Bennett, Galsworthy and, somewhat different from the others— not an Englishman, remember, but a Pole who chose to write in English—Joseph Conrad. There were also A.E. Housman (*A Shropshire Lad*), and the various Georgian poets, Rupert Brooke and the others. There were also the innumerable comic writers, Sir James Barrie, W.W. Jacobs, Barry Pain and many others. If you read all those writers I've just mentioned, you would get a not misleading picture of the English mind before 1914. There were other literary tendencies at work, there were various Irish writers, for instance, and in a quite different vein, much nearer to our own time, there was the American novelist Henry James, but the main stream was the one I've indicated. But what is the common denominator between writers who are individually as far apart as Bernard Shaw and A.E. Housman, or Thomas Hardy and H.G. Wells? I think the basic fact about nearly all English writers of that time is their complete unawareness of anything outside the contemporary English scene. Some are better writers than others, some are politically conscious and some aren't, but they are all alike in being untouched by any European influence. This is true even of novelists like Bennett and Galsworthy, who derived in a very superficial sense from French and perhaps Russian models. All of these writers have a background of ordinary, respectable, middle-class English life, and a half-conscious belief that this kind of life will go on for ever, getting more humane and more enlightened all the time. Some of them, like Hardy and Housman, are pessimistic in outlook, but they all at least believe that what is called progress would be desirable if it were possible. Also—a thing that generally goes with lack of aesthetic sensibility—they are all uninterested in the past, at any rate the remote past. It is very rare to find in a writer of that time anything we should now regard as a sense of history. Even Thomas Hardy, when he attempts a huge poetic drama based on the Napoleonic wars—*The Dynasts*, it's called—sees it all from the angle of a patriotic school textbook. Still more, they're all aesthetically uninterested in the past. Arnold Bennett, for instance, wrote a great deal of literary criticism, and it's clear that he is almost unable to see any merit in any book earlier than the nineteenth century, and indeed hasn't much interest in any writer other than his contemporaries. To Bernard Shaw most of the past is simply a mess which ought to be swept away in the name of progress, hygiene, efficiency and what not. H.G. Wells, though later on he was to write a history of the world, looks at the past with the same sort of surprised disgust as a civilised man contemplating a tribe of cannibals. All of these people, whether they liked their own age or not, at least thought it was better than what had gone before, and took the literary standards of their own time for granted. The basis of all Bernard Shaw's attacks on Shakespeare is really the charge—quite true, of course—that Shakespeare wasn't an enlightened member of the Fabian Society. If any of these writers had been told that the writers immediately subsequent to them would hark back to the English poets of the sixteenth and seventeenth centuries, to the French poets of the mid-nineteenth century and to the philosophers of the Middle Ages, they would have thought it a kind of dilettantism.

But now look at the writers who begin to attract notice—some of them had begun writing rather earlier, of course—immediately after the last war: Joyce, Eliot, Pound, Huxley, Lawrence, Wyndham Lewis. Your first impression of them, compared with the others—this is true even of Lawrence—is that something has been punctured. To begin with, the notion of progress has gone by the board. They don't any longer believe that progress happens or that it ought to happen, they don't any longer believe that men are getting better and better by having lower mortality rates, more effective birth control, better plumbing, more aeroplanes and faster motor cars. Nearly all of them are homesick for the remote past, or some period of the past, from D.H. Lawrence's ancient Etruscans onwards. All of them are politically reactionary, or at best are uninterested in politics. None of them cares twopence about the various hole-and-corner reforms which had seemed important to their predecessors, such as female suffrage, temperance reform, birth control or prevention of cruelty to animals. All of them are more friendly, or at least less hostile, towards the Christian churches than the previous generation had been. And nearly all of them seem to be aesthetically alive in a way that hardly any English writer since the Romantic Revival had been.

Now, one can best illustrate what I have been saying by means of individual examples, that is, by comparing outstanding books of more or less comparable type in the two periods. As a first example, compare H.G. Wells's short stories—there's a large number of them collected together under the title of *The Country of the Blind*— with D.H. Lawrence's short stories, such as those in *England, my England* and *The Prussian Officer*.

This isn't an unfair comparison, since each of these writers was at his best, or somewhere near his best, in the short story, and each of them was expressing a new vision of life which had a great effect on the young of his generation. The ultimate subject-matter of H.G. Wells's stories is, first of all, scientific discovery, and beyond that the petty snobberies and tragi-comedies of contemporary English life, especially lower-middle-class life. His basic "message", to use an expression I don't like, is that Science can solve all the ills that humanity is heir to, but that man is at present too blind to see the possibility of his own powers. The alternation between ambitious Utopian themes and light comedy, almost in the W.W. Jacobs vein, is very marked in Wells's work. He writes about journeys to the moon and to the bottom of the sea, and also he writes about small shopkeepers dodging bankruptcy and fighting to keep their end up in the frightful snobbery of provincial towns. The connecting link is Wells's belief in Science. He is saying all the time, if only that small shopkeeper could acquire a scientific outlook, his troubles would be ended. And of course he believes that this is going to happen, probably in the quite near future. A few more million pounds for scientific research, a few more generations scientifically educated, a few more superstitions shovelled into the dustbin, and the job is done. Now, if you turn to Lawrence's stories, you don't find this belief in Science—rather a hostility towards it, if anything—and you don't find any marked interest in the future, certainly not in a rationalised hedonistic future of the kind that Wells deals in. You don't even find the notion that the small shopkeeper, or any of the other victims of our society, would be better off if he were better educated. What you do find is a persistent implication that man has thrown away his birthright by becoming civilised. The ultimate subject-matter of nearly all Lawrence's books is the failure of contemporary men, especially in the English-speaking countries, to live their lives intensely enough. Naturally he fixes first on their sexual lives, and it is a fact that most of Lawrence's books centre round sex. But he isn't, as is sometimes supposed, demanding more of what people call sexual liberty. He is completely disillusioned about that, and he hates the so-called sophistication of bohemian intellectuals just as much as he hates the puritanism of the middle class. What he is saying is simply that modern men aren't fully alive, whether they fail through having too narrow standards or through not having any. Granted that they can be fully alive, he doesn't much care what social or political or economic system they live under. He takes the structure of existing society, with its class distinctions and so on, almost for granted in his stories, and doesn't show any very urgent wish to change it. All he asks is that men shall live more simply, nearer to the earth, with more sense of the magic of things like vegetation, fire, water, sex, blood, than they can in a world of celluloid and concrete where the gramophones never stop playing. He imagines—quite likely he is wrong—that savages or primitive peoples live more intensely than civilised men, and he builds up a mythical figure who is not far from being the Noble Savage over again. Finally, he projects these virtues on to the Etruscans, an ancient pre-Roman people who lived in northern Italy and about whom we don't, in fact, know anything. From the point of view of H.G. Wells all this abandonment of Science and

Progress, this actual wish to revert to the primitive, is simply heresy and nonsense. And yet one must admit that whether Lawrence's view of life is true or whether it is perverted, it is at least an advance on the Science worship of H.G. Wells or the shallow Fabian progressivism of writers like Bernard Shaw. It is an advance in the sense that it results from seeing through the other attitude and not from falling short of it. Partly that was the effect of the war of 1914–18, which succeeded in debunking both Science, Progress and civilised man. Progress had finally ended in the biggest massacre in history, Science was something that created bombing planes and poison gas, civilised man, as it turned out, was ready to behave worse than any savage when the pinch came. But Lawrence's discontent with modern machine civilisation would have been the same, no doubt, if the war of 1914–18 had never happened.

Now I want to make another comparison, between James Joyce's great novel *Ulysses*, and John Galsworthy's at any rate very large novel sequence *The Forsyte Saga*. This time it isn't a fair comparison, in effect it's a comparison between a good book and a bad one, and it also isn't quite correct chronologically, because the later parts of *The Forsyte Saga* were written in the nineteen-twenties. But the parts of it that anyone is likely to remember were written about 1910, and for my purpose the comparison is relevant, because both Joyce and Galsworthy are making efforts to cover an enormous canvas and get the spirit and social history of a whole epoch between the covers of a single book. *The Man of Property* may not seem to us *now* a very profound criticism of society, but it seemed so to its contemporaries, as you can see by what they wrote about it.

Joyce wrote *Ulysses* in the seven years between 1914 and 1921, working away all through the war, to which he probably paid little or no attention, and earning a miserable living as a teacher of languages in Italy and Switzerland. He was quite ready to work seven years in poverty and complete obscurity so as to get his great book on to paper. But what is it that it was so urgently important for him to express? Parts of *Ulysses* aren't very easily intelligible, but from the book as a whole you get two main impressions. The first is that Joyce is interested to the point of obsession with technique. This has been one of the main characteristics of modern literature, though more recently it has been a diminishing one. You get a parallel development in the plastic arts, painters, and even sculptors, being more and more interested in the material they work in, in the brush-marks of a picture, for instance, as against its design, let alone its subject-matter. Joyce is interested in mere words, the sounds and associations of words, even the pattern of words on the paper, in a way that wasn't the case with any of the preceding generation of writers, except to some extent the Polish-English writer, Joseph Conrad. With Joyce you are back to the conception of style, of fine writing, or poetic writing, perhaps even to purple passages. A writer like Bernard Shaw, on the other hand, would have said as a matter of course that the sole use of words is to express exact meanings as shortly as possible. And apart from this technical obsession, the other main theme of *Ulysses* is the squalor, even the meaninglessness of modern life after the triumph of the machine and the collapse of religious belief. Joyce—an Irishman, remember, and it's worth noting that the best English writers during the nineteen-twenties were in many cases not Englishmen—is writing as a Catholic who has lost his faith but has retained the mental framework which he acquired in his Catholic childhood and boyhood. *Ulysses*, which is a very long novel, is a description of the events of a single day, as seen mostly through the eyes of an out-at-elbow Jewish commercial traveller. At the time when the book came out there was a great outcry and Joyce was accused of deliberately exploiting the sordid, but as a matter of fact, considering what everyday human life is like when you contemplate it in detail, it doesn't seem that he overdid either the squalor or the silliness of the day's events. What you do feel all through, however, is the conviction from which Joyce can't escape, that the whole of this modern world which he is describing has no meaning in it now that the teachings of the Church are no longer credible. He is yearning after the religious faith which the two or three generations preceding him had had to fight against in the name of religious liberty. But finally the main interest of the book is technical. Quite a considerable proportion of it consists of pastiche or parody—parodies of everything from the Irish legends of the Bronze Age down to contemporary newspaper reports. And one can see there that, like all the characteristic writers of his time, Joyce doesn't derive from the English nineteenth-century writers but from Europe and from the remoter past. Part of his mind is in the Bronze Age, another part in the Middle Ages, another part in the England of Elizabeth. The twentieth century, with its hygiene and its motor-cars, doesn't particularly appeal to him.

Now look again at Galsworthy's book, *The Forsyte Saga*, and you see how comparatively narrow its range is. I have said already that this isn't a fair comparison, and indeed from a strictly literary point of view it's a ridiculous one, but it will do as an illustration, in the sense that both books are intended to give a comprehensive picture of existing society. Well, the thing that strikes one about Galsworthy is that though he's trying to be iconoclastic, he has been utterly unable to move his mind outside the wealthy bourgeois society he is attacking. With only slight modifications he takes all its values for granted. All he conceives to be wrong is that human beings are a little too inhumane, a little too fond of money, and aesthetically not quite sensitive enough. When he sets out to depict what he conceives as the desirable type of human being, it turns out to be simply a cultivated, humanitarian version of the upper-middle-class *rentier*, the sort of person who in those days used to haunt picture galleries in Italy and subscribe heavily to the Society for the Prevention of Cruelty to Animals. And this fact—the fact that Galsworthy hasn't any really deep aversion to the social types he thinks he is attacking—gives you the clue to his weakness. It is, that he has no contact with anything outside contemporary English society. He may think he doesn't like it, but he is part of it. Its money and security, the ring of battleships that separated it from Europe, have been too much for him. At the bottom of his heart he despises foreigners, just as much as any illiterate business-man in Manchester. The feeling you have with Joyce or Eliot, or even Lawrence, that they have got the whole of human history inside their heads and can look outwards from their own place and time towards Europe and the past, isn't to be found in Galsworthy or in any characteristic English writer in the period before 1914.

Finally, one more brief comparison. Compare almost any of H.G. Wells's Utopia books, for instance *A Modern Utopia*, or *The Dream*, or *Men Like Gods*, with Aldous Huxley's *Brave New World*. Again it's rather the same contrast, the contrast between the over-confident and the deflated, between the man who believes innocently in Progress and the man who happens to have been born later and has therefore lived to see that Progress, as it was conceived in the early days of the aeroplane, is just as much of a swindle as reaction. The obvious explanation of this sharp difference between the dominant writers before and after the war of 1914–18 is the war itself. Some such development would have happened in any case as the insufficiency of modern materialistic civilisation revealed itself, but the war speeded the process, partly by showing how very shallow the veneer of civilisation is, partly by making England less prosperous and therefore less isolated. After 1918 you couldn't live in such a narrow and padded world as you did when Britannia ruled not only the waves but also the markets. One effect of the ghastly history of the last twenty years has been to make a great deal of ancient literature seem much more modern. A lot that has happened in Germany since the rise of Hitler might have come straight out of the later volumes of Gibbon's *Decline and Fall of the Roman Empire*. Recently I saw Shakespeare's *King John* acted —the first time I had seen it, because it is a play which isn't acted very often. When I had read it as a boy it seemed to me archaic, something dug out of a history book and not having anything to do with our own time. Well, when I saw it acted, what with its intrigues and doublecrossings, non-aggression pacts, quislings, people changing sides in the middle of a battle, and what not, it seemed to me extraordinarily up to date. And it was rather the same thing that happened in the literary development between 1910 and 1920. The prevailing temper of the time gave a new reality to all sorts of themes which had seemed out of date and puerile when Bernard Shaw and his Fabians were—so they thought—turning the world into a sort of super garden city. Themes like revenge, patriotism, exile, persecution, race hatred, religious faith, loyalty, leader worship, suddenly seemed real again. Tamerlane and Genghis Khan seem credible figures now, and Machiavelli seems a serious thinker, as they didn't in 1910. We have got out of a backwater and back into history. I haven't an unqualified admiration for the writers of the early nineteen-twenties, the writers among whom Eliot and Joyce are chief names. Those who followed them have had to undo a great deal of what they did. Their revulsion from a shallow conception of progress drove them politically in the wrong direction, and it isn't an accident that Ezra Pound, for instance, is now shouting antisemitism on the Rome radio. But one must concede that their writings are more grown-up, and have a wider scope, than what went immediately before them. They broke the cultural circle in which England had existed for something like a century. They re-established contact with Europe, and they brought back the sense of history and the possibility of tragedy. On that basis all subsequent English literature that matters twopence has rested, and the development that Eliot and the others started, back in the closing years of the last war, has not yet run its course.

Broadcast talk in the BBC Eastern Service, 10 March 1942; printed in the *Listener*, 19 March 1942; reprinted in *Talking to India*, 1943.

## 32. The British Crisis: London Letter to *Partisan Review*

London
8 May 1942

Dear Editors,

When I last wrote to you things had begun to go wrong in the Far East but nothing was happening politically. Now, I am fairly certain, we are on the edge of the political crisis which I have been expecting for the better part of two years. The situation is very complicated and I dare say that even before this reaches you much will have happened to falsify my predictions, but I will make the best analysis I can.

The basic fact is that people are now as fed up and as ready for a radical policy as they were at the time of Dunkirk, with the difference that they now have, or are inclined to think they have, a potential leader in Stafford Cripps. I don't mean that people in significant numbers are crying out for the introduction of Socialism, merely that the mass of the nation wants certain things that aren't obtainable under a capitalist economy and is willing to pay almost any price to get them. Few people, for instance, seem to me to feel urgently the need for nationalisation of industry, but all except the interested minority would accept nationalisation without a blink if they were told authoritatively that you can't have efficient war-production otherwise. The fact is that "Socialism", called by that name, isn't by itself an effective rallying cry. To the mass of the people "Socialism" just means the discredited Parliamentary Labour Party, and one feature of the time is the widespread disgust with all the old political parties. But what then do people want? I should say that what they articulately want is more social equality, a complete clean-out of the political leadership, an aggressive war strategy and a tighter alliance with the USSR. But one has to consider the background of these desires before trying to predict what political development is now possible.

The war has brought the class nature of their society very sharply home to English people, in two ways. First of all there is the unmistakable fact that all real power depends on class privilege. You can only get certain jobs if you have been to one of the right schools, and if you fail and have to be sacked, then somebody else from one of the right schools takes over, and so it continues. This may go unnoticed when things are prospering, but becomes obvious in moments of disaster. Secondly, there are the hardships of war which are, to put it mildly, tempered for anyone with over £2,000 a year. I don't want to bore you with a detailed account of the way in which the food rationing is evaded, but you can take it that whereas ordinary people have to live on an uninteresting diet and do without many luxuries they are accustomed to, the rich go short of absolutely nothing except, perhaps, wines, fruit and sugar. You can be almost unaffected by food rationing without even breaking the law, though there is also a lively Black Market. Then there is bootleg petrol and, quite obviously, widespread evasion of Income Tax. This does not go unnoticed, but nothing happens because the will to crack down on it is not there while money and political power more or less coincide. To give just one example. At long last, and against much opposition in high places, the Ministry of Food is about to cut down "luxury feeding" by limiting the sum of money that can be spent on a meal in a hotel or restaurant. Already, before the law is even passed, ways of evading it have been thought out, and these are discussed almost undisguisedly in the newspapers.

There are other tensions which the war has brought out but which are somewhat less obvious than the jealousy caused by the Black Market or the discontent of soldiers blancoing their gas-masks under the orders of twerps of officers. One is the growing resentment felt by the underpaid armed forces (at any rate the army) against the high wages of the munition workers. If this were dealt with by raising the soldier's pay to the munition-worker's level the result would be either inflation or the diversion of labour from war production to consumption goods. The only real remedy is to cut down the civilian worker's wages as well, which could

only be made acceptable by the most drastic income cuts all round
—briefly, "war-Communism". And apart from the class struggle in
its ordinary sense there are deeper jealousies within the bourgeoisie
than foreigners sometimes realise. If you talk with a BBC accent you
can get jobs that a proletarian couldn't get, but it is almost impossible
to get beyond a certain point unless you belong socially to the Upper
Crust. Everywhere able men feel themselves bottled down by incompetent idiots from the county families. Bound up with this is the
crushing feeling we have all had in England these last twenty years
that if you have brains "they" (the Upper Crust) will see to it that you
are kept out of any really important job. During the years of investment capital we produced like a belt of fat the huge blimpocracy
which monopolises official and military power and has an instinctive
hatred of intelligence. This is probably a more important factor in
England than in a "new" country like the USA. It means that our
military weakness goes beyond the inherent weakness of a capitalist
state. When in England you find a gifted man in a really commanding
position it is usually because he happens to have been born into an
aristocratic family (examples are Churchill, Cripps, Mountbatten),
and even so he only gets there in moments of disaster when others
don't want to take responsibility. Aristocrats apart, those who are
branded as "clever" can't get their hands on the real levers of power,
and they know it. Of course "clever" individuals do occur in the
upper strata, but basically it is a class issue, middle class against
upper class.

### THE POLITICAL LEADERSHIP

The statement in the March-April *PR* that "the reins of power
are still firmly in the hands of Churchill" is an error. Churchill's
position is very shaky. Up to the fall of Singapore it would have
been true to say that the mass of the people liked Churchill while
disliking the rest of his Government, but in recent months his
popularity has slumped heavily. In addition he has the right-wing
Tories against him (the Tories on the whole have always hated
Churchill, though they had to pipe down for a long period), and
Beaverbrook is up to some game which I do not fully understand
but which must have the object of bringing himself into power. I
wouldn't give Churchill many more months of power, but whether
he will be replaced by Cripps, Beaverbrook or somebody like Sir
John Anderson is still uncertain.

The reason why nearly everyone who was anti-Nazi supported Churchill from the collapse of France onwards was that there was nobody else—i.e. nobody who was already well enough known to be able to step into power and who at the same time could be trusted not to surrender. It is idle to say that in 1940 we ought to have set up a Socialist government; the mass basis for such a thing probably existed, but not the leadership. The Labour Party had no guts, the pinks were defeatist, the Communists effectively pro-Nazi, and in any case there did not exist on the Left one single man of really nation-wide reputation. In the months that followed what was wanted was chiefly obstinacy, of which Churchill had plenty. Now, however, the situation has altered. The strategic situation is probably far better than it was in 1940, but the mass of the people don't think so, they are disgusted by defeats some of which they realise were unnecessary, and they have been gradually disillusioned by perceiving that in spite of Churchill's speeches the old gang stays in power and nothing really alters. For the first time since Churchill came to power the Government has begun losing by-elections. Of the five most recent it has lost three, and in the two which it didn't lose one opposition candidate was anti-war (ILP) and the other was regarded as a defeatist. In all these elections the polls were extremely low, in one case reaching the depth-record of 24 per cent of the electorate. (Most wartime polls have been low, but one has to write off something for the considerable shift of population.) There is a most obvious loss of the faith in the old parties, and there is a new factor in the presence of Cripps, who enjoys at any rate for the moment a considerable personal reputation. Just at the moment when things were going very badly he came back from Russia in a blaze of undeserved glory. People had by this time forgotten the circumstances in which the Russo-German war broke out and credited Cripps with having "got Russia in on our side". He was, however, cashing in on his earlier political history and on having never sold out his political opinions. There is good reason to think that at that moment, with no party machine under his control, he did not realise how commanding his personal position was. Had he appealed directly to the public, through the channels open to him, he could probably then and there have forced a more radical policy on the Government, particularly in the direction of a generous settlement with India. Instead he made the mistake of entering the Government and the almost equally bad one of going to India with an offer which was certain to be turned down. I can't put in print the little I know about the inner history of the Cripps-Nehru negotiations, and in any case the story is too complex to be written about in a letter of this length. The important thing is to what extent this failure has discredited Cripps. The people most interested in ditching the negotiations were the pro-Japanese faction in the Indian Congress Party, and the British right-wing Tories. Halifax's speech made in New York at the time was interpreted here as an effort to tread on as many Indian toes as possible and thus make a get-together between Cripps and Nehru more difficult. Similar efforts are being made from the opposite end at this moment. The upshot is that Cripps's reputation is damaged in India but not in this country—or, if damaged, then by his entry into the Government rather than by the failure in Delhi.

I can't yet give you a worth-while opinion as to whether Cripps is the man the big public think him, or are half-inclined to think him. He is an enigmatic man who has been politically unstable, and those who know him only agree upon the fact that he is personally honest. His position rests purely upon the popular belief in him, for he has the Labour Party machine more or less against him, and the Tories are only temporarily supporting him because they want to use him against Churchill and Beaverbrook and imagine that they can make him into another tame cat like Attlee. Some of the factory workers are inclined to be suspicious of him (one comment reported to me was "Too like Mosley"—meaning too much the man of family who "goes to the people") and the Communists hate him because he is suspected of being anti-Stalin. Beaverbrook already appears to be instituting an attack on Cripps and his newspapers are making use of anti-Stalinist remarks dropped by Cripps in the past. I note that the Germans, to judge from their wireless, would be willing to see Cripps in power if at that price they could get rid of Churchill. They probably calculate that since Cripps has no party machine to rely on he would soon be levered out by the right-wing Tories and make way for Sir John Anderson, Lord Londonderry or someone of that kind. I can't yet say with certainty that Cripps is not merely a second-rate figure to whom the public have tied their hopes, a sort of bubble blown by popular discontent. But at any rate, the way people talked about him when he came back from Moscow was symptomatically important.

## WAR STRATEGY

There is endless talk about a Second Front, those who are for and those who are against being divided roughly along political lines. Much that is said is extremely ignorant, but even people with little military knowledge are able to see that in the last few months we have lost by useless defensive actions a force which, if grouped in one place and used offensively, might have achieved something. Public opinion often seems to be ahead of the so-called experts in matters of grand strategy, sometimes even tactics and weapons. I don't myself know whether the opening of a second front is feasible, because I don't know the real facts about the shipping situation; the only clue I have to the latter is that the food situation hasn't altered during the past year. Official policy seems to be to discountenance the idea of a Second Front, but just possibly that is only military deception. The right-wing papers make much play with our bombing raids on Germany and suggest that we can tie down a million troops along the coast of Europe by continuous commando raids. The latter is nonsense, as the commandos can't do much when the nights get short, and after our own experiences few people here believe that bombing can settle anything. In general the big public is offensive-minded and is always pleased when the government shows by violating international law (e.g. Oran, Syria, Madagascar) that it is taking the war seriously. Nevertheless the idea of attacking Spain or Spanish Morocco (much the most hopeful area for a Second Front in my opinion) is seldom raised. It is agreed by all observers that the army, i.e. rank and file and a lot of the junior officers, is exceedingly browned off, but this does not seem to be the case with the navy and RAF, and it is easy to get recruits for the dangerous corps such as the commandos and parachute troops. An anonymous pamphlet attacking the blimpocracy, button-polishing, etc recently sold enormously, and this line is also run by the *Daily Mirror,* the soldiers' favourite paper, which was nearly suppressed a few weeks back for its criticisms of the higher command. On the other hand the pamphlets which used to appear earlier in the war, complaining about the hardships of army life, seem to have faded out. Perhaps symptomatically important is the story now widely circulated, that the real reason why the higher-ups have stuck out against adopting dive-bombers is that these are cheap to manufacture and don't represent much profit. I know nothing as to the truth of this story, but I record the fact that many people believe it. Churchill's speech a few days back in which he referred to possible use of poison gas by the Germans was interpreted as a warning that gas warfare will begin soon. Usual comment: "I hope we start using it first." People seem to me to have got tougher in their attitude, in spite of general discontent and the lack of positive war aims. It is hard to assess how much the man in the street cared about the Singapore disaster. Working-class people seemed to me to be more impressed by the escape of the German warships from Brest. The opinion seems general that Germany is the real enemy, and newspaper efforts to work up a hate over Japanese atrocities failed. My impression is that people will go on fighting indefinitely so long as Germany is in the field, but that if Germany should be knocked out they would not continue the war against Japan unless a real and intelligible war aim were produced.

### THE RUSSIAN ALLIANCE

I have referred in earlier letters to the great growth of pro-Russian feeling. It is difficult, however, to be sure how deep this goes. A Trotskyist said to me recently that he thought that by their successful resistance the Russians had won back all the credit they lost by the Hitler-Stalin pact and the Finnish war. I don't believe this is so. What has happened is that the USSR has gained a lot of admirers it did not previously have, but many who used to be its uncritical adherents have grown cannier. One notices here a gulf between what is said publicly and privately. In public nobody says a word against the USSR, but in private, apart from the "disillusioned" Stalinists that one is always meeting, I notice a more sceptical attitude among thinking people. One sees this especially in conversations about the Second Front. The official attitude of the pinks is that if we open up a Second Front the Russians will be so grateful that they will be our comrades to the last. In reality, to open a Second Front without a clear agreement beforehand would simply give the Russians the opportunity to make a separate peace; for if we succeeded in drawing the Germans away from their territories, what reason would they have for going on fighting? Another theory favoured in left-wing papers is that the more fighting we do the more say we shall have in the post-war settlement. This again is an illusion; those who dictate the peace treaties are those who have remained strongest, which usually means those who have managed to avoid fighting (e.g. the USA in the last war). Considerations of this kind seldom find their way into print but are admitted readily enough in private. I think people have not altogether forgotten the Russo-German Pact and that fear of another double-cross partly explains their desire for a closer alliance. But there is also much sentimental boosting of Russia, based on ignorance and played up by all kinds of crooks who are utterly anti-Socialist but see that the Red Army is a popular line. I must take back some of the favourable references I made in earlier letters to the Beaverbrook press. After giving his journalists a free hand for a year or more, during which some of them did good work in enlightening the big public, Beaverbrook has again cracked the whip and is setting his team at work to attack Churchill and, more directly, Cripps. He is simultaneously yapping against fuel-rationing, petrol-rationing and other restrictions on private capitalism, and posing as more Stalinist than the Stalinists. Most of the right-wing press adopts the more cautious line of praising "the great Russian people" (historic parallels with Napoleon etc) while keeping silent about the nature of the Russian régime. The "International" is at last being played on the wireless. Molotov's speech on the German atrocities was issued as a White Paper, but in deference to somebody's feelings (I don't know whether Stalin's or the King's) the royal arms were omitted from the cover. People in general want to think well of Russia, though still vaguely hostile to Communism. They would welcome a joint declaration of war aims and a close co-ordination of strategy. I think many people realise that a firm alliance with Russia is difficult while the Munich crew are still more or less in power, but much fewer grasp that the comparative political backwardness of the USA presents another difficulty.

### REVOLUTION OR DISASTER

Well, that is the set-up as I see it. It seems to me that we are back to the "revolutionary situation" which existed but was not utilised after Dunkirk. From that time until quite recently one's thoughts necessarily moved in some such progression as this:

We can't win the war with our present social and economic structure.

The structure won't change unless there is a rapid growth in popular consciousness.

The only thing that promotes this growth is military disasters.

One more disaster and we shall lose the war.

In the circumstances all one could do was to "support" the war, which involved supporting Churchill, and hope that in some way it would all come right on the night—i.e. that the mere necessities of war, the inevitable drift towards a centralised economy and a more equal standard of living, would force the régime gradually to the Left and allow the worst reactionaries to be levered out. No one in his senses supposed that the British ruling classes would legislate themselves out of existence, but they might be manoeuvred into a position where their continuance in power was quite obviously in the Nazi interest. In that case the mass of the nation would swing against them and it would be possible to get rid of them with little or no violence. Before writing this off as a hopelessly "reformist" strategy it is worth remembering that England is literally within gunshot of the continent. Revolutionary defeatism, or anything approaching it, is nonsense in our geographical situation. If there were even a week's serious disorganisation in the armed forces the Nazis would be here, after which one might as well stop talking about revolution.

To some small extent things have happened as I foresaw. One can after all discern the outlines of a revolutionary world war. Britain has been forced into alliance with Russia and China and into restoring Abyssinia and making fairly generous treaties with the Middle Eastern countries, and because of, among other things, the need to raise a huge air force a serious breach has been made in the class system. The defeats in the Far East have gone a long way towards killing the old conception of imperialism. But there was a sort of gap in the ladder which we never got over and which it was perhaps impossible to get over while no revolutionary party and no able left-wing leadership existed. This may or may not have been altered by the emergence of Cripps. I think it is certain that a new political party will have to arise if anything is to be changed, and the obvious bankruptcy of the old parties may hasten this. Maybe Cripps will lose his lustre quite quickly if he does not get out of the Government. But at present, in his peculiar isolated position, he is the likeliest man for any new movement to crystallise round. If he fails, God save us from the other probable alternatives to Churchill.

I suppose as usual I have written too much. There is not much change in our everyday lives here. The nation went on to brown bread a few weeks back. The basic petrol ration stops next month, which in theory means the end of private motoring. The new luxury taxes are terrific. Cigarettes now cost a shilling for ten and the cheapest beer tenpence a pint (fourpence in 1936). Everyone seems to be working longer and longer hours. Now and again at intervals of weeks one gets one's head above water for a moment and notices with surprise that the earth is still going round the sun. One day I noticed crocuses in the parks, another day pear blossom, another day hawthorn. One seems to catch vague glimpses of these things through a mist of war news.

Yours ever

George Orwell

*Partisan Review*, July–August 1942

## 33. Review

*The Sword and the Sickle* by Mulk Raj Anand

In this war we have one weapon which our enemies cannot use against us, and that is the English language. Several other languages are spoken by larger numbers of people, but there is no other that has any claim to be a world-wide lingua franca. The Japanese administrators in the Philippines, the Chinese delegates in India, the Indian nationalists in Berlin, are all obliged to do their business in English. Therefore, although Mr Anand's novel would still be interesting on its own merits if it had been written by an Englishman, it is impossible to read it without remembering every few pages that it is also a cultural curiosity. The growth, especially during the last few years, of an English-language Indian literature is a strange phenomenon, and it will have its effect on the post-war world, if not on the outcome of the war itself.

This novel is a sequel to *The Village* and *Across the Black Waters*. The Sikh sepoy who has fought in France and spent years as a prisoner in Germany comes home to find himself—partly because he is suspected of disaffection and partly because that is the normal fate of all soldiers in all wars—cheated out of the reward that he had imagined that he was fighting for. The rest of the story deals mostly with the peasant movement and the beginnings of the Indian Communist Party. Now, any book about India written by an Indian must at this date almost unavoidably be the story of a grievance, and I notice that Mr Anand has already got himself into trouble by what is wrongly described as his bitterness. In reality, the book's comparative lack of bitterness is a roundabout demonstration of the English "bad conscience" towards India. In a novel on the same subject by an English intellectual, what would you expect to find? An endless masochistic denunciation of his own race, and a series of traditional caricatures of Anglo-Indian society, with its unbearable club life, its chota pegs, etc etc. In the scene as the Indian sees it, however, the English hardly enter. They are merely a permanent evil, something taken almost for granted, like the climate, and though the ultimate objective is to get rid of British rule, it is almost forgotten among the weaknesses and internecine struggles of the revolutionaries themselves. European characters barely appear in the story—a reminder that in India only about one person in a thousand is technically white—and of the few that do it cannot be said that they are treated worse than the other characters. They are not treated sympathetically either, for on the whole the characterisation is harsh and derisive (to give just one example, Mr Gandhi's head is described as resembling "a raw purple turnip"), and the whole book is full of the Indian melancholy and of the horribly ugly, degrading scenes which offend one's eyes all the time in the starved countries of the East. Although it ends on a comparatively hopeful note this novel does not break the rule that books about India are depressing. Probably they must be so, quite apart from the question-mark they raise in the English conscience, because while the world remains in anything like its present shape the central problem of India, its poverty, is not soluble. How much of the special atmosphere of English-language Indian literature is due to its subject-matter is uncertain, but in reading Mr Anand's work, or that of Ahmed Ali and several others, it is difficult not to feel that by this time another dialect, comparable perhaps to Irish-English, has grown up. One quotation will do to illustrate this:

> Conscious of his responsibility for the misadventures into which he had led them, Lalu bent down and strained to lever the dead bodies with trembling hands. A sharp odour of decomposing flesh shot up to his nostrils from Chandra's body, while his hands were smeared with blood from Nandu's neck. He sat up imagining the smell to be a whiff of the foul virulence of bacterial decay, ensuing from the vegetation of the forest through which

they had come. But, as he bent down again, there was no dis-
guising the stink of the corpse. And, in a flash, he realised that
though Nandu's blood was hot now, it would soon be cold and
the body would stink if it was carried all the way to Allahabad.

There is a vaguely un-English flavour about this ("shot up to his
nostrils", for instance, is not quite an English idiom), and yet it is
obviously the work of a man who is not only at ease with the English
language but thinks in it and would probably write in it by prefer-
ence. This raises the question of the future, if any, of English-
language Indian literature. At present English is to a great extent
the official and business language of India: five million Indians are
literate in it and millions more speak a debased version of it; there
is a huge English-language Indian press, and the only English
magazine devoted wholly to poetry is edited by Indians. On average,
too, Indians write and even pronounce English far better than any
European race. Will this state of affairs continue? It is inconceivable
that the present relationship between the two countries will last
much longer, and when it vanishes the economic inducements for
learning English will also tend to disappear. Presumably, therefore,
the fate of the English language in Asia is either to fade out or to
survive as a pidgin language useful for business and technical purposes. It might survive, in dialect form, as the mother tongue of
the small Eurasian community, but it is difficult to believe that it
has a literary future. Mr Anand and Ahmed Ali are much better
writers than the average run of English novelists, but they are not
likely to have many successors. Why, then, is it that their books
have at this moment an importance that goes beyond their literary
merit? Partly because they are interpreting Asia to the west, but
more, I think, because they act as a westernising influence among
their own countrymen. And at present there are reasons why the
second function is more important than the first.

Anyone who has to deal in propaganda knows that a sudden
change came over the Indian scene as soon as Japan entered the war.
Many, perhaps most, Indian intellectuals are emotionally pro-Japanese. From their point of view Britain is the enemy, China means
nothing to them, Russia is an object of lip-service only. But is it
the case that the Indian anti-British intelligentsia actually wishes to
see China permanently enslaved, the Soviet Union destroyed,
Europe a Nazi concentration camp? No, that is not fair either: it

is merely that the nationalism of defeated peoples is necessarily revengeful and short-sighted. If you discuss this question with an Indian you get an answer something like this: "Half of me is a Socialist but the other half is a Nationalist. I know what Fascism means, I know very well that I ought to be on your side, but I hate your people so much that if we can get rid of them I hardly care what happens afterwards. I tell you that there are moments when all I want is to see China, Japan and India get together and destroy western civilisation, not only in Asia, but in Europe." This outlook is widespread among the coloured peoples. Its emotional roots are obvious enough, the various disguises in which it is wrapped are easily seen through, but it is there, and it contains a great danger, to us and to the world. The only answer to the self-pity and race-hatred common among Indians is to point out that others besides Indians are oppressed. The only answer to nationalism is international Socialism, and the contact of Indians—to a lesser extent, of all Asiatics—with Socialist literature and Socialist thought generally, is through the English language. As a general rule, Indians are reliably anti-Fascist in proportion as they are westernised. That is why at the beginning of this review I described the English language as a weapon of war. It is a funnel for ideas deadly to the Fascist view of life. Mr Anand does not like us very much, and some of his colleagues hate us very bitterly; but so long as they voice their hatred in English they are in a species of alliance with us, and an ultimate decent settlement with the Indians whom we have wronged but also helped to awaken remains possible.

*Horizon,* July 1942

# 34. Pacifism and the War

*A Controversy*, by D. S. Savage, George Woodcock, Alex Comfort,
George Orwell.

D.S. SAVAGE:[1]

A few brief comments on George Orwell's March-April *London Letter*.

It is fashionable nowadays to equate Fascism with Germany. We must fight Fascism, therefore we must fight Germany. Thus Mr Orwell: "the greater part of the very young intelligentsia . . . don't feel the horror of Fascism that we who are somewhat older feel," also: "there is no real answer to the charge that pacifism is objectively pro-Fascist." *Answer:* Fascism is not a force confined to any one nation. We can just as soon get it here as anywhere else. The characteristic markings of Fascism are: curtailment of individual and minority liberties; abolition of private life and private values and substitution of State life and public values (patriotism); external imposition of discipline (militarism); prevalence of mass-values and mass-mentality; falsification of intellectual activity under State pressure. These are all tendencies of present-day Britain. The pacifist opposes every one of these, and might therefore be called the *only genuine opponent* of Fascism.

Don't let us be misled by *names*. Fascism is quite capable of calling itself democracy or even Socialism. It's the reality under the name that matters. War demands totalitarian organisation of society. Germany organised herself on that basis prior to embarking on war. Britain now finds herself compelled to take the same measures after involvement in war. Germans call it National Socialism. We call it democracy. The result is the same.

Let us assume that Mr Orwell means "objectively pro-German". (If so, his loose terminology is surely indicative of very loose thinking.) Who is "objective"?—Mr Orwell, a partisan of one particular side in the struggle? According to this type of reasoning, a German or Japanese pacifist would be "objectively pro-British". This is puerile. Mr Orwell is assuming that the pacifist shares his chauvinistic predilections. On the contrary, we regard the war as a disaster to humanity. Who is to say that a British victory will be less

[1] D.S. Savage, poet, whose critical works include *The Personal Principle* and *Hamlet and the Pirates*.

disastrous than a German one? The last British victory was pretty meaningless.

Mr Orwell, in all his recent writings on the subject, shows a total inability to grasp the real nature of pacifism. Let me try, in a few words, to enlighten him.

Mr Orwell is himself a "politician", with a politician's outlook on things. He consequently sees pacifism primarily as a political phenomenon. That is just what it isn't. Primarily it is a moral phenomenon. Political movements are based on programme and organisation. With pacifism, programme and organisation are quite subsidiary. Pacifism springs from conscience—i.e. from within the individual human being. "*Peace News*," says Orwell, "follows its old tradition of opposing war for different and incompatible reasons." There are certainly innumerable reasons why war should be opposed, but the chief reason is the diabolical nature of modern warfare, with its diabolical repercussions upon human personality and values. I am not referring only to the act of warfare itself, but the whole complex of events which is war. The corruption and hollowness revealed in the prosecution of this war are too contemptible for words. Certainly I will accept my share of responsibility for them, but I won't fight in a war to *extend* that corruption and hollowness.

Perhaps I ought to try and give expression to what many of us pacifists feel about Germany in relation to ourselves, since Mr Orwell brings up this point. Needless to say, we have no love for Fascism, and our entire attitude is one of personal resistance to all forms of Fascism, as they impinge upon us in concrete form. (Whereas Orwell swallows the concrete encroachments and waves his arms at a distant bogey.) Not only will we not fight, nor lend a hand with the war, but the "intellectuals" among us would scorn to mentally compromise themselves with the Government. Orwell dislikes the French intellectuals licking up Hitler's crumbs, but what's the difference between them and our intellectuals who are licking up Churchill's? However: we "don't believe in any 'defence of democracy', are inclined to prefer Germany to Britain, and don't feel the horror of Fascism that we who are somewhat older feel". I can only speak for myself, of course, but surely the "defence of democracy" is best served by defending one's own concrete liberties, not by equating democracy with Britain, and allowing all democracy to be destroyed in order that we may fight better—for "Britain"; and Orwell should not need to be told what, or who, "Britain" now is.

I am not greatly taken in by Britain's "democracy", particularly as it is gradually vanishing under the pressure of the war. Certainly I would never fight and kill for such a phantasm. I do not greatly admire the part "my country" has played in world events. I consider that spiritually Britain has lost all meaning; she once stood for something, perhaps, but who can pretend that the *idea* of "Britain" now counts for anything in the world? This is not cynicism. I feel identified with my country in a deep sense, and want her to regain her meaning, her soul, if that be possible: but the unloading of a billion tons of bombs on Germany won't help this forward an inch. The pretence exists in some quarters that, although Britain has been a sick nation, now, engaged in war, she has "found her soul", and by this one gathers that the sickness was exemplified by Chamberlain and the soul-finding by Churchill. Unfortunately, deep changes do not occur so easily as that. England does not even know what she is fighting for, only what she is fighting against. The pacifists' "championing" of Hitler referred to by Orwell is simply a recognition by us that Hitler and Germany contain a real historical dynamic, whereas we do not. Whereas the rest of the nation is content with calling down obloquy on Hitler's head, we regard this as superficial. Hitler requires, not condemnation, but understanding. This does not mean that we like, or defend him. Personally I do not care for Hitler. He is, however, "realler" than Chamberlain, Churchill, Cripps, etc, in that he is the vehicle of raw historical forces, whereas they are stuffed dummies, waxwork figures, living in unreality. We do not desire a German "victory"; we would not lift a finger to help either Britain or Germany to "win"; but there would be a profound justice, I feel, however terrible, in a German victory. (In actuality, any ruler would find us rather awkward customers, one no less than another.)

Now, how about Mr Orwell's own position, and the position of people like him? I would ask him to consider, first, the company he keeps. Who are his leaders? What is the actual social system which he is fighting to defend? What hopes has he of diverting the stream of history the way *he* wants it to go? Brave words and muddled thinking cannot disguise the fact that Mr Orwell, like all the other supporters of the war, shipping magnates, coal owners, proletarians, university professors, Sunday journalists, trade union leaders, Church dignitaries, scoundrels and honest men, is being swept along by history, not directing it. Like them, he will be deposited, along with other detritus, where history decides, not where he thinks. Mr Orwell is, I believe, a man of integrity, an honest man. But that does not make up for his superficiality. And can we afford superficiality, at any time, still less times like these?

11 May 1942
Dry Drayton, England

GEORGE WOODCOCK:[1]

I hope you will allow me to comment in your columns on certain references in George Orwell's London Letter to the review *Now*, of which I am editor.

Orwell suggests that this paper has a Fascist tendency, and names two of its contributors, Hugh Ross Williamson and the Duke of Bedford, to prove his case. In fact, *Now* was established early in the war as a review for publishing literary matter and also as a forum for controversial writing which could not readily find publication under wartime conditions. Not all the writers were opposed to the war, and of the fifty odd contributors to the seven numbers, only two, those named by Orwell, were even reputed to have Fascist tendencies. Neither of these men contributed more than one article to the review. The remaining writers included Anarchists, Stalinists, Trotskyists, pacifists and *New Statesman* moderates. Julian Huxley and Herbert Read, two of its best-known contributors, can hardly be accused of Fascism!

The reference to the article by Julian Symons is, in my opinion, unjust. Orwell gives no idea of its subject and does not quote a single sentence to prove his assertion that it is "vaguely Fascist"! No one in England, except Orwell and possibly the Stalinists, would think of suggesting that Julian Symons has any Fascist tendencies. On the contrary, he has been consistently anti-Fascist, and the article mentioned, which attacks *Now's* former lack of a definite political line, is Marxist in tendency.

I do not propose to defend Hugh Ross Williamson or the Duke of Bedford—although I would mention that neither of them belonged

[1] George Woodcock (1912–   ), Anarchist, editor of *Now* 1940–7, author of *William Godwin*, *Anarchism* and *The Crystal Spirit*. At present Professor of English at the University of British Columbia and since 1959, editor of *Canadian Literature*. After this controversy he and Orwell corresponded and remained friends until Orwell's death.

to the BUF and that the People's Party, although it may have contained former Fascists, was not a Fascist party and contained many honest pacifists and Socialists, like Ben Greene, whose wrongful imprisonment and maltreatment in gaol caused a major scandal. I would also point out that if we are to expose antecedents, Orwell himself does not come off very well. Comrade Orwell, the former police official of British imperialism (from which the Fascists learnt all they know) in those regions of the Far East where the sun at last sets for ever on the bedraggled Union Jack! Comrade Orwell, former fellow-traveller of the pacifists and regular contributor to the pacifist *Adelphi*—which he now attacks! Comrade Orwell, former extreme left-winger, ILP partisan and defender of Anarchists (see *Homage to Catalonia*)! And now Comrade Orwell who returns to his old imperialist allegiances and works at the BBC conducting British propaganda to fox the Indian masses! It would seem that Orwell himself shows to a surprising degree the overlapping of left-wing, pacifist and reactionary tendencies of which he accuses others!

Adverting to *Now*, I would mention that this review has abandoned its position as an independent forum, and has now become the cultural review of the British Anarchist movement. Perhaps Mr Orwell will regard this as another proof of his mystic and blimpish trinity.

Finally, I would point out two inaccuracies in Orwell's letter. The Anarchist pamphlet to which he refers is entitled *The Russian Myth*, and the editor of the *Adelphi* during the earlier part of the war was not John Middleton Murry, but the late Max Plowman.

19 May 1942
Richmond, England

ALEX COMFORT:[1]

I see that Mr Orwell is intellectual-hunting again, in your pages this time, and that he has made the discovery that almost every writer under thirty in this country has his feet already on the slippery slope to Fascism, or at least to compromise. It seems I am a "pure pacifist of the other-cheek" variety, a piece of horticultural eulogy I'm glad I did not miss, and that I deserve a spanking for associating with such disreputables as the Duke of Bedford and the—perfectly harmless—Ross Williamson. The trouble is that some of your American readers may not realise Mr Orwell's status in this country

[1] Alex Comfort (1920–    ), poet, novelist, pamphleteer and medical biologist.

and take his commentary seriously. We all like him here, though the standard of his pamphleteering is going down of late, and we know him as the preacher of a doctrine of Physical Courage as an Asset to the Left-wing Intellectual, and so forth. I think we all agree that he is pretty thoroughly out of touch with any writing under thirty years of age, and his last two public performances—a reproof in sorrow to my book *No Such Liberty*, and this "London Letter" of his—suggest that he still has not grasped why most of the post-'thirties poets are pacifists, or what their pacifism would entail if Hitler arrived here.

Mr Orwell calls us "objectively pro-Fascist". I suppose he means that we are letting anti-Fascism go by default. If we suggest to him that we, who have the single intention of salvaging English artistic culture when the crash comes, are the only people likely to continue to hold genuinely anti-Fascist values, he will not be convinced. But perhaps he will grant that Hitler's greatest and irretrievable victory over here was when he persuaded the English people that the only way to lick Fascism was to imitate it. He puts us in a dilemma which cannot be practically rebutted, only broken away from—"If I win, you have political Fascism victorious: if you want to beat me, you must assimilate as much of its philosophy as you can, so that I am bound to win either way." Accordingly we began feverishly jamming into our national life all the minor pieces of Fascist practice which did not include Socialist methods, sitting on the press "because this is Total War", making our soldiers jab blood bladders while loud-speakers howl propaganda at them, because the German army consisted of efficient yahoos. The only people who said that to defeat Fascism one must (a) try to understand it and (b) refuse to accept its tenets oneself were the pacifists. It looks as if Mr Orwell and his warlike friends were being not objectively but constructively supporters of the entire philosophical apparatus which they quite genuinely detest.

What, again, does Mr Orwell imagine the rôle of the artist should be in occupied territory? He should protest with all his force, where and when he can, against such evils as he sees—but can he do this more usefully by temporarily accepting the *status quo*, or by skirmishing in Epping Forest with a pocket full of hand-grenades? I think that English writers honour, and will follow when the opportunity comes, the example of integrity which Gide has set. We are going to be entrusted with the job of saving what remains of the structure of civilised values from Hitler or alternatively from Churchill and his bladder-prickers. The men who, like Orwell, could have helped, are calling us Fascists and presumably dancing round the ruins of Munster Cathedral. We prefer not to join them, and if, in the pursuit of our task we find ourselves obliged to publish in the same paper as the Devil himself, the others having politely refused us as unorthodox, we shall have very few qualms.

18 May 1942
Brentwood, England

GEORGE ORWELL:
Since I don't suppose you want to fill an entire number of *PR* with squalid controversies imported from across the Atlantic, I will lump together the various letters you have sent on to me (from Messrs Savage, Woodcock and Comfort), as the central issue in all of them is the same. But I must afterwards deal separately with some points of fact raised in various of the letters.

*Pacifism.* Pacifism is objectively pro-Fascist. This is elementary common sense. If you hamper the war effort of one side you automatically help that of the other. Nor is there any real way of remaining outside such a war as the present one. In practice, "he that is not with me is against me". The idea that you can somehow remain aloof from and superior to the struggle, while living on food which British sailors have to risk their lives to bring you, is a bourgeois illusion bred of money and security. Mr Savage remarks that "according to this type of reasoning, a German or Japanese pacifist would be 'objectively pro-British'." But of course he would be! That is why pacifist activities are not permitted in those countries (in both of them the penalty is, or can be, beheading) while both the Germans and the Japanese do all they can to encourage the spread of pacifism in British and American territories. The Germans even run a spurious "freedom" station which serves out pacifist propaganda indistinguishable from that of the PPU. They would stimulate pacifism in Russia as well if they could, but in that case they have tougher babies to deal with. In so far as it takes effect at all, pacifist propaganda can only be effective *against* those countries where a certain amount of freedom of speech is still permitted; in other words it is helpful to totalitarianism.

I am not interested in pacifism as a "moral phenomenon". If Mr Savage and others imagine that one can somehow "overcome" the

German army by lying on one's back, let them go on imagining it, but let them also wonder occasionally whether this is not an illusion due to security, too much money and a simple ignorance of the way in which things actually happen. As an ex-Indian civil servant, it always makes me shout with laughter to hear, for instance, Gandhi named as an example of the success of non-violence. As long as twenty years ago it was cynically admitted in Anglo-Indian circles that Gandhi was very useful to the British Government. So he will be to the Japanese if they get there. Despotic governments can stand "moral force" till the cows come home; what they fear is physical force. But though not much interested in the "theory" of pacifism, I *am* interested in the psychological processes by which pacifists who have started out with an alleged horror of violence end up with a marked tendency to be fascinated by the success and power of Nazism. Even pacifists who wouldn't own to any such fascination are beginning to claim that a Nazi victory is desirable in itself. In the letter you sent on to me, Mr Comfort considers that an artist in occupied territory ought to "protest against such evils as he sees", but considers that this is best done by "temporarily accepting the *status quo*" (like Déat or Bergery, for instance?) A few weeks back he was hoping for a Nazi victory because of the stimulating effect it would have upon the arts:

> As far as I can see, no therapy short of complete military defeat has any chance of re-establishing the common stability of literature and of the man in the street. One can imagine the greater the adversity the greater the sudden realisation of a stream of imaginative work, and the greater the sudden katharsis of poetry, from the isolated interpretation of war as calamity to the realisation of the imaginative and actual tragedy of Man. When we have access again to the literature of the war years in France, Poland and Czechoslovakia, I am confident that that is what we shall find. (From a letter to *Horizon*.)

I pass over the money-sheltered ignorance capable of believing that literary life is still going on in, for instance, Poland, and remark merely that statements like this justify me in saying that our English pacifists are tending towards active pro-Fascism. But I don't particularly object to that. What I object to is the intellectual cowardice of people who are objectively and to some extent emotionally pro-Fascist, but who don't care to say so and take refuge behind the formula "I am just as anti-Fascist as anyone, but—". The result of this is that so-called peace propaganda is just as dishonest and intellectually disgusting as war propaganda. Like war propaganda, it concentrates on putting forward a "case", obscuring the opponent's point of view and avoiding awkward questions. The line normally followed is "Those who fight against Fascism go Fascist themselves". In order to evade the quite obvious objections that can be raised to this, the following propaganda-tricks are used:

1. The Fascising processes occurring in Britain as a result of war are systematically exaggerated.

2. The actual record of Fascism, especially its pre-war history, is ignored or pooh-poohed as "propaganda". Discussion of what the world would actually be like if the Axis dominated it is evaded.

3. Those who want to struggle against Fascism are accused of being wholehearted defenders of capitalist "democracy". The fact that the rich everywhere tend to be pro-Fascist and the working class are nearly always anti-Fascist is hushed up.

4. It is tacitly pretended that the war is only between Britain and Germany. Mention of Russia and China, and their fate if Fascism is permitted to win, is avoided. (You won't find one word about Russia or China in the three letters you sent to me.)

Now as to one or two points of fact which I must deal with if your correspondents' letters are to be printed in full.

*My past and present.* Mr Woodcock tries to discredit me by saying that (a) I once served in the Indian Imperial Police, (b) I have written articles for the *Adelphi* and was mixed up with the Trotskyists in Spain, and (c) that I am at the BBC "conducting British propaganda to fox the Indian masses". With regard to (a), it is quite true that I served five years in the Indian Police. It is also true that I gave up that job, partly because it didn't suit me but mainly because I would not any longer be a servant of imperialism. I am against imperialism because I know something about it from the inside. The whole history of this is to be found in my writings, including a novel[1] which I think I can claim was a kind of prophecy of what happened this year in Burma. (b) Of course I have written for the *Adelphi*. Why not? I once wrote an article for a vegetarian paper. Does that make me a vegetarian? I was associated with the Trotskyists in Spain. It was chance that I was serving in the POUM militia and not another, and I largely disagreed with the POUM "line" and told its

[1] *Burmese Days.*

leaders so freely, but when they were afterwards accused of pro-Fascist activities I defended them as best I could. How does this contradict my present anti-Hitler attitude? It is news to me that Trotskyists are either pacifists or pro-Fascists. (c) Does Mr Wood-cock really know what kind of stuff I put out in the Indian broad-casts? He does not—though I would be quite glad to tell him about it. He is careful not to mention what other people are associated with these Indian broadcasts. One for instance is Herbert Read, whom he mentions with approval. Others are T.S. Eliot, E.M. Forster, Reginald Reynolds, Stephen Spender, J.B.S. Haldane, Tom Wintringham. Most of our broadcasters are Indian left-wing intellectuals, from Liberals to Trotskyists, some of them bitterly anti-British. They don't do it to "fox the Indian masses" but because they know what a Fascist victory would mean to the chances of India's independence. Why not try to find out what I am doing before accusing my good faith?

*"Mr Orwell is intellectual-hunting again"* (Mr Comfort). I have never attacked "the intellectuals" or "the intelligentsia" *en bloc*. I have used a lot of ink and done myself a lot of harm by attacking the successive literary cliques which have infested this country, not because they were intellectuals but precisely because they were *not* what I mean by true intellectuals. The life of a clique is about five years and I have been writing long enough to see three of them come and two go—the Catholic gang, the Stalinist gang, and the present pacifist or, as they are sometimes nicknamed, Fascifist gang. My case against all of them is that they write mentally dishonest propaganda and degrade literary criticism to mutual arse-licking. But even with these various schools I would differentiate between individuals. I would never think of coupling Christopher Dawson with Arnold Lunn, or Malraux with Palme Dutt, or Max Plowman with the Duke of Bedford. And even the work of one individual can exist at very different levels. For instance Mr Comfort himself wrote one poem I value greatly ("The Atoll in the Mind"), and I wish he would write more of them instead of lifeless propaganda tracts dressed up as novels. But this letter he has chosen to send you is a different matter. Instead of answering what I have said he tries to prejudice an audience to whom I am little known by a misrepresentation of my general line and sneers about my "status" in England. (A writer isn't judged by his "status", he is judged by his work.) That is on a par with "peace" propaganda which has to avoid

mention of Hitler's invasion of Russia, and it is not what I mean by
intellectual honesty. It is just because I do take the function of the
intelligentsia seriously that I don't like the sneers, libels, parrot
phrases and financially profitable back-scratching which flourish in
our English literary world, and perhaps in yours also.

12 July 1942
London, England

*Partisan Review*, September–October 1942

## 35. London Letter to *Partisan Review*

London, England
29 August 1942

Dear Editors,
I write this letter at a moment when it is almost certain to be over-
taken and swamped by events. We are still in the same state of
frozen crisis as we were three months ago. Cripps is still enig-
matically in office, gradually losing credit with the Left but believed
by many to be waiting his moment to leave the Government and
proclaim a revolutionary policy. Such a development as there has
been is definitely in a reactionary direction. Many people besides
myself have noticed an all-round increase in blimpishness, a drive
against giving the war an anti-Fascist colour, a general shedding of
the phony radicalism of the past two years. The India business
twitched the masks off many faces, including Lord Rothermere's.
This seems to violate the principle that every régime moves to the
Left in moments of disaster, and vice versa, for one could hardly
describe the last six months as triumphant. But something or other
appears to have made the Blimps feel much more sure of themselves.

There are a few minor political happenings to record. Sir Richard
Acland's fairly radical Forward March group (a sort of Christian
Socialism) has amalgamated with Priestley's somewhat less radical
1941 Committee and the movement is calling itself Common
Wealth.[1] I believe the amalgamation happened somewhat against

[1] The "1941 Committee" was founded early in 1941 by a group of left-wing
publicists, politicians and notabilities. J. B. Priestley, the novelist, whose broadcasts in 1940 had made him a national figure, was chairman of the discussions,
though Orwell is echoing a popular misapprehension when he calls it "Priestley's

Acland's will. They have now been joined by Tom Wintringham, a useful demagogue, but I don't think these people should be taken seriously, though they have won one by-election. Trotskyism has at last got itself into the news owing to the threatened prosecution of a weekly paper, the *Socialist Appeal*. I believe this is still running, though in danger of suppression. I managed to get hold of one copy of it—the usual stuff, but not a bad paper. The group responsible for it are said to number 500. The Rothermere press is especially active in chasing the Trotskyists. The *Sunday Dispatch* denounces Trotskyism in almost exactly the terms used by the orthodox Communists. The *Sunday Dispatch* is one of the very worst of the gutter papers (murders, chorus girls' legs and the Union Jack) and belongs to the press which before the war outdid all others in kow-towing to Fascism, describing Hitler as late as the early months of 1939 as "a great gentleman". The *Daily Worker* has been de-suppressed and is to reappear on 7 September. This was the necessary sequel to lifting the ban on the Communist press in India. Communist literature at the moment is chiefly concerned with urging the opening of a second front, but pamphlets are also issued attacking all MPs of whatever party who vote against the Government. The anti-Trotskyist pamphlets now being issued are barely distinguishable from those of the Spanish civil war period, but go somewhat further in mendacity. The Indian issue makes a certain amount of stir here,

---

Committee". Its aim was to bring pressure to bear on the Coalition Government, through publications and lobbying, in favour of immediate left-wing political and economic changes. Dissension within the Committee led to its dissolution and what remained of it merged with Acland's "Forward March" in July 1942 to form a new political party, Common Wealth.

Sir Richard Acland (1906– ), became a Liberal MP in 1935. At the outbreak of war he announced his conversion to Socialism or, as he preferred to call it, Common Ownership. After the publication of his successful book *Unser Kampf* and his *Manifesto of the Ordinary Man* he formed a small movement called Forward March. Common Wealth's policies were those of Utopian Socialism but Acland eschewed the conventional Marxist vocabulary and insisted that the basis of a Socialist revolution must be moral and not economic. Common Wealth supported the war effort and, apart from the anti-war Independent Labour Party, formed the only organised Socialist opposition to the political truce and the Churchill Government. As a party it won by-elections during the war but fared disastrously in the 1945 General Election when most of its 23 candidates, including Acland, lost their deposits against Labour opposition. Afterwards Acland and most of its other leaders joined Labour, and Common Wealth (which still exists) disappeared from political prominence.

but less than one would expect because all the big newspapers have conspired to misrepresent it and the Indian intellectuals in this country go out of their way to antagonise those likeliest to help them. The Vansittart controversy rumbles on in books, pamphlets, correspondence columns and the monthly reviews. "Independent" candidates, some of them plain mountebanks, tour the country, fighting by-elections. Several of them have a distinct Fascist tinge. Nevertheless there is no sign of any Fascist mass movement emerging.

That seems to me the whole of the political news. It has been in my mind for some time past that you might be interested to hear something about the minor social changes occurring in this country —what one might call the mechanical results of war. The price of nearly everything is controlled, and controlled rather low, which leads to black-marketing of luxury foods, but this is perhaps less damaging to morale than the shameless profiteering that went on last time. The interesting point is whether the food restrictions are affecting public health and in what direction they are altering the national diet. A certain number of people with small fixed incomes —Old Age Pensioners are the extreme instance—are now in desperate financial straits, and the allowances paid to soldiers' wives are wretched enough, but as a whole the purchasing power of the working class has increased. My own opinion is that on average people are better nourished than they used to be. Against this is the increase in tuberculosis, which may have a number of causes but must be due in some cases to malnutrition. But though it is difficult to be sure with no standard of comparison, I can't help feeling that people in London have better complexions than they used, and are more active, and that one sees less grossly fat people. English working people before the war, even when very highly paid, lived on the most unwholesome diet it is possible to imagine, and the rationing necessarily forces them back to simpler food. It is strange to learn, for instance, that with an adult milk ration of three pints a week, milk consumption has actually increased since the war. The most sensational drop has been in the consumption of sugar and tea. Plenty of people in England before the war ate several pounds of sugar a week. Two ounces of tea is a miserable ration by English standards, though alleviated by the fact that small children who don't drink tea draw their ration. The endlessly stewing teapot was one of the bases of English life in the era of the dole, and though I miss the tea myself I have no doubt we are better without it. The wheatmeal bread is also an improvement, though working people don't as a rule like it.

War and consequent abandonment of imports tend to reduce us to the natural diet of these islands, that is, oatmeal, herrings, milk, potatoes, green vegetables and apples, which is healthy if rather dull. I am not certain how much of our own food we are now producing, but it would be of the order of 60 or 70 per cent. Six million extra acres have been ploughed in England since the war, and nine million in Great Britain as a whole. After the war Britain must necessarily become more of an agricultural country, because, however the war ends, many markets will have disappeared owing to industrialisation in India, Australia, etc. In that case we shall have to return to a diet resembling that of our ancestors, and perhaps these war years are not a bad preparation. The fact that, owing to evacuation, hundreds of thousands of town-born children are now growing up in the country may help to make the return to an agricultural way of life easier.

The clothes rationing is now beginning to take effect in a general shabbiness. I had expected it to accentuate class differences, because it is a thoroughly undemocratic measure, hardly affecting well-to-do people who have large stocks of clothes already. Also, the rationing only regulates the number of garments you can buy and has nothing to do with the price, so that you give up the same number of coupons for a hundred-guinea mink coat and a thirty-shilling waterproof. However, it now seems rather "the thing" for people not in uniform to look shabby. Evening dress has practically disappeared so far as men are concerned. Corduroy trousers and, in women, bare legs are on the increase. There hasn't yet been what one could call a revolutionary change in clothing, but there may be one owing to the sheer necessity of cutting down wastage of cloth. The Board of Trade tinkers with the problem by, for example, suppressing the turn-ups of trouser ends, but is already contemplating putting everyone into battledress. The quality of cloth is deteriorating, though less than I had expected. Cosmetics are becoming scarce. Cigarettes have lost their cellophane and greaseproof wrappings and are sold in cheap paper packets or loose. Writing paper gets more and more like toilet paper while toilet paper resembles sheet tin. Crockery is somewhat scarce and a hideous white "utility" hardware, the sort of thing you would expect to see in prison, is being produced. All articles which are not controlled, for instance furniture, linen, clocks, tools, rocket to fantastic prices. Now that the basic petrol ration has stopped private cars are very much rarer on the roads. In the country many people are taking to pony-traps again. In London there are no conveyances, except very occasional taxis, after midnight. It is becoming a common practice when you dine at anybody else's house to sleep there. What with the air raids and fire-watching people are so used to sleeping out of their beds that they can kip down anywhere. The fuel shortage hasn't yet made itself felt, but it is going to do so about January. For long past the coal owners have been successfully sabotaging the attempts to introduce fuel rationing, and it is considered that this winter we shall be 25 million tons of coal short. Buildings everywhere are growing very shabby, not only from air-raid damage but from lack of repairs. Plaster peeling off, windows patched with linen or cardboard, empty shops in every street. Regency London is becoming almost ruinous. The beautiful but flimsy houses, no longer lived in, are falling to pieces with damp and neglect. On the other hand the parks are improved out of recognition by the removal of the railings for scrap iron. As a rule these have gone from the gardens in the squares as well, but in places the rich and powerful manage to cling to their railings and keep the populace out. Generally speaking, where there is money, there are railings.

One periodical reminder that things *have changed* in England since the war is the arrival of American magazines, with their enormous bulk, sleek paper and riot of brilliantly-coloured adverts urging you to spend your money on trash. English adverts of before the war were no doubt less colourful and enterprising than the American ones, but their mental atmosphere was similar, and the sight of a full-page ad on shiny paper gives one the sensation of stepping back into 1939. Periodicals probably give up to advertisements as great a proportion of their dwindled bulk as before, but the total amount of advertisement is far smaller and the government ads constantly gain on the commercial ones. Everywhere there are enormous hoardings standing empty. In the Tube stations you can see an interesting evolutionary process at work, the commercial ads growing smaller and smaller (some of them only about 1 ft by 2 ft) and the official ones steadily replacing them. This, however, only reflects the dwindling of internal trade and does not point to any deep change of outlook. An extraordinary feature of the time is advertisements for products which no longer exist. To give just one example:

the word IRON in large letters, with underneath it an impressive picture of a tank, and underneath that a little essay on the importance of collecting scrap iron for salvage; at the bottom, in tiny print, a reminder that after the war Iron Jelloids will be on sale as before. This throws a sort of sidelight on the strange fact, recently reported by the Mass Observers and confirmed by my own limited experience, that many factory-workers are actually *afraid* of the war ending, because they foresee a prompt return to the old conditions, with three million unemployed, etc. The idea that *whatever happens* old-style capitalism is doomed and we are in much more danger of forced labour than of unemployment, hasn't reached the masses except as a vague notion that "things will be different". The advertisements that seem to have been least changed by the war are those for theatres and patent medicines. Certain drugs are unobtainable, but the British have lost none of their old enthusiasm for medicine-taking, and the consumption of aspirin, phenacetin, etc has no doubt increased. All pubs without exception sell aspirins, and various new proprietary drugs have appeared. One is named Blitz, the lightning pick-me-up.

Once again I may have seemed to talk to you about very trivial things, but these minor changes in our habits, all tending towards a more equal way of life and a lessened reliance on imported luxuries, could have their importance in the difficult transition period which must occur if Britain becomes a Socialist country. We are growing gradually used to conditions that would once have seemed intolerable and getting to have less of the consumer mentality which both Socialists and capitalists did their best to inculcate in times of peace. Since the introduction of Socialism is almost certain to mean a drop in the standard of living during the first few years, perhaps this is just as well. But of course the changes in our food and clothes have no meaning unless there is a structural change as well. For many of the same processes occurred during the last war as are occurring now. Then too food was short and money plentiful, agriculture revived, women in vast numbers moved into industry, trade union membership swelled, government interference with private life increased, and the class system was shaken up because of the need for great numbers of officers. But there had been no real shift of power and in 1919 we went back to "normal" with startling speed. I cannot believe that the same thing will happen this time, but I cannot say either that I see concrete evidence that it won't happen. At present the only insurance against it seems to me to lie in what one might call the mechanics of the situation. Old-style capitalism can't win the war, and the events of the past three years suggest that we can't develop a native version of Fascism. Therefore, now as two years ago, one can predict the future in the form of an "either—or": either we introduce Socialism, or we lose the war. The strange, perhaps disquieting, fact is that it was as easy to make this prophecy in 1940 as it is now, and yet the essential situation has barely altered. We have been two years on the burning deck and somehow the magazine never explodes.

There are now many American soldiers in the streets. They wear on their faces a look of settled discontent. I don't know how far this may be the normal expression of the American countenance, as against the English countenance, which is mild, vague and rather worried. In the Home Guard we have orders to be punctilious about saluting the officers, which I'm afraid I don't do and which they don't seem to expect. I believe some of the provincial towns have been almost taken over by the American troops. There is already a lot of jealousy, and sooner or later something will have to be done about the differences in pay. An American private gets five times as much as an English one, which has its effect on the girls. Also, working-class girls probably find it rather thrilling to hear the accent they are so used to in the movies emerging from a living face. I don't think the foreign troops here can complain about the way the women have treated them. The Poles have already done their bit towards solving our birth-rate problem.

Yours ever

George Orwell

*Partisan Review*, November–December 1942

## 36. Review

*Burnt Norton, East Coker, The Dry Salvages* by T.S. Eliot

There is very little in Eliot's later work that makes any deep impression on me. That is a confession of something lacking in myself, but it is not, as it may appear at first sight, a reason for simply shutting up and saying no more, since the change in my own reaction probably points to some external change which is worth investigating.

I know a respectable quantity of Eliot's earlier work by heart. I did not sit down and learn it, it simply stuck in my mind as any passage of verse is liable to do when it has really rung the bell. Sometimes after only one reading it is possible to remember the whole of a poem of, say, twenty or thirty lines, the act of memory being partly an act of reconstruction. But as for these three latest poems, I suppose I have read each of them two or three times since they were published, and how much do I verbally remember? "Time and the bell have buried the day", "At the still point of the turning world", "The vast waters of the petrel and the porpoise", and bits of the passage beginning "O dark dark dark. They all go into the dark". (I don't count "In my end is my beginning", which is a quotation.) That is about all that sticks in my head of its own accord. Now one cannot take this as proving that *Burnt Norton* and the rest are worse than the more memorable early poems, and one might even take it as proving the contrary, since it is arguable that that which lodges itself most easily in the mind is the obvious and even the vulgar. But it is clear that something has departed, some kind of current has been switched off, the later verse does not *contain* the earlier, even if it is claimed as an improvement upon it. I think one is justified in explaining this by a deterioration in Mr Eliot's subject-matter. Before going any further, here are a couple of extracts, just near enough to one another in meaning to be comparable. The first is the concluding passage of *The Dry Salvages*:

> And right action is freedom
> From past and future also.
> For most of us, this is the aim
> Never here to be realised;
> Who are only undefeated
> Because we have gone on trying;
> We, content at the last
> If our temporal reversion nourish
> (Not too far from the yew-tree)
> The life of significant soil.

Here is an extract from a much earlier poem:

> Daffodil bulbs instead of balls
> Stared from the sockets of his eyes!
> He knew that thought clings round dead limbs
> Tightening its lusts and luxuries;

. . . .

> He knew the anguish of the marrow,
> The ague of the skeleton;
> No contact possible to flesh
> Allayed the fever of the bone.

The two passages will bear comparison since they both deal with the same subject, namely death. The first of them follows upon a longer passage in which it is explained, first of all, that scientific research is all nonsense, a childish superstition on the same level as fortune-telling, and then that the only people ever likely to reach an understanding of the universe are saints, the rest of us being reduced to "hints and guesses". The keynote of the closing passage is "resignation". There is a "meaning" in life and also in death; unfortunately we don't know what it is, but the fact that it exists should be a comfort to us as we push up the crocuses, or whatever it is that grows under the yew-trees in country churchyards. But now look at the other two stanzas I have quoted. Though fathered on to somebody else, they probably express what Mr Eliot himself felt about death at that time, at least in certain moods. They are not voicing resignation. On the contrary, they are voicing the pagan attitude towards death, the belief in the next world as a shadowy place full of thin, squeaking ghosts, envious of the living, the belief that however bad life may be, death is worse. This conception of death seems to have been general in antiquity, and in a sense it is general now. "The anguish of the marrow, the ague of the skeleton", Horace's famous ode *"Eheu fugaces"*, and Bloom's unuttered thoughts during Paddy Dignam's funeral, are all very much of a muchness. So long as man regards himself as an individual, his attitude towards death must be one of simple resentment. And however unsatisfactory this may be, if it is intensely felt it is more likely to produce good literature than a religious faith which is not really *felt* at all, but merely accepted against the emotional grain. So far as they can be compared, the two passages I have quoted seem to me to bear this out. I do not think it is questionable that the second of them is superior as verse, and also more intense in feeling, in spite of a tinge of burlesque.

What are these three poems, *Burnt Norton* and the rest, "about"? It is not so easy to say what they are about, but what they appear on the surface to be about is certain localities in England and America with which Mr Eliot has ancestral connections. Mixed up with this is a rather gloomy musing upon the nature and purpose of life, with the rather indefinite conclusion I have mentioned above. Life has a "meaning", but it is not a meaning one feels inclined to grow lyrical about; there is faith, but not much hope, and certainly no enthusiasm. Now the subject-matter of Mr Eliot's early poems was very different from this. They were not hopeful, but neither were they depressed or depressing. If one wants to deal in antitheses, one might say that the later poems express a melancholy faith and the earlier ones a glowing despair. They were based on the dilemma of modern man, who despairs of life and does not want to be dead, and on top of this they expressed the horror of an over-civilised intellectual confronted with the ugliness and spiritual emptiness of the machine age. Instead of "not too far from the yew-tree" the keynote was "weeping, weeping multitudes", or perhaps "the broken fingernails of dirty hands". Naturally these poems were denounced as "decadent" when they first appeared, the attacks only being called off when it was perceived that Eliot's political and social tendencies were reactionary. There was, however, a sense in which the charge of "decadence" could be justified. Clearly these poems were an end-product, the last gasp of a cultural tradition, poems which spoke only for the cultivated third-generation *rentier*, for people able to feel and criticise but no longer able to act. E.M. Forster praised "Prufrock" on its first appearance because "it sang of people who were ineffectual and weak" and because it was "innocent of public spirit" (this was during the other war, when public spirit was a good deal more rampant than it is now). The qualities by which any society which is to last longer than a generation actually has to be sustained—industry, courage, patriotism, frugality, philoprogenitiveness—obviously could not find any place in Eliot's early poems. There was only room for *rentier* values, the values of people too civilised to work, fight or even reproduce themselves. But that was the price that had to be paid, at any rate at that time, for writing a poem worth reading. The mood of lassitude, irony, disbelief, disgust, and not the sort of beefy enthusiasm demanded by the Squires and Herberts, was what sensitive people actually felt. It is fashionable to say that in verse only the words count and the "meaning" is irrelevant, but in fact every poem contains a prose meaning, and when the poem is any good it is a meaning which the poet urgently wishes to express. All art is to some extent propaganda. "Prufrock" is an expression of futility, but it is also a poem of wonderful vitality and power, culminating in a sort of rocket-burst in the closing stanzas:

> I have seen them riding seaward on the waves
> Combing the white hair of the waves blown back
> When the wind blows the water white and black.
>
> We have lingered in the chambers of the sea
> By sea-girls wreathed with seaweed red and brown,
> Till human voices wake us, and we drown.

There is nothing like that in the later poems, although the *rentier* despair on which these lines are founded has been consciously dropped.

But the trouble is that conscious futility is something only for the young. One cannot go on "despairing of life" into a ripe old age. One cannot go on and on being "decadent", since decadence means falling and one can only be said to be falling if one is going to reach the bottom reasonably soon. Sooner or later one is obliged to adopt a positive attitude towards life and society. It would be putting it too crudely to say that every poet in our time must either die young, enter the Catholic Church, or join the Communist Party, but in fact the escape from the consciousness of futility is along those general lines. There are other deaths besides physical death, and there are other sects and creeds besides the Catholic Church and the Communist Party, but it remains true that after a certain age one must either stop writing or dedicate oneself to some purpose not wholly aesthetic. Such a dedication necessarily means a break with the past:

>                    every attempt
> Is a wholly new start, and a different kind of failure
> Because one has only learnt to get the better of words
> For the thing one no longer has to say, or the way in which
> One is no longer disposed to say it. And so each venture
> Is a new beginning, a raid on the inarticulate
> With shabby equipment always deteriorating
> In the general mess of imprecision of feeling,
> Undisciplined squads of emotion.

Eliot's escape from individualism was into the Church, the Anglican Church as it happened. One ought not to assume that the gloomy Pétainism to which he now appears to have given himself over was the unavoidable result of his conversion. The Anglo-Catholic movement does not impose any political "line" on its followers, and a reactionary or austro-Fascist tendency had always been apparent in his work, especially his prose writings. In theory it is still possible to be an orthodox religious believer without being intellectually crippled in the process; but it is far from easy, and in practice books by orthodox believers usually show the same cramped, blinkered outlook as books by orthodox Stalinists or others who are mentally unfree. The reason is that the Christian churches still demand assent to doctrines which no one seriously believes in. The most obvious case is the immortality of the soul. The various "proofs" of personal immortality which can be advanced by Christian apologists are psychologically of no importance; what matters, psychologically, is that hardly anyone nowadays *feels* himself to be immortal. The next world may be in some sense "believed in" but it has not anywhere near the same actuality in people's minds as it had a few centuries ago. Compare for instance the gloomy mumblings of these three poems with "Jerusalem my happy home"; the comparison is not altogether pointless. In the second case you have a man to whom the next world is as real as this one. It is true that his vision of it is incredibly vulgar—a choir practice in a jeweller's shop—but he believes in what he is saying and his belief gives vitality to his words. In the other case you have a man who does not really *feel* his faith, but merely assents to it for complex reasons. It does not in itself give him any fresh literary impulse. At a certain stage he feels the need for a "purpose", and he wants a "purpose" which is reactionary and not progressive; the immediately available refuge is the Church, which demands intellectual absurdities of its members; so his work becomes a continuous nibbling round those absurdities, an attempt to make them acceptable to himself. The Church has not now any living imagery, any new vocabulary to offer:

> The rest
> Is prayer, observance, discipline, thought and action.

Perhaps what we need is prayer, observance, etc but you do not make a line of poetry by stringing those words together. Mr Eliot speaks also of

> the intolerable wrestle
> With words and meanings. The poetry does not matter.

I do not know, but I should imagine that the struggle with meanings would have loomed smaller, and the poetry would have seemed to matter more, if he could have found his way to some creed which did not start off by forcing one to believe the incredible.

There is no saying whether Mr Eliot's development could have been much other than it has been. All writers who are any good develop throughout life, and the general direction of their development is determined. It is absurd to attack Eliot, as some left-wing critics have done, for being a "reactionary" and to imagine that he might have used his gifts in the cause of democracy and Socialism. Obviously a scepticism about democracy and a disbelief in "progress" are an integral part of him; without them he could not have written a line of his works. But it is arguable that he would have done better to go much further in the direction implied in his famous "Anglo-Catholic and Royalist" declaration. He could not have developed into a Socialist, but he might have developed into the last apologist of aristocracy.

Neither feudalism nor indeed Fascism is necessarily deadly to poets, though both are to prose writers. The thing that is really deadly to both is Conservatism of the half-hearted modern kind.

It is at least imaginable that if Eliot had followed wholeheartedly the anti-democratic, anti-perfectionist strain in himself he might have struck a new vein comparable to his earlier one. But the negative Pétainism, which turns its eyes to the past, accepts defeat, writes off earthly happiness as impossible, mumbles about prayer and repentance and thinks it a spiritual advance to see life as "a pattern of living worms in the guts of the women of Canterbury"—that, surely, is the least hopeful road a poet could take.

*Poetry London*, October–November 1942; reprinted in *Little Reviews Anthology*, edited by Denys Val Baker, 1943.

# 37. An Unpublished Letter[1] to the Editor of *The Times*

10a Mortimer Crescent
NW6.
12 October 1942

Sir,

May I be allowed to offer one or two reflections on the British Government's decision to retaliate against German prisoners,[2] which seems so far to have aroused extraordinarily little protest?

By chaining up German prisoners in response to similar action by the Germans, we descend, at any rate in the eyes of the ordinary observer, to the level of our enemies. It is unquestionable when one thinks of the history of the past ten years that there *is* a deep moral difference between democracy and Fascism, but if we go on the principle of an eye for an eye and a tooth for a tooth we simply cause that difference to be forgotten. Moreover, in the matter of ruthlessness we are unlikely to compete successfully with our enemies. As the Italian radio has just proclaimed, the Fascist principle is two eyes for an eye and a whole set of teeth for one tooth. At some point or another public opinion in England will flinch from the implications of this statement, and it is not very difficult to foresee what will happen. As a result of our action the Germans will chain up more British prisoners, we shall have to follow suit by chaining up more Axis prisoners, and so it will continue till logically all the prisoners on either side will be in chains. In practice, of course, we shall become disgusted with the process first, and we shall announce that the chaining up will now cease, leaving, almost certainly, more British than Axis prisoners in fetters. We shall thus have acted both barbarously and weakly, damaging our own good name without succeeding in terrorising the enemy.

It seems to me that the civilised answer to the German action would be something like this: "You proclaim that you are putting thousands of British prisoners in chains because some half-dozen

---

[1] Text taken from a carbon copy.

[2] In August the British and Canadians had made a short raid on Dieppe. The Germans alleged that during the raids the British had tied the hands of German prisoners and that, in reprisal, they were putting a number of British prisoners of war in chains. Whereupon the British Government declared their intention of putting equal numbers of German prisoners in chains.

Germans or thereabouts were temporarily tied up during the
Dieppe raid. This is disgusting hypocrisy, in the first place because
of your own record during the past ten years, in the second place
because troops who have taken prisoners have got to secure them
somehow until they can get them to a place of safety, and to tie
men's hands in such circumstances is totally different from chaining up a helpless prisoner who is already in an internment camp. At
this moment, we cannot stop you maltreating our prisoners, though
we shall probably remember it at the peace settlement, but don't
fear that we shall retaliate in kind. You are Nazis, we are civilised
men. This latest act of yours simply demonstrates the difference."

At this moment this may not seem a very satisfying reply, but
I suggest that to anyone who looks back in three months' time, it
will seem better than what we are doing at present and it is the duty
of those who can keep their heads to protest before the inherently
silly process of retaliation against the helpless is carried any further.

Yours truly,
[George Orwell]

## 38. BBC Internal Memorandum

From: Eric Blair, Indian Section
Subject: Weekly News Commentary
To: Eastern Service Director

Confidential
15 October 1942

With reference to the suggestion that I should write and broadcast
the weekly news review [to India] in English over my own name,
i.e. George Orwell. The four speakers who are at present doing this
in rotation have contracts up to 7 November, after which I will gladly
take this on. But there are one or two points which it would be better
to define clearly beforehand.

If I broadcast as George Orwell I am as it were selling my literary
reputation, which so far as India is concerned probably arises chiefly
from books of anti-imperialist tendency, some of which have been
banned in India. If I gave broadcasts which appeared to endorse
unreservedly the policy of the British Government I should quite

soon be written off as "one more renegade" and should probably miss my potential public, at any rate among the student population. I am not thinking about my personal reputation, but clearly we should defeat our own object in these broadcasts if I could not preserve my position as an independent and more or less "agin the government" commentator. I would therefore like to be sure in advance that I can have reasonable freedom of speech. I think this weekly commentary is only likely to be of value if I can make it from an anti-Fascist rather than imperialist standpoint and avoid mention of subjects on which I could not conscientiously agree with current Government policy.

I do not think this is likely to cause trouble, as the chief difficulty is over Indian internal politics, which we rarely mention in our weekly news commentaries. These commentaries have always followed what is by implication a "left" line, and in fact have contained very little that I would not sign with my own name. But I can imagine situations arising in which I should have to say that I could not in honesty do the commentary for that week, and I should like the position to be defined in advance.[1]

## 39. Letter[2] to T.S. Eliot

[The British Broadcasting Corporation
Broadcasting House,
London, W1]
16 October 1942

Dear Eliot,

I wonder if you would like to take part in a programme on Tuesday November 3rd. We have a magazine number once a month which is called "Voice" and pretends to be a magazine in broadcast form. Where it is possible we try to get poets to read their own work. We usually arrange each number round a central theme and we think next time of having an American number. You are I think the only American poet at present in England, though there may perhaps be others, in which case I should be glad to hear about

---

[1] The BBC authorities were agreeable to Orwell's proposal. He had joined the Eastern Service (Indian Section) of the BBC in the summer of 1941.

[2] Text taken from a carbon copy.

them. In any case we would like it very much if you would take
part and read something of your own, either one or two poems taking
anything up to five minutes in all. The other people who will probably be taking part are Herbert Read, William Empson, myself and
Mulk Raj Anand,[1] though we will try to dig up some American
writers if we can. Please do this if the date is at all possible for you.
It will only mean giving up the morning of that particular day.

Yours sincerely,
[Geo. Orwell]
Talks Producer
Indian Section

## 40. Review

*The British Way in Warfare* by B.H. Liddell Hart

This collection of revised and reprinted essays written from about
1932 onwards, is largely a history of the development of the British
army in the years between the two wars. Its opening chapters, however, contain a survey of Britain's "traditional grand strategy" which
is the most interesting and provocative part of the book and the
most important at this moment. The battle for mechanisation has
been won, at any rate on paper, but the controversy over the Second
Front is still raging, and Captain Liddell Hart's theories are
extremely relevant to it.

What is the "traditional strategy" which we have abandoned and
which Captain Liddell Hart implies that we should return to?
Briefly, the strategy of indirect attack and limited aims. It was
practised with great success in Britain's predatory wars of the
eighteenth century and only dropped in the decade before 1914,
when Britain entered into an all-in alliance with France. Its technique is essentially commercial. You attack your enemy chiefly by
means of blockade, privateering, and sea-borne "commando" raids.
You avoid raising a mass army and leave the land fighting as far as
possible to continental allies whom you keep going by means of

<hr>

[1] Mulk Raj Anand (1905–   ), Indian novelist and critic who broadcast for
Indian Section of the BBC during the war. He was appointed Chairman of the
Lalit Kala Akademi, New Delhi, 1966.

subsidies. While your allies are doing your fighting for you you capture your enemy's overseas trade and occupy his outlying colonies. At the first suitable moment you make peace, either retaining the territories you have captured or using them as bargaining counters. This was, in fact, Britain's characteristic strategy for something like two hundred years, and the term *perfide Albion* was thoroughly justified except in so far as the behaviour of other States was morally similar. The wars of the eighteenth century were waged in a spirit so mercenary that the normal process is reversed, and they seem more "ideological" to posterity than they did to the people who fought in them. But in any case the "limited aims" strategy is not likely to be successful unless you are willing to betray your allies whenever it pays to do so.

In 1914–18, as is well known, we broke with our past, subordinated our strategy to that of an ally, and lost a million dead. Commenting on this Captain Liddell Hart says: "I can find in the conditions of the war no satisfying explanation of our change. . . . No fundamental cause for a change of historic policy seems to appear. Hence one is inclined to find it in a change of fashion—in the military mode of thought inspired by Clausewitz." Clausewitz is the evil genius of military thought. He taught, or is supposed to have taught, that the proper strategy is to attack your strongest enemy, that nothing is solved except by battle, and that "blood is the price of victory". Fascinated by this theory, Britain "made her navy a subsidiary weapon, and grasped the glittering sword of continental manufacture".

Now there is something unsatisfactory in tracing an historical change to an individual theorist, because a theory does not gain ground unless material conditions favour it. If Britain ceased, at any rate for four years, from being *perfide Albion*, there were deeper reasons than Sir Henry Wilson's tie-up with the French General Staff. To begin with it is very doubtful whether our "traditional" strategy is workable any longer. In the past it really depended on the balance of power, more and more precarious from 1870 onwards, and on geographical advantages which modern technical developments have lessened. After 1890 Britain was no longer the only naval power, and moreover the whole scope of naval warfare had diminished. With the abandonment of sail navies became less mobile, the inland seas were inaccessible after the invention of the marine mine, and blockade lost part of its power owing to the science of substitutes and the mechanisation of agriculture. After the rise of modern Germany it was hardly possible for us to dispense with European alliances, and one of the things allies are apt to insist on is that you do your fair share of the fighting. Money subsidies have no meaning when war involves the total effort of every belligerent nation.

The real shortcoming of these stimulating essays, however, lies in Captain Liddell Hart's unwillingness to admit that war has changed its character. "Limited aims" strategy implies that your enemy is very much the same kind of person as yourself; you want to get the better of him, but it is not necessary for your safety to annihilate him or even to interfere with his internal politics. These conditions existed in the eighteenth century and even in the later phases of the Napoleonic wars, but have disappeared in the atomised world in which we are now living. Writing in 1932 or thereabouts, Captain Liddell Hart is able to say, "Has there ever been such a thing as absolute war since nations ceased to exterminate or enslave the defeated?" The trouble is that they haven't ceased. Slavery, which seemed as remote as cannibalism in 1932, is visibly returning in 1942, and in such circumstances it is impossible to wage the old style of limited profit-making war, intent only on "safeguarding British interests" and making peace at the first opportune moment. As Mussolini has truly said, democracy and totalitarianism cannot exist side by side. It is a curious fact, not much remarked on, that in the present war Britain has, up to date, waged the kind of war that Captain Liddell Hart advocates. We have fought no large-scale continental campaign, we have used up one ally after another, and we have acquired territories far larger and, potentially, far richer than those we have lost. Yet neither Captain Liddell Hart nor anyone else would argue from this that the war has gone well for us. Nobody advocates that we should simply wipe up the remaining French and Italian colonies and then make a negotiated peace with Germany because even the most ignorant person sees that such a peace would not be final. Our survival depends on the destruction of the present German political system, which implies the destruction of the German army. It is difficult not to feel that Clausewitz was right in teaching that "you must concentrate against the main enemy, who must be overthrown first", and that "the armed forces form the true objective", at least in any war where there is a genuine ideological issue.

To some extent Captain Liddell Hart's tactical theories are separable from his strategic ones, and here his prophecies have been all too well justified by events. No military writer in our time has done more to enlighten public opinion. But his justified war with the Blimps has perhaps overcoloured his judgment. The people who scoffed at mechanisation and still labour to reduce military training to a routine of barking and stamping are also in favour of mass armies, frontal attacks, bayonet charges and, in general, meaningless bloodshed. Disgusted by the spectacle of Passchendaele, Captain Liddell Hart seems to have ended by believing that wars can be won on the defensive or without fighting—and even, indeed, that a war is better half-won than won outright. That holds good only when your enemy thinks likewise, a state of affairs which disappeared when Europe ceased to be ruled by an aristocracy.

*New Statesman and Nation,* 21 November 1942

# 41. Looking Back on the Spanish War

i

First of all the physical memories, the sounds, the smells and the surfaces of things.

It is curious that more vividly than anything that came afterwards in the Spanish war I remember the week of so-called training that we received before being sent to the front—the huge cavalry barracks in Barcelona with its draughty stables and cobbled yards, the icy cold of the pump where one washed, the filthy meals made tolerable by pannikins of wine, the trousered militia-women chopping firewood, and the roll-call in the early mornings where my prosaic English name made a sort of comic interlude among the resounding Spanish ones, Manuel Gonzalez, Pedro Aguilar, Ramon Fenellosa, Roque Ballaster, Jaime Domenech, Sebastian Viltron, Ramon Nuvo Bosch. I name those particular men because I remember the faces of all of them. Except for two who were mere riff-raff and have doubtless become good Falangists by this time, it is probable that all of them are dead. Two of them I know to be dead. The eldest would have been about twenty-five, the youngest sixteen.

One of the essential experiences of war is never being able to escape from disgusting smells of human origin. Latrines are an overworked subject in war literature, and I would not mention them if it were not that the latrine in our barracks did its necessary bit towards puncturing my own illusions about the Spanish civil war. The Latin type of latrine, at which you have to squat, is bad enough at its best, but these were made of some kind of polished stone so slippery that it was all you could do to keep on your feet. In addition they were always blocked. Now I have plenty of other disgusting things in my memory, but I believe it was these latrines that first brought home to me the thought, so often to recur: "Here we are, soldiers of a revolutionary army, defending democracy against Fascism, fighting a war which is *about* something, and the detail of our lives is just as sordid and degrading as it could be in prison, let alone in a bourgeois army." Many other things reinforced this impression later; for instance, the boredom and animal hunger of trench life, the squalid intrigues over scraps of food, the mean, nagging quarrels which people exhausted by lack of sleep indulge in.

The essential horror of army life (whoever has been a soldier will know what I mean by the essential horror of army life) is barely affected by the nature of the war you happen to be fighting in. Discipline, for instance, is ultimately the same in all armies. Orders have to be obeyed and enforced by punishment if necessary, the relationship of officer and man has to be the relationship of superior and inferior. The picture of war set forth in books like *All Quiet on the Western Front* is substantially true. Bullets hurt, corpses stink, men under fire are often so frightened that they wet their trousers. It is true that the social background from which an army springs will colour its training, tactics and general efficiency, and also that the consciousness of being in the right can bolster up morale, though this affects the civilian population more than the troops. (People forget that a soldier anywhere near the front line is usually too hungry, or frightened, or cold, or, above all, too tired to bother about the political origins of the war.) But the laws of nature are not suspended for a "red" army any more than for a "white" one. A louse is a louse and a bomb is a bomb, even though the cause you are fighting for happens to be just.

Why is it worth while to point out anything so obvious? Because the bulk of the British and American intelligentsia were manifestly unaware of it then, and are now. Our memories are short nowadays, but look back a bit, dig out the files of *New Masses* or the *Daily Worker*, and just have a look at the romantic warmongering muck that our left-wingers were spilling at that time. All the stale old phrases! And the unimaginative callousness of it! The sang-froid with which London faced the bombing of Madrid! Here I am not bothering about the counter-propagandists of the Right, the Lunns, Garvins *et hoc genus*; they go without saying. But here were the very people who for twenty years had hooted and jeered at the "glory" of war, at atrocity stories, at patriotism, even at physical courage, coming out with stuff that with the alteration of a few names would have fitted into the *Daily Mail* of 1918. If there was one thing that the British intelligentsia were committed to, it was the debunking version of war, the theory that war is all corpses and latrines and never leads to any good result. Well, the same people who in 1933 sniggered pityingly if you said that in certain circumstances you would fight for your country, in 1937 were denouncing you as a Trotsky-Fascist if you suggested that the stories in *New Masses* about freshly wounded men clamouring to get back into the fighting might be exaggerated. And the Left intelligentsia made their swing-over from "War is hell" to "War is glorious" not only with no sense of incongruity but almost without any intervening stage. Later the bulk of them were to make other transitions equally violent. There must be a quite large number of people, a sort of central core of the intelligentsia, who approved the "King and Country" declaration in 1935, shouted for a "firm line" against Germany in 1937, supported the People's Convention in 1940, and are demanding a Second Front now.

As far as the mass of the people go, the extraordinary swings of opinion which occur nowadays, the emotions which can be turned on and off like a tap, are the result of newspaper and radio hypnosis. In the intelligentsia I should say they result rather from money and mere physical safety. At a given moment they may be "pro-war" or "anti-war", but in either case they have no realistic picture of war in their minds. When they enthused over the Spanish war they knew, of course, that people were being killed and that to be killed is unpleasant, but they did feel that for a soldier in the Spanish Republican army the experience of war was somehow not degrading. Somehow the latrines stank less, discipline was less irksome. You have only to glance at the *New Statesman* to see that they believed that; exactly similar blah is being written about the Red army at this moment. We have become too civilised to grasp the obvious. For the truth is very simple. To survive you often have to fight, and to fight you have to dirty yourself. War is evil, and it is often the lesser evil. Those who take the sword perish by the sword, and those who don't take the sword perish by smelly diseases. The fact that such a platitude is worth writing down shows what the years of *rentier* capitalism have done to us.

## ii

In connection with what I have just said, a footnote on atrocities.

I have little direct evidence about the atrocities in the Spanish civil war. I know that some were committed by the Republicans, and far more (they are still continuing) by the Fascists. But what impressed me then, and has impressed me ever since, is that atrocities are believed in or disbelieved in solely on grounds of political predilection. Everyone believes in the atrocities of the enemy and disbelieves in those of his own side, without ever bothering to examine the evidence. Recently I drew up a table of atrocities during the period between 1918 and the present; there was never a year when atrocities were not occurring somewhere or other, and there was hardly a single case when the Left and the Right believed in the same stories simultaneously. And stranger yet, at any moment the situation can suddenly reverse itself and yesterday's proved-to-the-hilt atrocity story can become a ridiculous lie, merely because the political landscape has changed.

In the present war we are in the curious situation that our "atrocity campaign" was done largely before the war started, and done mostly by the Left, the people who normally pride themselves on their incredulity. In the same period the Right, the atrocity-mongers of 1914–18, were gazing at Nazi Germany and flatly refusing to see any evil in it. Then as soon as war broke out it was the pro-Nazis of yesterday who were repeating horror stories, while the anti-Nazis suddenly found themselves doubting whether the Gestapo really existed. Nor was this solely the result of the Russo-German Pact. It was partly because before the war the Left had wrongly believed that Britain and Germany would never fight and were therefore able to be anti-German and anti-British simultaneously; partly also because official war propaganda, with its disgusting hypocrisy and self-righteousness, always tends to make thinking people sympathise with the enemy. Part of the price we paid for the systematic lying of 1914–18 was the exaggerated pro-German reaction which followed. During the years 1918–33 you were hooted at in left-wing circles if you suggested that Germany bore even a fraction of responsibility for the war. In all the denunciations of Versailles I listened to during those years I don't think I ever once heard the question, "What would have happened if Germany had won?" even mentioned, let alone discussed. So also with atrocities. The truth, it is felt, becomes untruth when your enemy utters it. Recently I noticed that the very people who swallowed any and every horror story about the Japanese in Nanking in 1937 refused to believe exactly the same stories about Hong Kong in 1942. There was even a tendency to feel that the Nanking atrocities had become, as it were, retrospectively untrue because the British Government now drew attention to them.

But unfortunately the truth about atrocities is far worse than that they are lied about and made into propaganda. The truth is that they happen. The fact often adduced as a reason for scepticism—that the same horror stories come up in war after war—merely makes it rather more likely that these stories are true. Evidently they are widespread fantasies, and war provides an opportunity of putting them into practice. Also, although it has ceased to be fashionable to say so, there is little question that what one may roughly call the "whites" commit far more and worse atrocities than the "reds". There is not the slightest doubt, for instance, about the behaviour of the Japanese in China. Nor is there much doubt about the long tale of Fascist outrages during the last ten years in Europe. The volume of testimony is enormous, and a respectable proportion of it comes from the German press and radio. These things really happened, that is the thing to keep one's eye on. They happened even though Lord Halifax said they happened. The raping and butchering in Chinese cities, the tortures in the cellars of the Gestapo, the elderly Jewish professors flung into cesspools, the machine-gunning of refugees along the Spanish roads—they all happened, and they did not happen any the less because the *Daily Telegraph* has suddenly found out about them when it is five years too late.

### iii

Two memories, the first not proving anything in particular, the second, I think, giving one a certain insight into the atmosphere of a revolutionary period.

Early one morning another man and I had gone out to snipe at the Fascists in the trenches outside Huesca. Their line and ours here lay three hundred yards apart, at which range our aged rifles would not shoot accurately, but by sneaking out to a spot about a hundred yards from the Fascist trench you might, if you were lucky, get a shot at someone through a gap in the parapet. Unfortunately the ground between was a flat beetfield with no cover except a few ditches, and it was necessary to go out while it was still dark and return soon after dawn, before the light became too good. This time no Fascists appeared, and we stayed too long and were caught by the dawn. We were in a ditch, but behind us were two hundred yards of flat ground with hardly enough cover for a rabbit. We were still trying to nerve ourselves to make a dash for it when there was an uproar and a blowing of whistles in the Fascist trench. Some of our aeroplanes were coming over. At this moment a man, presumably carrying a message to an officer, jumped out of the trench and ran along the top of the parapet in full view. He was half-dressed and was holding up his trousers with both hands as he ran. I refrained from shooting at him. It is true that I am a poor shot and unlikely to hit a running man at a hundred yards, and also that I was thinking chiefly about getting back to our trench while the Fascists had their attention fixed on the aeroplanes. Still, I did not shoot partly because of that detail about the trousers. I had come here to shoot at "Fascists"; but a man who is holding up his trousers isn't a "Fascist", he is visibly a fellow creature, similar to yourself, and you don't feel like shooting at him.

What does this incident demonstrate? Nothing very much, because it is the kind of thing that happens all the time in all wars. The other is different. I don't suppose that in telling it I can make it moving to you who read it, but I ask you to believe that it is moving to me, as an incident characteristic of the moral atmosphere of a particular moment in time.

One of the recruits who joined us while I was at the barracks was a wild-looking boy from the back streets of Barcelona. He was ragged and barefooted. He was also extremely dark (Arab blood, I dare say), and made gestures you do not usually see a European make; one in particular—the arm outstretched, the palm vertical—was a gesture characteristic of Indians. One day a bundle of cigars, which you could still buy dirt cheap at that time, was stolen out of my bunk. Rather foolishly I reported this to the officer, and one of the scallywags I have already mentioned promptly came forward and said quite untruly that twenty-five pesetas had been stolen from his bunk. For some reason the officer instantly decided that the brown-faced boy must be the thief. They were very hard on stealing in the militia, and in theory people could be shot for it. The wretched boy allowed himself to be led off to the guardroom to be searched. What most struck me was that he barely attempted to protest his innocence. In the fatalism of his attitude you could see the desperate poverty in which he had been bred. The officer ordered him to take his clothes off. With a humility which was horrible to me he stripped himself naked, and his clothes were searched. Of course neither the cigars nor the money were there; in fact he had not stolen them. What was most painful of all was that he seemed no less ashamed after his innocence had been established. That night I took him to the pictures and gave him brandy and chocolate. But that too was horrible—I mean the attempt to wipe out an injury with money. For a few minutes I had half believed him to be a thief, and that could not be wiped out.

Well, a few weeks later at the front I had trouble with one of the men in my section. By this time I was a "cabo", or corporal, in command of twelve men. It was static warfare, horribly cold, and the chief job was getting sentries to stay awake and at their posts. One day a man suddenly refused to go to a certain post, which he said quite truly was exposed to enemy fire. He was a feeble creature, and I seized hold of him and began to drag him towards his post. This roused the feelings of the others against me, for Spaniards, I think, resent being touched more than we do. Instantly I was surrounded by a ring of shouting men: "Fascist! Fascist! Let that man go! This isn't a bourgeois army. Fascist!" etc etc. As best I could in my bad Spanish I shouted back that orders had got to be obeyed, and the row developed into one of those enormous arguments by means of which discipline is gradually hammered out in revolutionary armies. Some said I was right, others said I was wrong. But the point is that the one who took my side the most warmly of all was the brown-faced boy. As soon as he saw what was happening he sprang into the ring and began passionately defending me. With his strange, wild, Indian gesture he kept exclaiming, "He's the best corporal we've got!" (*¡No hay cabo como el!*) Later on he applied for leave to exchange into my section.

Why is this incident touching to me? Because in any normal circumstances it would have been impossible for good feelings ever to be re-established between this boy and myself. The implied accusation of theft would not have been made any better, probably somewhat worse, by my efforts to make amends. One of the effects of safe and civilised life is an immense oversensitiveness which makes all the primary emotions seem somewhat disgusting. Generosity is as painful as meanness, gratitude as hateful as ingratitude. But in Spain in 1936 we were not living in a normal time. It was a time when generous feelings and gestures were easier than they ordinarily are. I could relate a dozen similar incidents, not really communicable but bound up in my own mind with the special atmosphere of the time, the shabby clothes and the gay-coloured revolutionary posters, the universal use of the word "comrade", the anti-Fascist ballads printed on flimsy paper and sold for a penny, the phrases like "international proletarian solidarity", pathetically repeated by ignorant men who believed them to mean something. Could you feel friendly towards somebody, and stick up for him in a quarrel, after you had been ignominiously searched in his presence for property you were supposed to have stolen from him? No, you couldn't; but you might if you had both been through some emotionally widening experience. That is one of the by-products of revolution, though in this case it was only the beginnings of a revolution, and obviously foredoomed to failure.

iv

The struggle for power between the Spanish Republican parties is an unhappy, far-off thing which I have no wish to revive at this date. I only mention it in order to say: believe nothing, or next to nothing, of what you read about internal affairs on the Government side. It is all, from whatever source, party propaganda—that is to say, lies. The broad truth about the war is simple enough. The Spanish bourgeoisie saw their chance of crushing the labour movement, and took it, aided by the Nazis and by the forces of reaction all over the world. It is doubtful whether more than that will ever be established.

I remember saying once to Arthur Koestler, "History stopped in 1936," at which he nodded in immediate understanding. We were both thinking of totalitarianism in general, but more particularly of the Spanish civil war. Early in life I had noticed that no event is ever correctly reported in a newspaper, but in Spain, for the first time, I saw newspaper reports which did not bear any relation to the facts, not even the relationship which is implied in an ordinary lie. I saw great battles reported where there had been no fighting, and complete silence where hundreds of men had been killed. I saw troops who had fought bravely denounced as cowards and traitors, and others who had never seen a shot fired hailed as the heroes of imaginary victories; and I saw newspapers in London retailing these lies and eager intellectuals building emotional superstructures over events that had never happened. I saw, in fact, history being written not in terms of what happened but of what ought to have happened according to various "party lines". Yet in a way, horrible as all this was, it was unimportant. It concerned secondary issues—namely, the struggle for power between the Comintern and the Spanish left-wing parties, and the efforts of the Russian Government to prevent revolution in Spain. But the broad picture of the war which the Spanish Government presented to the world was not untruthful. The main issues were what it said they were. But as for the Fascists and their backers, how could they come even as near to the truth as that? How could they possibly mention their real aims? Their version of the war was pure fantasy, and in the circumstances it could not have been otherwise.

The only propaganda line open to the Nazis and Fascists was to represent themselves as Christian patriots saving Spain from a Russian dictatorship. This involved pretending that life in Government Spain was just one long massacre (*vide* the *Catholic Herald* or the *Daily Mail*—but these were child's play compared with the continental Fascist press), and it involved immensely exaggerating the scale of Russian intervention. Out of the huge pyramid of lies which the Catholic and reactionary press all over the world built up, let me take just one point—the presence in Spain of a Russian army. Devout Franco partisans all believed in this; estimates of its strength went as high as half a million. Now, there was no Russian army in Spain. There may have been a handful of airmen and other technicians, a few hundred at the most, but an army there was not. Some thousands of foreigners who fought in Spain, not to mention millions of Spaniards, were witnesses of this. Well, their testimony made no impression at all upon the Franco propagandists, not one of whom had set foot in Government Spain. Simultaneously these people refused utterly to admit the fact of German or Italian intervention, at the same time as the German and Italian press were openly boasting about the exploits of their "legionaries". I have chosen to mention only one point, but in fact the whole of Fascist propaganda about the war was on this level.

This kind of thing is frightening to me, because it often gives me the feeling that the very concept of objective truth is fading out of the world. After all, the chances are that those lies, or at any rate similar lies, will pass into history. How will the history of the Spanish war be written? If Franco remains in power his nominees will write the history books, and (to stick to my chosen point) that Russian army which never existed will become historical fact, and schoolchildren will learn about it generations hence. But suppose Fascism is finally defeated and some kind of democratic government restored in Spain in the fairly near future; even then, how is the history of the war to be written? What kind of records will Franco have left behind him? Suppose even that the records kept on the Government side are recoverable—even so, how is a true history of the war to be written? For, as I have pointed out already, the Government also dealt extensively in lies. From the anti-Fascist angle one could write a broadly truthful history of the war, but it would be a partisan history, unreliable on every minor point. Yet, after all, *some* kind of history will be written, and after those who actually remember the war are dead, it will be universally accepted. So for all practical purposes the lie will have become truth.

I know it is the fashion to say that most of recorded history is lies anyway. I am willing to believe that history is for the most part inaccurate and biased, but what is peculiar to our own age is the abandonment of the idea that history *could* be truthfully written. In the past people deliberately lied, or they unconsciously coloured what they wrote, or they struggled after the truth, well knowing that they must make many mistakes; but in each case they believed that "the facts" existed and were more or less discoverable. And in practice there was always a considerable body of fact which would have been agreed to by almost everyone. If you look up the history of the last war in, for instance, the *Encyclopaedia Britannica*, you will find that a respectable amount of the material is drawn from German sources. A British and a German historian would disagree deeply on many things, even on fundamentals, but there would still be that body of, as it were, neutral fact on which neither would seriously challenge the other. It is just this common basis of agreement, with its implication that human beings are all one species of animal, that totalitarianism destroys. Nazi theory indeed specifically denies that such a thing as "the truth" exists. There is, for instance, no such thing as "science". There is only "German science",

"Jewish science" etc. The implied objective of this line of thought is a nightmare world in which the Leader, or some ruling clique, controls not only the future but *the past*. If the Leader says of such and such an event, "It never happened"—well, it never happened. If he says that two and two are five—well, two and two are five. This prospect frightens me much more than bombs—and after our experiences of the last few years that is not a frivolous statement.

But is it perhaps childish or morbid to terrify oneself with visions of a totalitarian future? Before writing off the totalitarian world as a nightmare that can't come true, just remember that in 1925 the world of today would have seemed a nightmare that couldn't come true. Against that shifting phantasmagoric world in which black may be white tomorrow and yesterday's weather can be changed by decree, there are in reality only two safeguards. One is that however much you deny the truth, the truth goes on existing, as it were, behind your back, and you consequently can't violate it in ways that impair military efficiency. The other is that so long as some parts of the earth remain unconquered, the liberal tradition can be kept alive. Let Fascism, or possibly even a combination of several Fascisms, conquer the whole world, and those two conditions no longer exist. We in England underrate the danger of this kind of thing, because our traditions and our past security have given us a sentimental belief that it all comes right in the end and the thing you most fear never really happens. Nourished for hundreds of years on a literature in which Right invariably triumphs in the last chapter, we believe half-instinctively that evil always defeats itself in the long run. Pacifism, for instance, is founded largely on this belief. Don't resist evil, and it will somehow destroy itself. But why should it? What evidence is there that it does? And what instance is there of a modern industrialised state collapsing unless conquered from the outside by military force?

Consider for instance the re-institution of slavery. Who could have imagined twenty years ago that slavery would return to Europe? Well, slavery has been restored under our noses. The forced-labour camps all over Europe and North Africa where Poles, Russians, Jews and political prisoners of every race toil at road-making or swamp-draining for their bare rations, are simple chattel slavery. The most one can say is that the buying and selling of slaves by individuals is not yet permitted. In other ways—the breaking-up of families, for instance—the conditions are probably worse than they were on the American cotton plantations. There is no reason for thinking that this state of affairs will change while any totalitarian domination endures. We don't grasp its full implications, because in our mystical way we feel that a régime founded on slavery *must* collapse. But it is worth comparing the duration of the slave empires of antiquity with that of any modern state. Civilisations founded on slavery have lasted for such periods as four thousand years.

When I think of antiquity, the detail that frightens me is that those hundreds of millions of slaves on whose backs civilisation rested generation after generation have left behind them no record whatever. We do not even know their names. In the whole of Greek and Roman history, how many slaves' names are known to you? I can think of two, or possibly three. One is Spartacus and the other is Epictetus. Also, in the Roman room at the British Museum there is a glass jar with the maker's name inscribed on the bottom, "*Felix fecit*". I have a vivid mental picture of poor Felix (a Gaul with red hair and a metal collar round his neck), but in fact he may not have been a slave; so there are only two slaves whose names I definitely know, and probably few people can remember more. The rest have gone down into utter silence.

v

The backbone of the resistance against Franco was the Spanish working class, especially the urban trade union members. In the long run—it is important to remember that it is only in the long run—the working class remains the most reliable enemy of Fascism, simply because the working class stands to gain most by a decent reconstruction of society. Unlike other classes or categories, it can't be permanently bribed.

To say this is not to idealise the working class. In the long struggle that has followed the Russian Revolution it is the manual workers who have been defeated, and it is impossible not to feel that it was their own fault. Time after time, in country after country, the organised working-class movements have been crushed by open, illegal violence, and their comrades abroad, linked to them in theoretical solidarity, have simply looked on and done nothing; and underneath this, secret cause of many betrayals, has lain the fact that between white and coloured workers there is not even lip-service to solidarity. Who can believe in the class-conscious international proletariat after the events of the past ten years? To the British working class the massacre of their comrades in Vienna, Berlin,

Madrid, or wherever it might be, seemed less interesting and less important than yesterday's football match. Yet this does not alter the fact that the working class will go on struggling against Fascism after the others have caved in. One feature of the Nazi conquest of France was the astonishing defections among the intelligentsia, including some of the left-wing political intelligentsia. The intelligentsia are the people who squeal loudest against Fascism, and yet a respectable proportion of them collapse into defeatism when the pinch comes. They are far-sighted enough to see the odds against them, and more-over they can be bribed—for it is evident that the Nazis think it worth while to bribe intellectuals. With the working class it is the other way about. Too ignorant to see through the trick that is being played on them, they easily swallow the promises of Fascism, yet sooner or later they always take up the struggle again. They must do so, because in their own bodies they always discover that the promises of Fascism cannot be fulfilled. To win over the working class permanently, the Fascists would have to raise the general standard of living, which they are unable and probably unwilling to do. The struggle of the working class is like the growth of a plant. The plant is blind and stupid, but it knows enough to keep pushing upwards towards the light, and it will do this in the face of endless discouragements. What are the workers struggling for? Simply for the decent life which they are more and more aware is now technically possible. Their consciousness of this aim ebbs and flows. In Spain, for a while, people were acting consciously, moving towards a goal which they wanted to reach and believed they could reach. It accounted for the curiously buoyant feeling that life in Government Spain had during the early months of the war. The common people knew in their bones that the Republic was their friend and Franco was their enemy. They knew that they were in the right, because they were fighting for something which the world owed them and was able to give them.

One has to remember this to see the Spanish war in its true perspective. When one thinks of the cruelty, squalor, and futility of war—and in this particular case of the intrigues, the persecutions, the lies and the misunderstandings—there is always the temptation to say: "One side is as bad as the other. I am neutral." In practice, however, one cannot be neutral, and there is hardly such a thing as a war in which it makes no difference who wins. Nearly always one side stands more or less for progress, the other side more or less for reaction. The hatred which the Spanish Republic excited in millionaires, dukes, cardinals, play-boys, Blimps and what not would in itself be enough to show one how the land lay. In essence it was a class war. If it had been won, the cause of the common people everywhere would have been strengthened. It was lost, and the dividend-drawers all over the world rubbed their hands. That was the real issue; all else was froth on its surface.

vi

The outcome of the Spanish war was settled in London, Paris, Rome, Berlin—at any rate not in Spain. After the summer of 1937 those with eyes in their heads realised that the Government could not win the war unless there was some profound change in the international set-up, and in deciding to fight on Negrin and the others may have been partly influenced by the expectation that the world war which actually broke out in 1939 was coming in 1938. The much-publicised disunity on the Government side was not a main cause of defeat. The Government militias were hurriedly raised, ill-armed and unimaginative in their military outlook, but they would have been the same if complete political agreement had existed from the start. At the outbreak of war the average Spanish factory-worker did not even know how to fire a rifle (there had never been universal conscription in Spain), and the traditional pacifism of the Left was a great handicap. The thousands of foreigners who served in Spain made good infantry, but there were very few experts of any kind among them. The Trotskyist thesis that the war could have been won if the revolution had not been sabotaged was probably false. To nationalise factories, demolish churches, and issue revolutionary manifestos would not have made the armies more efficient. The Fascists won because they were the stronger; they had modern arms and the others hadn't. No political strategy could offset that.

The most baffling thing in the Spanish war was the behaviour of the great powers. The war was actually won for Franco by the Germans and Italians, whose motives were obvious enough. The motives of France and Britain are less easy to understand. In 1936 it was clear to everyone that if Britain would only help the Spanish Government, even to the extent of a few million pounds' worth of arms, Franco would collapse and German strategy would be severely dislocated. By that time one did not need to be a clair-voyant to foresee that war between Britain and Germany was coming; one could even foretell within a year or two when it would come. Yet in the most mean, cowardly, hypocritical way the British ruling class did all they could to hand Spain over to Franco and the Nazis. Why? Because they were pro-Fascist, was the obvious answer. Undoubtedly they were, and yet when it came to the final show-down they chose to stand up to Germany. It is still very uncertain what plan they acted on in backing Franco, and they may have had no clear plan at all. Whether the British ruling class are wicked or merely stupid is one of the most difficult questions of our time, and at certain moments a very important question. As to the Russians, their motives in the Spanish war are completely inscrutable. Did they, as the pinks believed, intervene in Spain in order to defend democracy and thwart the Nazis? Then why did they intervene on such a niggardly scale and finally leave Spain in the lurch? Or did they, as the Catholics maintained, intervene in order to foster revolution in Spain? Then why did they do all in their power to crush the Spanish revolutionary movements, defend private property and hand power to the middle class as against the working class? Or did they, as the Trotskyists suggested, intervene simply in order to *prevent* a Spanish revolution? Then why not have backed Franco? Indeed, their actions are most easily explained if one assumes that they were acting on several contradictory motives. I believe that in the future we shall come to feel that Stalin's foreign policy, instead of being so diabolically clever as it is claimed to be, has been merely opportunistic and stupid. But at any rate, the Spanish civil war demonstrated that the Nazis knew what they were doing and their opponents did not. The war was fought at a low technical level and its major strategy was very simple. That side which had arms would win. The Nazis and the Italians gave arms to their Spanish Fascist friends, and the western democracies and the Russians didn't give arms to those who should have been their friends. So the Spanish Republic perished, having "gained what no republic missed".

Whether it was right, as all left-wingers in other countries undoubtedly did, to encourage the Spaniards to go on fighting when they could not win is a question hard to answer. I myself think it was right, because I believe that it is better even from the point of view of survival to fight and be conquered than to surrender without fighting. The effects on the grand strategy of the struggle against Fascism cannot be assessed yet. The ragged, weaponless armies of the Republic held out for two and a half years, which was undoubtedly longer than their enemies expected. But whether that dislocated the Fascist time-table, or whether, on the other hand, it merely postponed the major war and gave the Nazis extra time to get their war machine into trim, is still uncertain.

### vii

I never think of the Spanish war without two memories coming into my mind. One is of the hospital ward at Lerida and the rather sad voices of the wounded militiamen singing some song with a refrain that ended:

> *Una resolucion,*
> *Luchar hast' al fin!*

Well, they fought to the end all right. For the last eighteen months of the war the Republican armies must have been fighting almost without cigarettes, and with precious little food. Even when I left Spain in the middle of 1937, meat and bread were scarce, tobacco a rarity, coffee and sugar almost unobtainable.

The other memory is of the Italian militiaman who shook my hand in the guardroom, the day I joined the militia. I wrote about this man at the beginning of my book on the Spanish war,[1] and do not want to repeat what I said there. When I remember—oh, how vividly!—his shabby uniform and fierce, pathetic, innocent face, the complex side-issues of the war seem to fade away and I see clearly that there was at any rate no doubt as to who was in the right. In spite of power politics and journalistic lying, the central issue of the war was the attempt of people like this to win the decent life which they knew to be their birthright. It is difficult to think of this particular man's probable end without several kinds of bitterness. Since I met him in the Lenin Barracks he was probably a Trotskyist or an Anarchist, and in the peculiar conditions of our time, when people of that sort are not killed by the Gestapo they are usually killed by the GPU. But that does not affect the long-term issues. This man's face, which I saw only for a minute or two, remains with me as a sort of visual reminder of what the war was really about. He symbolises for me the flower of the European working class, harried by the police of all countries, the people who fill the mass graves of the Spanish battlefields and are now, to the tune of several millions, rotting in forced-labour camps.

[1] *Homage to Catalonia.*

When one thinks of all the people who support or have supported Fascism, one stands amazed at their diversity. What a crew! Think of a programme which at any rate for a while could bring Hitler, Pétain, Montagu Norman, Pavelitch, William Randolph Hearst, Streicher, Buchman, Ezra Pound, Juan March, Cocteau, Thyssen, Father Coughlin, the Mufti of Jerusalem, Arnold Lunn, Antonescu, Spengler, Beverley Nichols, Lady Houston, and Marinetti all into the same boat! But the clue is really very simple. They are all people with something to lose, or people who long for a hierarchical society and dread the prospect of a world of free and equal human beings. Behind all the ballyhoo that is talked about "godless" Russia and the "materialism" of the working class lies the simple intention of those with money or privileges to cling to them. Ditto, though it contains a partial truth, with all the talk about the worthlessness of social reconstruction not accompanied by a "change of heart". The pious ones, from the Pope to the yogis of California, are great on the "change of heart", much more reassuring from their point of view than a change in the economic system. Pétain attributes the fall of France to the common people's "love of pleasure". One sees this in its right perspective if one stops to wonder how much pleasure the ordinary French peasant's or working-man's life would contain compared with Pétain's own. The damned impertinence of these politicians, priests, literary men, and what not who lecture the working-class Socialist for his "materialism"! All that the working man demands is what these others would consider the indispensable minimum without which human life cannot be lived at all. Enough to eat, freedom from the haunting terror of unemployment, the knowledge that your children will get a fair chance, a bath once a day, clean linen reasonably often, a roof that doesn't leak, and short enough working hours to leave you with a little energy when the day is done. Not one of those who preach against "materialism" would consider life livable without these things. And how easily that minimum could be attained if we chose to set our minds to it for only twenty years! To raise the standard of living of the whole world to that of Britain would not be a greater undertaking than the war we are now fighting. I don't claim, and I don't know who does, that that would solve anything in itself. It is merely that privation and brute labour have to be abolished before the real problems of humanity can be tackled. The major problem of our time is the decay of the belief in personal immortality, and it cannot be dealt with while the

average human being is either drudging like an ox or shivering in
fear of the secret police. How right the working classes are in their
"materialism"! How right they are to realise that the belly comes
before the soul, not in the scale of values but in point of time!
Understand that, and the long horror that we are enduring becomes
at least intelligible. All the considerations that are likely to make one
falter—the siren voices of a Pétain or of a Gandhi, the inescapable
fact that in order to fight one has to degrade oneself, the equivocal
moral position of Britain, with its democratic phrases and its coolie
empire, the sinister development of Soviet Russia, the squalid farce
of left-wing politics—all this fades away and one sees only the
struggle of the gradually awakening common people against the
lords of property and their hired liars and bumsuckers. The question
is very simple. Shall people like that Italian soldier be allowed to live
the decent, fully human life which is now technically achievable, or
shan't they? Shall the common man be pushed back into the mud, or
shall he not? I myself believe, perhaps on insufficient grounds, that
the common man will win his fight sooner or later, but I want it to
be sooner and not later—some time within the next hundred years,
say, and not some time within the next ten thousand years. That was
the real issue of the Spanish war, and of the present war, and perhaps
of other wars yet to come.

I never saw the Italian militiaman again, nor did I ever learn
his name. It can be taken as quite certain that he is dead. Nearly
two years later, when the war was visibly lost, I wrote these verses
in his memory:

> The Italian soldier shook my hand
> Beside the guard-room table;
> The strong hand and the subtle hand
> Whose palms are only able
>
> To meet within the sound of guns,
> But oh! what peace I knew then
> In gazing on his battered face
> Purer than any woman's!
>
> For the flyblown words that make me spew
> Still in his ears were holy,
> And he was born knowing what I had learned
> Out of books and slowly.

The treacherous guns had told their tale
And we both had bought it,
But my gold brick was made of gold—
Oh! who ever would have thought it?

Good luck go with you, Italian soldier!
But luck is not for the brave;
What would the world give back to you?
Always less than you gave.

Between the shadow and the ghost,
Between the white and the red,
Between the bullet and the lie,
Where would hide your head?

For where is Manuel Gonzalez,
And where is Pedro Aguilar,
And where is Ramon Fenellosa?
The earthworms know where they are.

Your name and your deeds were forgotten
Before your bones were dry,
And the lie that slew you is buried
Under a deeper lie;

But the thing that I saw in your face
No power can disinherit:
No bomb that ever burst
Shatters the crystal spirit.

Written [Autumn 1942]; Sections i, ii, iii, and vii printed in *New Road*, [June?] 1943; full version in SJ; EYE; CE.

## 42. Letter to George Woodcock

10a Mortimer Crescent
NW6
2 December 1942

Dear Woodcock,

I'm sorry I didn't get round to answering your letter earlier, but I am very busy these days. I am afraid I answered rather roughly in the *Partisan Review* controversy,[1] I always do when I am attacked—however, no malice either side, I hope.

I can't help smiling at your (a) not accepting the fee after doing a broadcast for the BBC & (b) "suspecting a trap" when asked to b'cast. As a matter of fact it was Mulk's[2] idea to ask you. That particular b'cast is a bit of private lunacy we indulge in once a month & I would be surprised if it is listened-in to by 500 people. In any case there is no question of getting to the Indian *masses* with any sort of b'cast, because they don't possess radios, certainly not shortwave sets. In our outfit we are really only b'casting for the students, who, however, won't listen to anything except news & perhaps music while the political situation is what it is.

I am sorry that what I said abt "financially profitable" rankled—I didn't mean it to apply to you or any of the others personally, merely to the whole process of literary racketeering abt which doubtless you know as well as I do.

As to the ethics of b'casting & in general letting oneself be used by the British governing class. It's of little value to argue abt it, it is chiefly a question of whether one considers it more important to down the Nazis first or whether one believes doing this is meaningless unless one achieves one's own revolution first. But for heaven's sake don't think I don't see how they are using me. A subsidiary point is that one can't effectively remain outside the war & by working inside an institution like the BBC one can perhaps deodorise it to some small extent. I doubt whether I shall stay in this job very much longer, but while here I consider I have kept our propaganda slightly less disgusting than it might otherwise have been. I am trying to get some of our b'casts for the Indian section published in book form.[3] If this goes through you may see from the book that our b'casts, though of course much as all radio stuff is, aren't as bad as they might be. To appreciate this you have to be as I am in constant touch with propaganda Axis & Allied. Till then you don't realise what muck & filth is normally flowing through the air. I consider I have kept our little corner of it fairly clean.

Yours
Geo. Orwell

[1] See 34.
[2] Mulk Raj Anand.
[3] Published as *Talking to India*, edited by George Orwell, 1943.

1943

# 43. W.B. Yeats

One thing that Marxist criticism has not succeeded in doing is to trace the connection between "tendency" and literary style. The subject-matter and imagery of a book can be explained in sociological terms, but its texture seemingly cannot. Yet some such connection there must be. One knows, for instance, that a Socialist would not write like Chesterton or a Tory imperialist like Bernard Shaw, though *how* one knows it is not easy to say. In the case of Yeats, there must be some kind of connection between his wayward, even tortured style of writing and his rather sinister vision of life. Mr Menon[1] is chiefly concerned with the esoteric philosophy underlying Yeats's work, but the quotations which are scattered all through his interesting book serve to remind one how artificial Yeats's manner of writing was. As a rule, this artificiality is accepted as Irishism, or Yeats is even credited with simplicity because he uses short words, but in fact one seldom comes on six consecutive lines of his verse in which there is not an archaism or an affected turn of speech. To take the nearest example:

> Grant me an old man's Frenzy,
> My self must I remake
> Till I am Timon and Lear
> Or that William Blake
> Who beat upon the wall
> Till Truth obeyed his call.

The unnecessary "that" imports a feeling of affectation, and the same tendency is present in all but Yeats's best passages. One is seldom long away from a suspicion of "quaintness", something that links up not only with the 'nineties, the Ivory Tower and the "calf covers of pissed-on green", but also with Rackham's drawings, Liberty art-fabrics and the *Peter Pan* never-never land, of which, after all, "The Happy Townland" is merely a more appetising example. This does not matter, because, on the whole, Yeats gets away with it, and if his straining after effect is often irritating, it can also produce phrases ("the chill, footless years", "the mackerel-crowded seas") which suddenly overwhelm one like a girl's face seen across a

---

[1] *The Development of William Butler Yeats* by V.K. Narayana Menon.

room. He is an exception to the rule that poets do not use poetical language:

> How many centuries spent
> The sedentary soul
> In toils of measurement
> Beyond eagle or mole,
> Beyond hearing or seeing,
> Or Archimedes' guess,
> To raise into being
> That loveliness?

Here he does not flinch from a squashy vulgar word like "loveliness", and after all it does not seriously spoil this wonderful passage. But the same tendencies, together with a sort of raggedness which is no doubt intentional, weaken his epigrams and polemical poems. For instance (I am quoting from memory) the epigram against the critics who damned *The Playboy of the Western World*:

> Once when midnight smote the air
> Eunuchs ran through Hell and met
> On every crowded street to stare
> Upon great Juan riding by;
> Even like these to rail and sweat,
> Staring upon his sinewy thigh.

The power which Yeats has within himself gives him the analogy ready made and produces the tremendous scorn of the last line, but even in this short poem there are six or seven unnecessary words. It would probably have been deadlier if it had been neater.

Mr Menon's book is incidentally a short biography of Yeats, but he is above all interested in Yeats's philosophical "system", which in his opinion supplies the subject-matter of more of Yeats's poems than is generally recognised. This system is set forth fragmentarily in various places, and at full length in *A Vision*, a privately printed book which I have never read but which Mr Menon quotes from extensively. Yeats gave conflicting accounts of its origin, and Mr Menon hints pretty broadly that the "documents" on which it was ostensibly founded were imaginary. Yeats's philosophical system, says Mr Menon, "was at the back of his intellectual life almost from the beginning. His poetry is full of it. Without it his later poetry becomes almost completely unintelligible." As soon as we begin to read about the so-called system we are in the middle of a hocus-pocus of Great Wheels, gyres, cycles of the moon, reincarnation, disembodied spirits, astrology and what not. Yeats hedges as to the literalness with which he believed in all this, but he certainly dabbled in spiritualism and astrology, and in earlier life had made experiments in alchemy. Although almost buried under explanations, very difficult to understand, about the phases of the moon, the central idea of his philosophical system seems to be our old friend, the cyclical universe, in which everything happens over and over again. One has not, perhaps, the right to laugh at Yeats for his mystical beliefs—for I believe it could be shown that *some* degree of belief in magic is almost universal—but neither ought one to write such things off as mere unimportant eccentricities. It is Mr Menon's perception of this that gives his book its deepest interest. "In the first flush of admiration and enthusiasm," he says, "most people dismissed the fantastical philosophy as the price we have to pay for a great and curious intellect. One did not quite realise where he was heading. And those who did, like Pound and perhaps Eliot, approved the stand that he finally took. The first reaction to this did not come, as one might have expected, from the politically-minded young English poets. They were puzzled because a less rigid or artificial system than that of *A Vision* might not have produced the great poetry of Yeats's last days." It might not, and yet Yeats's philosophy has some very sinister implications, as Mr Menon points out.

Translated into political terms, Yeats's tendency is Fascist. Throughout most of his life, and long before Fascism was ever heard of, he had had the outlook of those who reach Fascism by the aristocratic route. He is a great hater of democracy, of the modern world, science, machinery, the concept of progress—above all, of the idea of human equality. Much of the imagery of his work is feudal, and it is clear that he was not altogether free from ordinary snobbishness. Later these tendencies took clearer shape and led him to "the exultant acceptance of authoritarianism as the only solution. Even violence and tyranny are not necessarily evil because the people, knowing not evil and good, would become perfectly acquiescent to tyranny. . . . Everything must come from the top. Nothing can come from the masses." Not much interested in politics, and no doubt disgusted by his brief incursions into public life, Yeats nevertheless makes political pronouncements. He is too big a man to share the illusions of Liberalism, and as early as 1920 he foretells in a justly

famous passage ("The Second Coming") the kind of world that we
have actually moved into. But he appears to welcome the coming age,
which is to be "hierarchical, masculine, harsh, surgical", and is
influenced both by Ezra Pound and by various Italian Fascist writers.
He describes the new civilisation which he hopes and believes will
arrive: "an aristocratic civilisation in its most completed form, every
detail of life hierarchical, every great man's door crowded at dawn
by petitioners, great wealth everywhere in a few men's hands, all
dependent upon a few, up to the Emperor himself, who is a God
dependent on a greater God, and everywhere, in Court, in the
family, an inequality made law." The innocence of this statement is as
interesting as its snobbishness. To begin with, in a single phrase,
"great wealth in a few men's hands", Yeats lays bare the central
reality of Fascism, which the whole of its propaganda is designed to
cover up. The merely political Fascist claims always to be fighting for
justice: Yeats, the poet, sees at a glance that Fascism means injustice,
and acclaims it for that very reason. But at the same time he fails to
see that the new authoritarian civilisation, if it arrives, will not be
aristocratic, or what he means by aristocratic. It will not be ruled by
noblemen with Van Dyck faces, but by anonymous millionaires,
shiny-bottomed bureaucrats and murdering gangsters. Others who
have made the same mistake have afterwards changed their views,
and one ought not to assume that Yeats, if he had lived longer, would
necessarily have followed his friend Pound, even in sympathy. But
the tendency of the passage I have quoted above is obvious, and its
complete throwing overboard of whatever good the past two
thousand years have achieved is a disquieting symptom.

How do Yeat's political ideas link up with his leaning towards
occultism? It is not clear at first glance why hatred of democracy and
a tendency to believe in crystal-gazing should go together. Mr Menon
only discusses this rather shortly, but it is possible to make two
guesses. To begin with, the theory that civilisation moves in recurring
cycles is one way out for people who hate the concept of human
equality. If it is true that "all this", or something like it, "has
happened before", then science and the modern world are debunked
at one stroke and progress becomes for ever impossible. It does not
much matter if the lower orders are getting above themselves, for,
after all, we shall soon be returning to an age of tyranny. Yeats is by
no means alone in this outlook. If the universe is moving round on a
wheel, the future must be foreseeable, perhaps even in some detail. It

is merely a question of discovering the laws of its motion, as the early astronomers discovered the solar year. Believe that, and it becomes difficult not to believe in astrology or some similar system. A year before the war, examining a copy of *Gringoire*, the French Fascist weekly, much read by army officers, I found in it no less than thirty-eight advertisements of clairvoyants. Secondly, the very concept of occultism carries with it the idea that knowledge must be a secret thing, limited to a small circle of initiates. But the same idea is integral to Fascism. Those who dread the prospect of universal suffrage, popular education, freedom of thought, emancipation of women, will start off with a predilection towards secret cults. There is another link between Fascism and magic in the profound hostility of both to the Christian ethical code.

No doubt Yeats wavered in his beliefs and held at different times many different opinions, some enlightened, some not. Mr Menon repeats for him Eliot's claim that he had the longest period of development of any poet who has ever lived. But there is one thing that seems constant, at least in all of his work that I can remember, and that is his hatred of modern western civilisation and desire to return to the Bronze Age, or perhaps to the Middle Ages. Like all such thinkers, he tends to write in praise of ignorance. The Fool in his remarkable play, *The Hour-Glass*, is a Chestertonian figure, "God's fool", the "natural born innocent", who is always wiser than the wise man. The philosopher in the play dies on the knowledge that all his lifetime of thought has been wasted (I am quoting from memory again):

> The stream of the world has changed its course,
> And with the stream my thoughts have run
> Into some cloudly, thunderous spring
> That is its mountain-source;
> Ay, to a frenzy of the mind,
> That all that we have done's undone
> Our speculation but as the wind.[1]

Beautiful words, but by implication profoundly obscurantist and reactionary; for if it is really true that a village idiot, as such, is wiser than a philosopher, then it would be better if the alphabet had never

[1] The last three lines actually read:

> Aye, to some frenzy of the mind
> For all that we have done's undone
> Our speculation but as the wind.

been invented. Of course, all praise of the past is partly sentimental, because we do not live in the past. The poor do not praise poverty. Before you can despise the machine, the machine must set you free from brute labour. But that is not to say that Yeats's yearning for a more primitive and more hierarchical age was not sincere. How much of all this is traceable to mere snobbishness, product of Yeats's own position as an impoverished offshoot of the aristocracy, is a different question. And the connection between his obscurantist opinions and his tendency towards "quaintness" of language remains to be worked out; Mr Menon hardly touches upon it.

This is a very short book, and I would greatly like to see Mr Menon go ahead and write another book on Yeats, starting where this one leaves off. "If the greatest poet of our times is exultantly ringing in an era of Fascism, it seems a somewhat disturbing symptom," he says on the last page, and leaves it at that. It is a disturbing symptom, because it is not an isolated one. By and large the best writers of our time have been reactionary in tendency, and though Fascism does not offer any real return to the past, those who yearn for the past will accept Fascism sooner than its probable alternatives. But there are other lines of approach, as we have seen during the past two or three years. The relationship between Fascism and the literary intelligentsia badly needs investigating, and Yeats might well be the starting-point. He is best studied by someone like Mr Menon, who can approach a poet primarily as a poet, but who also knows that a writer's political and religious beliefs are not excrescences to be laughed away, but something that will leave their mark even on the smallest detail of his work.

*Horizon*, January 1943; CTE; DD; CE.


# 44. Letter from England to *Partisan Review*

3 January 1943

Dear Editors,

It is just on two years since I wrote you my first letter. I wrote that one to the tune of AA guns, when we were in desperate straits and also on what appeared to be the edge of rapid political advance. I begin this one at a time when the military situation is enormously better but the political outlook is blacker than it has ever been. My last letter but one, which I wrote in May of this year, you headed on your own initiative "The British Crisis". Well, that crisis is over and the forces of reaction have won hands down. Churchill is firm in the saddle again, Cripps has flung away his chances, no other left-wing leader or movement has appeared, and what is more important, it is hard to see how any revolutionary situation can recur till the western end of the war is finished. We have had two opportunities, Dunkirk and Singapore, and we took neither. Before trying to predict the consequences of this, let me sketch out the main tendencies of this year as I see them.

Although the individual incidents don't fit in so neatly as they might, the rule has held good that the Government moves to the right in moments of success and to the Left in moments of disaster. Collapse in the Far East—Cripps taken into the Government, Cripps's mission to India (this was probably so framed as to make sure that it should not be accepted, but was at least a big concession to popular feeling in this country). American victories in the Pacific, German failure to reach Alexandria—Indian Congress leaders arrested. British victory in Egypt, American invasion of North Africa—tie-up with Darlan and fresh bum-kissing for Franco. But over the whole year—indeed I have mentioned it in earlier letters—there has been visible a steady growth of blimpishness and a more conscious elbowing-out of the "reds" who were useful when morale needed pepping up but can now be dispensed with. The sudden sacking of Cripps merely symbolises a process which is occurring all over the place. Apart from the general rightward swing there have been two other developments which seem to me significant. One is the Second Front agitation, which reached its peak about July and thereafter took on a more definitely political colour than before. The North African campaign has temporarily silenced the clamour for a Second Front, but in the preceding months the controversy had not really been a military one but was a struggle between pro-Russians and anti-Russians. The other development is the growth of anti-American feeling, together with increased American control over British policy. The popular attitude towards America has I believe changed in the last few months, and I will return to this in a moment. Meanwhile the growing suspicion that we may all have underrated the strength of capitalism and that the Right may, after all, be able to win the war off its own bat without resorting to any radical change, is very depressing to anyone who thinks. Cynicism about "after the war" is widespread, and the "we're all in it together" feeling of 1940 has faded away. The great political topic of the last few weeks has been the Beveridge Report on Social Security. People seem to feel that this very moderate measure of reform is almost too good to be true. Except for the tiny interested minority, everyone is pro-Beveridge—including left-wing papers which a few years ago would have denounced such a scheme as semi-Fascist—and at the same time no one believes that Beveridge's plan will actually be adopted. The usual opinion is that "they" (the Government) will make a pretence of accepting the Beveridge Report and then simply let it drop. The sense of impotence seems to be growing and is reflected in the lower and lower voting figures at by-elections. The last public demonstrations of any magnitude were those demanding a Second Front in the late summer. No demonstrations against the Darlan deal, though disapproval of it was almost general; nor over the India business, though, again, popular feeling is pro-Congress. The extreme Left still tends to be defeatist, except as regards the Russian front, and at each stage of the African campaign its press has clung almost desperately to a pessimistic interpretation of events. I think it is worth noting that the military experts favoured by the Left are all of them defeatist, and haven't suffered in reputation when their gloomy prophecies are falsified, any more than the cheery optimists favoured by the Right. However, this comes partly from jealousy and "opposition mentality": few people now really believe in a German victory. As to the real moral of the last three years—that the Right has more guts and ability than the Left—no one will face up to it.

Now a word about Anglo-American relations. In an earlier letter I tried to indicate very briefly the various currents of pro- and anti-American feeling in this country. Since then there has been an obvious growth of animosity against America, and this now extends to people who were previously pro-American, such as the literary intelligentsia. It is important to realise that for about fifteen years Britain has differed from most countries in having no nationalist intelligentsia worth speaking of. The average English intellectual is anti-British, and though chiefly worshipping the USSR has also tended to look on America as being not only more efficient and up-to-date than Britain, but more genuinely democratic. During the period 1935–9 the Left intelligentsia were taken in to a surprising extent by the "anti-Fascist" antics in which so many American newspapers indulged. There was also a tendency to crouch culturally

towards America and urge the superiority of the American language
and even the American accent. This attitude is changing, however,
as it begins to be grasped that the USA is potentially imperialist and
politically a long way behind Britain. A favourite saying nowadays
is that whereas Chamberlain appeased Germany, Churchill appeases
America. It is, indeed, obvious enough that the British ruling class is
being propped up by American arms, and may thereby get a new
lease of life it would not otherwise have had. People now blame the
USA for every reactionary move, more even than is justified. For
instance, even quite well-informed people believed the Darlan job
to have been "put over" by the Americans without our knowledge,
though in fact the British Government must have been privy to it.

There is also widespread anti-American feeling among the working class, thanks to the presence of the American soldiers, and, I
believe, very bitter anti-British feeling among the soldiers themselves.
I have to speak here on second-hand evidence, because it is almost
impossible to make contact with an American soldier. They are to be
seen everywhere in the streets, but they don't go to the ordinary pubs,
and even in the hotels and cocktail bars which they do frequent they
keep by themselves and hardly answer if spoken to. American
civilians who are in contact with them say that apart from the
normal grumbling about the food, the climate, etc, they complain of
being inhospitably treated and of having to pay for their amusements, and are disgusted by the dinginess, the old-fashionedness and
the general poverty of life in England. Certainly it cannot be pleasant
to be suddenly transferred from the comforts of American civilisation
to some smoky and rainy Midland town, battered by three years of
war and short of every kind of consumption goods. I doubt, however,
whether the average American would find England tolerable even in
peacetime. The cultural differences are very deep, perhaps irreconcilable, and the Americans obviously have the profoundest contempt
for England, rather like the contempt which the ordinary lowbrow
Englishman has for the Latin races. All who are in contact with the
American troops report them as saying that this is "their" war, they
have done all the fighting in it, the British are no good at anything
except running away, etc. The lack of contact between the Americans
and the locals is startling. It is now more than eight months since the
first American troops arrived, and I have not yet seen a British soldier
and an American soldier together. Officers very occasionally, soldiers
never. The early good impression which the American troops made

on the women seems to have worn off. One never sees them except
with tarts or near-tarts, and the same thing is reported from most
parts of the country. Relations are said to be better in Scotland, however, where the people are certainly more hospitable than in England.
Also, people seem to prefer the Negroes to the white Americans.

If you ask people why they dislike Americans, you get first of all
the answer that they are "always boasting" and then come upon a
more solid grievance in the matter of the soldiers' pay and food. An
American private soldier gets 10 shillings a day and all found, which
—with wages and income tax as they now are—means that the whole
American army is financially in the middle class, and fairly high up
in it. As to the food, I do not imagine that people would resent the
troops being better fed than civilians, since the British army is also
better fed, so far as the ingredients of food go, but the Americans are
given foodstuffs otherwise reserved for children, and also imported
luxuries which obviously waste shipping space. They are even
importing beer, since they will not drink English beer. People point
out with some bitterness that sailors have to be drowned in bringing
this stuff across. You can imagine also the petty jealousies centring
round the fact that American officers monopolise all the taxis, drink
up all the whisky and have inflated the rents of furnished rooms to
unheard-of levels. The usual comment is "I wouldn't mind if they
were fighting, not just talking." This is said out of spite, but it is a fact
that the attitude will change deeply if and when the American army
is engaged in Europe. At present the parallel with our own relations
with France during the phony war is all too obvious.

Whether this state of affairs could be altered by better propaganda
methods is disputable. I note that people newly returned from the
USA or with knowledge of conditions there, especially Canadians,
are concerned about Anglo-American relations and very anxious that
the British war effort should be more loudly boosted in the USA.
Britain's propaganda problems, however, are more complex than
most people realise. To take one example, it is politically necessary to
flatter the Dominions, which involves playing down the British. As a
result the Germans are able to say plausibly that Britain's fighting is
done for her by colonial troops, but this is held to be a lesser evil than
offending the Australians, who are only very loosely attached to the
Empire and culturally hostile to Britain. This dilemma presents itself
over and over again, in endless variations. As to America, some
propagandists actually hold that it is better for the Americans to be

anti-British, as this gives them a good opinion of themselves and "keeps their morale up". Others are dismayed because we are represented in America by people like Lord Halifax—who, it is feared, may be taken for a typical Englishman. The usual line is "Why can't we send over a few working men from Wigan or Bradford to show them we're ordinary decent people like themselves?" This seems to me sentimentality. It is true, of course, that Lord Halifax is just about as representative of Britain as a Red Indian chieftain is of the United States, but the theory that the common people of all nations love each other at sight is not backed up by experience. The common people nearly everywhere are xenophobe, because they cannot accustom themselves to foreign food and foreign habits. Holding left-wing opinions makes no difference to this, a fact which impressed itself on me in the Spanish civil war. The popular goodwill towards the USSR in this country partly depends on the fact that few Englishmen have ever seen a Russian. And one has only to look round the English-speaking world, with its labyrinth of cultural hatreds, to see that speaking the same language is no guarantee of friendship.

Whatever happens, Britain will not go the way that France went, and the growing animosity between British and Americans may not have any real importance till the war is over. But it might have a direct influence on events if—as is now widely expected—Germany is defeated some time in 1943 or 1944 and it then takes about two more years to settle Japan. In that case the war against Japan might quite easily be represented as "an American war", a more plausible variant of "a Jewish war". The masses in Britain have it fixed in their minds that Hitler is *the* enemy, and it is quite common to hear soldiers say "I'm packing up as soon as Germany is finished." That doesn't mean that they genuinely intend or would be able to do this, and I think in practice majority opinion would be for staying in the war, unless by that time Russia had changed sides again. But the question "What are we fighting for?" is bound to come up in a sharper form when Germany is knocked out, and there are pro-Japanese elements in this country which might be clever enough to make use of popular war weariness. From the point of view of the man in the street the war in the Far East is a war for the rubber companies and the Americans, and in that context American unpopularity might be important. The British ruling class has never stated its real war aims, which happen to be unmentionable, and so long as things went badly Britain was driven part of the way towards a revolutionary strategy. There was always the possibility, therefore, of democratising the war without losing it in the process. Now, however, the tide begins to turn and immediately the dreary world which the American millionaires and their British hangers-on intend to impose upon us begins to take shape. The British people, in the mass, don't want such a world, and might say so fairly vigorously when the Nazis are out of the way. What they want, so far as they formulate their thoughts at all, is some kind of United States of Europe dominated by a close alliance between Britain and the USSR. Sentimentally, the majority of people in this country would far rather be in a tie-up with Russia than with America, and it is possible to imagine situations in which the popular cause would become the anti-American cause. There were signs of this alignment in the reactions to the Darlan business. Whether any leader or party capable of giving a voice to these tendencies will arise even when Hitler is gone and Europe is in turmoil, I do not know. None is visible at this moment, and the reactionaries are tightening their grip everywhere. But one can at least foresee at what point a radical change will again become possible.

There is not much more news. Another Fascist party has started up, the British National Party. It is the usual stuff—anti-Bolshevik, anti-Big Business, etc. These people have got hold of some money from somewhere but do not appear to have a serious following. The Common Wealth people have quarrelled and split, but the main group is probably making headway. There have been further signs of the growth of a left-wing faction in the Church of England, which has had tendencies in this direction for some years past. These centre not, as one might expect in the "modernists" but in the Anglo-Catholics, dogmatically the extreme "right-wing" of the Church. The *Church Times*, which is more or less the official paper of the C of E[1] (enormous circulation in country vicarages), has for some years past been a mildly left-wing paper and politically quite intelligent. Parts of the Roman Catholic press have gone more markedly pro-Fascist since the Darlan affair. There is evidently a split in the Catholic intelligentsia over the whole question of Fascism, and they have been attacking one another in public in a way they usually avoid doing. There is still antisemitism, but no sign that it is growing. Our food is much as usual. The Christmas puddings, my clue to the shipping situation, were about the same colour as last year. It is getting hard

[1] Church of England.

to live with prices and taxes as they now are, and what between long working hours and then fire-watching, the Home Guard, ARP or what not, one seems to have less and less spare time, especially as all journeys now are slow and uncomfortable. Good luck for 1943.

*Partisan Review*, March–April 1943

# 45. Pamphlet Literature

One cannot adequately review fifteen pamphlets in a thousand words, and if I have picked out that number it is because between them they make a representative selection of eight out of the nine main trends in current pamphleteering. (The missing trend is pacifism: I don't happen to have a recent pacifist pamphlet by me.) I list them under their separate headings, with short comments, before trying to explain certain rather curious features in the revival of pamphleteering during recent years.

1. Anti-Left and crypto-Fascist: *A Soldier's New World*. 2d (Sub-titled, "An anti-crank pamphlet written in camp"; this wallops the highbrow and proves that the common man does not want Social-ism. Key phrase: "the Clever Ones have never learned to delight in simple things".) *Gollancz in the German Wonderland*. 1/- (Vansittar-tite). *World Order or World Ruin*. 6d (Anti-planning; G.D.H. Cole demolished.)

2. Conservative: *Bomber Command Continues*. 7d (Good speci-men of an official pamphlet.)

3. Social Democrat: *The Case of Austria*. 6d (Published by the Free Austrian Movement.)

4. Communist: *Clear out Hitler's Agents*. 2d (Sub-titled, "An exposure of Trotskyist disruption being organised in Britain"; ex-ceptionally mendacious.)

5. Trotskyist and Anarchist: *The Kronstadt Revolt*. 2d (Anarchist pamphlet, largely an attack on Trotsky.)

6. Non-party radical: *What's Wrong with the Army?* 6d (A Hurricane Book, well-informed and well-written anti-Blimp docu-ment.) *I, James Blunt*. 6d (Good flesh-creeper, founded on the justified assumption that the mass of the English people haven't yet heard of Fascism.) *Battle of Giants*. Unpriced, probably 6d (In-teresting specimen of popular non-Communist russophile literature).

7. Religious: *A Letter to a Country Clergyman.* 2d (Fabian pamphlet, left-wing Anglican.) *Fighters Ever.* 6d (Buchman vindicated.)

8. Lunatic: *Britain's Triumphant Destiny, or Righteousness no longer on the Defensive.* 6d (British Israel, profusely illustrated.) *When Russia Invades Palestine.* 1/- (British Israel. The author, A. J. Ferris, BA, has written a long series of pamphlets on kindred subjects, some of them enjoying enormous sales. His *When Russia Bombs Germany*, published in 1940, sold over 60,000.) *Hitler's Story and Programme to Conquer England*, by "Civis Britannicus Sum". 1/- (Specimen passage: "It is a grand thing to 'play the game', and to know that one is doing it. Then, when the day comes that stumps are drawn or the whistle blows for the last time:

> The *Great Scorer* will come to write against your name,
> Not if you have won or lost; but *How you Played the Game*.")

These few that I have named are only a drop in the ocean of pamphlet literature, and for the sake of giving a good cross-section I have included several that the average reader is likely to have heard of. What conclusions can one draw from this small sample? The interesting fact, not easily explicable, is that pamphleteering has revived upon an enormous scale since about 1935, and has done so without producing anything of real value. My own collection, made during the past six years, would run into several hundreds, but probably does not represent anywhere near 10 per cent of the total output. Some of these pamphlets have had huge sales, especially the religio-patriotic ones, such as those of Mr Ferris, BA, and the scurrilous ones, such as *Hitler's Last Will and Testament*, which is said to have sold several millions. Directly-political pamphlets sometimes sell in big numbers, but the circulation of any pamphlet which is "party line" (any party) is likely to be spurious. Looking through my collection, I find that it is practically all trash, interesting only to bibliophiles. Though I have classified current pamphlets under nine headings they could be finally reduced to two main schools, roughly describable as Party Line and Astrology. There is totalitarian rubbish and paranoiac rubbish, but in each case it *is* rubbish. Even the well-informed Fabian pamphlets are hopelessly dull, considered as reading matter. The liveliest pamphlets are almost always non-party, a good example being *Bless 'em All*, which should be regarded as a pamphlet, though it costs one and sixpence.

The reason why the badness of contemporary pamphlets is somewhat surprising is that the pamphlet ought to be *the* literary form of an age like our own. We live in a time when political passions run high, channels of free expresssion are dwindling, and organised lying exists on a scale never before known. For plugging the holes in history the pamphlet is the ideal form. Yet lively pamphlets are very few, and the only explanation I can offer—a rather lame one—is that the publishing trade and the literary papers have never gone to the trouble of making the reading public pamphlet-conscious. One difficulty of collecting pamphlets is that they are not issued in any regular manner, cannot always be procured even in the libraries of museums, and are seldom advertised and still more seldom reviewed. A good writer with something he passionately wanted to say—and the essence of pamphleteering is to have something you want to say *now*, to as many people as possible—would hesitate to cast it in pamphlet form, because he would hardly know how to set about getting it published, and would be doubtful whether the people he wanted to reach would ever read it. Probably he would water his idea down into a newspaper article or pad it out into a book. As a result by far the greater number of pamphlets are either written by lonely lunatics who publish at their own expense, or belong to the sub-world of the crank religions, or are issued by political parties. The normal way of publishing a pamphlet is through a political party, and the party will see to it that any "deviation"—and hence any literary value—is kept out. There have been a few good pamphlets in fairly recent years. D.H. Lawrence's *Pornography and Obscenity* was one, Potocki de Montalk's *Snobbery with Violence* was another, and some of Wyndham Lewis's essays in *The Enemy* really come under this heading. At present the most hopeful symptom is the appearance of the non-party left-wing pamphlet, such as the Hurricane Books. If productions of this type were as sure of being noticed in the press as are novels or books of verse, something would have been done towards bringing the pamphlet back to the attention of its proper public, and the level of the whole genre might rise. When one considers how flexible a form the pamphlet is, and how badly some of the events of our time need documenting, this is a thing to be desired.

*New Statesman and Nation*, 9 January 1943

## 46. London Letter to *Partisan Review*

[Late May? 1943]

Dear Editors,
I begin my letter just after the dissolution of the Comintern, and before the full effects of this have become clear. Of course the immediate results in Britain are easy to foretell. Obviously the Communists will make fresh efforts to affiliate with the Labour Party (this has already been refused by the LP Executive), obviously they will be told that they must dissolve and join as individuals, and obviously, once inside the Labour Party, they will try to act as an organised faction, whatever promises they may have given beforehand. The real interest lies in trying to foresee the long-term effects of the dissolution on a Communist Party of the British type.

Weighing up the probabilities, I think the Russian gesture should be taken at its face-value—that is, Stalin is genuinely aiming at a closer tie-up with the USA and Britain and not merely "deceiving the bourgeoisie" as his followers like to believe. But that would not of itself alter the behaviour of the British Communists. For after all, their subservience to Moscow during the last fifteen years did not rest on any real authority. The British Communists could not be shot or exiled if they chose to disobey, and so far as I know they have not even had any money from Moscow in recent years. Moreover the Russians made it reasonably clear that they despised them. Their obedience depended on the mystique of the Revolution, which had gradually changed itself into a nationalistic loyalty to the Russian state. The English left-wing intelligentsia worship Stalin because they have lost their patriotism and their religious belief without losing the need for a god and a fatherland. I have always held that many of them would transfer their allegiance to Hitler if Germany won. So long as "Communism" merely means furthering the interests of the Russian Foreign Office, it is hard to see that the disappearance of the Comintern makes any difference. Nearly always one can see at a glance what policy is needed, even if there is no central organisation to hand out directives.

However, one has got to consider the effect on the working-class membership, who have a different outlook from the salaried hacks at the top of the Party. To these people the open declaration that the International is dead must make a difference, although it was in fact a ghost already. And even in the central committee of the Party there are differences in outlook which might widen if after a while the British Communist Party came to think of itself as an independent party. One must allow here for the effects of self-deception. Even long-term Communists often won't admit to themselves that they are merely Russian agents, and therefore don't necessarily see what move is required until the instructions arrive from Moscow. Thus, as soon as the Franco-Russian military pact was signed, it was obvious that the French and British Communists must go all patriotic, but to my knowledge some of them failed to grasp this. Or again, after the signing of the Russo-German Pact several leading members refused to accept the anti-war line and had to do some belly-crawling before their mutiny was forgiven. In the months that followed the two chief publicists of the Party became extremely sympathetic to the Nazi *Weltanschauung*, evidently to the dismay of some of the others. The line of division is between deracinated intellectuals like Palme Dutt and trade union men like Pollitt and Hannington. After all the years they have had on the job none of these men can imagine any occupation except boosting Soviet Russia, but they might differ as to the best way of doing it if Russian leadership has really been withdrawn. All in all, I should expect the dissolution of the Comintern to produce appreciable results, but not immediately. I should say that for six months, perhaps more, the British Communists will carry on as always, but that thereafter rifts will appear and the Party will either wither away or develop into a looser, less russophile organisation under more up-to-date leadership.

There remains the bigger puzzle of why the Comintern was dissolved. If I am right and the Russians did it to inspire confidence, one must assume that the rulers of Britain and the USA wanted the dissolution and perhaps demanded it as part of the price of a Second Front. But in Britain at any rate there has been little sign in the past dozen years that the ruling class seriously objected to the existence of the Communist Party. Even during the People's Convention period they showed it an astonishing amount of tolerance. At all other times from 1935 onwards it has had powerful support from one or other section of the capitalist press. A thing that it is difficult to be sure about is where the Communists get their money from. It is not likely that they get all of it from their declared supporters, and I believe they tell the truth in saying that they get nothing from Moscow. The difference is that they are "helped" from time to time by wealthy English people who see the value of an organisation which

acts as an eel-trap for active Socialists. Beaverbrook for instance is
credited, rightly or wrongly, with having financed the Communist
Party during the past year or two. This is perhaps not less significant
as a rumour than it would be as a fact. When one thinks of the history
of the past twenty years it is hard not to feel that the Comintern has
been one of the worst enemies the working class has had. Yet the
Upper Crust is evidently pleased to see it disappear—a fact which I
record but cannot readily explain.

The other important political development during these past
months has been the growth of Common Wealth, Sir Richard
Acland's party. I mentioned this in earlier letters but underrated its
importance. It is now a movement to be seriously reckoned with and
is hated by all the other parties alike.

Acland's programme, which is set forth almost in baby language in
many leaflets and pamphlets, could be described as Socialism minus
the class war and with the emphasis on the moral instead of the
economic motive. It calls for nationalisation of all major resources,
immediate independence (not Dominion status) for India, pooling
of raw materials as between "have" and "have not" countries,
international administration of backward areas, and a composite
army drawn from as many countries as possible to keep the peace
after the war is done. All in all this programme is not less drastic than
that of the extremist parties of the Left, but it has some unusual
features which are worth noticing, since they explain the advance
Common Wealth has made during the past few months.

In the first place the whole class-war ideology is scrapped. Though
all property-owners are to be expropriated, they are to receive
fractional compensation—in effect, the bourgeois is to be given a
small life-pension instead of a firing-squad. The idea of "proletarian
dictatorship" is specifically condemned; the middle class and the
working class are to amalgamate instead of fighting one another. The
Party's literature is aimed chiefly at winning over the middle class,
both the technical middle class and the "little man" (farmers, shopkeepers, etc). Secondly, the economic side of the programme lays the
emphasis on increasing production rather than equalising consumption.
Thirdly, an effort is made to synthesise patriotism with an internationalist outlook. Stress is laid on the importance of following British
tradition and "doing things in our own way". Parliament, apparently,
is to be preserved in much its present form, and nothing is said against
the Monarchy. Fourthly, Common Wealth does not describe itself as

"Socialist" and carefully avoids Marxist phraseology. It declares itself willing to collaborate with any other party whose aims are sufficiently similar. (With the Labour Party the test is that the LP shall break the electoral truce.) Fifthly—and perhaps most important of all—Common Wealth propaganda has a strong ethical tinge. Its best-known poster consists simply of the words "Is it expedient?" crossed out and replaced by "Is it right?" Anglican priests are much to the fore in the movement though the Catholics seem to be opposing it.

Whether this movement has a future I am still uncertain, but its growth since I last wrote to you has been very striking. Acland's candidates are fighting by-elections all over the country. Although they have only won two so far, they have effected a big turn-over of votes against Government candidates, and what is perhaps more significant, the whole poll seems to rise wherever a Common Wealth candidate appears. The ILP has been conducting a distant flirtation with Common Wealth, but the other Left parties are hostile and perhaps frightened. The usual criticism is that Common Wealth is only making progress because of the electoral truce—in other words, because the Labour Party is what it is. In addition it is said that the membership of the party is wholly middle-class. Acland himself claims to have a good nucleus of followers in the factories and still more in the forces. The Communists, of course, have labelled Common Wealth as Fascist. They and the Conservatives now work together at by-elections.

The programme I have roughly outlined has elements both of demagogy and of Utopianism, but it takes very much better account of the actual balance of forces than any of the older Left parties have done. It might have a chance of power if another revolutionary situation arises, either through military disaster or at the end of the war. Some who know Acland declare that he has a "fuehrer complex" and that if he saw the movement growing beyond his control he would split it sooner than share authority. I don't believe this to be so, but neither do I believe that Acland by himself could bring a nationwide movement into being. He is not a big enough figure, and not in any way a man of the people. Although of aristocratic and agricultural background (he is a fifteenth baronet) he has the manners and appearance of a civil servant, with a typical upper-class accent. For a popular leader in England it is a serious disability to be a gentleman, which Churchill, for instance, is not. Cripps is a gentleman, but to offset this he has his notorious "austerity", the Gandhi touch, which Acland just misses, in spite of his ethical and religious slant. I think this movement should be watched with attention. It might develop into the new Socialist party we have all been hoping for, or into something very sinister: it has some rather doubtful followers already.

Finally a word about antisemitism, which could now be said to have reached the stature of a "problem". I said in my last letter that it was not increasing, but I now think it is. The danger signal, which is also a safeguard, is that everyone is very conscious of it and it is discussed interminably in the press.

Although Jews in England have always been socially looked down on and debarred from a few professions (I doubt whether a Jew would be accepted as an officer in the navy, for instance), antisemitism is primarily a working-class thing, and strongest among Irish labourers. I have had some glimpses of working-class antisemitism through being three years in the Home Guard—which gives a good cross-section of society—in a district where there are a lot of Jews. My experience is that middle-class people will laugh at Jews and discriminate against them to some extent, but only among working people do you find the full-blown belief in the Jews as a cunning and sinister race who live by exploiting the Gentiles. After all that has happened in the last ten years it is a fearful thing to hear a working man saying, "Well, I reckon 'Itler done a good job when 'e turned 'em all out," but I have heard just that, and more than once. These people never seem to be aware that Hitler has done anything to the Jews except "turned 'em all out"; the pogroms, the deportations, etc have simply escaped their notice. It is questionable, however, whether the Jew is objected to as a Jew or simply as a foreigner. No religious consideration enters. The English Jew, who is often strictly orthodox but entirely anglicised in his habits, is less disliked than the European refugee who has probably not been near a synagogue for thirty years. Some people actually object to the Jews on the ground that Jews are Germans!

But in somewhat different forms antisemitism is now spreading among the middle class as well. The usual formula is "Of course I don't want you to think I'm antisemitic, but—" —and here follows a catalogue of Jewish misdeeds. Jews are accused of evading military service, infringing the food laws, pushing their way to the front of queues, etc etc. More thoughtful people point out that the Jewish refugees use this country as a temporary asylum but show no loyalty towards it. Objectively this is true, and the tactlessness of some of the refugees is almost incredible. (For example, a remark by a German

Jewess overheard during the Battle of France: "These English police are not nearly so smart as our SS men.") But arguments of this kind are obviously rationalisations of prejudice. People dislike the Jews so much that they do not want to remember their sufferings, and when you mention the horrors that are happening in Germany or Poland, the answer is always "Oh yes, of course that's dreadful, but—" —and out comes the familiar list of grievances. Not all of the intelligentsia are immune from this kind of thing. Here the get-out is usually that the refugees are all "petty bourgeois"; and so the abuse of Jews can proceed under a respectable disguise. Pacifists and others who are anti-war sometimes find themselves forced into antisemitism.

One should not exaggerate the danger of this kind of thing. To begin with, there is probably less antisemitism in England now than there was thirty years ago. In the minor novels of that date you find it taken for granted far oftener than you would nowadays that a Jew is an inferior or a figure of fun. The "Jew joke" has disappeared from the stage, the radio and the comic papers since 1934. Secondly, there is a great awareness of the prevalence of antisemitism and a conscious effort to struggle against it. But the thing remains, and perhaps it is one of the inevitable neuroses of war. I am not particularly impressed by the fact that it does not take violent forms. It is true that no one wants to have pogroms and throw elderly Jewish professors into cesspools, but then there is very little crime or violence in England anyway. The milder form of antisemitism prevailing here can be just as cruel in an indirect way, because it causes people to avert their eyes from the whole refugee problem and remain uninterested in the fate of the surviving Jews of Europe. Because two days ago a fat Jewess grabbed your place on the bus, you switch off the wireless when the announcer begins talking about the ghettoes of Warsaw; that is how people's minds work nowadays.

That is all the political news I have. Life goes on much as before. I don't notice that our food is any different, but the food situation is generally considered to be worse. The war hits one a succession of blows in unexpected places. For a long time razor blades were unobtainable, now it is boot polish. Books are being printed on the most villainous paper and in tiny print, very trying to the eyes. A few people are wearing wooden-soled shoes. There is an alarming amount of drunkenness in London. The American soldiers seem to be getting on better terms with the locals, perhaps having become more resigned to the climate etc. Air raids continue, but on a pitiful scale. I notice that many people feel sympathy for the Germans now that it is they who are being bombed—a change from 1940, when people saw their houses tumbling about them and wanted to see Berlin scraped off the map.

George Orwell

*Partisan Review*, July–August 1943

## 47. Literature and the Left

"When a man of true Genius appears in the World, you may know him by this infallible Sign, that all the Dunces are in Conspiracy against him." So wrote Jonathan Swift, 200 years before the publication of *Ulysses*.

If you consult any sporting manual or yearbook you will find many pages devoted to the hunting of the fox and the hare, but not a word about the hunting of the highbrow. Yet this, more than any other, is the characteristic British sport, in season all the year round and enjoyed by rich and poor alike, with no complications from either class-feeling or political alignment.

For it should be noted that in its attitude toward "highbrows"— that is, towards any writer or artist who makes experiments in technique—the Left is no friendlier than the Right. Not only is "highbrow" almost as much a word of abuse in the *Daily Worker* as in *Punch*, but it is exactly those writers whose work shows both originality and the power to endure that Marxist doctrinaires single out for attack. I could name a long list of examples, but I am thinking expecially of Joyce, Yeats, Lawrence and Eliot. Eliot, in particular, is damned in the left-wing press almost as automatically and perfunctorily as Kipling—and that by critics who only a few years back were going into raptures over the already forgotten masterpieces of the Left Book Club.

If you ask a "good party man" (and this goes for almost any party of the Left) what he objects to in Eliot, you get an answer that ultimately reduces to this. Eliot is a reactionary (he has declared himself a royalist, an Anglo-Catholic, etc), and he is also a "bourgeois intellectual", out of touch with the common man: therefore he is a bad writer. Contained in this statement is a half-conscious confusion of ideas which vitiates nearly all politico-literary criticism.

To dislike a writer's politics is one thing. To dislike him because he forces you to think is another, not necessarily incompatible with the first. But as soon as you start talking about "good" and "bad" writers you are tacitly appealing to literary tradition and thus dragging in a totally different set of values. For what is a "good" writer? Was Shakespeare "good"? Most people would agree that he was. Yet Shakespeare is, and perhaps was even by the standards of his own time, reactionary in tendency; and he is also a difficult writer, only doubtfully accessible to the common man. What, then, becomes of the notion that Eliot is disqualified, as it were, by being an Anglo-Catholic royalist who is given to quoting Latin?

Left-wing literary criticism has not been wrong in insisting on the importance of subject-matter. It may not even have been wrong, considering the age we live in, in demanding that literature shall be first and foremost propaganda. Where it has been wrong is in making what are ostensibly literary judgements for political ends. To take a crude example, what Communist would dare to admit in public that Trotsky is a better writer than Stalin—as he is, of course? To say "X is a gifted writer, but he is a political enemy and I shall do my best to silence him" is harmless enough. Even if you end by silencing him with a tommy-gun you are not really sinning against the intellect. The deadly sin is to say "X is a political enemy: therefore he is a bad writer." And if anyone says that this kind of thing doesn't happen, I answer merely: look up the literary pages of the left-wing press, from the *News Chronicle* to the *Labour Monthly*, and see what you find.

There is no knowing just how much the Socialist movement has lost by alienating the literary intelligentsia. But it has alienated them, partly by confusing tracts with literature, and partly by having no room in it for a humanistic culture. A writer can vote Labour as easily as anyone else, but it is very difficult for him to take part in the Socialist movement *as a writer*. Both the book-trained doctrinaire and the practical politician will despise him as a "bourgeois intellectual", and will lose no opportunity of telling him so. They will have much the same attitude towards his work as a golfing stockbroker would have. The illiteracy of politicians is a special feature of our age—as G.M. Trevelyan put it, "In the seventeenth century Members of Parliament quoted the Bible, in the eighteenth and nineteenth centuries, the classics, and in the twentieth century nothing"—and its corollary is the [political] impotence of writers. In the years following the last war the best English writers were reactionary in tendency, though most of them took no direct part in politics. After them, about 1930, there came a generation of writers who tried very hard to be actively useful in the left-wing movement. Numbers of them joined the Communist Party, and got there exactly the same reception as they would have got in the Conservative Party. That is, they were first regarded with patronage and suspicion, and then, when it was found that they would not or could not turn themselves into gramophone records, they were thrown out on their ears. Most of them retreated into individualism. No doubt they still vote Labour, but their talents are lost to the movement; and—a more sinister development—after them there comes a new generation of writers who, without being strictly non-political, are outside the Socialist movement from the start. Of the very young writers who are now beginning their careers, the most gifted are pacifists; a few may even have a leaning towards Fascism. There is hardly one to whom the mystique of the Socialist movement appears to mean anything. The ten-year-long struggle against Fascism seems to them meaningless and uninteresting, and they say so frankly. One could explain this in a number of ways, but the contemptuous attitude of the Left towards "bourgeois intellectuals" is likely to be part of the reason.

Gilbert Murray relates somewhere or other that he once lectured on Shakespeare to a Socialist debating society. At the end he called for questions in the usual way, to receive as the sole question asked: "Was Shakespeare a capitalist?" The depressing thing about this story is that it might well be true. Follow up its implications, and you perhaps get a glimpse of the reason why Céline wrote *Mea Culpa* and Auden is watching his navel in America.

*Tribune*, 4 June 1943

## 48. *Letter to an American Visitor*, by Obadiah Hornbooke[1]

> Columbian poet, whom we've all respected
> From a safe distance for a year or two,
> Since first your *magnum opus* was collected—
> It seems a pity no one welcomed you

[1] Pseudonym of Alex Comfort.

Except the slippery professional few,
Whose news you've read, whose posters you've inspected;
Who gave America Halifax, and who
Pay out to scribes and painters they've selected
    Doles which exceed a fraction of the debts
    Of all our pimps in hardware coronets.


You've seen the ruins, heard the speeches, swallowed
    The bombed-out hospitals and cripples' schools—
You've heard (on records) how the workers hollowed
And read in poker-work GIVE US THE TOOLS:
    You know how, with the steadfastness of mules,
The Stern Determination of the People
    Goes sailing through a paradise of fools
Like masons shinning up an endless steeple—
    A climb concluding after many days
    In a brass weathercock that points all ways.


The land sprouts orators. No doubt you've heard
    How every buffer, fool and patrioteer
Applies the Power of the Spoken Word
    And shoves his loud posterior in your ear;
    So Monkey Hill competes with Berkeley Square—
The BBC as bookie, pimp and vet
    Presenting Air Vice-Marshals set to cheer
Our raided towns with vengeance (though I've yet
    To hear from any man who lost his wife
    Berlin or Lübeck brought her back to life).


You've heard of fighting on the hills and beaches
    And down the rabbit holes with pikes and bows—
You've heard the Baron's bloody-minded speeches
    (Each worth a fresh Division to our foes)
That smell so strong of murder that the crows
Perch on the Foreign Office roof and caw
    For German corpses laid in endless rows,
"A Vengeance such as Europe never saw"—
    The maniac Baron's future contribution
    To peace perpetual through retribution . . .

You've heard His Nibs decanting year by year
  The dim productions of his bulldog brain,
While homes and factories sit still to hear
  The same old drivel dished up once again—
  You heard the Churches' cartwheels to explain
That bombs are Christian when the English drop them—
  The Union bosses scrapping over gain
While no one's the temerity to stop them
    Or have the racketeers who try to bleed 'em
    Flogged, like the Indians for demanding freedom.

They found you poets—quite a decent gallery
  Of painters who don't let their chances slip;
And writers who prefer a regular salary
  To steer their writings by the Party Whip—
  Hassall's been tipped to have the Laureateship:
Morton is following Goebbels, not St Paul.
  There's Elton's squeaky pump still gives a drip,
And Priestley twists his proletarian awl
    Cobbling at shoes that Mill and Rousseau wore
    And still the wretched tool contrives to bore.

They found you critics—an astounding crowd:
  (Though since their work's their living, I won't say
Who howled at Eliot, hooted Treece, were loud
  In kicking Auden when he slipped away
  Out of the looney-bin to find, they say,
A quiet place where men with minds could write:
  But since Pearl Harbour, in a single day
The same old circus chase him, black is white,
    And once again by day and night he feels
    The packs of tripehounds yelling at his heels).

I say, they found you artists, well selected,
  Whom we export to sell the British case:
We keep our allied neighbours well protected
  From those who give the thing a different face—
  One man's in jail, one in a "medical place";
Another working at a farm with pigs on:
    We take their leisure, close their books, say grace,
And like that bus-conducting lad Geoff Grigson

We beat up every buzzard, kite and vulture,
And dish them out to you as English Culture.

Once in a while, to every Man and Nation,
  There comes, as Lowell said, a sort of crisis
Between the Ministry of Information
  And what your poor artistic soul advises:
  They catch the poets, straight from Cam or Isis:
"Join the brigade, or be for ever dumb—
  Either cash in on your artistic lysis
Or go on land work if you won't succumb:
    Rot in the Army, sickened and unwilling":
    So can you wonder that they draw their shilling?

You met them all. You don't require a list
  Of understrapping ghosts who once were writers—
Who celebrate the size of Britain's fist,
  Write notes for sermons, dish out pep to mitres,
  Fake letters from the Men who Fly our Fighters.
Cheer when we blast some enemy bungalows—
  Think up atrocities, the artful blighters,
To keep the grindstone at the public's nose—
    Combining moral uplift and pornography,
    Produced with arty paper and typography.

They find their leisure to fulfil their promise,
  Their work is praised, *funguntur vice cotis;*
And Buddy Judas cracks up Doubting Thomas.
  Their ways are paved with favourable notice
  (Look how unanimous the Tory vote is).
They write in papers and review each other,
  You'd never guess how bloody full the boat is;
I shan't forgive MacNeice his crippled brother
    Whom just a year ago on New Year's Day
    The Germans murdered in a radio play.

O for another Dunciad—a POPE
  To purge this dump with his gigantic boot—
Drive fools to water, aspirin or rope—
  Make idle lamp-posts bear their fitting fruit:

Private invective's far too long been mute—
O for another vast satiric comet
To blast this wretched tinder, branch and root.
The servile stuff that makes a true man vomit—
   Suck from the works to which they cling like leeches,
   Those resurrection-puddings, Churchill's speeches.

God knows—for there is libel—I can't name
How many clammy paws of these you've shaken,
Been told our English spirit is the same
From Lord Vansittart back to pseudo-Bacon—
Walked among licensed writers, and were taken
To Grub Street, Malet Street, and Portland Place,
Where every question that you ask will waken
The same old salesman's grin on every face
   Among the squads of columbines and flunkeys,
   Set on becoming Laureate of Monkeys.

We do not ask, my friend, that you'll forget
The squirts and toadies when you were presented,
The strength-through-joy brigades you will have met
Whose mouths are baggy and whose hair is scented—
Only recall we were not represented.
We wrote our own refusals, and we meant them.
Our work is plastered and ourselves resented—
Our heads are bloody, but we have not bent them.
   We hold no licences, like ladies' spaniels;
   We live like lions in this den of Daniels.

O friend and writer, deafened by the howls
That dying systems utter, mad with fear
In darkness, with a sinking of the bowels,
Where all the devils of old conscience leer—
Forget the gang that met you on the pier,
Grinning and stuffed with all the old excuses
For starving Europe, and the crocodile tear
Turned on for visitors who have their uses.
   We know the capers of the simian crew.
   We send our best apologies to you.

*Tribune*, 4 June 1943

## As One Non-Combatant to Another

## (A Letter to "Obadiah Hornbooke")

O poet strutting from the sandbagged portal
Of that small world where barkers ply their art,
And each new "school" believes itself immortal,
Just like the horse that draws the knacker's cart:
O captain of a clique of self-advancers,
Trained in the tactics of the pamphleteer,
Where slogans serve for thoughts and sneers for answers—
You've chosen well your moment to appear
And hold your nose amid a world of horror
Like Dr Bowdler walking through Gomorrah.

In the Left Book Club days you wisely lay low,
But when "Stop Hitler!" lost its old attraction
You bounded forward in a Woolworth's halo
To cash in on the anti-war reaction;
You waited till the Nazis ceased from frightening,
Then, picking a safe audience, shouted "Shame!"
Like a Prometheus you defied the lightning,
But didn't have the nerve to sign your name.[1]
You're a true poet, but as saint and martyr
You're a mere fraud, like the Atlantic Charter.

Your hands are clean, and so were Pontius Pilate's,
But as for "bloody heads", that's just a metaphor;
The bloody heads are on Pacific islets
Or Russian steppes or Libyan sands—it's better for
The health to be a CO than a fighter,
To chalk a pavement doesn't need much guts,
It pays to stay at home and be a writer
While other talents wilt in Nissen huts;
"We live like lions"—yes, just like a lion,
Pensioned on scraps in a safe cage of iron.

[1] In a footnote to Orwell's reply the Editor of *Tribune* stated: "In fairness to 'Mr Hornbooke' it should be stated that he was willing to sign his name if we insisted, but preferred a pseudonym".

For while you write the warships ring you round
And flights of bombers drown the nightingales,
And every bomb that drops is worth a pound
To you or someone like you, for your sales
Are swollen with those of rivals dead or silent,
Whether in Tunis or the BBC,
And in the drowsy freedom of this island
You're free to shout that England isn't free;
They even chuck you cash, as bears get buns,
For crying "Peace!" behind a screen of guns.

In 'seventeen to snub the nosing bitch
Who slipped you a white feather needed cheek,
But now, when every writer finds his niche
Within some mutual-admiration clique,
Who cares what epithets by Blimps are hurled?
Who'd give a damn if handed a white feather?
Each little mob of pansies is a world,
Cosy and warm in any kind of weather;
In such a world it's easy to "object",
Since that's what both your friends and foes expect.

At times it's almost a more dangerous deed
*Not* to object; I know, for I've been bitten.
I wrote in nineteen-forty that at need
I'd fight to keep the Nazis out of Britain;
And Christ! how shocked the pinks were! Two years later
I hadn't lived it down; one had the effrontery
To write three pages calling me a "traitor",
So black a crime it is to love one's country.
Yet where's the pink that would have thought it odd of me
To write a shelf of books in praise of sodomy?

Your game is easy, and its rules are plain:
Pretend the war began in 'thirty-nine,
Don't mention China, Ethiopia, Spain,
Don't mention Poles  except to say they're swine;
Cry havoc when we bomb a German city,
When Czechs get killed don't worry in the least,
Give India a perfunctory squirt of pity
But don't enquire what happens further East;

Don't mention Jews—in short, pretend the war is
Simply a racket "got up" by the Tories.

Throw in a word of "anti-Fascist" patter
From time to time, by way of reinsurance,
And then go on to prove it makes no matter
If Blimps or Nazis hold the world in durance;
And that we others who "support" the war
Are either crooks or sadists or flag-wavers
In love with drums and bugles, but still more
Concerned with cadging Brendan Bracken's favours;
Or fools who think that bombs bring back the dead,
A thing not even Harris ever said.

If you'd your way we'd leave the Russians to it
And sell our steel to Hitler as before;
Meanwhile you save your soul, and while you do it,
Take out a long-term mortgage on the war.
For after war there comes an ebb of passion,
The dead are sniggered at—and there you'll shine,
You'll be the very bull's-eye of the fashion,
You almost might get back to 'thirty-nine,
Back to the dear old game of scratch-my-neighbour
In sleek reviews financed by coolie labour.

But you don't hoot at Stalin—that's "not done"—
Only at Churchill; I've no wish to praise him,
I'd gladly shoot him when the war is won,
Or now, if there were someone to replace him.
But unlike some, I'll pay him what I owe him;
There was a time when empires crashed like houses,
And many a pink who'd titter at your poem
Was glad enough to cling to Churchill's trousers.
Christ! how they huddled up to one another
Like day-old chicks about their foster-mother!

I'm not a fan for "fighting on the beaches",
And still less for the "breezy uplands" stuff,
I seldom listen-in to Churchill's speeches,
But I'd far sooner hear that kind of guff
Than your remark, a year or so ago,

That if the Nazis came you'd knuckle under
And peaceably "accept the *status quo*".
Maybe you would! But I've a right to wonder
Which will sound better in the days to come,
"Blood, toil and sweat" or "Kiss the Nazi's bum".

But your chief target is the radio hack,
The hired pep-talker—he's a safe objective,
Since he's unpopular and can't hit back.
It doesn't need the eye of a detective
To look down Portland Place and spot the whores,
But there are men (I grant, not the most heeded)
With twice your gifts and courage three times yours
Who do that dirty work because it's needed;
Not blindly, but for reasons they can balance,
They wear their seats out and lay waste their talents.

All propaganda's lying, yours or mine;
It's lying even when its facts are true;
That goes for Goebbels or the "party line",
Or for the Primrose League or PPU.
But there are truths that smaller lies can serve,
And dirtier lies that scruples can gild over;
To waste your brains on war may need more nerve
Than to dodge facts and live in mental clover;
It's mean enough when other men are dying,
But when you lie, it's much to know you're lying.

That's thirteen stanzas, and perhaps you're puzzled
To know why I've attacked you—well, here's why:
Because your enemies all are dead or muzzled,
You've never picked on one who might reply.
You've hogged the limelight and you've aired your virtue,
While chucking sops to every dangerous faction,
The Left will cheer you and the Right won't hurt you;
What did you risk? Not even a libel action.
If you would show what saintly stuff you're made of,
Why not attack the cliques you *are* afraid of?

Denounce Joe Stalin, jeer at the Red Army,
Insult the Pope—you'll get some come-back there;
It's honourable, even if it's barmy,
To stamp on corns all round and never care.

> But for the half-way saint and cautious hero,
> Whose head's unbloody even if "unbowed",
> My admiration's somewhere near to zero;
> So my last words would be: Come off that cloud,
> Unship those wings that hardly dared to flitter,
> And spout your halo for a pint of bitter.

George Orwell

*Tribune*, 18 June 1943

## 49. Letter to Alex Comfort

10a Mortimer Crescent<br>
London NW6<br>
Sunday [11? July 1943]

Dear Comfort,

Very many thanks for sending me the copy of *New Road*.[1] I am afraid I was rather rude to you in our *Tribune* set-to,[2] but you yourself weren't altogether polite to certain people. I was only making a *political* and perhaps moral reply, and as a piece of verse your contribution was immensely better, a thing most of the people who spoke to me about it hadn't noticed. I think no one noticed that your stanzas had the same rhyme going right the way through. There is no respect for virtuosity nowadays. You ought to write something longer in that genre, something like the "Vision of Judgement". I believe there could be a public for that kind of thing again nowadays.

As to *New Road*. I am much impressed by the quantity and the general level of the verse you have got together. I should think half the writers were not known to me before. Apropos of Aragon and others, I have thought over what you said about the reviving effect of defeat upon literature and also upon national life. I think you may well be right, but it seems to me that such a revival is only *against* something, i.e. against foreign oppression, and can't lead beyond a certain point unless that oppression is ultimately to be broken, which

---

[1] *New Road: New Directions in European Art and Letters*, 1943–49, an occasional anthology of prose and verse, whose first two numbers were edited by Alex Comfort and John Bayliss.

[2] *Letter to an American Visitor* by "Obadiah Hornbooke" and Orwell's reply.

must be by military means. I suppose however one might accept defeat in a mystical belief that it will ultimately break down of its own accord. The really wicked thing seems to me to wish for a "negotiated" peace, which means back to 1939 or even 1914. I have written a long article on this for *Horizon* apropos of Fielden's[1] book on India, but I am not certain Connolly will print it.[2]

I am going to try to get Forster to talk about *New Road*, together with the latest number of *New Writing*, in one of his monthly book talks to India. If he doesn't do it this month he might next. There is no sales value there, but it extends your publicity a little and by talking about these things on the air in wartime one has the feeling that one is keeping a tiny lamp alight somewhere. You ought to try to get a few copies of the book to India. There is a small public for such things among people like Ahmed Ali[3] and they are starved for books at present. We have broadcast quite a lot of contemporary verse to India, and they are now doing it to China with a commentary in Chinese. We also have some of our broadcasts printed as pamphlets in India and sold for a few annas, a thing that could be useful but is terribly hard to organise in the face of official inertia and obstruction. I saw you had a poem by Tambimuttu.[4] If you are bringing out other numbers you ought to get some of the other Indians to write for you. There are several quite talented ones and they are very embittered because they think people snub them and won't print their stuff. It is tremendously important from several points of view to try to promote decent cultural relations between Europe and Asia. Nine tenths of what one does in this direction is simply wasted labour, but now and again a pamphlet or a broadcast or something gets to the person it is intended for, and this does more good than fifty speeches by politicians. William Empson has worn himself out for two years trying to get them to broadcast

[1] Lionel Fielden (1896–   ), author of *Beggar My Neighbour* and *The Natural Bent*; went to India in 1935; Controller of Broadcasting in India 1935–40 which became AIR (All India Radio); returned to the BBC London, 1940, as Indian News Editor.

[2] See 51.

[3] Ahmed Ali, a Pakistani writer, author of *Twilight in Delhi* and *Ocean of Night*. During the war he was the BBC's Listener and Research Director and Representative in India. After the partition of India he joined the Pakistani diplomatic corps. He is now a Professor at the University of Karachi.

[4] Tambimuttu, a Sinhalese poet, who founded and edited *Poetry London*, 1939–51.

intelligent stuff to China, and I think has succeeded to some small extent. It was thinking of people like him that made me rather angry about what you said of the BBC, though God knows I have the best means of judging what a mixture of whoreshop and lunatic asylum it is for the most part.

Yours sincerely
Geo. Orwell

## 50. Letter to Rayner Heppenstall

The British Broadcasting Corporation
Broadcasting House, London, W1
24 August 1943

Dear Rayner,

Thanks for yours. I hope your new post isn't too bloody. I'll try & fit in a talk for you in our next literary lot, but that will be 6 weeks or more from now—schedule is full up till then.

I wonder would you feel equal to featurising a story? We do that now abt once in 3 weeks. I featurised the first 2 myself, choosing Anatole France's *Crainquebille* & Ignazio Silone's *The Fox* (these are ½ hour programmes). I am probably going to hand the job of featurising future ones over to Lionel Fielden, but he won't necessarily do it every time. The chief difficulty is picking suitable stories, as they must be *a.* approximately right length, *b.* have a strong plot, *c.* not too many characters & *d.* not be too local, as these are for India. Have you any ideas? I could send you a specimen script & no doubt you could improve on my technique of featurisation.

Re cynicism, you'd be cynical yourself if you were in this job. However I am definitely leaving it probably in abt 3 months. Then by some time in 1944 I might be near-human again & able to write something serious. At present I'm just an orange that's been trodden on by a very dirty boot.

Yours
Eric

## 51. Review

*Beggar My Neighbour* by Lionel Fielden

If you compare commercial advertising with political propaganda, one thing that strikes you is its relative intellectual honesty. The advertiser at least knows what he is aiming at—that is, money—whereas the propagandist, when he is not a lifeless hack, is often a neurotic working off some private grudge and actually desirous of the exact opposite of the thing he advocates. The ostensible purpose of Mr Fielden's book is to further the cause of Indian independence. It will not have that effect, and I do not see much reason for thinking that he himself wishes for anything of the kind. For if someone is genuinely working for Indian independence, what is he likely to do? Obviously he will start by deciding what forces are potentially on his side, and then, as cold-bloodedly as any toothpaste advertiser, he will think out the best method of appealing to them. This is not Mr Fielden's manner of approach. A number of motives are discernible in his book, but the immediately obvious one is a desire to work off various quarrels with the Indian Government, All India Radio and various sections of the British press. He does indeed marshal a number of facts about India, and towards the end he even produces a couple of pages of constructive suggestions, but for the most part his book is simply a nagging, irrelevant attack on British rule, mixed up with tourist-like gush about the superiority of Indian civilisation. On the fly-leaf, just to induce that matey atmosphere which all propagandists aim at, he signs his dedicatory letter "among the European barbarians", and then a few pages later introduces an imaginary Indian who denounces western civilisation with all the shrillness of a spinster of thirty-nine denouncing the male sex:

> . . . an Indian who is intensely proud of his own traditions, and regards Europeans as barbarians who are continually fighting, who use force to dominate other peaceful peoples, who think chiefly in terms of big business, whisky, and bridge; as people of comparatively recent growth, who, while they put an exaggerated value on plumbing, have managed to spread tuberculosis and venereal disease all over the world . . . he will say that to sit in the water in which you have washed, instead of bathing yourself in running water, is not clean, but dirty and disgusting; he will show, and I shall agree with him absolutely, that the English

are a dirty and even a smelly nation compared with the Indians;
he will assert, and I am not at all sure that he is wrong, that the
use of half-washed forks, spoons and knives by different people
for food is revoltingly barbaric when compared with the exquisite manipulation of food by Indian fingers; he will be
confident that the Indian room, with its bare walls and beautiful
carpets, is infinitely superior to the European clutter of uncomfortable chairs and tables, etc etc etc.

The whole book is written in this vein, more or less. The same
nagging, hysterical note crops up every few pages, and where a
comparison can be dragged in it is dragged in, the upshot always
being that the East is Good and the West is Bad. Now before
stopping to inquire what service this kind of thing really does to
the cause of Indian freedom, it is worth trying an experiment. Let
me rewrite this passage as it might be uttered by an Englishman
speaking up for his own civilisation as shrilly as Mr Fielden's
Indian. It is important to notice that what he says is not more dishonest or more irrelevant than what I have quoted above:

... an Englishman who is intensely proud of his own traditions,
and regards Indians as an unmanly race who gesticulate like
monkeys, are cruel to women and talk incessantly about money;
as a people who take it upon them to despise western science
and consequently are rotten with malaria and hookworm ... he
will say that in a hot climate washing in running water has its
points, but that in cold climates all Orientals either wash as we
do or as in the case of many Indian hill tribes—not at all; he will
show, and I shall agree with him absolutely, that no western
European can walk through an Indian village without wishing
that his smell organs had been removed beforehand; he will
assert, and I am not at all sure that is he wrong, that eating with
your fingers is a barbarous habit since it cannot be done without
making disgusting noises; he will be confident that the English
room, with its comfortable armchairs and friendly book-
shelves, is infinitely superior to the bare Indian interior where the
mere effort of sitting with no support to your back makes for
vacuity of mind, etc etc etc.

Two points emerge here. To begin with, no English person would
now write like that. No doubt many people think such thoughts,

and even utter them behind closed doors, but to find anything of the kind in print you would have to go back ten years or so. Secondly, it is worth asking, what would be the effect of this passage on an Indian who happened to take it seriously? He would be offended, and very rightly. Well then, isn't it just possible that passages like the one I quoted from Mr Fielden might have the same effect on a British reader? No one likes hearing his own habits and customs abused. This is not a trivial consideration, because at this moment books about India have, or could have, a special importance. There is no political solution in sight, the Indians cannot win their freedom and the British Government will not give it, and all one can for the moment do is to push public opinion in this country and America in the right direction. But that will not be done by any propaganda that is merely anti-European. A year ago, soon after the Cripps mission had failed, I saw a well-known Indian nationalist address a small meeting at which he was to explain why the Cripps offer had been refused. It was a valuable opportunity, because there were present a number of American newspaper correspondents who, if handled tactfully, might cable to America a sympathetic account of the Congress Party's case. They had come there with fairly open minds. Within about ten minutes the Indian had converted all of them into ardent supporters of the British Government, because instead of sticking to his subject he launched into an anti-British tirade quite obviously founded on spite and inferiority complex. That is just the mistake that a toothpaste advertiser would not make. But then the toothpaste advertiser is trying to sell toothpaste and not to get his own back on that Blimp who turned him out of a first-class carriage fifteen years ago.

However, Mr Fielden's book raises wider issues than the immediate political problem. He upholds the East against the West on the ground that the East is religious, artistic and indifferent to "progress", while the West is materialistic, scientific, vulgar and warlike. The great crime of Britain is to have forced industrialisation on India. (Actually, the real crime of Britain during the last thirty years has been to do the opposite.) The West looks on work as an end in itself, but at the same time is obsessed with a "high standard of living" (it is worth noticing that Mr Fielden is anti-Socialist, russophobe and somewhat contemptuous of the English working class), while India wants only to live in ancestral simplicity in a world freed from the machine. India must be independent, and at the same time must be de-industrialised. It is also suggested a number of times, though not in very clear terms, that India ought to be neutral in the present war. Needless to say, Mr Fielden's hero is Gandhi, about whose financial background he says nothing. "I have a notion that the legend of Gandhi may yet be a flaming inspiration to the millions of the East, and perhaps to those of the West. But it is, for the time being, the East which provides the fruitful soil, because the East has not yet fallen prone before the Golden Calf. And it may be for the East, once again, to show mankind that human happiness does not depend on that particular form of worship, and that the conquest of materialism is also the conquest of war." Gandhi makes many appearances in the book, playing rather the same part as "Frank" in the literature of the Buchmanites.

Now, I do not know whether or not Gandhi will be a "flaming inspiration" in years to come. When one thinks of the creatures who *are* venerated by humanity it does not seem particularly unlikely. But the statement that India "ought" to be independent, *and* de-industrialised, *and* neutral in the present war, is an absurdity. If one forgets the details of the political struggle and looks at the strategic realities, one sees two facts which are in seeming conflict. The first is that whatever the "ought" of the question may be, India is very unlikely ever to be independent in the sense in which Britain or Germany is now independent. The second is that India's *desire* for independence is a reality and cannot be talked out of existence.

In a world in which national sovereignty exists, India cannot be a sovereign state, because she is unable to defend herself. And the more she is the cow and spinning-wheel paradise imagined by Mr Fielden, the more this is true. What is now called independence means the power to manufacture aeroplanes in large numbers. Already there are only five genuinely independent states in the world, and if present trends continue there will in the end be only three. On a long-term view it is clear that India has little chance in a world of power politics, while on a short-term view it is clear that the necessary first step towards Indian freedom is an Allied victory. Even that would only be a short and uncertain step, but the alternatives must lead to India's continued subjection. If we are defeated, Japan or Germany takes over India and that is the end of the story. If there is a compromise peace (Mr Fielden seems to hint at times that this is desirable), India's chances are no better, because in such circumstances we should inevitably cling to any territories we had captured or not lost. A compromise peace is always a peace of "grab what you can". Mr Fielden brings forward his imaginary Indian to suggest that if India were neutral Japan might leave her alone; I doubt whether any responsible Indian nationalist has said anything quite so stupid as that. The other idea, more popular in left-wing circles, that India could defend herself better on her own than with our help, is a sentimentality. If the Indians were militarily superior to ourselves they would have driven us out long ago. The much-quoted example of China is very misleading here. India is a far easier country to conquer than China, if only because of its better communications, and in any case Chinese resistance depends on help from the highly industrialised states and would collapse without it. One must conclude that for the next few years India's destiny is linked with that of Britain and the USA. It might be different if the Russians could get their hands free in the West or if China were a great military power; but that again implies a complete defeat of the Axis, and points away from the neutrality which Mr Fielden seems to think desirable. The idea put forward by Gandhi himself, that if the Japanese came they could be dealt with by sabotage and "non-co-operation", is a delusion, nor does Gandhi show any very strong signs of believing in it. Those methods have never seriously embarrassed the British and would make no impression on the Japanese. After all, where is the Korean Gandhi?

But against this is the *fact* of Indian nationalism, which is not to be exorcised by the humbug of White Papers or by a few phrases out of Marx. And it is nationalism of an emotional, romantic, even chauvinistic kind. Phrases like "the sacred soil of the Motherland", which now seem merely ludicrous in Britain, come naturally enough to an Indian intellectual. When the Japanese appeared to be on the point of invading India, Nehru actually used the phrase, "Who dies if India live?" So the wheel comes full circle and the Indian rebel quotes Kipling. And nationalism at this level works indirectly in favour of Fascism. Extremely few Indians are at all attracted by the idea of a federated world, the only kind of world in which India could actually be free. Even those who pay lip-service to federalism usually want only an eastern federation, thought of as a military alliance against the West. The idea of the class struggle has little appeal anywhere in Asia, nor do Russia and China evoke much loyalty in India. As for the Nazi domination of Europe, only a handful of Indians are able to see that it affects their own destiny in any way. In some of the smaller Asiatic countries the "my country right or wrong" nationalists were exactly the ones who went over to the Japanese—a step which may not have been wholly due to ignorance.

But here there arises a point which Mr Fielden hardly touches on, and that is: we don't know to what extent Asiatic nationalism is simply the product of our own oppression. For a century all the major oriental nations except Japan have been more or less in subjection, and the hysteria and shortsightedness of the various nationalist movements may be the result simply of that. To realise that national sovereignty is the enemy of national freedom may be a great deal easier when you are not being ruled by foreigners. It is not certain that this is so, since the most nationalist of the oriental nations, Japan, is also the one that has never been conquered, but at least one can say that if the solution is not along these lines, then there *is* no solution. Either power politics must yield to common decency, or the world must go spiralling down into a nightmare of which we can already catch some dim glimpses. And the necessary first step, before we can make our talk about world federation sound even credible, is that Britain shall get off India's back. This is the only large-scale decent action that is possible in the world at this moment. The immediate preliminaries would be: abolish the Viceroyalty and the India Office, release the Congress prisoners, and declare India formally independent. The rest is detail.[1]

But how are we to bring any such thing about? If it is done at this time, it can only be a voluntary act. Indian independence has no asset except public opinion in Britain and America, which is only a potential asset. Japan, Germany and the British Government are all on the other side, and India's possible friends, China and the USSR, are fighting for their lives and have little bargaining power. There remain the peoples of Britain and America, who are in a position to put pressure on their own governments if they see a reason for doing so. At the time of the Cripps mission, for instance, it would have been quite easy for public opinion in this country to force the Government into making a proper offer, and similar opportunities may recur. Mr Fielden, by the way, does his best to throw doubt on Cripps's personal honesty, and also lets it appear that the Congress

---

[1] Of course the necessary corollary would be a military alliance for the duration of the war. But it is not likely that there would be any difficulty in securing this. Extremely few Indians really want to be ruled by Japan or Germany. [Author's footnote.]

Working Committee were unanimously against accepting the Cripps proposals, which was not the case. In fact, Cripps extorted the best terms he could get from the Government; to get better ones he would have had to have public opinion actively and intelligently behind him. Therefore the first job is—win over the ordinary people of this country. Make them see that India matters, and that India has been shamefully treated and deserves restitution. But you are not going to do that by insulting them. Indians, on the whole, grasp this better than their English apologists. After all, what is the probable effect of a book which irrelevantly abuses every English institution, rapturises over the "wisdom of the East" like an American schoolmarm on a conducted tour, and mixes up pleas for Indian freedom with pleas for surrender to Hitler? At best it can only convert the converted, and it may deconvert a few of those. The net effect must be to strengthen British imperialism, though its motives are probably more complex than this may seem to imply.

On the surface, Mr Fielden's book is primarily a plea for "spiritu-ality" as against "materialism". On the one hand an uncritical reverence for everything oriental; on the other a hatred of the West generally, and of Britain in particular, hatred of science and the machine, suspicion of Russia, contempt for the working-class conception of Socialism. The whole adds up to Parlour Anarchism— a plea for the simple life, based on dividends. Rejection of the machine is, of course, always founded on tacit acceptance of the machine, a fact symbolised by Gandhi as he plays with his spinning-wheel in the mansion of some cotton millionaire. But Gandhi also comes into the picture in another way. It is noticeable that both Gandhi and Mr Fielden have an exceedingly equivocal attitude towards the present war. Although variously credited in this country with being a "pure" pacifist and a Japanese agent, Gandhi has, in fact, made so many conflicting pronouncements on the war that it is difficult to keep track of them. At one moment his "moral support" is with the Allies, at another it is withdrawn, at one moment he thinks it best to come to terms with the Japanese, at another he wishes to oppose them by non-violent means—at the cost, he thinks, of several million lives—at another he urges Britain to give battle in the West and leave India to be invaded, at another he "has no wish to harm the Allied cause" and declares that he does not want the Allied troops to leave India. Mr Fielden's views on the war are less compli-cated, but equally ambiguous. In no place does he state whether or not he wishes the Axis to be defeated. Over and over again he urges that an Allied victory can lead to no possible good result, but at the same time he disclaims "defeatism" and even argues that Indian neutrality would be useful to us in a *military* sense, i.e. that we could fight better if India were not a liability. Now, if this means anything, it means that he wants a compromise, a negotiated peace; and though he fails to say so, I do not doubt that that is what he does want. But curiously enough, this is the *imperialist* solution. The appeasers have always wanted neither defeat nor victory but a compromise with the other imperialist powers; and they too have known how to use the manifest folly of war as an argument.

For years past the more intelligent imperialists have been in favour of compromising with the Fascists, even if they had to give away a good deal in order to do so, because they have seen that only thus could imperialism be salvaged. Some of them are not afraid to hint this fairly broadly even now. If we carry the war to a destructive conclusion, the British Empire will either be lost, or democratised, or pawned to America. On the other hand it could and probably would survive in something like its present form if there were other sated imperialist powers which had an interest in preserving the existing world system. If we came to an understanding with Germany and Japan we might diminish our possessions (even that isn't certain: it is a little-noticed fact that *in territory* Britain and the USA have gained more than they have lost in this war), but we should at least be confirmed in what we had already. The world would be split up between three or four great imperial powers who, for the time being, would have no motive for quarrelling. Germany would be there to neutralise Russia, Japan would be there to prevent the development of China. Given such a world system, India could be kept in subjection almost indefinitely. And more than this, it is doubtful whether a compromise peace *could* follow any other lines. So it would seem that Parlour Anarchism is [not] something very innocuous after all. Objectively it only demands what the worst of the appeasers want, subjectively it is of a kind to irritate the possible friends of India in this country. And does not this bear a sort of resemblance to the career of Gandhi, who has alienated the British public by his extremism and aided the British Government by his moderation? Impossibilism and reaction are usually in alliance, though not, of course, conscious alliance.

Hypocrisy is a very rare thing, true villainy is perhaps as difficult as virtue. We live in a lunatic world in which opposites are constantly changing into one another, in which pacifists find themselves worshipping Hitler, Socialists become nationalists, patriots become quislings, Buddhists pray for the success of the Japanese army, and the Stock Market takes an upward turn when the Russians stage an offensive. But though these people's motives are often obvious enough when seen from the outside, they are not obvious to themselves. The scenes imagined by Marxists, in which wicked rich men sit in little secret rooms and hatch schemes for robbing the workers, don't happen in real life. The robbery takes place, but it is committed by sleepwalkers. Now, one of the finest weapons that the rich have ever evolved for use against the poor is "spirituality". If you can induce the working man to believe that his desire for a decent standard of living is "materialism", you have got him where you want him. Also, if you can induce the Indian to remain "spiritual" instead of taking up with vulgar things like trade unions, you can ensure that he will always remain a coolie. Mr Fielden is indignant with the "materialism" of the western working class, whom he accuses of being even worse in this respect than the rich and of wanting not only radios but even motor cars and fur coats. The obvious answer is that these sentiments don't come well from someone who is in a comfortable and privileged position himself. But that is only an answer, not a diagnosis, for the problem of the disaffected intelligentsia would be hardly a problem at all if ordinary dishonesty were involved.

In the last twenty years western civilisation has given the intellectual security without responsibility, and in England, in particular, it has educated him in scepticism while anchoring him almost immovably in the privileged class. He has been in the position of a young man living on an allowance from a father whom he hates. The result is a deep feeling of guilt and resentment, not combined with any genuine desire to escape. But some psychological escape, some form of self-justification there must be, and one of the most satisfactory is transferred nationalism. During the nineteen-thirties the normal transference was to Soviet Russia, but there are other alternatives, and it is noticeable that pacifism and anarchism, rather than Stalinism, are now gaining ground among the young. These creeds have the advantage that they aim at the impossible and therefore in effect demand very little. If you throw in a touch of oriental mysticism and Buchmanite raptures over Gandhi, you have everything that a disaffected intellectual needs. The life of an English gentleman and the moral attitudes of a saint can be enjoyed simultaneously. By merely transferring your allegiance from England to India (it used to be Russia), you can indulge to the full in all the chauvinistic sentiments which would be totally impossible if you recognised them for what they were. In the name of pacifism you can compromise with Hitler, and in the name of "spirituality" you can keep your money. It is no accident that those who wish for an inconclusive ending to the war tend to extol the East as against the West. The actual facts don't matter very much. The fact that the eastern nations have shown themselves at least as warlike and bloodthirsty as the western ones, that so far from rejecting industrialism, the East is adopting it as swiftly as it can—this is irrelevant, since what is wanted is the mythos of the peaceful, religious and patriarchal East to set against the greedy and materialistic West. As soon as you have "rejected" industrialism, and hence Socialism, you are in that strange no man's land where the Fascist and the pacifist join forces. There is indeed a sort of apocalyptic truth in the statement of the German radio that the teachings of Hitler and Gandhi are the same. One realises this when one sees Middleton Murry praising the Japanese invasion of China and Gerald Heard proposing to institute the Hindu caste system in Europe at the same time as the Hindus themselves are abandoning it. We shall be hearing a lot about the superiority of eastern civilisation in the next few years. Meanwhile this is a mischievous book, which will be acclaimed in the left-wing press and welcomed for quite different reasons by the more intelligent Right.

*Horizon*, September 1943; *Partisan Review*, Winter 1944

## 52. Letter to L.F. Rushbrook-Williams

BBC
24 September 1943

Dear Mr Rushbrook-Williams,[1]
In confirmation of what I said to you earlier in private, I want to tender my resignation from the BBC, and should be much obliged if you would forward this to the proper quarter.

[1] L.F. Rushbrook-Williams, Eastern Service Director at the BBC.

I believe that in speaking to you I made my reasons clear, but I should like to put them on paper lest there should be any mistake. I am not leaving because of any disagreement with BBC policy and still less on account of any kind of grievance. On the contrary I feel that throughout my association with the BBC I have been treated with the greatest generosity and allowed very great latitude. On no occasion have I been compelled to say on the air anything that I would not have said as a private individual. And I should like to take this opportunity of thanking you personally for the very understanding and generous attitude you have always shown towards my work.

I am tendering my resignation because for some time past I have been conscious that I was wasting my own time and the public money on doing work that produces no result. I believe that in the present political situation the broadcasting of British propaganda to India is an almost hopeless task. Whether these broadcasts should be continued at all is for others to judge, but I myself prefer not to spend my time on them when I could be occupying myself with journalism which does produce some measurable effect. I feel that by going back to my normal work of writing and journalism I could be more useful than I am at present.

I do not know how much notice of resignation I am supposed to give. The *Observer* have again raised the project of my going to North Africa. This has to be approved by the War Office and may well fall through again, but I mention it in case I should have to leave at shorter notice than would otherwise be the case. I will in any case see to it that the programmes are arranged for some time ahead.[1]

Yours sincerely
Eric Blair

[1] Orwell officially left the BBC on 24 November 1943.

## 53. Letter to Philip Rahv

10a Mortimer Crescent
London NW6
14 October 1943

Dear Philip Rahv,[1]

I have thought over your request for the names of possible contributors, but I must tell you that it is extremely difficult to think of any at present. No new people who are worth much seem to be coming along, and nearly everyone is either in the forces or being drained dry by writing muck for one of the ministries. You say the Comfort crew have been plaguing the life out of you, which I can well imagine, but I don't know which of them you have actually contacted. I think the best of this lot are Comfort himself, [Henry] Treece, Alun Lewis, Alan Rook, William Rodgers, G.S. Frazer[2] [*sic*], Roy Fuller, Kathleen Raine. You will have seen the work of these in *Poetry London* if it gets to the USA. I could obtain the addresses of these or others at need, except that Frazer, I believe, is in the Middle East.

Of older people I suppose you have the addresses of [Herbert] Read and [T.S.] Eliot and of the [Stephen] Spender-[Louis] MacNeice lot, who can in any case be contacted through *Horizon*. E.M. Forster has seen and likes *PR*, and would I should think do you something if you wanted. His address is West Hackhurst, Abinger Hammer, Nr Dorking, Surrey. William Empson who does still occasionally write something can be found care of the BBC. I don't know whether you know Mark Benney,[3] some of whose stuff is quite good. I haven't his address but could find it out (you could send it care of me if you wanted to write to him). Ditto with Jack Common[4] whose stuff you have possibly seen. You *might* get something very interesting out of Hugh Slater[5] (address 106 George Street, Nr

[1] Philip Rahv (1908– ), American critic and editor. Author of *Image and Idea*; one of the founders of *Partisan Review*, which he has co-edited since 1934.

[2] G.S. Fraser.

[3] Mark Benney became famous with his book, *Low Company: Describing the Evolution of a Burglar* (1936), which he had written in prison. He became a figure on the London literary scene for a time and shortly after the war went to America to teach sociology.

[4] Jack Common (1903– ), writer and editor, had met Orwell around 1930 through the *Adelphi* and had remained a friend.

[5] Hugh (Humphrey) Slater (1906–58), painter, author and ex-Communist. Involved in anti-Nazi politics in Berlin in the early 'thirties. Went to Spain as

Baker Street, London W1). If you are interested in Indian writers, I think the best is Ahmed Ali, whose address is care of BBC, New Delhi. He might do you something very good about present-day conditions in India especially among the younger intelligentsia. I know he is very overworked but he has recently published a book so he must have some spare time. Roy Campbell, who as you know was previously a Fascist and fought for Franco (i.e. for the Carlists) in Spain, but has latterly changed all his views, has been silent for some time but may be about due to begin writing again and I could get his address at need. I am sorry I cannot suggest more names but this place is a literary desert at present.

I am leaving the BBC at the end of next month and unless anything intervenes am going to take over the literary editorship of the *Tribune*. This *may* leave me some time to do a little of my own work as well, which the BBC doesn't. You may be interested to hear that I have contacted several American soldiers via *PR*. A chap called Julius Horowitz brought a message from Clement Greenberg[1] whom he had met in the army somewhere, and a boy named John Schloss who had read my letters in *PR* rang me up at the office and we met for a few drinks. Another fellow named Harry Milton who was with my lot in Spain and whom I think you may possibly know is also here. I wonder whether a Canadian airman named David Martin, who went across recently to finish his training, has shown up at your office. He said he would do so if in New York, and he has a message from me.

I hope all goes well.

Yours
Geo. Orwell

PS. How about the extra copies of *PR*? Is it now possible to send them? If so there is no doubt we could whack up the British circulation a bit. The last I heard was it was being done in some devious way through *Horizon*, but they were not getting enough copies to

---

political journalist and fought for the Republicans 1936–8, becoming Chief of Operations in the International Brigade. Helped Tom Wintringham to found Osterley Park training centre for the Home Guard in 1940. Edited *Polemic* (1945–7) to which Orwell contributed several pieces.

[1] Clement Greenberg (1909–  ), American art critic and editor; associate editor *Partisan Review* 1940–3; edited *Jewish Contemporary Review* (which later became *Commentary*) 1945–57.

supply all those who wanted to subscribe. The people who *are* getting it are most enthusiastic about it.

## 54. Who Are the War Criminals?

On the face of it, Mussolini's collapse was a story straight out of Victorian melodrama. At long last Righteousness had triumphed, the wicked man was discomfited, the mills of God were doing their stuff. On second thoughts, however, this moral tale is less simple and less edifying. To begin with, what crime, if any, has Mussolini committed? In power politics there are no crimes, because there are no laws. And, on the other hand, is there any feature in Mussolini's *internal* régime that could be seriously objected to by any body of people likely to sit in judgement on him? For, as the author of this book[1] abundantly shows—and this in fact is the main purpose of the book—there is not one scoundrelism committed by Mussolini between 1922 and 1940 that has not been lauded to the skies by the very people who are now promising to bring him to trial.

For the purposes of his allegory "Cassius" imagines Mussolini indicted before a British court, with the Attorney General as prosecutor. The list of charges is an impressive one, and the main facts—from the murder of Matteotti to the invasion of Greece, and from the destruction of the peasants' co-operatives to the bombing of Addis Ababa—are not denied. Concentration camps, broken treaties, rubber truncheons, castor oil—everything is admitted. The only troublesome question is: How can something that was praiseworthy at the time when you did it—ten years ago, say—suddenly become reprehensible now? Mussolini is allowed to call witnesses, both living and dead, and to show by their own printed words that from the very first the responsible leaders of British opinion have encouraged him in everything that he did. For instance, here is Lord Rothermere in 1928:

> In his own country [Mussolini] was the antidote to a deadly poison. For the rest of Europe he has been a tonic which has done to all incalculable good. I can claim with sincere satisfaction to have been the first man in a position of public

[1] *The Trial of Mussolini* by "Cassius".

influence to put Mussolini's splendid achievement in its right light.
. . . He is the greatest figure of our age.

Here is Winston Churchill in 1927:

> If I had been an Italian I am sure I should have been whole-
> heartedly with you in your triumphant struggle against the
> bestial appetites and passions of Leninism. . . . [Italy] has
> provided the necessary antidote to the Russian poison. Here-
> after no great nation will be unprovided with an ultimate means
> of protection against the cancerous growth of Bolshevism.

Here is Lord Mottistone in 1935:

> I did not oppose [the Italian action in Abyssinia]. I wanted to
> dispel the ridiculous illusion that it was a nice thing to sym-
> pathise with the underdog. . . . I said it was a wicked thing to
> send arms or connive to send arms to these cruel, brutal
> Abyssinians and still to deny them to others who are playing an
> honourable part.

Here is Mr Duff Cooper in 1938:

> Concerning the Abyssinian episode, the less said now the better.
> When old friends are reconciled after a quarrel, it is always
> dangerous for them to discuss its original causes.

Here is Mr Ward Price, of the *Daily Mail*, in 1932:

> Ignorant and prejudiced people talk of Italian affairs as if that
> nation were subject to some tyranny which it would willingly
> throw off. With that rather morbid commiseration for fanatical
> minorities which is the rule with certain imperfectly informed
> sections of British public opinion, this country long shut its
> eyes to the magnificent work that the Fascist régime was doing.
> I have several times heard Mussolini himself express his grati-
> tude to the *Daily Mail* as having been the first British newspaper
> to put his aims fairly before the world.

And so on, and so on, and so on. Hoare, Simon, Halifax, Neville
Chamberlain, Austen Chamberlain, Hore-Belisha, Amery, Lord
Lloyd and various others enter the witness-box, all of them ready
to testify that, whether Mussolini was crushing the Italian trade

unions, non-intervening in Spain, pouring mustard gas on the Abyssinians, throwing Arabs out of aeroplanes or building up a navy for use against Britain, the British Government and its official spokesmen supported him through thick and thin. We are shown Lady (Austen) Chamberlain shaking hands with Mussolini in 1924, Chamberlain and Halifax banqueting with him and toasting "the Emperor of Abyssinia" in 1939, Lord Lloyd buttering up the Fascist régime in an official pamphlet as late as 1940. The net impression left by this part of the trial is quite simply that Mussolini is not guilty. Only later, when an Abyssinian, a Spaniard and an Italian anti-Fascist give their evidence, does the real case against him begin to appear.

Now, the book is a fanciful one, but this conclusion is realistic. It is immensely unlikely that the British Tories will ever put Mussolini on trial. There is nothing that they could accuse him of except his declaration of war in 1940. If the "trial of war criminals" that some people enjoy dreaming about ever happens, it can only happen after revolutions in the Allied countries. But the whole notion of finding scapegoats, of blaming individuals, or parties, or nations for the calamities that have happened to us, raises other trains of thought, some of them rather disconcerting.

The history of British relations with Mussolini illustrates the structural weakness of a capitalist state. Granting that power politics are not moral, to attempt to buy Italy out of the Axis—and clearly this idea underlay British policy from 1934 onwards—was a natural strategic move. But it was not a move which Baldwin, Chamberlain and the rest of them were capable of carrying out. It could only have been done by being so strong that Mussolini would not dare to side with Hitler. This was impossible, because an economy ruled by the profit motive is simply not equal to rearming on a modern scale. Britain only began to arm when the Germans were in Calais. Before that, fairly large sums had, indeed, been voted for armaments, but they slid peaceably into the pockets of the shareholders and the weapons did not appear. Since they had no real intention of curtailing their own privileges, it was inevitable that the British ruling class should carry out every policy half-heartedly and blind themselves to the coming danger. But the moral collapse which this entailed was something new in British politics. In the nineteenth and early twentieth centuries, British politicians might be hypocritical, but hypocrisy implies a moral code. It was something new when Tory MPs cheered the news that British ships had been bombed by Italian aeroplanes, or when members of the House of Lords lent themselves to organised libel campaigns against the Basque children who had been brought here as refugees.

When one thinks of the lies and betrayals of those years, the cynical abandonment of one ally after another, the imbecile optimism of the Tory press, the flat refusal to believe that the dictators meant war, even when they shouted it from the housetops, the inability of the moneyed class to see anything wrong whatever in concentration camps, ghettos, massacres and undeclared wars, one is driven to feel that moral decadence played its part as well as mere stupidity. By 1937 or thereabouts it was not possible to be in doubt about the nature of the Fascist régimes. But the lords of property had decided that Fascism was on their side and they were willing to swallow the most stinking evils so long as their property remained secure. In their clumsy way they were playing the game of Machiavelli, of "political realism", of "anything is right which advances the cause of the Party"—the Party in this case, of course, being the Conservative Party.

All this "Cassius" brings out, but he does shirk its corollary. Throughout his book it is implied that only Tories are immoral. "Yet there is still another England," he says. "This other England detested Fascism from the day of its birth. . . . This was the England of the Left, the England of Labour." True, but only part of the truth. The actual behaviour of the Left has been more honourable than its theories. It has fought against Fascism, but its representative thinkers have entered just as deeply as their opponents into the evil world of "realism" and power politics.

"Realism" (it used to be called dishonesty) is part of the general political atmosphere of our time. It is a sign of the weakness of "Cassius's" position that one could compile a quite similar book entitled *The Trial of Winston Churchill*, or *The Trial of Chiang Kai-Shek*, or even *The Trial of Ramsay MacDonald*. In each case you would find the leaders of the Left contradicting themselves almost as grossly as the Tory leaders quoted by "Cassius". For the Left has also been willing to shut its eyes to a great deal and to accept some very doubtful allies. We laugh now to hear the Tories abusing Mussolini when they were flattering him five years ago, but who would have foretold in 1927 that the Left would one day take Chiang Kai-Shek to its bosom? Who would have foretold just after the General

Strike that ten years later Winston Churchill would be the darling of the *Daily Worker*? In the years 1935–9, when almost any ally against Fascism seemed acceptable, left-wingers found themselves praising Mustapha Kemal and then developing a tenderness for Carol of Rumania.

Although it was in every way more pardonable, the attitude of the Left towards the Russian régime has been distinctly similar to the attitude of the Tories towards Fascism. There has been the same tendency to excuse almost anything "because they're on our side". It is all very well to talk about Lady Chamberlain photographed shaking hands with Mussolini; the photograph of Stalin shaking hands with Ribbentrop is much more recent. On the whole, the intellectuals of the Left defended the Russo-German Pact. It was "realistic", like Chamberlain's appeasement policy, and with similar consequences. If there is a way out of the moral pigsty we are living in, the first step towards it is probably to grasp that "realism" does *not* pay, and that to sell out your friends and sit rubbing your hands while they are destroyed is not the last word in political wisdom.

This fact is demonstrable in any city between Cardiff and Stalingrad, but not many people can see it. Meanwhile it is a pamphleteer's duty to attack the Right, but not to flatter the Left. It is partly because the Left have been too easily satisfied with themselves that they are where they are now.

Mussolini, in "Cassius's" book, after calling his witnesses, enters the box himself. He sticks to his Machiavellian creed: Might is Right, *vae victis!* He is guilty of the only crime that matters, the crime of failure, and he admits that his adversaries have a right to kill him—but not, he insists, a right to blame him. Their conduct has been similar to his own, and their moral condemnations are all hypocrisy. But thereafter come the other three witnesses, the Abyssinian, the Spaniard and the Italian, who are morally upon a different plane, since they have never temporised with Fascism nor had a chance to play at power politics; and all three of them demand the death penalty.

Would they demand it in real life? Will any such thing ever happen? It is not very likely, even if the people who have a real right to try Mussolini should somehow get him into their hands. The Tories, of course, though they would shrink from a real inquest into the origins of the war, are not sorry to have the chance of pushing the whole blame onto a few notorious individuals like Mussolini and Hitler. In this way the Darlan-Badoglio manoeuvre is made easier. Mussolini is a good scapegoat while he is at large, though he would be an awkward one in captivity. But how about the common people? Would they kill their tyrants, in cold blood and with the forms of law, if they had the chance?

It is a fact that there have been very few such executions in history. At the end of the last war an election was won partly on the slogan "Hang the Kaiser", and yet if any such thing had been attempted the conscience of the nation would probably have revolted. When tyrants are put to death, it should be by their own subjects; those who are punished by a foreign authority, like Napoleon, are simply made into martyrs and legends.

What is important is not that these political gangsters should be made to suffer, but that they should be made to discredit themselves. Fortunately they do do so in many cases, for to a surprising extent the war-lords in shining armour, the apostles of the martial virtues, tend not to die fighting when the time comes. History is full of ignominious getaways by the great and famous. Napoleon surrendered to the English in order to get protection from the Prussians, the Empress Eugénie fled in a hansom cab with an American dentist, Ludendorff resorted to blue spectacles, one of the more unprintable Roman emperors tried to escape assassination by locking himself in the lavatory, and during the early days of the Spanish civil war one leading Fascist made his escape from Barcelona, with exquisite fitness, through a sewer.

It is some such exit that one would wish for Mussolini, and if he is left to himself perhaps he will achieve it. Possibly Hitler also. It used to be said of Hitler that when his time came he would never fly or surrender, but would perish in some operatic manner, by suicide at the very least. But that was when Hitler was successful; during the last year, since things began to go wrong, it is difficult to feel that he has behaved with dignity or courage. "Cassius" ends his book with the judge's summing-up, and leaves the verdict open, seeming to invite a decision from his readers. Well, if it were left to me, my verdict on both Hitler and Mussolini would be: not death, unless it is inflicted in some hurried unspectacular way. If the Germans and Italians feel like giving them a summary court-martial and then a firing-squad, let them do it. Or better still, let the pair of them escape with a suitcaseful of bearer securities and settle down as the accredited bores of some Swiss *pension*. But no martyrising, no

St Helena business. And, above all, no solemn hypocritical "trial of war criminals", with all the slow cruel pageantry of the law, which after a lapse of time has so strange a way of focusing a romantic light on the accused and turning a scoundrel into a hero.

*Tribune*, 22 October 1943

## 55. Mark Twain—The Licensed Jester

Mark Twain has crashed the lofty gates of the Everyman Library, but only with *Tom Sawyer* and *Huckleberry Finn*, already fairly well known under the guise of "children's books" (which they are not). His best and most characteristic books, *Roughing It*, *The Innocents at Home*, and even *Life on the Mississippi*, are little remembered in this country, though no doubt in America the patriotism which is everywhere mixed up with literary judgement keeps them alive.

Although Mark Twain produced a surprising variety of books, ranging from a namby-pamby "life" of Joan of Arc to a pamphlet so obscene that it has never been publicly printed, all that is best in his work centres about the Mississippi river and the wild mining towns of the West. Born in 1835 (he came of a Southern family, a family just rich enough to own one or perhaps two slaves), he had had his youth and early manhood in the golden age of America, the period when the great plains were opened up, when wealth and opportunity seemed limitless, and human beings felt free, indeed *were* free, as they had never been before and may not be again for centuries. *Life on the Mississippi* and the two other books that I have mentioned are a ragbag of anecdotes, scenic descriptions and social history both serious and burlesque, but they have a central theme which could perhaps be put into these words: "This is how human beings behave when they are not frightened of the sack". In writing these books Mark Twain is not consciously writing a hymn to liberty. Primarily he is interested in "character", in the fantastic, almost lunatic variations which human nature is capable of when economic pressure and tradition are both removed from it. The raftsmen, Mississippi pilots, miners and bandits whom he describes are probably not much exaggerated, but they are as different from modern men, and from one another, as the gargoyles of a medieval cathedral. They could develop their strange and sometimes sinister individuality because of the lack of any outside pressure. The State hardly existed, the churches were weak and spoke with many voices, and land was to be had for the taking. If you disliked your job you simply hit the boss in the eye and moved further west; and moreover, money was so plentiful that the smallest coin in circulation was worth a shilling. The American pioneers were not supermen, and they were not especially courageous. Whole towns of hardy gold miners let themselves be terrorised by bandits whom they lacked the public spirit to put down. They were not even free from class distinctions. The desperado who stalked through the streets of the mining settlement, with a Derringer pistol in his waistcoat pocket and twenty corpses to his credit, was dressed in a frock coat and shiny top-hat, described himself firmly as a "gentleman" and was meticulous about table manners. But at least it was not the case that a man's destiny was settled from his birth. The "log cabin to White House" myth was true while the free land lasted. In a way, it was for this that the Paris mob had stormed the Bastille, and when one reads Mark Twain, Bret Harte and Whitman it is hard to feel that their effort was wasted.

However, Mark Twain aimed at being something more than a chronicler of the Mississippi and the Gold Rush. In his own day he was famous all over the world as a humorist and comic lecturer. In New York, London, Berlin, Vienna, Melbourne and Calcutta vast audiences rocked with laughter over jokes which have now, almost without exception, ceased to be funny. (It is worth noticing that Mark Twain's lectures were only a success with Anglo-Saxon and German audiences. The relatively grown-up Latin races—whose own humour, he complained, always centred round sex and politics —never cared for them.) But in addition, Mark Twain had some pretensions to being a social critic, even a species of philosopher. He had in him an iconoclastic, even revolutionary vein which he obviously wanted to follow up and yet somehow never did follow up. He might have been a destroyer of humbugs and a prophet of democracy more valuable than Whitman, because healthier and more humorous. Instead he became that dubious thing a "public figure", flattered by passport officials and entertained by royalty, and his career reflects the deterioration in American life that set in after the civil war.

Mark Twain has sometimes been compared with his contemporary, Anatole France. This comparison is not so pointless as it may sound. Both men were the spiritual children of Voltaire, both had an ironical, sceptical view of life, and a native pessimism overlaid by gaiety; both knew that the existing social order is a swindle and its cherished beliefs mostly delusions. Both were bigoted atheists and convinced (in Mark Twain's case this was Darwin's doing) of the unbearable cruelty of the universe. But there the resemblance ends. Not only is the Frenchman enormously more learned, more civilised, more alive aesthetically, but he is also more courageous. He does attack the things he disbelieves in; he does not, like Mark Twain, always take refuge behind the amiable mask of the "public figure" and the licensed jester. He is ready to risk the anger of the Church and to take the unpopular side in a controversy—in the Dreyfus case, for example. Mark Twain, except perhaps in one short essay "What is Man?", never attacks established beliefs in a way that is likely to get him into trouble. Nor could he ever wean himself from the notion, which is perhaps especially an American notion, that success and virtue are the same thing.

In *Life on the Mississippi* there is a queer little illustration of the central weakness of Mark Twain's character. In the earlier part of this mainly autobiographical book the dates have been altered. Mark Twain describes his adventures as a Mississippi pilot as though he had been a boy of about seventeen at the time, whereas in fact he was a young man of nearly thirty. There is a reason for this. The same part of the book describes his exploits in the civil war, which were distinctly inglorious. Moreover, Mark Twain started by fighting, if he can be said to have fought, on the Southern side, and then changed his allegiance before the war was over. This kind of behaviour is more excusable in a boy than in a man, whence the adjustment of the dates. It is also clear enough, however, that he changed sides because he saw that the North was going to win; and this tendency to side with the stronger whenever possible, to believe that might *must* be right, is apparent throughout his career. In *Roughing It* there is an interesting account of a bandit named Slade, who, among countless other outrages, had committed 28 murders. It is perfectly clear that Mark Twain admires this disgusting scoundrel. Slade was successful; therefore he was admirable. This outlook, no less common today, is summed up in the significant American expression "to *make good*".

In the money-grubbing period that followed the civil war it was hard for anyone of Mark Twain's temperament to refuse to be a success. The old, simple, stump-whittling, tobacco-chewing democracy which Abraham Lincoln typified was perishing: it was now the age of cheap immigrant labour and the growth of Big Business. Mark Twain mildly satirised his contemporaries in *The Gilded Age*, but he also gave himself up to the prevailing fever, and made and lost vast sums of money. He even for a period of years deserted writing for business; and he squandered his time on buffooneries, not merely lecture tours and public banquets, but, for instance, the writing of a book like *A Connecticut Yankee in King Arthur's Court*, which is a deliberate flattery of all that is worst and most vulgar in American life. The man who might have been a kind of rustic Voltaire became the world's leading after-dinner speaker, charming alike for his anecdotes and his power to make businessmen feel themselves public benefactors.

It is usual to blame Mark Twain's wife for his failure to write the books he ought to have written, and it is evident that she did tyrannise over him pretty thoroughly. Each morning, Mark Twain would show her what he had written the day before, and Mrs Clemens (Mark Twain's real name was Samuel Clemens) would go over it with the blue pencil, cutting out everything that she thought unsuitable. She seems to have been a drastic blue-penciller even by nineteenth-century standards. There is an account in W.D. Howells's book *My Mark Twain* of the fuss that occurred over a terrible expletive that had crept into *Huckleberry Finn*. Mark Twain appealed to Howells, who admitted that it was "just what Huck would have said," but agreed with Mrs Clemens that the word could not possibly be printed. The word was "hell". Nevertheless, no writer is really the intellectual slave of his wife. Mrs Clemens could not have stopped Mark Twain writing any book he really wanted to write. She may have made his surrender to society easier, but the surrender happened because of that flaw in his own nature, his inability to despise success.

Several of Mark Twain's books are bound to survive, because they contain invaluable social history. His life covered the great period of American expansion. When he was a child it was a normal day's outing to go with a picnic lunch and watch the hanging of an Abolitionist, and when he died the aeroplane was ceasing to be a novelty. This period in America produced relatively little literature, and but for Mark Twain our picture of a Mississippi paddle-steamer, or a stage-coach crossing the plains, would be much dimmer than it is. But most people who have studied his work have come away with a feeling that he might have done something more. He gives all the while a strange impression of being about to say something and then funking it, so that *Life on the Mississippi* and the rest of them seem to be haunted by the ghost of a greater and much more coherent book. Significantly, he starts his autobiography by remarking that a man's inner life is indescribable. We do not know what he would have said —it is just possible that the unprocurable pamphlet, *1601*, would supply a clue but we may guess that it would have wrecked his reputation and reduced his income to reasonable proportions.

*Tribune*, 26 November 1943

## 56. Poetry and the Microphone

About a year ago I and a number of others were engaged in broadcasting literary programmes to India, and among other things we broadcast a good deal of verse by contemporary and near-contemporary English writers—for example, Eliot, Herbert Read, Auden, Spender, Dylan Thomas, Henry Treece, Alex Comfort, Robert Bridges, Edmund Blunden, D.H. Lawrence. Whenever it was possible we had poems broadcast by the people who wrote them. Just why these particular programmes (a small and remote outflanking movement in the radio war) were instituted there is no need to explain here, but I should add that the fact that we were broadcasting to an Indian audience dictated our technique to some extent. The essential point was that our literary broadcasts were aimed at the Indian university students, a small and hostile audience, unapproachable by anything that could be described as British propaganda. It was known in advance that we could not hope for more than a few thousand listeners at the most, and this gave us an excuse to be more "highbrow" than is generally possible on the air.

If you are broadcasting poetry to people who know your language but don't share your cultural background, a certain amount of comment and explanation is unavoidable, and the formula we usually followed was to broadcast what purported to be a monthly literary magazine. The editorial staff were supposedly sitting in their office, discussing what to put into the next number. Somebody suggested one poem, someone else suggested another, there was a short discussion and then came the poem itself, read in a different voice, preferably the author's own. This poem naturally called up another, and so the programme continued, usually with at least half a minute of discussion between any two items. For a half-hour programme, six voices seemed to be the best number. A programme of this sort was necessarily somewhat shapeless, but it could be given a certain appearance of unity by making it revolve round a single central theme. For example, one number of our imaginary magazine was devoted to the subject of war. It included two poems by Edmund Blunden, Auden's "September 1941", extracts from a long poem by G.S. Fraser ("A Letter to Anne Ridler"), Byron's "Isles of Greece" and an extract from T.E. Lawrence's *Revolt in the Desert*. These half-dozen items, with the arguments that preceded and followed them, covered reasonably well the possible attitudes towards war. The poems and the prose extract took about twenty minutes to broadcast, the arguments about eight minutes.

This formula may seem slightly ridiculous and also rather patronising, but its advantage is that the element of mere instruction, the textbook motif, which is quite unavoidable if one is going to broadcast serious and sometimes "difficult" verse, becomes a lot less forbidding when it appears as an informal discussion. The various speakers can ostensibly say to one another what they are in reality saying to the audience. Also, by such an approach you at least give a poem a context, which is just what poetry lacks from the average man's point of view. But of course there are other methods. One which we frequently used was to set a poem in music. It is announced that in a few minutes' time such and such a poem will be broadcast; then the music plays for perhaps a minute, then fades out into the poem, which follows without any title or announcement, then the music is faded again and plays up for another minute or two—the whole thing taking perhaps five minutes. It is necessary to choose appropriate music, but needless to say, the real purpose of the music is to insulate the poem from the rest of the programme. By this method you can have, say, a Shakespeare sonnet within three minutes of a news bulletin without, at any rate to my ear, any gross incongruity.

These programmes that I have been speaking of were of no great value in themselves, but I have mentioned them because of the ideas they aroused in myself and some others about the possibilities of the radio as a means of popularising poetry. I was early struck by the fact that the broadcasting of a poem by the person who wrote it does not merely produce an effect upon the audience, if any, but also on the poet himself. One must remember that extremely little in the way of broadcasting poetry has been done in England, and that many people who write verse have never even considered the idea of reading it aloud. By being set down at a microphone, especially if this happens at all regularly, the poet is brought into a new relationship with his work, not otherwise attainable in our time and country. It is a commonplace that in modern times—the last two hundred years, say—poetry has come to have less and less connection either with music or with the spoken word. It needs print in order to exist at all, and it is no more expected that a poet, as such, will know how to sing or even to declaim than it is expected that an architect will know how to plaster a ceiling. Lyrical and rhetorical poetry have almost ceased to be written, and a hostility towards poetry on the part of the common man has come to be taken for granted in any country where everyone can read. And where such a breach exists it is always inclined to widen, because the concept of poetry as primarily something printed, and something intelligible only to a minority, encourages obscurity and "cleverness". How many people do not feel quasi-instinctively that there must be something wrong with any poem whose meaning can be taken in at a single glance? It seems unlikely that these tendencies will be checked unless it again becomes normal to read verse aloud, and it is difficult to see how this can be brought about except by using the radio as a medium. But the special advantage of the radio, its power to select the right audience, and to do away with stage-fright and embarrassment, ought here to be noticed.

In broadcasting your audience is conjectural, but it is an audience of *one*. Millions may be listening, but each is listening alone, or as a member of a small group, and each has (or ought to have) the feeling that you are speaking to him individually. More than this, it is reasonable to assume that your audience is sympathetic, or at least interested, for anyone who is bored can promptly switch you off by turning a knob. But though presumably sympathetic, the audience *has no power over you*. It is just here that a broadcast differs from a speech or a lecture. On the platform, as anyone used to public speaking knows, it is almost impossible not to take your tone from the audience. It is always obvious within a few minutes what they will respond to and what they will not, and in practice you are almost compelled to speak for the benefit of what you

estimate as the stupidest person present, and also to ingratiate yourself by means of the ballyhoo known as "personality". If you don't
do so, the result is always an atmosphere of frigid embarrassment.
That grisly thing, a "poetry reading", is what it is because there will
always be some among the audience who are bored or all but
frankly hostile and who can't remove themselves by the simple act
of turning a knob. And it is at bottom the same difficulty—the fact
that a theatre audience is not a selected one—that makes it impossible
to get a decent performance of Shakespeare in England. On the air
these conditions do not exist. The poet *feels* that he is addressing
people to whom poetry means something, and it is a fact that poets
who are used to broadcasting can read into the microphone with a
virtuosity they would not equal if they had a visible audience in front
of them. The element of make-believe that enters here does not
greatly matter. The point is that in the only way now possible the
poet has been brought into a situation in which reading verse aloud
seems a natural unembarrassing thing, a normal exchange between
man and man: also he has been led to think of his work as *sound*
rather than as a pattern on paper. By that much the reconciliation
between poetry and the common man is nearer. It already exists at
the poet's end of the aether-waves, whatever may be happening at
the other end.

However, what is happening at the other end cannot be disregarded. It will be seen that I have been speaking as though the
whole subject of poetry were embarrassing, almost indecent, as
though popularising poetry were essentially a strategic manoeuvre,
like getting a dose of medicine down a child's throat or establishing
tolerance for a persecuted sect. But unfortunately that or something
like it is the case. There can be no doubt that in our civilisation poetry
is by far the most discredited of the arts, the only art, indeed, in
which the average man refuses to discern *any* value. Arnold Bennett
was hardly exaggerating when he said that in the English-speaking
countries the word "poetry" would disperse a crowd quicker than a
fire-hose. And as I have pointed out, a breach of this kind tends to
widen simply because of its existence, the common man becoming
more and more anti-poetry, the poet more and more arrogant and
unintelligible, until the divorce between poetry and popular culture is
accepted as a sort of law of nature, although in fact it belongs only
to our own time and to a comparatively small area of the earth. We
live in an age in which the average human being in the highly

civilised countries is aesthetically inferior to the lowest savage. This state of affairs is generally looked upon as being incurable by any *conscious* act, and on the other hand is expected to right itself of its own accord as soon as society takes a comelier shape. With slight variations the Marxist, the Anarchist and the religious believer will all tell you this, and in broad terms it is undoubtedly true. The ugliness amid which we live has spiritual and economic causes and is not to be explained by the mere going-astray of tradition at some point or other. But it does not follow that no improvement is possible within our present framework, nor that an aesthetic improvement is not a necessary part of the general redemption of society. It is worth stopping to wonder, therefore, whether it would not be possible even now to rescue poetry from its special position as the most hated of the arts and win for it at least the same degree of toleration as exists for music. But one has to start by asking, in what way and to what extent is poetry unpopular?

On the face of it, the unpopularity of poetry is as complete as it could be. But on second thoughts, this has to be qualified in a rather peculiar way. To begin with, there is still an appreciable amount of folk poetry (nursery rhymes etc) which is universally known and quoted and forms part of the background of everyone's mind. There is also a handful of ancient songs and ballads which have never gone out of favour. In addition there is the popularity, or at least the toleration, of "good bad" poetry, generally of a patriotic or senti-mental kind. This might seem beside the point if it were not that "good bad" poetry has all the characteristics which, ostensibly, make the average man dislike true poetry. It is in verse, it rhymes, it deals in lofty sentiments and unusual language—all this to a very marked degree, for it is almost axiomatic that bad poetry is more "poetical" than good poetry. Yet if not actively liked it is at least tolerated. For example, just before writing this I have been listening to a couple of BBC comedians doing their usual turn before the 9 o'clock news. In the last three minutes one of the two comedians suddenly announces that he "wants to be serious for a moment" and proceeds to recite a piece of patriotic balderdash entitled "A Fine Old English Gentleman", in praise of His Majesty the King. Now, what is the reaction of the audience to this sudden lapse into the worst sort of rhyming heroics? It cannot be very violently negative, or there would be a sufficient volume of indignant letters to stop the BBC doing this kind of thing. One must conclude that though the big public is hostile to *poetry*, it is not strongly hostile to *verse*. After all, if rhyme and metre were disliked for their own sakes, neither songs nor dirty limericks could be popular. Poetry is disliked because it is associated with untelligibility, intellectual pretentiousness and a general feeling of Sunday-on-a-weekday. Its name creates in advance the same sort of bad impression as the word "God", or a parson's dog-collar. To a certain extent, popularising poetry is a question of breaking down an acquired inhibition. It is a question of getting people to listen instead of uttering a mechanical raspberry. If true poetry could be introduced to the big public in such a way as to make it seem *normal*, as that piece of rubbish I have just listened to presumably seemed normal, then part of the prejudice against it might be overcome.

It is difficult to believe that poetry can ever be popularised again without some deliberate effort at the education of public taste, involving strategy and perhaps even subterfuge. T.S. Eliot once suggested that poetry, particularly dramatic poetry, might be brought back into the consciousness of ordinary people through the medium of the music hall; he might have added the pantomime, whose vast possibilities do not seem ever to have been completely explored. "Sweeney Agonistes" was perhaps written with some such idea in mind, and it would in fact be conceivable as a music-hall turn, or at least as a scene in a revue. I have suggested the radio as a more hopeful medium, and I have pointed out its technical advantages, particularly from the point of view of the poet. The reason why such a suggestion sounds hopeless at first hearing is that few people are able to imagine the radio being used for the dissemination of anything except tripe. People listen to the stuff that does actually dribble from the loudspeakers of the world, and conclude that it is for that and nothing else that the wireless exists. Indeed the very word "wireless" calls up a picture either of roaring dictators or of genteel throaty voices announcing that three of our aircraft have failed to return. Poetry on the air sounds like the Muses in striped trousers. Nevertheless one ought not to confuse the capabilities of an instrument with the use it is actually put to. Broadcasting is what it is, not because there is something inherently vulgar, silly and dishonest about the whole apparatus of microphone and transmitter, but because all the broadcasting that now happens all over the world is under the control of governments or great monopoly companies which are actively interested in maintaining the *status quo* and therefore in preventing the common man from becoming too intelligent. Something of the same kind has happened to the cinema, which, like the radio, made its appearance during the monopoly stage of capitalism and is fantastically expensive to operate. In all the arts the tendency is similar. More and more the channels of production are under the control of bureaucrats, whose aim is to destroy the artist or at least to castrate him. This would be a bleak outlook if it were not that the totalitarianisation which is now going on, and must undoubtedly continue to go on, in every country of the world, is mitigated by another process which it was not easy to foresee even as short a time as five years ago.

This is, that the huge bureaucratic machines of which we are all part are beginning to work creakily because of their mere size and their constant growth. The tendency of the modern state is to wipe out the freedom of the intellect, and yet at the same time every state, especially under the pressure of war, finds itself more and more in need of an intelligentsia to do its publicity for it. The modern state needs, for example, pamphlet-writers, poster artists, illustrators, broadcasters, lecturers, film producers, actors, song composers, even painters and sculptors, not to mention psychologists, sociologists, bio-chemists, mathematicians and what not. The British Government started the present war with the more or less openly declared intention of keeping the literary intelligentsia out of it; yet after three years of war almost every writer, however undesirable his political history or opinions, has been sucked into the various Ministries or the BBC and even those who enter the armed forces tend to find themselves after a while in Public Relations or some other essentially literary job. The Government has absorbed these people, unwillingly enough, because it found itself unable to get on without them. The ideal, from the official point of view, would have been to put all publicity into the hands of "safe" people like A.P. Herbert or Ian Hay: but since not enough of these were available, the existing intelligentsia had to be utilised, and the tone and even to some extent the content of official propaganda have been modified accordingly. No one acquainted with the Government pamphlets, ABCA[1] lectures, documentary films and broadcasts to occupied countries which have been issued during the past two years imagines that our rulers would sponsor this kind of thing if they could help it. Only, the bigger the machine of government becomes, the more loose

[1] The Army Bureau of Current Affairs.

ends and forgotten corners there are in it. This is perhaps a small consolation, but it is not a despicable one. It means that in countries where there is already a strong liberal tradition, bureaucratic tyranny can perhaps never be complete. The striped-trousered ones will rule, but so long as they are forced to maintain an intelligentsia, the intelligentsia will have a certain amount of autonomy. If the Government needs, for example, documentary films, it must employ people specially interested in the technique of the film, and it must allow them the necessary minimum of freedom; consequently, films that are all wrong from the bureaucratic point of view will always have a tendency to appear. So also with painting, photography, script-writing, reportage, lecturing and all the other arts and half-arts of which a complex modern state has need.

The application of this to the radio is obvious. At present the loudspeaker is the enemy of the creative writer, but this may not necessarily remain true when the volume and scope of broadcasting increase. As things are, although the BBC does keep up a feeble show of interest in contemporary literature, it is harder to capture five minutes on the air in which to broadcast a poem than twelve hours in which to disseminate lying propaganda, tinned music, stale jokes, faked "discussions" or what-have-you. But that state of affairs may alter in the way I have indicated, and when that time comes serious experiment in the broadcasting of verse, with complete disregard for the various hostile influences which prevent any such thing at present, would become possible. I don't claim it as certain that such an experiment would have very great results. The radio was bureaucratised so early in its career that the relationship between broadcasting and literature has never been thought out. It is not certain that the microphone is the instrument by which poetry could be brought back to the common people and it is not even certain that poetry would gain by being more of a spoken and less of a written thing. But I do urge that these possibilities exist, and that those who care for literature might turn their minds more often to this much-despised medium, whose powers for good have perhaps been obscured by the voices of Professor Joad and Doctor Goebbels.

Written [Autumn 1943]; _New Saxon Pamphlet_, [No. 3, March 1945], SJ; EYE; CE.

# War-time Diaries

## 57. War-time Diary: *28 May 1940–28 August 1941*

[During the first three years of the War Orwell kept two diaries covering
the periods 28 May 1940 to 28 August 1941 and 14 March 1942 to 15
November 1942. Both were handwritten, but the first diary no longer exists
in that form, the version of it printed here being the selection that Orwell
himself typed up from it. The cuts he made are indicated by five dots. Any
cuts made by the editors to avoid repetitions or libel are indicated by three
dots or by four dots to coincide with the end of a sentence.

The second diary is taken direct from the handwritten original but the
editors have made some cuts to avoid wounding the feelings of the people
mentioned and these cuts are indicated by three or four dots as the case
may be.

Orwell refers to many people in these diaries by initials, but only where
the editors are certain who is being referred to have the initials been supplied
with names.]

*28 May 1940*
This is the first day on which newspaper posters are definitely dis-
continued. . . . . Half of the front page of the early *Star*[1] devoted to
news of the Belgian surrender, the other half to news to the effect
that the Belgians are holding out and the King is with them. This is
presumably due to paper shortage. Nevertheless of the early *Star's*
eight pages, six are devoted to racing.

For days past there has been no real news and little possibility of
inferring what is really happening. The seeming possibilities were: (*i*)
that the French were really about to counter-attack from the south
(*ii*) that they hoped to do so but that the German bombers were
making it impossible to concentrate an army (*iii*) that the forces in
the north were confident of being able to hold on, and it was thought
better not to counter-attack till the German attack had spent itself,
or (*iv*) that the position in the north was in reality hopeless and the
forces there could only fight their way south, capitulate, be destroyed
entirely or escape by sea, probably losing very heavily in the process.

[1] A London evening newspaper of the time.

Now only the fourth alternative seems possible. The French com-
muniqués speak of stabilising the line along the Somme and Aisne,
as though the forces cut off in the north did not exist. Horrible
though it is, I hope the BEF[1] is cut to pieces sooner than capitulate.

People talk a little more of the war, but very little. As always
hitherto, it is impossible to overhear any comments on it in pubs etc.
Last night E[2] and I went to the pub to hear the 9 o'clock news. The
barmaid was not going to have turned it on if we had not asked her,
and to all appearances nobody listened.

## 29 May

One has to gather any major news nowadays by means of hints and
allusions. The chief sensation last night was that the 9 o'clock news
was preceded by a cheer-up talk (quite good) by Duff Cooper,[3] to
sugar the pill, and that Churchill said in his speech that he would
report again on the situation some time at the beginning of next
week, and that the House must prepare itself for "dark and heavy
tidings". This presumably means that they are going to attempt a
withdrawal, but whether the "dark tidings" mean enormous casualties, a surrender of part of the BEF, or what, nobody knows. Heard
the news between acts at a more or less highbrow play at the Torch
Theatre. The audience listened a good deal more attentively than
would have been the case in a pub.

E says the people in the Censorship Department where she works
lump all "red" papers together and look on the *Tribune*[4] as being in
exactly the same class as the *Daily Worker*.[5] Recently when the *Daily
Worker* and *Action*[6] were prohibited from export, one of her fellow-
workers asked her, "Do you know this paper, the *Daily Worker and
Action*?"

---

[1] The British Expeditionary Force, i.e. the British troops in France at the
time of the fall of France.

[2] Eileen, Orwell's wife.

[3] Alfred Duff Cooper (1890–1954), Conservative politician, diplomat and author.
After his resignation as First Lord of the Admiralty through disagreement with
Chamberlain over Munich, he became the figurehead of the patriotic Right.
Churchill made him Minister of Information in his Government in May 1940.
Always a francophile, Duff Cooper became Ambassador to France at the end of
the war and was created Viscount Norwich.

[4] The Socialist weekly, then edited by Raymond Postgate.

[5] The English Communist Party daily newspaper.

[6] The journal of the British Union of Fascists.

Current rumours: That Beaverbrook[1] since his appointment has got 2000 extra aeroplanes into the air by cutting through bottlenecks. That the air raids, possibly on London, are due to begin in 2 days' time. That Hitler's plan for invading England is to use thousands of speed-boats which can ride over the minefields. That there is a terrible shortage of rifles (this from several sources). That the morale of the ordinary German infantry of the line is pitiably low. That at the time of the Norway business the War Office were so ill-informed as not even to know that the Norwegian nights are short, and imagined that troops which had to disembark in broad daylight would have the cover of darkness.

*30 May*

The BEF are falling back on Dunkirk. Impossible not only to guess how many may get away, but how many are there. Last night a talk on the radio by a colonel who had come back from Belgium, which unfortunately I did not hear, but which from E's account of it contained interpolations put in by the broadcaster himself to let the public know the army had been let down (a) by the French (not counter-attacking), and (b) by the military authorities at home, by equipping them badly. No word anywhere in the press of recriminations against the French, and Duff Cooper's broadcast of two nights ago especially warned against this. . . . . Today's map looks as if the French contingent in Belgium are sacrificing themselves to let the BEF get away.

Borkenau[2] says England is now definitely in the first stage of revolution. Commenting on this, Connolly[3] related that recently a ship was coming away from northern France with refugees on board and a few ordinary passengers. The refugees were mostly children who were in a terrible state after having been machine-gunned etc etc. Among the passengers was Lady ——, who tried to push herself to the head of the queue to get on the boat, and when ordered back said indignantly, "Do you know who I am?" The steward answered, "I don't care who you are, you bloody bitch. You can take your turn in the queue." Interesting if true.

[1] In May Lord Beaverbrook, the newspaper proprietor, had been appointed Minister of Aircraft Production by Churchill.

[2] Franz Borkenau, writer and refugee from Hitler Germany, author of *The Spanish Cockpit* and *The Communist International*. See I, 101 and 138.

[3] Cyril Connolly (1903– ), the writer and critic, a life-long friend of Orwell, editor of *Horizon* 1940–50.

Still no evidence of any interest in the war. Yet the by-elections, responses to appeals for men, etc show what people's feelings are. It is seemingly quite impossible for them to grasp that they are in danger, although there is good reason to think that the invasion of England may be attempted within a few days, and all the papers are saying this. They will grasp nothing until the bombs are dropping. Connolly says they will then panic, but I don't think so.

### 31 May

Last night to see Denis Ogden's play *The Peaceful Inn*. The most fearful tripe. The interesting point was that though the play was cast in 1940, it contained no reference direct or indirect to the war.

Struck by the fewness of the men who even now have been called up. As a rule, looking round the street, it is impossible to see a uniform. . . . . Barbed wire entanglements are being put up at many strategic points, e.g. beside the Charles I statue in Trafalgar Square. . . . . Have heard on so many sides of the shortage of rifles that I believe it must be true.

### 1 June

Last night to Waterloo and Victoria to see whether I could get any news of [Eric].[1] Quite impossible, of course. The men who have been repatriated have orders not to speak to civilians and are in any case removed from the railway stations as promptly as possible. Actually I saw very few British soldiers, i.e. from the BEF, but great numbers of Belgian or French refugees, a few Belgian or French soldiers, and some sailors, including a few naval men. The refugees seemed mostly middling people of the shopkeeper-clerk type, and were in quite good trim, with a certain amount of personal belongings. One family had a parrot in a huge cage. One refugee woman was crying, or nearly so, but most seemed only bewildered by the crowds and the general strangeness. A considerable crowd was watching at Victoria and had to be held back by the police to let the refugees and others get to the street. The refugees were greeted in silence but all sailors of any description enthusiastically cheered. A naval officer, in a uniform that had been in the water and parts of a soldier's equipment, hurried

---

[1] Laurence (Eric) O'Shaughnessy, Eileen Blair's brother to whom she was greatly attached, an eminent heart and chest surgeon and a major in the Royal Army Medical Corps, was killed in Flanders while awaiting evacuation from Dunkirk. His death was announced in *The Times*, 8 June 1940.

towards a bus, smiling and touching his tin hat to either side as the women shouted at him and clapped him on the shoulder.

Saw a company of Marines marching through the station to entrain for Chatham. Was amazed by their splendid physique and bearing, the tremendous stamp of boots and the superb carriage of the officers, all taking me back to 1914, when all soldiers seemed like giants to me.

This morning's papers claim variously four-fifths and three-quarters of the BEF already removed. Photos, probably selected or faked, show the men in good trim with their equipment fairly intact.

*2 June*

Impossible to tell how many of the BEF have really been repatriated, but statements appearing in various papers suggest that it is about 150,000 and that the number that originally advanced into Belgium was about 300,000. No indication as to how many French troops were with them. There are hints in several papers that it may be intended to hang on to Dunkirk instead of evacuating it completely. This would seem quite impossible without tying down a great number of aeroplanes to that one spot. But if 150,000 have really been removed, it will presumably be possible to remove large numbers more. Italy's entry into the war is now predicted at any time after June 4th, presumably with some kind of peace offer to give it a pretext. . . . . General expectation that some attempt will now be made to invade England, if only as a diversion, while Germany and Italy endeavour to polish off France. . . . . The possibility of a landing in Ireland is evidently believed in by many people including de Valera. This idea has barely been mentioned until the last few days, although it was an obvious one from the start.

The usual Sunday crowds drifting to and fro, perambulators, cycling clubs, people exercising dogs, knots of young men loitering at street corners, with not an indication in any face or in anything that one can overhear that these people grasp that they are likely to be invaded within a few weeks, though today all the Sunday papers are telling them so. The response to renewed appeals for evacuation of children from London has been very poor. Evidently the reasoning is, "The air raids didn't happen last time, so they won't happen this time." Yet these people will behave bravely enough when the time comes, if only they are told what to do.

Rough analysis of advertisements in today's issue of the *People*:[1]

[1] A popular Sunday newspaper.

Paper consists of 12 pages = 84 columns. Of this, just about 26½ columns (over ¼) is advertisements. These are divided up as follows:

*Food and drink:* 5¾ columns.
*Patent medicines:* 9⅓.
*Tobacco:* 1.
*Gambling:* 2⅛.
*Clothes:* 1½.
*Miscellaneous:* 6¾.

Of 9 food and drink adverts, 6 are for unnecessary luxuries. Of 29 adverts for medicines, 19 are for things which are either fraudulent (baldness cured etc), more or less deleterious or of the blackmail type ("Your child's stomach needs ——"). Benefit of doubt has been allowed in the case of a few medicines. Of 14 miscellaneous adverts, 4 are for soap, 1 for cosmetics, 1 for a holiday resort and 2 are government advertisements, including a large one for national savings. Only 3 adverts in all classes are cashing in on the war.

*3 June*
From a letter from Lady Oxford[1] to the *Daily Telegraph*, on the subject of war economies:

"Since most London houses are deserted there is little entertaining. . . . . in any case, most people have to part with their cooks and live in hotels."

Apparently nothing will ever teach these people that the other 99% of the population exists.

*6 June*
Both Borkenau and I considered that Hitler was likely to make his next attack on France, not England, and as it turns out we were right. Borkenau considers that the Dunkirk business has proved once for all that aeroplanes cannot defeat warships if the latter have planes of their own. The figures given out were 6 destroyers and about 25 boats of other kinds lost in the evacuation of nearly 350,000 men. The number of men evacuated is presumably truthful, and even if one doubled the number of ships lost it would not be a great loss for such a large undertaking, considering that the circumstances were about as favourable to the aeroplanes as they could well be.

Borkenau thinks Hitler's plan is to knock out France and demand

[1] Margot Asquith (1864–1945), widow of Herbert Henry Asquith, Prime Minister 1908–16, created Earl of Oxford and Asquith 1925.

the French fleet as part of the peace terms. After that the invasion of England with sea-borne troops might be feasible.

Huge advert on the side of a bus: "FIRST AID IN WARTIME FOR HEALTH, STRENGTH AND FORTITUDE. WRIGLEY'S CHEWING GUM".

*7 June*

Although newspaper posters are now suppressed, one fairly frequently sees the paper-sellers displaying a poster. It appears that old ones are resuscitated and used, and ones with captions like "RAF raids on Germany" or "Enormous German losses" can be used at almost all times.

*8 June*

In the middle of a fearful battle in which, I suppose, thousands of men are being killed every day, one has the impression that there is no news. The evening papers are the same as the morning ones, the morning ones are the same as those of the night before, and the radio repeats what is in the papers. As to truthfulness of news, however, there is probably more suppression than downright lying. Borkenau considers that the effect of the radio has been to make war comparatively truthful, and that the only large-scale lying hitherto has been the German claims of British ships sunk. These have certainly been fantastic. Recently one of the evening papers which had made a note of the German announcements pointed out that in about 10 days the Germans claimed to have sunk 25 capital ships, i.e. 10 more than we ever possessed.

Stephen Spender said to me recently, "Don't you feel that any time during the past ten years you have been able to foretell events better than, say, the Cabinet?" I had to agree to this. Partly it is a question of not being blinded by class interests etc, e.g. anyone not financially interested could see at a glance the strategic danger to England of letting Germany and Italy dominate Spain, whereas many right-wingers, even professional soldiers, simply could not grasp this most obvious fact. But where I feel that people like us understand the situation better than so-called experts is not in any power to foretell specific events, but in the power to grasp what *kind* of world we are living in. At any rate, I have known since about 1931 (Spender says he has known since 1929) that the future must be catastrophic. I could not say exactly what wars and revolutions would happen, but they never surprised me when they came. Since 1934 I have known war between England and Germany was coming, and since 1936 I have known it with complete certainty. I could feel it in my belly, and the chatter of the pacifists on the one hand, and the Popular Front people who pretended to fear that Britain was preparing for war against Russia on the other, never deceived me. Similarly, such horrors as the Russian purges never surprised me, because I had always felt that—not *exactly* that, but something *like* that—was implicit in Bolshevik rule. I could feel it in their literature.

. . . . . Who would have believed seven years ago that Winston Churchill had any kind of political future before him? A year ago Cripps[1] was the naughty boy of the Labour Party, who expelled him and refused even to hear his defence. On the other hand, from the Conservative point of view he was a dangerous Red. Now he is ambassador in Moscow, the Beaverbrook press having led the cry for his appointment. Impossible to say yet whether he is the right man. If the Russians are disposed to come round to our side, he probably is, but if they are still hostile, it would have been better to send a man who does not admire the Russian régime.

### 10 June

Have just heard, though it is not in the papers, that Italy has declared war. . . . . . The allied troops are withdrawing from Norway, the reason given being that they can be used elsewhere and Narvik after its capture was rendered useless to the Germans. But in fact Narvik will not be necessary to them till the winter, it wouldn't have been much use anyway when Norway had ceased to be neutral, and I shouldn't have thought the allies had enough troops in Norway to make much difference. The real reason is probably so as not to have to waste warships.

This afternoon I remembered very vividly that incident with the taxi-driver in Paris in 1936,[2] and was going to have written something

---

[1] Sir Stafford Cripps (1889–1952), started his career as a successful lawyer, becoming a Labour MP in 1931. Frequently in trouble with the Labour Party leadership during the 'thirties, he was considered a brilliant theoretical mind, while his personal austerity and the rigidity of his Socialism gained him respect if not affection. He was Ambassador to Moscow 1940–42. He then joined the War Cabinet in February 1942 as Lord Privy Seal and Leader of the House of Commons and in March–April went as special envoy to India. In October of the same year became Minister of Aircraft Production. In the post-war Labour Government he was Chancellor of the Exchequer 1947–50.

[2] See III, 67, where Orwell describes the incident referred to.

about it in this diary. But now I feel so saddened that I can't write it. Everything is disintegrating. It makes me writhe to be writing book reviews etc at such a time, and even angers me that such time-wasting should still be permitted. The interview at the War Office on Saturday *may* come to something, if I am clever at faking my way past the doctor. If once in the army, I know by the analogy of the Spanish war, that I shall cease to care about public events. At present I feel as I felt in 1936 when the Fascists were closing in on Madrid, only far worse. But I will write about the taxi-driver some time.

*12 June*

E and I last night walked through Soho to see whether the damage to Italian shops etc was as reported. It seemed to have been exaggerated in the newspapers, but we did see, I think, 3 shops which had had their windows smashed. The majority had hurriedly labelled themselves "British". Gennari's, the Italian grocer's, was plastered all over with printed placards saying "This establishment is entirely British". The Spaghetti House, a shop specialising in Italian food-stuffs, had renamed itself "British Food Shop". Another shop proclaimed itself Swiss, and even a French restaurant had labelled itself British. The interesting thing is that all these placards must evidently have been printed beforehand and kept in readiness.

. . . . . Disgusting though these attacks on harmless Italian shopkeepers are, they are an interesting phenomenon, because English people, i.e. people of a kind who would be likely to loot shops, don't as a rule take a spontaneous interest in foreign politics. I don't think there was anything of this kind during the Abyssinian war, and the Spanish war simply did not touch the mass of the people. Nor was there any popular move against the Germans resident in England until the last month or two. The low-down, cold-blooded meanness of Mussolini's declaration of war at that moment must have made an impression even on people who as a rule barely read the newspapers.

*13 June*

Yesterday to a group conference of the LDV,[1] held in the Committee Room at Lord's. . . . . Last time I was at Lord's[2] must have been at the Eton-Harrow match in 1921. At that time I should have felt that to go into the Pavilion, not being a member of the MCC,[2] was on a par

[1] Local Defence Volunteers, which later became the Home Guard.
[2] Marylebone Cricket Club, whose grounds are at Lord's, London.

with pissing on the altar, and years later would have had some vague idea that it was a legal offence for which you could be prosecuted.

I notice that one of the posters recruiting for the Pioneers, of a foot treading on a swastika with the legend "Step on it", is cribbed from a Government poster of the Spanish war, i.e. cribbed as to the idea. Of course it is vulgarised and made comic, but its appearance at any rate shows that the Government are beginning to be willing to learn.

The Communist candidate in the Bow[1] by-election got about 500 votes. This a a new depth-record, though the Blackshirts have often got less (in one case about 150). The more remarkable because Bow was Lansbury's[2] seat, and might be expected to contain a lot of pacifists. The whole poll was very low, however.

*14 June*

The Germans are definitely in Paris, one day ahead of schedule. It can be taken as a certainty that Hitler will go to Versailles. Why don't they mine it and blow it up while he is there? Spanish troops have occupied Tangier, obviously with a view to letting the Italians use it as a base. To conquer Spanish Morocco from French Morocco would probably be easy at this date, and to do so, ditto the other Spanish colonies, and set up Negrin[3] or someone of his kind as an alternative government, would be a severe blow at Franco. But even the present British Government would never think of doing such a thing. One has almost lost the power of imagining that the Allied governments can ever take the initiative.

Always, as I walk through the Underground stations, sickened by the advertisements, the silly staring faces and strident colours, the general frantic struggle to induce people to waste labour and material by consuming useless luxuries or harmful drugs. How much rubbish this war will sweep away, if only we can hang on throughout the summer. War is simply a reversal of civilised life; its motto is "Evil be thou my good", and so much of the good of modern life is actually evil that it is questionable whether on balance war does harm.

---

[1] A working-class constituency in the East End of London.

[2] George Lansbury (1859–1940), Labour MP and leader of the Labour Party 1931–5, a fervent advocate of pacifism.

[3] Juan Negrin, Prime Minister of the Spanish Government during the last phase of the civil war, after which he set up a Spanish Government in exile.

*15 June*

It has just occurred to me to wonder whether the fall of Paris means the end of the Albatross Library,[1] as I suppose it does. If so, I am £30 to the bad. It seems incredible that people still attach any importance to long-term contracts, stocks and shares, insurance policies, etc in such times as these. The sensible thing to do now would be to borrow money right and left and buy solid goods. A short while back E made enquiries about the hire-purchase terms for sewing machines and found they had agreements stretching over two and a half years.

P.W[2] related that Unity Mitford,[3] besides having tried to shoot herself while in Germany, is going to have a baby. Whereupon a little man with a creased face, whose name I forget, exclaimed, "The Fuehrer wouldn't do such a thing!"

*16 June*

This morning's papers make it reasonably clear that, at any rate until after the Presidential election, the USA will not do anything, i.e. will not declare war, which in fact is what matters. For, if the USA is not actually in the war, there will never be sufficient control of either business or labour to speed up production of armaments. In the last war this was the case even when the USA was a belligerent.

It is impossible even yet to decide what to do in the case of German conquest of England. The one thing I will not do is to clear out, at any rate not further than Ireland, supposing that to be feasible. If the fleet is intact and it appears that the war is to be continued from America and the Dominions, then one must remain alive if possible, if necessary in the concentration camp. If the USA is going to submit to conquest as well, there is nothing for it but to die fighting, but one

[1] One of the earliest paperback publishers in Paris producing books in English for the continental market. Their publications included many of the most interesting books of the time, several of which were banned in Britain.

[2] Victor William (Peter) Watson (1908–56), a rich young man who after much travel decided in about 1939 to devote his life to the arts. He was co-founder with his friend Cyril Connolly of the magazine *Horizon* which he financed himself besides providing all the material for the art section. In 1948 he was one of the founders of the Institute of Contemporary Arts. He was always an admirer of Orwell's writing.

[3] The Hon. Unity Valkyrie Mitford (1914–48), fourth daughter of the second Lord Redesdale. From 1934, when she first met Hitler, she was his admirer. In January 1940 she was brought back to England from Germany suffering from bullet wounds in the head. Thereafter she lived in retirement.

must above all die *fighting* and have the satisfaction of killing some-body else first.

Talking yesterday to M, one of the Jewish members of my LDV section, I said that if and when the present crisis passed there would be a revolt in the Conservative Party against Churchill and an attempt to force wages down again, etc. He said that in that case there would be revolution, "or at least he hoped so". M is a manufacturer and I imagine fairly well off.

### 17 June

The French have surrendered. This could be foreseen from last night's broadcast and in fact should have been foreseeable when they failed to defend Paris, the one place where it might have been possible to stop the German tanks. Strategically all turns on the French fleet, of which there is no news yet. . . . .

Considerable excitement today over the French surrender, and people everywhere to be heard discussing it. Usual line, "Thank God we've got a navy". A Scottish private, with medals of the last war, partly drunk, making a patriotic speech in a carriage in the Underground, which the other passengers seemed rather to like. Such a rush on evening papers that I had to make four attempts before getting one.

Nowadays, when I write a review, I sit down at the typewriter and type it straight out. Till recently, indeed till six months ago, I never did this and would have said that I could not do it. Virtually all that I wrote was written at least twice, and my books as a whole three times—individual passages as many as five or ten times. It is not really that I have gained in facility, merely that I have ceased to care, so long as the work will pass inspection and bring in a little money. It is a deterioration directly due to the war.

Considerable throng at Canada House, where I went to make enquiries, as G[1] contemplates sending her child to Canada. Apart from mothers, they are not allowing anyone between 16 and 60 to leave, evidently fearing a panic rush.

### 20 June

Went to the office of the —— to see what line they are taking about home defence. C, who is now in reality the big noise there, was

---

[1] Gwen O'Shaughnessy, widow of Laurence (Eric), Eileen Blair's brother.

rather against the "arm the people" line and said that its dangers outweighed its possible advantages. If a German invading force finds civilians armed it may commit such barbarities as will cow the people altogether and make everyone anxious to surrender. He said it was dangerous to count on ordinary people being courageous and instanced the case of some riot in Glasgow when a tank was driven round the town and everyone fled in the most cowardly way. The circumstances were different, however, because the people in that case were unarmed and, as always in internal strife, conscious of fighting with ropes round their necks. . . . . C said that he thought Churchill, though a good man up to a point, was incapable of doing the necessary thing and turning this into a revolutionary war, and for that reason shielded Chamberlain and Co and hesitated to bring the whole nation into the struggle. I don't of course think Churchill sees it in quite the same colours as we do, but I don't think he would jib at any step (e.g. equalisation of incomes, independence for India) which he thought necessary for winning the war. Of course it's possible that today's secret session *may* achieve enough to get Chamberlain and Co out for good. I asked C what hope he thought there was of this, and he said none at all. But I remember that the day the British began to evacuate Namsos[1] I asked Bevan[2] and Strauss,[3] who had just come from the House, what hope there was of this business unseating Chamberlain, and they also said none at all. Yet a week or so later the new government was formed.

The belief in direct treachery in the higher command is now widespread, enough so to be dangerous. . . . . Personally I believe that such conscious treachery as exists is only in the pro-Fascist element of the aristocracy and perhaps in the army command. Of course the

[1] Seaport in Norway held by the British, April–May 1940, during the unsuccessful Norway campaign.

[2] Aneurin (Nye) Bevan (1897–1960), Labour Member of Parliament and Minister of Health in the post-war Labour Government. One of England's greatest orators, he was loved by the Left and feared and disliked by the Right. He resigned from the Labour Cabinet in 1951 over a split in policy but remained a member of the Party and the symbol of its Socialist aspirations. As a director of *Tribune* he gave Orwell freedom to write exactly as he pleased even when he wrote against the Labour line of the moment, e.g., when Orwell denounced the Soviet régime during the crucial phases of the Russo-British war effort. In 1949 Orwell said to a friend, "If only I could become Nye's *éminence grise* we'd soon have this country on its feet."

[3] G.R. Strauss, a Labour MP and co-director, with his friend Aneurin Bevan, of *Tribune*.

unconscious sabotage and stupidity which have got us into this situation, e.g. the idiotic handling of Italy and Spain, is a different matter. R.H[1] says that private soldiers back from Dunkirk whom he has spoken to all complain of the conduct of their officers, saying that the latter cleared off in cars and left them in the soup, etc etc. This sort of thing is always said after a defeat and may or may not be true. One could verify it by studying the lists of casualites, if and when they are published in full. But it is not altogether bad that that sort of thing should be said, provided it doesn't lead to sudden panic, because of the absolute need for getting the whole thing onto a new class basis. In the new armies middle-class people are bound to predominate as officers, they did so even, for instance, in the Spanish militias, but it is a question of unblimping. Ditto with the LDV. Under the stress of emergency we shall unblimp if we have time, but time is all.

A thought that occurred to me yesterday: how is it that England, with one of the smallest armies in the world, has so many retired colonels?

I notice that all the "left" intellectuals I meet believe that Hitler, if he gets here, will take the trouble to shoot people like ourselves and will have very extensive lists of undesirables. C[2] says there is a move on foot to get our police records (no doubt we all have them) at Scotland Yard destroyed. Some hope! The police are the very people who would go over to Hitler once they were certain he had won. Well, if only we can hold out for a few months, in a year's time we shall see red militia billeted in the Ritz, and it would not particularly surprise me to see Churchill or Lloyd George at the head of them.

Thinking always of my island in the Hebrides, which I suppose I shall never possess nor even see. Compton Mackenzie says even now most of the islands are uninhabited (there are 500 of them, only 10 per cent inhabited at normal times), and most have water and a little cultivable land, and goats will live on them. According to R.H. a woman who rented an island in the Hebrides in order to avoid air raids was the first air-raid casualty of the war, the RAF dropping a bomb there by mistake. Good if true.

The first air raid of any consequence on Great Britain the night before last. Fourteen killed, seven German aeroplanes claimed shot

[1] Rayner Heppenstall.
[2] Cyril Connolly.

down. The papers have photos of three wrecked German planes, so possibly the claim is true.

### 21 June

No real news. I see from yesterday's paper that Chiappe[1] has been elected president of the Paris Municipal Council, presumably under German pressure. So much for the claim that Hitler is the friend of the working classes, enemy of plutocracy, etc.

Yesterday the first drill of our platoon of the LDV. They were really admirable, only 3 or 4 in the whole lot (about 60 men) who were not old soldiers. Some officers who were there and had, I think, come to scoff were quite impressed.

### 22 June

No real news yet of the German terms to France. They are said to be "so complicated" as to need long discussion. I suppose one may assume that what is really happening is that the Germans on the one side and Pétain and Co on the other are trying to hammer out a formula that will induce the French commanders in the colonies and the navy to surrender. Hitler has in reality no power over these except through the French government. . . . . I think we have all been rather hasty in assuming that Hitler will now invade England, indeed it has been so generally expected that one might almost infer from this that he wouldn't do it. . . . . If I were him I should march across Spain, seize Gibraltar and then clean up North Africa and Egypt. If the British have a fluid force of say ¼ million men, the proper course would be to transfer it to French Morocco, then suddenly seize Spanish Morocco and hoist the Republican flag. The other Spanish colonies could be mopped up without much trouble. Alas, no hope of any such thing happening.

The Communists are apparently swinging back to an anti-Nazi position. This morning picked up a leaflet denouncing the "betrayal" of France by Pétain and Co, although till a week or two ago these people were almost openly pro-German.

### 24 June

The German armistice terms are much as expected. . . . . What is interesting about the whole thing is the extent to which the traditional

[1] Jean Chiappe (1878–1940), Corsican head of the Paris Police 1927–34; pro-Fascist, responsible for severely repressive measures against the Left.

pattern of loyalties and honour is breaking down. Pétain, ironically enough, is the originator (at Verdun) of the phrase "ils ne passeront pas", so long an anti-Fascist slogan. Twenty years ago any Frenchman who would have signed such an armistice would have had to be either an extreme left-winger or an extreme pacifist, and even then there would have been misgivings. Now the people who are virtually changing sides in the middle of the war are the professional patriots. To Pétain, Laval, Flandin and Co the whole war must have seemed like a lunatic internecine struggle at the moment when your real enemy is waiting to slosh you. . . . . It is therefore practically certain that high-up influences in England are preparing for a similar sell-out, and while e.g. —— is at —— there is no certainty that they won't succeed even without the invasion of England. The one good thing about the whole business is that the bottom is being knocked out of Hitler's pretence of being the poor man's friend. The people actually willing to do a deal with him are bankers, generals, bishops, kings, big industrialists, etc etc. . . . . Hitler is the leader of a tremendous counter-attack of the capitalist class, which is forming itself into a vast corporation, losing its privileges to some extent in doing so, but still retaining its power over the working class. When it comes to resisting such an attack as this, anyone who is *of* the capitalist class must be treacherous or half-treacherous, and will swallow the most fearful indignities rather than put up a real fight. . . . . Whichever way one looks, whether it is at the wider strategic aspects or the most petty details of local defence, one sees that any real struggle means revolution. Churchill evidently can't see or won't accept this, so he will have to go. But whether he goes in time to save England from conquest depends on how quickly the people at large can grasp the essentials. What I fear is that they will never move until it is too late.

Strategically, all turns upon hanging on until the winter. By that time, with huge armies of occupation everywhere, food almost certainly running short and the difficulty of forcing the conquered populations to work, Hitler must be in an awkward position. It will be interesting to see whether he rehabilitates the suppressed French Communist party and tries to use it against the working class in northern France as he has used Pétain against the Blimp class.

If the invasion happens and fails, all is well, and we shall have a definitely left-wing government and a conscious movement against the governing class. I think, though, people are in error in imagining that Russia would be more friendly towards us if we had a revolutionary government. After Spain, I cannot help feeling that Russia, i.e. Stalin, must be hostile to any country that is genuinely undergoing revolution. They would be moving in opposite directions. A revolution starts off with wide diffusion of the ideas of liberty, equality, etc. Then comes the growth of an oligarchy which is as much interested in holding onto its privileges as any other governing class. Such an oligarchy must necessarily be hostile to revolutions elsewhere, which inevitably reawaken the ideas of liberty and equality. This morning's *News Chronicle* announces that saluting of superior ranks has been reinstituted in the Red army. A revolutionary army would *start* by abolishing saluting, and this tiny point is symptomatic of the whole situation. Not that saluting and such things are not probably necessary.

Orders to the LDV that *all* revolvers are to be handed over to the police, as they are needed for the army. Clinging to useless weapons like revolvers, when the Germans have sub-machine-guns, is typical of the British army, but I believe the real reason for the order is to prevent weapons getting into "the wrong" hands.

Both E and G insistent that I should go to Canada if the worst comes to the worst, in order to stay alive and keep up propaganda. I will go if I have some function, e.g. if the government were transferred to Canada and I had some kind of job, but not as a refugee, nor as an expatriate journalist squealing from a safe distance. There are too many of these exiled "anti-Fascists" already. Better to die if necessary, and maybe even as propaganda one's death might achieve more than going abroad and living more or less unwanted on other people's charity. Not that I want to die; I have so much to live for, in spite of poor health and having no children.

Another government leaflet this morning, on treatment of air-raid casualties. The leaflets are getting much better in tone and language, and the broadcasts are also better, especially Duff Cooper's, which in fact are ideal for anyone down to the £5 a week level. But there is still nothing in really demotic speech, nothing that will move the poorer working class or even be quite certainly intelligible. Most educated people simply don't realise how little impression abstract words make on the average man. When Acland was sending round his asinine "Manifesto of Plain Men" (written by himself and signed on the dotted line by "plain men" whom he selected) he told me he had the first draft vetted by the Mass Observers, who tried it on

working men, and found that the most fantastic misunderstandings
arose. . . . . The first sign that things are really happening in England
will be the disappearance of that horrible plummy voice from the
radio. Watching in public bars, I have noticed that working men only
pay attention to the broadcasts when some bit of demotic speech
creeps in. E however claims, with some truth I think, that uneducated people are often moved by a speech in solemn language
which they don't actually understand but feel to be impressive, e.g.
Mrs A is impressed by Churchill's speeches, though not understanding them word for word.

*25 June*

Last night an air-raid warning about 1 am. It was a false alarm as
regards London, but evidently there was a real raid somewhere. We
got up and dressed, but did not go to the shelter. This is what everyone did, i.e. got up and then simply stood about talking, which seems
very foolish. But it seems natural to get up when one hears the siren,
and then in the absence of gunfire or other excitement one is ashamed
to go to the shelter.

I saw in one of yesterday's papers that gas masks are being issued
in America, though people have to pay for them. Gas masks are
probably useless to the civilian population in England and almost
certainly so in America. The issue of them is simply a symbol of
national solidarity, the first step towards wearing a uniform. . . . . As
soon as war started the carrying or not carrying of a gas mask
assumed social and political implications. In the first few days people
like myself who refused to carry one were stared at and it was generally assumed that the non-carriers were "left". Then the habit wore
off, and the assumption was that a person who carried a gas mask
was of the ultra-cautious type, the suburban rate-payer type. With
the bad news the habit has revived and I should think 20 per cent
now carry them. But you are still a little stared at if you carry one
without being in uniform. Until the big raids have happened and it is
grasped that the Germans don't, in fact, use gas, the extent to which
masks are carried will probably be a pretty good index of the
impression the war news is making on the public.

Went this afternoon to the recruiting office to put my name down
for the Home Service Battalions. Have to go again on Friday to be
medically examined, but as it is for men from 30 to 50 I suppose the
standards are low. The man who took my name etc, was the usual

imbecile, an old soldier with medals of the last war, who could barely write. In writing capital letters, he more than once actually wrote them upside down.

*27 June*

It appears that the night before last, during the air-raid alarm, many people all over London were woken by the All Clear signal, took that for the warning and went to the shelters and stayed there till morning, waiting for the All Clear. This after ten months of war and God knows how many explanations of the air-raid precautions.

The fact that the Government hasn't this time had to do a recruiting campaign has had a deadening effect on propaganda. . . . . A striking thing is the absence of any propaganda posters of a general kind, dealing with the struggle against Fascism, etc. If only someone would show the MOI the posters used in the Spanish war, even the Franco ones for that matter. But how can these people possibly rouse the nation *against Fascism* when they themselves are subjectively pro-Fascist and were buttering up Mussolini till almost the moment when Italy entered the war? Butler,[1] answering questions about the Spanish occupation of Tangier, says HM Government has "accepted the word" of the Spanish Government that the Spaniards are only doing so in order to preserve Tangier's neutrality—this after Falangist demonstrations in Madrid to celebrate the "conquest" of Tangier. . . . . This morning's papers publish a "denial" that Hoare[2] in Madrid is asking questions about an armistice. In other words he *is* doing so. Only question—can we get rid of these people in the next few weeks, before it is too late?

The unconscious treacherousness of the British ruling class in what is in effect a class war is too obvious to be worth mentioning. The difficult question is how much *deliberate* treachery exists. . . . . L.M,[3] who knows or at least has met all these people, says that with individual exceptions like Churchill the entire British aristocracy is

---

[1] R.A. Butler (1902– ), Conservative politician, Under-Secretary of State for Foreign Affairs 1938–41. Chancellor of the Exchequer and later Foreign Secretary in the Conservative Government of 1951–64.

[2] Sir Samuel Hoare, Bt, Viscount Templewood (1880–1959), politician and lawyer of extreme right-wing views, at this time British Ambassador to Spain. As Secretary of State for Foreign Affairs in 1935 he appeased Italy in the Italo-Ethiopian war, negotiating the Hoare-Laval Pact handing Ethiopia over to Italy despite existing international agreements.

[3] L.H. Myers (1881–1944), the novelist, author of *The Near and the Far*.

utterly corrupt and lacking in the most ordinary patriotism, caring in fact for nothing except preserving their own standards of life. He says they are also intensely class-conscious and recognise clearly the community of their interests with those of rich people elsewhere. The idea that Mussolini might fall has always been a nightmare to them, he says. Up to date L.M's predictions about the war, made the day it began, have been very correct. He said nothing would happen all the winter, Italy would be treated with great respect and then suddenly come in against us, and the German aim would be to force on England a puppet government through which Hitler could rule Britain without the mass of the public grasping what was happening. . . . . The only point where L.M proved wrong is that like myself he assumed Russia would continue to collaborate with Germany, which now looks as if it may not happen. But then the Russians probably did not expect France to collapse so suddenly. If they can bring it off, Pétain and Co are working towards the same kind of doublecross against Russia as Russia previously worked against England. It was interesting that at the time of the Russo-German Pact nearly everyone assumed that the pact was all to Russia's advantage and that Stalin had in some way "stopped" Hitler, though one had only to look at the map in order to see that this was not so. . . . . In western Europe Communism and Left extremism generally are now almost entirely a form of masturbation. People who are in fact without power over events console themselves by pretending that they are in some way controlling events. From the Communist point of view, nothing matters so long as they can persuade themselves that Russia is on top. It now seems doubtful whether the Russians gained much more from the pact than a breathing-space, though they did this much better than we did at Munich. Perhaps England and the USSR will be forced into alliance after all, an interesting instance of real interests overriding the most hearty ideological hatred.

The *New Leader*[1] is now talking about the "betrayal" by Pétain and Co and the "workers' struggle" against Hitler. Presumably they would be in favour of a "workers'" resistance if Hitler invaded England. And what will the workers fight with? With weapons. Yet the ILP clamour simultaneously for sabotage in the arms factories. These people live almost entirely in a masturbation fantasy, conditioned by the fact that nothing they say or do will ever influence events, not even the turning-out of a single shell.

[1] The organ of the Independent Labour Party.

*28 June*

Horribly depressed by the way things are turning out. Went this morning for my medical board and was turned down, my grade being C in which they aren't at present taking any men in any corps. .... What is appalling is the unimaginativeness of a system which can find *no* use for a man who is below the average level of fitness but at least is not an invalid. An army needs an immense amount of clerical work, most of which is done by people who are perfectly healthy and only half-literate. .... One could forgive the government for failing to employ the intelligentsia, who on the whole are politically unreliable, if they were making any attempt to mobilise the man-power of the nation and change people over from the luxury trades to productive work. This simply isn't happening, as one can see by looking down any street.

The Russians entered Bessarabia today. Practically no interest aroused, and the few remarks I could overhear were mildly approving or at least not hostile. Cf the intense popular anger over the invasion of Finland. I don't think the difference is due to a perception that Finland and Rumania are different propositions. It is probably because of our own desperate straits and the notion that this move may embarrass Hitler—as I believe it must, though evidently sanctioned by him.

*29 June*

The British Government has recognised de Gaulle, but apparently in some equivocal manner, i.e. it has not stated that it will not recognise the Pétain government.

One very hopeful thing is that the press is on our side and retains its independence. .... But contained in this is the difficulty that the "freedom" of the press really means that it depends on vested interests and largely (through its advertisements) on the luxury trades. Newspapers which would resist direct treachery can't take a strong line about cutting down luxuries when they live by advertising chocolates and silk stockings.

*30 June*

This afternoon a parade in Regent's Park of the LDV of the whole "zone", i.e. 12 platoons of theoretically about 60 men each (actually a little under strength at present). Predominantly old soldiers and, allowing for the dreadful appearance that men drilling in mufti always present, not a bad lot. Perhaps 25 per cent are working class.

If that percentage exists in the Regent's Park area, it must be much higher in some others. What I do not yet know is whether there has been any tendency to avoid raising LDV contingents in very poor districts where the whole direction would have to be in working-class hands. At present the whole organisation is in an anomalous and confused state, which has many different possibilities. Already people are spontaneously forming local defence squads, and hand-grenades are probably being manufactured by amateurs. The higher-ups are no doubt thoroughly frightened by these tendencies. . . . . The General inspecting the parade was the usual senile imbecile, actually decrepit, and made one of the most uninspiring speeches I ever heard. The men, however, very ready to be inspired. Loud cheering at the news that rifles have arrived at last.

Yesterday the news of Balbo's[1] death was on the posters as Connolly and the Ms and I walked down the street. C and I thoroughly pleased, C relating how Balbo and his friends had taken the Chief of the Senussi up in an aeroplane and thrown him out, and even the Ms (all but pure pacifists) were not ill-pleased, I think. E also delighted. Later in the evening (I spent the night at Crooms Hill)[2] we found a mouse which had slipped down into the sink and could not get up the sides. We went to great pains to make a sort of staircase of boxes of soap flakes etc, by which it could climb out, but by this time it was so terrified that it fled under the lead strip at the edge of the sink and would not move, even when we left it alone for half an hour or so. In the end E gently took it out with her fingers and let it go. This sort of thing does not matter. . . . . but when I remember how the *Thetis* disaster[3] upset me, actually to the point of interfering with my appetite, I do think it a dreadful effect of war that one is actually pleased to hear of an enemy submarine going to the bottom.

*1 July*

. . . . Rumours in all today's papers that Balbo was actually bumped off by his own side, as in the case of General von Fritsch.[4] Nowadays

[1] Marshal Balbo, the head of the Italian Air Force responsible for the bombing of Abyssinia in the Italo-Ethiopian War, 1935–6.

[2] In Greenwich. The home of Gwen O'Shaughnessy.

[3] In June 1939 the British submarine *Thetis* failed to surface from its first dive immediately after its launching. All the crew were drowned.

[4] General Werner von Fritsch (1880–1939), an old-guard member of the German General Staff who never concealed his contempt for Hitler. His death in action in 1939 was always thought to have been engineered by Hitler.

when any eminent person is killed in battle this suggestion inevitably arises. Cases in the Spanish war were Durruti[1] and General Mola.[2] The rumour about Balbo is based on a statement by the RAF that they know nothing about the air-fight in which Balbo is alleged to have been killed. If this is a lie, as it well may be, it is one of the first really good strokes the British propaganda has brought off.

*3 July*
Everywhere a feeling of something near despair among thinking people because of the failure of the Government to act and the continuance of dead minds and pro-Fascists in positions of command. Growing recognition that the only thing that would certainly right the situation is an unsuccessful invasion; and coupled with this a growing fear that Hitler won't after all attempt the invasion but will go for Africa and the Near East.

*5 July*
The almost complete lack of British casualties in the action against the French warships at Oran makes it pretty clear that the French seamen must have refused to serve the guns, or at any rate did so without much enthusiasm. . . . . In spite of the to-do in the papers about "French fleet out of action" etc etc, it appears from the list of ships actually given that about half the French navy is not accounted for, and no doubt more than half the submarines. But how many have actually fallen into German or Italian hands, and how many are still on the oceans, there is nothing in the papers to show. . . . . The frightful outburst of fury by the German radio (if rightly reported, actually calling on the English people to hang Churchill in Trafalgar Square) shows how right it was to make this move.

*10 July*
They have disabled the French battleship *Richelieu*, which was in Dakar harbour. But no move to seize any of the French West

[1] Buenaventura Durruti (1896–1936), head of the Spanish Anarchists at the beginning of the civil war, a gunman who became a General and popular leader. Killed in the defence of Madrid, possibly by Communists. His funeral gave rise to a great popular demonstration in Barcelona.

[2] General Mola (1887–1937), an equal colleague of Franco under General Sanjurjo, killed in the early stages of the Spanish civil war before the question of primacy with Franco could arise.

African ports, which no doubt are not strongly held. . . . . According
to Vernon Bartlett,[1] the Germans are going to make a peace offer
along the lines I foresaw earlier, i.e. England to keep out of Europe
but retain the Empire, and the Churchill Government to go out and
be replaced by one acceptable to Hitler. The presumption is that a
faction anxious to agree to this exists in England, and no doubt a
shadow cabinet has been formed. It seems almost incredible that
anyone should imagine that the mass of the people would tolerate
such an arrangement, unless they have been fought to a standstill
first. . . . . The Duke of Windsor has been shipped off as Governor of
the Bahamas, virtually a sentence of exile. . . . . The book Gollancz
has brought out, *Guilty Men*, the usual "indictment" of the Munich
crowd, is selling like hot cakes. According to *Time*, the American
Communists are working hand in glove with the local Nazis to
prevent American arms getting to England. One can't be sure how
much local freedom of action the various Communists have. Till
very recently it appeared that they had none. Of late however they
have sometimes pursued contradictory policies in different countries.
It is possible that they are allowed to abandon the "line" when strict
clinging to it would mean extinction.

*16 July*

No real news for some days, except the British Government's semi-
surrender to Japan, i.e. the agreement to stop sending war supplies
along the Burma road for a stated period. This however is not so
definite that it could not be revoked by a subsequent government. F
thinks it is the British Government's last effort (i.e. the last effort of
those with investments in Hong Kong etc) to appease Japan, after
which they will be driven into definitely supporting China. It may be
so. But what a way to do things—never to perform a decent action
until you are kicked into it and the rest of the world has ceased to
believe that your motives can possibly be honest.

W says that the London "left" intelligentsia are now completely
defeatist, look on the situation as hopeless and all but wish for
surrender. How easy it ought to have been to foresee, under their
Popular Front bawlings, that they would collapse when the real show
began.

[1] Vernon Bartlett (1894–   ), well-known liberal political journalist, for many
years on the *News Chronicle* where he reported on all the world crises connected
with Hitler, Mussolini and the Far East.

*22 July*

No real news for days past. The principal event of the moment is the pan-American conference, now just beginning, and the Russian absorption of the Baltic states, which must be directed against Germany. Cripps's wife and daughters are going to Moscow, so evidently he expects a long stay there. Spain is said to be importing oil in large quantities, obviously for German use, and we are not stopping it. Much hooey in the *News Chronicle* this morning about Franco desiring to keep out of war, trying to counter German influence etc etc. . . . . . It will be just as I said, Franco will play up his pretence of being pro-British, this will be used as a reason for handling Spain gently and allowing imports in any quantity, and ultimately Franco will come in on the German side.

*25 July*

No news, really. . . . . Various people who have sent their children to Canada are already regretting it. . . . . Casualties i.e. fatal ones, from air raids for last month were given out as about 340. If true, this is substantially less than the number of road deaths in the same period. . . . . . The LDV, now said to be 1,300,000 strong, is stopping recruiting and is to be renamed the Home Guard. There are rumours also that those acting as NCOs are to be replaced by men from the regular army. This seems to indicate either that the authorities are beginning to take the LDV seriously as a fighting force, or that they are afraid of it.

There are now rumours that Lloyd George is the potential Pétain of England. . . . . The Italian press makes the same claim and says that L.G's silence proves it true. It is of course fairly easy to imagine L.G playing this part out of sheer spite and jealousy because he has not been given a job, but much less easy to imagine him collaborating with the Tory clique who would in fact be in favour of such a course.

Constantly, as I walk down the street, I find myself looking up at the windows to see which of them would make good machine-gun nests. D says it is the same with him.

*28 July*

This evening I saw a heron flying over Baker Street. But this is not so improbable as the thing I saw a week or two ago, i.e. a kestrel killing a sparrow in the middle of Lord's cricket ground. I suppose it is possible that the war, i.e. the diminution of traffic tends to increase bird life in inner London.

The little man whose name I always forget used to know Joyce,[1] of the split-off Fascist party, commonly credited with being Lord Haw-Haw. He says that Joyce hated Mosley[2] passionately and talked about him in the most unprintable language. Mosley being Hitler's chief supporter in England, it is interesting that he should employ Joyce and not one of Mosley's men. This bears out what Borkenau said, that Hitler does not want a too-strong Fascist party to exist in England. Evidently the motive is always to split, and even to split the splitters. The German press is attacking the Pétain Government, with what motive is not absolutely certain, and so also are elements of the French press under German control. Doriot[3] is of course to the fore here. It was a shock to me when the *Sunday Times* also stated that the Germans in Paris are making use of Bergery.[4] But I accept this with caution, knowing how these small dissident Left parties are habitually lied about by the Right and the official Left alike.

*8 August*

The Italian attack on Egypt, or rather on British Somaliland, has begun. No real news yet, but the papers hint that Somaliland can't be held with the troops we have there. The important point is Perim, loss of which would practically close the Red Sea.

H.G. Wells knows Churchill well and says that he is a good man, not mercenary and not even a careerist. He has always lived "like a Russian commissar", "requisitions" his motor cars etc, but cares nothing about money. But —— says Churchill has a certain power

[1] William Joyce, known as Lord Haw-Haw supposedly from his way of speaking, was an American citizen who never acquired British nationality, although he spent most of his life in England and was a rabid nationalist. He became a Fascist for whom Sir Oswald Mosley's line was too mild. In August 1939 he went to Germany and in 1940 became a naturalised German. Throughout the early part of the war he broadcast propaganda to England from Germany. He was executed by the British at the end of the war.

[2] Sir Oswald Mosley, Bt. (1896–   ), politician, successively Conservative, Independent and Labour Member of Parliament. In 1931 he broke away from the Labour Party to form the New Party. Later he became fanatically pro-Hitler and turned his party into the British Union of Fascists.

[3] Jacques Doriot (1898–1945), French politician who, from being a Communist, became a Fascist leader and active collaborator with the Germans.

[4] Gaston Bergery, French deputé, an intellectual, who moved from the extreme Left to the extreme Right and, after the Fall of France, became a collaborator.

of shutting his eyes to facts and has the weakness of never wanting to let down a personal friend, which accounts for the non-sacking of various people. —— has already made a considerable row about the persecution of refugees. He considers that the centre of all the sabotage is the War Office. He believes that the jailing of anti-Fascist refugees is a perfectly conscious piece of sabotage based on the knowledge that some of these people are in touch with underground movements in Europe and might at some moment be able to bring about a "Bolshevik" revolution, which from the point of view of the governing class is much worse than defeat. He says that Lord S—— is the man most to blame. I asked him did he think it was a conscious action on Lord ——'s part, this being always the hardest thing to decide. He said he believed Lord —— knows perfectly well what he is doing.

Tonight to a lecture with lantern slides by an officer who had been in the Dunkirk campaign. Very bad lecture. He said the Belgians fought well and it was not true that they surrendered without warning (actually they gave three days' warning), but spoke badly of the French. He had one photograph of a regiment of Zouaves in full flight after looting houses, one man being dead drunk on the pavement.

### 9 August

The money situation is becoming completely unbearable. . . . . Wrote a long letter to the Income Tax people pointing out that the war had practically put an end to my livelihood while at the same time the government refused to give me any kind of job. The fact which is really relevant to a writer's position, the impossibility of writing books with this nightmare going on, would have no weight officially. . . . . Towards the government I feel no scruples and would dodge paying the tax if I could. Yet I would give my life for England readily enough, if I thought it necessary. No one is patriotic about taxes.

No real news for days past. Only air battles, in which, if the reports are true, the British always score heavily. I wish I could talk to some RAF officer and get some kind of idea whether these reports are truthful.

### 16 August

Things are evidently going badly in Somaliland, which is the flanking operation in the attack on Egypt. Enormous air battles over the

Channel, with, if the reports are anywhere near the truth, stupendous German losses. E.g. about 145 were reported shot down yesterday. .... The people in inner London could do with one real raid to teach them how to behave. At present everyone's behaviour is foolish in the extreme, everything except transport being held up but no precautions taken. For the first 15 seconds there is great alarm, blowing of whistles and shouts to children to go indoors, then people begin to congregate on the streets and gaze expectantly at the sky. In the daytime people are apparently ashamed to go into the shelters till they hear the bombs.

On Tuesday and Wednesday had two glorious days at Wallington.[1] No newspapers and no mention of the war. They were cutting the oats and we took Marx[2] out both days to help course the rabbits, at which Marx showed unexpected speed. The whole thing took me straight back to my childhood, perhaps the last bit of that kind of life that I shall ever have.

*19 August*

A feature of the air raids is the extreme credulity of almost everyone about damage done to distant places. George M arrived recently from Newcastle, which is generally believed here to have been seriously smashed about, and told us that the damage there was nothing to signify. On the other hand he arrived expecting to find London knocked to pieces and his first question on arrival was "whether we had had a very bad time". It is easy to see how people as far away as America can believe that London is in flames, England starving etc etc. And at the same time all this raises the presumption that our own raids on western Germany are much less damaging than is reported.

*20 August*

The papers are putting as good a face as possible upon the withdrawal from Somaliland, which is nevertheless a serious defeat, the first loss of British territory for centuries. .... It's a pity that the papers (at any rate the *News Chronicle*, the only one I have seen today) are so resolute in treating the news as good. This might have been made the start of another agitation which would have got some more of the duds out of the government.

[1] A village in Hertfordshire where Orwell had lived since 1936.
[2] The Orwells' dog.

Complaints among the Home Guards, now that air raids are getting commoner, because sentries have no tin hats. Explanation from Gen. Macnamara, who tells us that the regular army is still short of 300,000 tin hats—this after nearly a year of war.

*22 August*

The Beaverbrook press, compared with the headlines I saw on other papers, seems to be playing down the suggestion that Trotsky's murder was carried out by the GPU. In fact today's *Evening Standard*, with several separate items about Trotsky, didn't mention this suggestion. No doubt they still have their eye on Russia and want to placate the Russians at all costs, in spite of Low's[1] cartoons. But under this there may lie a much subtler manoeuvre. The men responsible for the [*Evening*] *Standard's* present pro-Russian policy are no doubt shrewd enough to know that a Popular Front "line" is not really the way to secure a Russian alliance. But they also know that the mass of leftish opinion in England still takes it for granted that a full anti-Fascist policy is the way to line up Russia on our side. To crack up Russia is therefore a way of pushing public opinion leftward. It is curious that I always attribute these devious motives to other people, being anything but cunning myself and finding it hard to use indirect methods even when I see the need for them.

Today in Portman Square saw a four-wheeler cab, in quite good trim, with a good horse and a cabman quite of the pre-1914 type.

*23 August*

This morning an air-raid warning about 3 am. Got up, looked at the time, then felt unable to do anything and promptly went to sleep again. They are talking of re-arranging the alarm system, and they will have to do so if they are to prevent every alarm from costing thousands of pounds in wasted time, lost sleep etc. The fact that at present the alarm sounds all over a wide area when the German planes are only operating in one part of it, means not only that people are unnecessarily woken up or taken away from work, but that an impression is spread that an air-raid alarm will *always* be false, which is obviously dangerous.

Have got my Home Guard uniform, after 2½ months.

[1] David Low (1891–1963), Kt. 1962, a political cartoonist of left-wing views who worked first for the *Evening Standard* and later for the *Manchester Guardian*.

Last night to a lecture by General ——, who is in command of about a quarter of a million men. He said he had been 41 years in the army. Was through the Flanders campaign, and no doubt *limogé* for incompetence. Dilating on the Home Guard being a static defensive force, he said contemptuously and in a rather marked way that he saw no use in our practising taking cover, "crawling about on our stomachs", etc etc evidently as a hit at the Osterley Park training school.[1] Our job, he said, was to die at our posts. Was also great on bayonet practice, and hinted that regular army ranks, saluting, etc, were to be introduced shortly. . . . . These wretched old Blimps, so obviously silly and senile, and so degenerate in everything except physical courage, are merely pathetic in themselves, and one would feel rather sorry for them if they were not hanging round our necks like millstones. The attitude of the rank and file at these would-be pep-talks—so anxious to be enthusiastic, so ready to cheer and laugh at the jokes, and yet all the time half feeling that there is something wrong—always strikes me as pathetic. The time has almost arrived when one will only have to jump up on the platform and tell them how they are being wasted and how the war is being lost, and by whom, for them to rise up and shovel the Blimps into the dustbin. When I watch them listening to one of these asinine talks, I always remember that passage in Samuel Butler's *Note-books* about a young calf he once saw eating dung. It could not quite make up its mind whether it liked the stuff or not, and all it needed was some experienced cow to give it a prod with her horn, after which it would have remembered for life that dung is not good to eat.

It occurred to me yesterday, how will the Russian state get on without Trotsky? Or the Communists elsewhere? Probably they will be forced to invent a substitute.

### 26 August

(Greenwich). The raid which occurred on the 24th was the first real raid on London so far as I am concerned, i.e. the first in which I could hear the bombs. We were watching at the front door when the East India docks were hit. No mention of the docks being hit in Sunday's papers, so evidently they do conceal it when important objectives are

---

[1] A training centre for the Home Guard, founded and run by Tom Wintringham with Hugh (Humphrey) Slater, where they taught guerilla warfare and street fighting based on their experiences in the International Brigade during the Spanish civil war.

hit. . . . . It was a loudish bang but not alarming and gave no impression of making the earth tremble, so evidently these are not very large
bombs that they are dropping. I remember the two big bombs that
dropped near Huesca when I was in the hospital at Monflorite. The
first, quite 4 kilometres away, made a terrific roar that shook the
houses and sent us all fleeing out of our beds in alarm. Perhaps that
was a 2,000 lb [sic] bomb and the ones at present being dropped are
500 lb ones. . . .

### 29 August

Air-raid alarms during the last 3 nights have totalled about 16–18
hours for the three nights. . . . . It is perfectly clear that these night
raids are intended chiefly as a nuisance, and as long as it is taken for
granted that at the sound of the siren everyone must dive for the
shelter, Hitler only needs to send his planes over half-a-dozen at a
time to hold up work and rob people of sleep to an indefinite extent.
However, this idea is already wearing off. . . . . For the first time in
20 years I have overheard bus conductors losing their tempers, and
being rude to passengers. E.g. the other night, a voice out of the
darkness: " 'Oo's conducting this bus, lady, me or you?" It took me
straight back to the end of the last war.

. . . . . E and I have paid the minimum of attention to raids and I
was honestly under the impression that they did not worry me at all
except because of the disorganisation, etc, that they cause. This
morning, however, putting in a couple of hours' sleep as I always do
when returning from guard duty, I had a very disagreeable dream of
a bomb dropping near me and frightening me out of my wits. Cf
the dream I used to have towards the end of our time in Spain, of
being on a grass bank with no cover and mortar shells dropping
round me.

### 31 August

Air-raid warnings, of which there are now half a dozen or thereabouts every 24 hours, becoming a great bore. Opinion spreading
rapidly that one ought simply to disregard the raids except when they
are known to be big-scale ones and in one's own area. Of the people
strolling in Regent's Park, I should say at least half pay no attention
to a raid warning. . . . . Last night just as we were going to bed, a
pretty heavy explosion. Later in the night woken up by a tremendous
crash, said to be caused by a bomb in Maida Vale. E and I merely

remarked on the loudness and fell asleep again. Falling asleep, with a vague impression of anti-aircraft guns firing, found myself mentally back in the Spanish war, on one of those nights when you had good straw to sleep on, dry feet, several hours' rest ahead of you, and the sound of distant gunfire, which acts as a soporific provided it *is* distant.

*1 September*
Recently bought a forage cap. . . . . It seems that forage caps over size 7 are a great rarity. Evidently they expect all soldiers to have small heads. This tallies with the remark made by some higher-up to R.R[1] in Paris when he tried to join the army—"Good God, you don't suppose we want intelligent men in the front line, do you?" All the Home Guard uniforms are made with 20-inch necks. . . . . Shops everywhere are beginning to cash in on the Home Guard, khaki shirts etc being displayed at fantastic prices with notices "Suitable for the Home Guard". Just as in Barcelona, in the early days when it was fashionable to be in the militia.

*3 September*
Yesterday talking with Mrs C who had recently come back from Cardiff. Raids there have been almost continuous, and finally it was decided that work in the docks must continue, raids or no raids. Almost immediately afterwards a German plane managed to drop a bomb straight into the hold of a ship, and according to Mrs C the remains of seven men working there "had to be brought up in pails." Immediately there was a dock strike, after which they had to go back to the practice of taking cover. This is the sort of thing that does not get into the papers. It is now stated on all sides that the casualties in the most recent raids, e.g. at Ramsgate, have been officially minimised, which greatly incenses the locals, who do not like to read about "negligible damage" when 100 people have been killed, etc etc. Shall be interested to see the figures for casualties for this month, i.e. August. I should say that up to about 2000 a month they would tell the truth, but would cover it up for figures over that.

Michael estimates that in his clothing factory, evidently a small individually-owned affair, time lost in air raids cost £50 last week.

[1] Richard Rees.

*7 September*

Air-raid alarms now frequent enough, and lasting long enough, for people habitually to forget whether the alarm is on at the moment, or whether the All Clear has sounded. Noise of bombs and gunfire, except when very close (which probably means within two miles) now accepted as a normal background to sleep or conversation. I have still not heard a bomb go off with the sort of bang that makes you feel you are personally involved.

In Churchill's speech, number killed in air raids during August given as 1075. Even if truthful, probably a large understatement as it includes only civilian casualties. . . . . The secretiveness officially practised about raids is extraordinary. Today's papers report that a bomb fell in a square "in central London". Impossible to find out which square it was, though thousands of people must know.

*10 September*

Can't write much of the insanities of the last few days. It is not so much that the bombing is worrying in itself as that the disorganisation of traffic, frequent difficulty of telephoning, shutting of shops whenever there is a raid on etc etc, combined with the necessity of getting on with one's ordinary work, wear one out and turn life into a constant scramble to catch up lost time. . . .

The delayed-action bombs are a great nuisance, but they appear to be successful in locating most of them and getting all the neighbouring people out until the bomb shall have exploded. All over South London, little groups of disconsolate-looking people wandering about with suitcases and bundles, either people who have been rendered homeless or, in more cases, who have been turned out by the authorities because of an unexploded bomb. . . . .

Most of last night in the public shelter, having been driven there by recurrent whistle and crash of bombs not very far away at intervals of about a quarter of an hour. Frightful discomfort owing to over-crowding, though the place was well-appointed, with electric light and fans. People, mostly elderly working class, grousing bitterly about the hardness of the seats and the longness of the night, but no defeatist talk. . . . .

People are now to be seen every night about dusk queuing up at the doors of the Shelters with their bedding. Those who come in first grab places on the floor and probably pass a reasonably good night.

Day raids apart, the raiding hours are pretty regularly 8 pm to 4.30 am i.e. dusk to just before dawn.

I should think 3 months of continuous raids at the same intensity as the last 4 nights would break down everyone's morale. But it is doubtful whether anyone could keep up the attack on such a scale for 3 months, especially when he is suffering much the same himself.

*12 September*

As soon as the air raids began seriously, it was noticeable that people were much readier than before to talk to strangers in the street. . . . . This morning met a youth of about 20, in dirty overalls, perhaps a garage hand. Very embittered and defeatist about the war, and horrified by the destruction he had seen in South London. He said that Churchill had visited the bombed area near the Elephant and at a spot where 20 out of 22 houses had been destroyed, remarked that it was "not so bad." The youth: "I'd have wrung his bloody neck if he'd said it to me." He was pessimistic about the war, considered Hitler was sure to win and would reduce London to much the same state as Warsaw. He spoke bitterly about the people rendered homeless in South London and eagerly took up my point when I said the empty houses in the West End should be requisitioned for them. He considered that all wars were fought for the profit of the rich, but agreed with me that this one would probably end in revolution. With all this, he was not unpatriotic. Part of his grouch was that he had tried to join the Air Force 4 times in the last 6 months, and always been put off.

Tonight and last night they have been trying the new device of keeping up a continuous AA barrage, apparently firing blind or merely by sound, though I suppose there is some kind of sound-detector which estimates the height at which they must make the shells burst. . . . . The noise is tremendous and almost continuous, but I don't mind it, feeling it to be on my side. Spent last night at Stephen Spender's place with a battery firing in the square at short intervals throughout the night. Slept through it easily enough, no bombs being audible in that place.

The havoc in the East End and South London is terrible, by all accounts. . . . . Churchill's speech last night referred very seriously to danger of imminent invasion. If invasion is actually attempted and this is not a feint, the idea is presumably either to knock out our air bases along the South Coast, after which the ground defences can be well bombed, at the same time causing all possible confusion in London and its southward communications, *or* to draw as much as possible of our defensive forces south before delivering the attack on Scotland or possibly Ireland.

Meanwhile our platoon of Home Guards, after 3½ months, have about 1 rifle for 6 men, no other weapons except incendiary bombs, and perhaps 1 uniform for 4 men. After all, they have stood out against letting the rifles be taken home by individual men. They are all parked in one place, where a bomb may destroy the whole lot of them any night.

### 14 September

On the first night of the barrage, which was the heaviest, they are said to have fired 500,000 shells, i.e. at an average cost of £5 per shell, £2½ millions worth. But well worth it, for the effect on morale.

### 15 September

This morning, for the first time, saw an aeroplane shot down. It fell slowly out of the clouds, nose foremost, just like a snipe that has been shot high overhead. Terrific jubilation among the people watching, punctuated every now and then by the question, "Are you sure it's a German?" So puzzling are the directions given, and so many the types of aeroplane, that no one even knows which are German planes and which are our own. My only test is that if a bomber is seen over London it must be a German, whereas a fighter is likelier to be ours.

### 17 September

Heavy bombing in this area last night till about 11 pm. . . . . I was talking in the hallway of this house to two young men and a girl who was with them. Psychological attitude of all 3 was interesting. They were quite openly and unashamedly frightened, talking about how their knees were knocking together, etc and yet at the same time excited and interested, dodging out of doors between bombs to see what was happening and pick up shrapnel splinters. Afterwards in Mrs C's little reinforced room downstairs, with Mrs C and her daughter, the maid, and three young girls who are also lodgers here. All the women, except the maid, screaming in unison, clasping each other and hiding their faces, every time a bomb went past, but between-whiles quite happy and normal, with animated conversation proceeding. The dog subdued and obviously frightened, knowing something to be wrong. Marx is also like this during raids, i.e. subdued and uneasy. Some dogs, however, go wild and savage during a raid and have had to be shot. They allege here, and E says the same thing about Greenwich, that all the dogs in the park now bolt for home when they hear the siren.

Yesterday, when having my hair cut in the City, asked the barber if he carried on during raids. He said he did. And even if he was shaving someone? I said. Oh, yes, he carried on just the same. And one day a bomb will drop near enough to make him jump, and he will slice half somebody's face off.

Later, accosted by a man, I should think some kind of commercial traveller, with a bad type of face, while I was waiting for a bus. He began a rambling talk about how he was getting himself and his wife out of London, how his nerves were giving way and he suffered from stomach trouble, etc etc. I don't know how much of this kind of thing there is. . . . . There has of course been a big exodus from the East End, and every night what amount to mass migrations to places where there is sufficient shelter accommodation. The practice of taking a 2d ticket and spending the night in one of the deep Tube stations, e.g. Piccadilly, is growing. . . . . Everyone I have talked to agrees that the empty furnished houses in the West End should be used for the homeless; but I suppose the rich swine still have enough pull to prevent this from happening. The other day 50 people from the East End, headed by some of the Borough Councillors, marched into the Savoy and demanded to use the air-raid shelter. The management didn't succeed in ejecting them till the raid was over, when they went voluntarily. When you see how the wealthy are *still* behaving, in what is manifestly developing into a revolutionary war, you think of St Petersburg in 1916.

(Evening). Almost impossible to write in this infernal racket. (Electric lights have just gone off. Luckily I have some candles.) So many streets in (lights on again) the quarter roped off because of unexploded bombs, that to get home from Baker Street, say 300 yards, is like trying to find your way to the heart of a maze.

### 21 September

Have been unable for some days to buy another volume to continue this diary because, of the three or four stationers' shops in the immediate neighbourhood, all but one are cordoned off because of unexploded bombs.

Regular features of the time: neatly swept-up piles of glass, litter of stone and splinters of flint, smell of escaping gas, knots of sight-seers waiting at the cordons.

Yesterday, at the entry to a street near here, a little crowd waiting with an ARP man in a black tin hat among them. A devastating roar, with a huge cloud of dust, etc. The man with the black hat comes running towards the ARP headquarters, where another with a white hat is emerging munching at a mouthful of bread and butter.

*The man with the black hat:* "Dorset Square, sir."

*The man with the white hat:* "OK." (Makes a tick in his notebook.)

Nondescript people wandering about, having been evacuated from their houses because of delayed-action bombs. Yesterday two girls stopping me in the street, very elegant in appearance except that their faces were filthily dirty: "Please, sir, can you tell us where we are?"

Withal, huge areas of London almost normal, and everyone quite happy in the daytime, never seeming to think about the coming night, like animals which are unable to foresee the future so long as they have a bit of food and a place in the sun.

*24 September*

Oxford Street yesterday, from Oxford Circus up to the Marble Arch, completely empty of traffic, and only a few pedestrians, with the late afternoon sun shining straight down the empty roadway and glittering on innumerable fragments of broken glass. Outside John Lewis's, a pile of plaster dress models, very pink and realistic, looking so like a pile of corpses that one could have mistaken them for that at a little distance. Just the same sight in Barcelona, only there it was plaster saints from desecrated churches.

Much discussion as to whether you would hear a bomb (i.e. its whistle) which was coming straight at you. All turns upon whether the bomb travels faster than sound. . . . . One thing I have worked out, I think satisfactorily, is that the further away from you a bomb falls, the longer the whistle you will hear. The short whizz is therefore the sound that should make you dive for cover. I think this is really the principle one goes on in dodging a shell, but there one seems to know by a kind of instinct.

The aeroplanes come back and come back, every few minutes. It is just like in an eastern country, when you keep thinking you have killed the last mosquito inside your net, and every time, as soon as you have turned the light out, another starts droning.

*27 September*
The *News Chronicle* today is markedly defeatist, as well it may be after yesterday's news about Dakar.[1] But I have a feeling that the *News Chronicle* is bound to become defeatist anyway and will be promptly to the fore when plausible peace terms come forward. These people have no definable policy and no sense of responsibility, nothing except a traditional dislike of the British ruling class, based ultimately on the Nonconformist conscience. They are only noise-makers, like the *New Statesman* etc. All these people can be counted on to collapse when the conditions of war become intolerable.

Many bombs last night, though I think none dropped within half a mile of this house. The commotion made by the mere passage of the bomb through the air is astonishing. The whole house shakes, enough to rattle objects on the table. Of course they are dropping very large bombs now. The unexploded one in Regent's Park is said to be "the size of a pillar box". Almost every night the lights go out at least once, not suddenly flicking off as when a connection is broken, but gradually fading out, and usually coming on again in about five minutes. Why it is that the lights dip when a bomb passes close by, nobody seems to know.

*15 October*
Writing this at Wallington, having been more or less ill for about a fortnight with a poisoned arm. Not much news—i.e. only events of world-wide importance; nothing that has much affected me personally.

There are now 11 evacuee children in Wallington (12 arrived, but one ran away and had to be sent home). They come from the East End. One little girl, from Stepney, said that her grandfather had been bombed out seven times. They seem nice children and to be settling down quite well. Nevertheless there are the usual complaints against them in some quarters, e.g. of the little boy who is with Mrs ——,

[1] In September 1940 a British expedition, co-operating with Free French forces under General de Gaulle, made an attempt to recapture the port of Dakar, West Africa, from the Vichy government. The expedition was a failure.

aged seven: "He's a dirty little devil, he is. He wets his bed and dirties his breeches. I'd rub his nose in it if I had charge of him, the dirty little devil."

Some murmurings about the number of Jews in Baldock. —— declares that Jews greatly predominate among the people sheltering in the Tubes. Must try and verify this.

Potato crop very good this year, in spite of the dry weather, which is just as well.

*19 October*
The unspeakable depression of lighting the fires every morning with papers of a year ago, and getting glimpses of optimistic headlines as they go up in smoke.

*21 October*
With reference to the advertisements in the Tube stations, "Be a Man" etc (asking able-bodied men not to shelter there but to leave the space for women and children), D says the joke going round London is that it was a mistake to print these notices in English.

Priestley,[1] whose Sunday night broadcasts were by implication Socialist propaganda, has been shoved off the air, evidently at the insistence of the Conservative Party. . . . . It looks rather as though the Margesson[2] crew are now about to stage a come-back.

*25 October*
The other night examined the crowds sheltering in Chancery Lane, Oxford Circus and Baker Street stations. *Not* all Jews, but, I think, a higher proportion of Jews than one would normally see in a crowd of this size. What is bad about Jews is that they are not only conspicuous, but go out of their way to make themselves so. A fearful

[1] J.B. Priestley (1894– ), prolific popular novelist, dramatist and man of letters. During 1940 and 1941 he gave a series of famous weekly talks on the radio urging the nation to determination and unity in the struggle against Hitler so as to make the country more democratic and egalitarian.

[2] D.R. Margesson (1890–1965), Conservative MP for Rugby 1924–42. Government Chief Whip 1931–40; doggedly loyal to each Prime Minister he served, backing Chamberlain until his downfall from the Premiership in May 1940. Under Churchill he continued as Joint Government Whip and after six months was appointed Secretary of State for War. He was created Viscount Margesson in 1942 after Churchill had relieved him of office in the spring of that year.

Jewish woman, a regular comic-paper cartoon of a Jewess, fought
her way off the train at Oxford Circus, landing blows on anyone
who stood in her way. It took me back to old days on the Paris
Métro.

Surprised to find that D, who is distinctly Left in his views, is
inclined to share the current feeling against the Jews. He says that
the Jews in business circles are turning pro-Hitler, or preparing to
do so. This sounds almost incredible, but according to D they will
always admire anyone who kicks them. What I do feel is that any
Jew, i.e. European Jew, would prefer Hitler's kind of social system
to ours, if it were not that he happens to persecute them. Ditto with
almost any Central European, e.g. the refugees. They make use of
England as a sanctuary, but they cannot help feeling the profoundest
contempt for it. You can see this in their eyes, even when they don't
say it outright. The fact is that the insular outlook and the continental
outlook are completely incompatible.

According to F, it is quite true that foreigners are more frightened
than English people during the raids. It is not their war, and therefore
they have nothing to sustain them. I think this might also account
for the fact—I am virtually sure it *is* a fact, though one mustn't
mention it—that working-class people are more frightened than
middle-class.

The same feeling of despair over impending events in France,
Africa, Syria, Spain—the sense of foreseeing what must happen and
being powerless to prevent it, and feeling with absolute certainty that a
British government *cannot* act in such a way as to get its blow in first.

Air raids much milder the last few days.

*16 November*
I never thought I should live to grow blasé about the sound of gunfire, but so I have.

*23 November*
The day before yesterday lunching with H.P, editor of ——. H.P
rather pessimistic about the war. Thinks there is no answer to the
New Order, i.e. this government is incapable of framing any answer,
and people here and in America could easily be brought to accept it.
I queried whether people would not for certain see any peace offer
along these lines as a trap. H.P: "Hell's bells, I could dress it up so
that they'd think it was the greatest victory in the history of the world.

I could make them eat it." That is true, of course. All depends on the form in which it is put to people. So long as our own newspapers don't do the dirty they will be quite indifferent to appeals from Europe. H.P, however, is certain that —— and Co are working for a sell-out. It appears that though —— is not submitted for censorship, all papers are now warned not to publish interpretations of the government's policy towards Spain. A few weeks back Duff Cooper had the press correspondents up and assured them "on his word of honour" that "things were going very well indeed in Spain". (The most one can say is that Duff Cooper's word of honour is worth more than Hoare's.)

H.P says that when France collapsed there was a Cabinet meeting to decide whether to continue the war or whether to seek terms. The vote was actually 50–50 except for one casting vote, and according to H.P this was *Chamberlain's*. If true, I wonder whether this will ever be made public. It was poor old Chamberlain's last public act, as one might say, poor old man.

Characteristic war-time sound, in winter: the musical tinkle of raindrops on your tin hat.

*28 November*

Lunching yesterday with C[1] editor of *France*. . . . . To my surprise he was in good spirits and had no grievances. I would have expected a French refugee to be grumbling endlessly about the food, etc. However, C knows England well and has lived here before.

He says there is much more resistance both in occupied and unoccupied France than people here realise. The press is playing it down, no doubt because of our continued relations with Vichy. He says that at the time of the French collapse no European looked on it as conceivable that England would go on fighting, and generally speaking Americans did not either. He is evidently somewhat of an anglophile and considers the monarchy a great advantage to England. According to him it has been a main factor in preventing the establishment of Fascism here. . . . . It is a fact that, on the whole, anti-Fascist opinion in England was pro-Edward; but C is evidently repeating what was current on the continent.

C was head of the press department during Laval's Government.

[1] Pierre Comert, French journalist and ex-diplomat, who came to England after the armistice in 1940.

Laval said to him in 1935 that England was now "only an appearance" and Italy was a really strong country, so that France must break with England and go in with Italy. On returning from signing the Franco-Russian pact he said that Stalin was the most powerful man in Europe. On the whole Laval's prophecies seem to have been falsified, clever though he is.

Completely conflicting accounts, from eye witnesses, about the damage to Coventry. It seems impossible to learn the truth about bombing at a distance. When we have a quiet night here, I find that many people are faintly uneasy, because feeling certain that they are getting it badly in the industrial towns. What every one feels at the back of his mind is that we are now hardened to it and the morale elsewhere is less reliable.

*1 December*
That bastard Chiappe is cold meat. Everyone delighted, as when Balbo died. This war is at any rate killing off a few Fascists.

*8 December*
Broadcasting the night before last. . . . . Met there a Pole who has only recently escaped from Poland by some underground route he would not disclose. . . . . He said that in the siege of Warsaw 95 per cent of the houses were damaged and about 25 per cent demolished. All services, electricity, water, etc broke down, and towards the end people had no defence whatever against the aeroplanes and, what was worse, the artillery. He described people rushing out to cut bits off a horse killed by shell-fire, then being driven back by fresh shells, then rushing out again. When Warsaw was completely cut off, the people were upheld by the belief that the English were coming to help them, rumours all the while of an English army in Danzig, etc etc. . . . .

During the bad period of the bombing, when everyone was semi-insane, not so much from the bombing itself as from broken sleep, interrupted telephone calls, the difficulty of communications, etc etc I found that scraps of nonsense poetry were constantly coming into my mind. They never got beyond a line or two and the tendency stopped when the bombing slacked off, but examples were:

> An old Rumanian peasant
> Who lived at Mornington Crescent

and

> And the key doesn't fit and the bell doesn't ring,
> But we all stand up for God save the King

and

> When the Borough Surveyor has gone to roost
> On his rod, his pole or his perch.

*29 December*

From a newspaper account of a raid (not ironical): "Bombs were falling like manna".

*2 January 1941*

The right-wing reaction is now in full swing, and Margesson's entry into the Cabinet is no doubt a deliberate cash-in on Wavell's victory in Egypt. Comically enough, a review of Wavell's life of Allenby which I wrote some months ago was printed in *Horizon*[1] just at the time when the news of Sidi Barrani came through. I said in the review that, as Wavell held so important a command, the chief interest of the book was the light that it threw on his own intellect, and left it to be inferred that I didn't think much of this. So the laugh was on me—though, God knows, I am glad enough to have been wrong.

The word "blitz" now used everywhere to mean any kind of attack on anything. Cf "strafe" in the last war. "Blitz" is not yet used as a verb, a development I am expecting.

*22 January*

—— is convinced, perhaps rightly, that the danger of the People's Convention racket is much under-estimated and that one must fight back and not ignore it. He says that thousands of simple-minded people are taken in by the appealing programme of the People's Convention and do not realise that it is a defeatist manoeuvre intended to help Hitler. He quoted a letter from the Dean of Canterbury[2] who said "I want you to understand that I am whole-heartedly

[1] *Horizon* (1940–50), a magazine of literature and art, edited by Cyril Connolly. Orwell's review of *Allenby: a Study in Greatness* by General Sir Archibald Wavell appeared in *Horizon*, December 1940.

[2] The Very Rev. Hewlett Johnson (1874–1966), Dean of Canterbury 1931–63. Publications include *The Socialist Sixth of the World*, *Soviet Strength* and *Christians and Communism*. He became known as "The Red Dean" for his pro-Russian sympathies.

for winning the war, and that I believe Winston Churchill to be the only possible leader for us till the war is over" (or words to that effect), and nevertheless supported the People's Convention. It appears that there are thousands like this.

Apropos of what —— says, it is at any rate a fact that the People's Convention crew have raised a lot of money from somewhere. Their posters are everywhere, also a lot of new ones from the *Daily Worker*. The space has not been paid for, but even so the printing, etc would cost a good deal. Yesterday I ripped down a number of these posters, the first time I have ever done such a thing. Cf in the summer when I chalked up "Sack Chamberlain" etc and in Barcelona, after the suppression of the POUM, when I chalked up *"Visca POUM"*. At any normal time it is against my instincts to write on a wall or to interfere with what anyone else has written.

The onion shortage has made everyone intensely sensitive to the smell of onions. A quarter of an onion shredded into a stew seems exceedingly strong. E the other day knew as soon as I kissed her that I had eaten onions some 6 hours earlier.

An instance of the sort of racketeering that goes on when any article whose price is not controlled becomes scarce—the price of alarm clocks. The cheapest now obtainable are 15/- —these the sort of rubbishy German-made clocks which used to sell for 3/6d. The little tin French ones which used to be 5/- are now 18/6d, and all others at corresponding prices.

The *Daily Express* has used "blitz" as a verb.

This morning's news—the defences of Tobruk pierced, and the *Daily Worker* suppressed. Only very doubtfully pleased about the latter.

## 26 January

Allocation of space in this week's *New Statesman*:

Fall of Tobruk (with 20,000 prisoners)—2 lines.

Suppression of the *Daily Worker* and the *Week*[1]—108 lines.

..... All thinking people uneasy about the lull at this end of the war, feeling sure that some new devilry is being prepared. But popular optimism is probably growing again and the cessation of raids for even a few days has its dangers. Listening-in the other day to somebody else's telephone conversation, as one is always doing nowadays owing to the crossing of wires, I heard two women talking

---

[1] A Communist newsletter for private subscribers, edited by Claud Cockburn.

to the effect of "it won't be long now", etc etc. The next morning, going into Mrs J's shop, I happened to remark that the war would probably last 3 years. Mrs J amazed and horrified. "Oh, you don't think so! Oh, it couldn't! Why, we've properly got them on the run now. We've got Bardia, and from there we can march on into Italy, and that's the way into Germany, isn't it?" Mrs J is, I should say, an exceptionally sharp, level-headed woman. Nevertheless she is unaware that Africa is on the other side of the Mediterranean.

*7 February*

There is now more and more division of opinion—the question is implicit from the start but people have only recently become aware of it—as to whether we are fighting the Nazis or the German people. This is bound up with the question of whether England should declare her war aims, or, indeed, have any war aims. All of what one might call respectable opinion is against giving the war any meaning whatever ("Our job is to beat the Boche—that's the only war aim worth talking about"), and this is probably bound to become official policy as well. Vansittart's[1] "hate Germany" pamphlet is said to be selling like hot cakes.

No definite news from France. It is obvious that Pétain will give in about taking Laval into the Cabinet. Then there will be a fresh to-do about the passage of troops through unoccupied France, bases in Africa, etc, another "firm stand", and then more giving in. All depends on the time factor, i.e. whether the Germans can obtain a footing in Africa before the Italian armies there finally collapse. Perhaps next the guns will be turned against Spain, and we shall be told that Franco is making a "firm stand" and that that shows how right the British Government were to take a conciliatory attitude towards Spain, until Franco gives in and attacks Gibraltar or allows the German armies to cross his territory. Or perhaps Laval, when in power, will for a short time resist the more extreme German demands, and then Laval will suddenly turn from a villain into a patriot who is making a "firm stand", like Pétain now. The thing

---

[1] Robert Vansittart (1881–1957), Kt. 1929, created Baron Vansittart of Denham, 1941, diplomat and writer, Permanent Under-Secretary of State for Foreign Affairs, 1930–8, chief diplomatic adviser to the Foreign Secretary 1938–41. Well known before and during the early part of the war for his outspoken criticism of Germany and the Germans. The pamphlet referred to here was *Black Record: Germans Past and Present*, 1941.

that British Conservatives *will not* understand is that the forces of the Right have no strength in them and exist only to be knocked down.

### 12 February

Arthur Koestler is being called up this week and will be drafted into the Pioneers, other sections of the forces being barred to him, as a German. What appalling stupidity, when you have a youngish gifted man who speaks I do not know how many languages and really knows something about Europe, especially the European political movements, to be unable to make any use of him except for shovelling bricks.

Appalled today by the havoc all round St Paul's, which I had not seen before. St Paul's, barely chipped, standing out like a rock. It struck me for the first time that it is a pity the cross on top of the dome is such an ornate one. It should be a plain cross, sticking up like the hilt of a sword.

Curiously enough, there don't seem to have been any repercussions to speak of about that old fool Ironside[1] taking the title of "Lord Ironside of Archangel". It really was an atrocious piece of impudence, a thing to protest against whatever one's opinion of the Russian régime.

### 1 March

The Bs, who only came up to London a few weeks ago and have seen nothing of the blitz, say that they find Londoners very much changed, everyone very hysterical, talking in much louder tones, etc etc. If this is so, it is something that happens gradually and that one does not notice while in the middle of it, as with the growth of a child. The only change I have definitely noticed since the air raids began is that people are much more ready to speak to strangers in the street. . . . . . The Tube stations don't now stink to any extent, the new metal bunks are quite good, and the people one sees there are reasonably well found as to bedding and seem contented and normal in all ways—but this is just what disquiets me. What is one to think of people who go on living this sub-human life night after night for months, including periods of a week or more when no aeroplane has

---

[1] Field Marshal Lord Ironside (1880–1959), Chief of the Imperial General Staff 1939–40, Head of the Home Defence Forces, 1940. In 1918 Ironside was Commander-in-Chief of the Allied Forces against the Bolsheviks at Archangel which led him to choose "of Archangel" as the title of his peerage.

come near London?..... It is appalling to see children still in all the
Tube stations, taking it all for granted and having great fun riding
round and round the Inner Circle. A little while back D.J was coming
to London from Cheltenham, and in the train was a young woman
with her two children who had been evacuated to somewhere in the
West Country and whom she was now bringing back. As the train
neared London an air raid began and the woman spent the rest of
the journey in tears. What had decided her to come back was the
fact that at that time there had been no raid on London for a week or
more, and so she had concluded that "it was all right now". What is
one to think of the mentality of such people?

*3 March*
Last night with G to see the shelter in the crypt under Greenwich
church. The usual wooden and sacking bunks, dirty (no doubt also
lousy when it gets warmer), ill-lighted and smelly, but not on this
particular night very crowded. The crypt is simply a system of narrow
passages running between vaults on which are the names of the
families buried in them, the most recent being about 1800. . . . . G
and the others insisted that I had not seen it at its worst, because on
nights when it is crowded (about 250 people) the stench is said to be
almost insupportable. I stuck to it, however, though none of the
others would agree with me, that it is far worse for children to be
playing about among vaults full of corpses than that they should have
to put up with a certain amount of living human smell.

*4 March*
At Wallington. Crocuses out everywhere, a few wallflowers budding,
snowdrops just at their best. Couples of hares sitting about in the
winter wheat and gazing at one another. Now and again in this war,
at intervals of months, you get your nose above water for a few
moments and notice that the earth is still going round the sun.

*14 March*
For the last few days there have been rumours everywhere, also hints
in the papers, that "something is going to happen" in the Balkans,
i.e. that we are going to send an expeditionary force to Greece. If
so, it must presumably be the army now in Libya, or the bulk of it.
I had heard a month back that Metaxas before he died asked us for
10 divisions and we offered him 4. It seems a terribly dangerous

thing to risk an army anywhere west of the Straits. To have any
worth-while ideas about the strategy of such a campaign, one would
have to know how many men Wavell disposes of and how many are
needed to hold Libya, how the shipping position stands, what the
communications from Bulgaria into Greece are like, how much of
their mechanised stuff the Germans have managed to bring across
Europe, and who effectively controls the sea between Sicily and
Tripoli. It would be an appalling disaster if, while our main force
was bogged in Salonika, the Germans managed to cross the sea
from Sicily and win back all the Italians have lost. Everyone who
thinks of the matter is torn both ways. To place an army in Greece
is a tremendous risk and doesn't offer much *positive* gain, except that
once Turkey is involved our warships can enter the Black Sea: on the
other hand if we let Greece down we have demonstrated once and for
all that we can't and won't help any European nation to keep its
independence. The thing I fear most is half-hearted intervention and
a ghastly failure, as in Norway. I am in favour of putting all our eggs
in one basket and risking a big defeat, because I don't think any
defeat or victory in the narrow military sense matters so much as
demonstrating that we are on the side of the weak against the strong.

The trouble is that it becomes harder and harder to understand
the reactions of European peoples, just as they seem incapable of
understanding ours. Numbers of Germans I have spoken to have
exclaimed on our appalling mistake at the beginning of the war in not
bombing Berlin promptly but merely scattering fatuous leaflets.
Yet I believe *all* English people were delighted at this gesture (we
should still have been so if we had known at the time what drivel the
leaflets were), because we saw it as a demonstration that we had no
quarrel with the common people of Germany. On the other hand, in
his book which we have just published, Haffner[1] exclaims that it is
folly on our part to let the Irish withhold vitally important bases and
that we should simply take these bases without more ado. He says
that the spectacle of our allowing a sham-independent country like
Ireland to defy us simply makes all Europe laugh at us. There you
have the European outlook, with its non-understanding of the
English-speaking peoples. Actually, if we took the Irish bases by

---

[1] Sebastian Haffner, anti-Hitler expatriate German journalist, correspondent
on German affairs for the *Observer*. Earlier in the year Orwell and T.R. Fyvel
had published his *Offensive Against Germany* in their series, Searchlight Books,
published by Secker & Warburg.

force, without a long course of propaganda beforehand, the effect on public opinion, not only in the USA but *in England*, would be disastrous.

I don't like the tone of official utterances about Abyssinia. They are mumbling about having a British "resident", as at the courts of Indian rajahs, when the Emperor is restored. The effect may be appalling if we let it be even plausibly *said* that we are swiping Abyssinia for ourselves. If the Italians are driven right out we have the chance to make the most tremendous gesture, demonstrating beyond argument that we are not simply fighting for our own hand. It would echo all round the world. But will they have the guts or decency to make it? One can't feel certain. One can foresee the specious arguments that will be put forward for grabbing Abyssinia for ourselves, the rot about slavery etc etc.

A considerable number of German planes shot down in the last few nights, probably because they have been clear nights and favourable to the fighters, but there is much excitement about some "secret weapon" that is said to be in use. The popular rumour is that it is a net made of wire which is shot into the air and in which the aeroplane becomes entangled.

*20 March*
Fairly heavy raids last night, but only 1 plane brought down, so no doubt the rumours about a "secret weapon" are all boloney.

A lot of bombs at Greenwich, one of them while I was talking to E over the 'phone. A sudden pause in the conversation and a tinkling sound:

*I:* "What's that?"
*E:* "Only the windows falling in."

The bomb had dropped in the park opposite the house, broke the cable of the barrage balloon and wounded one of the balloon barrage men and a Home Guard. Greenwich church was on fire and the people still sheltering in the crypt with the fire burning overhead and water flowing down, making no move to get out till made to do so by the wardens.

German consul in Tangier (the first time since 1914). It appears that in deference to American opinion we are going to let more food into France. Even if some kind of neutral commission is set up to supervise this it will do no good to the French. The Germans will

simply allow them to keep such wheat, etc. as we send in and withhold a corresponding quantity elsewhere. Even while we make ready
to allow the food ships in, there is no sign of the government extorting
anything in return—e.g. expulsion of German agents from North
Africa. The proper course would be to wait till France is on the verge
of starvation and the Pétain Government consequently rocking, and
then hand over a really large supply of food in return for some sub-
stantial concession, e.g. surrender of important units of the French
fleet. Any such policy totally unthinkable at present, of course. If
only one could be sure whether ——, —— and all their kind are really
traitors, or only fools.

Looking back through this diary, I see that of late I have written
in it at much longer intervals and much less about public events than
when I started it. The feeling of helplessness is growing in everyone.
One feels that the necessary swing of opinion cannot now happen
except at the price of another disaster, which we cannot afford and
which therefore one dare not hope for. The worst is that the crisis
now coming is going to be a crisis of hunger, which the English people
have no real experience of. Quite soon it is going to be a question of
whether to import arms or food. It is a mercy that the worst period
will come in the summer months, but it will be devilish difficult to
get the people to face hunger when, so far as they can see, there is no
purpose in the war whatever, and when the rich are still carrying on
just as before, as they will be, of course, unless dealt with forcibly. It
doesn't matter having no war aims when it is a question of repelling
invasion, because from the point of view of ordinary people keeping
foreigners out of England is quite a sufficient war aim. But how can
you ask them to starve their children in order to build tanks to fight
in Africa, when in all that they are told at present there is nothing to
make clear that fighting in Africa, or in Europe, has anything to do
with the defence of England?

On a wall in South London some Communist or Blackshirt had
chalked "Cheese, not Churchill". What a silly slogan. It sums up the
psychological ignorance of these people who even now have not
grasped that, whereas some people would die for Churchill, nobody
will die for cheese.

*23 March*
Yesterday attended a more or less compulsory Home Guard church
parade, to take part in the national day of prayer. There were also

contingents of the AFS,[1] Air Force cadets, WAAFs,[2] etc etc. Appalled by the jingoism and self-righteousness of the whole thing. . . . . I am not shocked by the Church condoning war, as many people profess to be—nearly always people who are not religious believers themselves, I notice. If you accept government, you accept war, and if you accept war, you must in most cases desire one side or the other to win. I can never work up any disgust over bishops blessing the colours of regiments, etc. All that kind of thing is founded on a sentimental idea that fighting is incompatible with loving your enemies. Actually you can only love your enemies if you are willing to kill them in certain circumstances. But what is disgusting about services like these is the absence of any kind of self-criticism. Apparently God is expected to help us on the ground that we are *better* than the Germans. In the set prayer composed for the occasion God is asked "to turn the hearts of our enemies, and to help us to forgive them; to give them repentance for their misdoings, and a readiness to make amends". Nothing about our enemies forgiving *us*. It seems to me that the Christian attitude would be that we are no better than our enemies—we are all miserable sinners, but that it so happens that it would be better if our cause prevailed and therefore that it is legitimate to pray for this. . . . . I suppose the idea is that it would be bad for morale to let people realise that the enemy has a case, though even that is a psychological error, in my opinion. But perhaps they aren't thinking primarily about the effect on the people taking part in the service but are simply looking for direct results from their nation-wide praying campaign, a sort of box barrage fired at the angels.

*24 March*

The reports of German heavy cruisers in the Atlantic somehow have the appearance of being a false rumour to draw British capital ships away. That might conceivably be a prelude to invasion. Expectation of invasion has much faded away, because it is generally felt that Hitler could not now conquer England with any force he would be able to bring here, unless British sea and air power had been greatly worn down beforehand. I think this is probably so and that Hitler will not attempt invasion until he has had a spectacular success else-where, because the invasion itself would appear as a failure and would need something to offset it. But I think that an unsuccessful

---

[1] Auxiliary Fire Service.
[2] Women's Auxiliary Air Force.

invasion meaning the loss of, say, 100,000 or even 500,000 men, might well do his job for him, because of the utter paralysis of industry and internal food supply it might cause. If a few hundred thousand men could be landed and could hold out for even three weeks they would have done more damage than thousands of air raids could do. But the effects of this would not be apparent immediately, and therefore Hitler is only likely to try it when things are going conspicuously well for him.

Evidently there is very serious shortage of Home Guard equipment, i.e. weapons. . . . . On the other hand, the captures of arms in Africa are said to be so enormous that experts are being sent out to inventory them. Drawings will then be made and fresh weapons manufactured to these specifications, the captured ones being sufficient as the nucleus for a whole new range of armaments.

*7 April*

Belgrade bombed yesterday, and the first official announcement this morning that there is a British army in Greece—150,000 men, so they say. So the mystery of where the British army in Libya has gone to is at last cleared up, though this had been obvious enough when the British retreated from Benghazi. Impossible to say yet whether the treaty of friendship between Jugoslavia and the USSR means anything or nothing, but it is difficult to believe that it doesn't point to a worsening of Russo-German relations. One will get another indication of the Russian attitude when and if the Emperor of Abyssinia is restored—i.e. whether the Russian Government recognises him and sends an ambassador to his court.

. . . . . Shortage of labour more and more apparent and prices of such things as textiles and furniture rising to a frightening extent. . . . . The secondhand furniture trade, after years of depression, is booming. . . . . It is evident that calling-up is now being consciously used as a way of silencing undesirables. The reserved age for journalists has been raised to 41—this won't bring them in more than a few hundred men, but can be used against individuals whenever desired. It would be comic if after having been turned down for the army on health grounds ten months ago it were suddenly found that my health had improved to just the point at which I was fit to be a private in the Pioneers.

. . . . . Thinking always of our army in Greece and the desperate risk it runs of being driven into the sea. One can imagine how the strategists of the Liddell Hart[1] type must be wringing their hands over this rash move. Politically it is right, however, if one looks 2–3 years ahead. The best one can say is that even in the narrow strategic sense it must offer some hope of success, or the generals concerned would have refused to undertake it. It is difficult to feel that Hitler has not mistimed his stroke by a month or thereabouts. Abyssinia at any rate is gone, and the Italian naval disaster can hardly have been intended. Also if war in the Balkans lasts even three months the effects on Germany's food supply in the autumn must be serious.

*8 April*
Have just read *The Battle of Britain*, the MOI's best best-seller (there was so great a run on it that copies were unprocurable for some days). It is said to have been compiled by Francis Beeding, the writer of thrillers. I suppose it is not as bad as it might be, but seeing that it is being translated into many languages and will undoubtedly be read all over the world—it is the first official account, at any rate in English, of the first great air battle in history—it is a pity that they did not have the sense to avoid the propagandist note altogether. The pamphlet is full of "heroic", "glorious exploits" etc, and the Germans are spoken of more or less slightingly. Why couldn't they simply give a cold, accurate account of the facts, which, after all, are favourable enough? For the sake of the bit of cheer-up that this pamphlet will accomplish in England, they throw away the chance of producing something that would be accepted all over the world as a standard authority and used to counteract German lies.

But what chiefly impresses me when reading *The Battle of Britain* and looking up the corresponding dates in this diary, is the way in which "epic" events never seem very important at the time. Actually I have a number of vivid memories of the day the Germans broke through and fired the docks (I think it must have been the 7th September), but mostly of trivial things. First of all, riding down in the bus to have tea with Connolly, and two women in front of me insisting that shell-bursts in the sky were parachutes, till I had a hard job of it not to chip in and correct them. Then sheltering in a doorway in Piccadilly from falling shrapnel, just as one might shelter from a cloudburst. Then a long line of German planes filing across the sky, and some very young RAF and naval officers running out of

---

[1] Captain B.H. Liddell Hart (1895–   ), military expert and author of numerous works on war and warfare. See 40.

one of the hotels and passing a pair of field glasses from hand to hand. Then sitting in Connolly's top-floor flat and watching the enormous fires beyond St Paul's, and the great plume of smoke from an oil drum somewhere down the river, and Hugh Slater sitting in the window and saying, "It's just like Madrid—quite nostalgic." The only person suitably impressed was Connolly, who took us up to the roof and, after gazing for some time at the fires, said "It's the end of capitalism. It's a judgement on us." I didn't feel this to be so, but was chiefly struck by the size and beauty of the flames. That night I was woken up by the explosions and actually went out into the street to see if the fires were still alight—as a matter of fact it was almost as bright as day, even in the N.W. quarter—but still didn't feel as though any important historical event were happening. Afterwards, when the attempt to conquer England by air bombardment had evidently been abandoned, I said to Fyvel,[1] "That was Trafalgar. Now there's Austerliz," but I hadn't seen this analogy at the time.

The *News Chronicle* very defeatist again, making a great outcry about the abandonment of Benghazi, with the implication that we ought to have gone for Tripoli while the going was good instead of withdrawing troops to use in Greece. And these are exactly the people who would have raised the loudest squeal if we had gone on with the conquest of the Italian empire and left the Greeks in the soup.

*9 April*

The budget has almost knocked the Balkan campaign out of the news. It is the former and not the latter that I overhear people everywhere discussing.

This evening's news has the appearance of being very bad. The Greek C in C has issued a statement that the Serbs have retreated and uncovered his left flank. The significance of this is that people don't officially say things like that—practically a statement that the Serbs have let the Greeks down—unless they feel things to be going very badly.

The Home Guard now have tommy guns, at any rate two per company. It seems a far cry from the time when we were going to be armed with shotguns—only there weren't any shotguns—and my

---

[1] T.R. (Tosco) Fyvel (1907–   ), writer, journalist and broadcaster; a friend of Orwell.

question as to whether we might hope for some machine-guns was laughed off as an absurdity.

*11 April*
Reported in yesterday's papers that Britain is arranging to lend £2,500,000 to Spain—as a reward for seizing Tangier, I suppose. This is a very bad symptom. Throughout the war it has always been when we were in exceptionally desperate straits that we have begun making concessions to the minor totalitarian powers.

*12 April*
The idea that the German troops in Libya, or some of them, got there via French ships and French African territory, is readily accepted by everyone that one suggests it to. Absolutely no mention of any such possibility in the press, however. Perhaps they are still being instructed to pipe down on criticisms of Vichy France.

The day before yesterday saw fresh-water fish (perch) for sale in a fishmonger's shop. A year ago English people, i.e. town people, wouldn't have touched such a thing.

*13 April*
No real news at all about either Greece or Libya. . . . . Of the two papers I was able to procure today, the *Sunday Pictorial* was blackly defeatist and the *Sunday Express* not much less so. Yesterday's *Evening Standard* had an article by "Our Military Correspondent". . . . . which was even more so. All this suggests that the newspapers may be receiving bad news which they are not allowed to pass on. . . . . God knows it is all a ghastly mess. The one thing that is perhaps encouraging is that all the military experts are convinced that our intervention in Greece is disastrous, and the military experts are always wrong.

When the campaign in the Near East is settled one way or the other, and the situation is in some way stabilised, I shall discontinue this diary. It covers the period between Hitler's spring campaigns of 1940 and 1941. Some time within the next month or two a new military and political phase must begin. The first six months of this diary covered the quasi-revolutionary period following on the disaster in France. Now we are evidently in for another period of disaster, but of a different kind, less intelligible to ordinary people and not necessarily producing any corresponding political improvement.

Looking back to the early part of this diary, I see how my
political predictions have been falsified, and yet, as it were, the
revolutionary changes that I expected *are* happening, but in slow
motion. I made an entry, I see, implying that private advertisements
would have disappeared from the walls within a year. They haven't,
of course—that disgusting Cough Syrup advert is still plastered all
over the place, also He's Twice the Man on Worthington and Somebody's Mother isn't Using Persil—but they are far fewer, and the
government posters far more numerous. Connolly said once that
intellectuals tend to be right about the direction of events but wrong
about their tempo, which is very true.

Registering on Saturday, with the 38 group, I was appalled to see
what a scrubby-looking lot they were. A thing that strikes one when
one sees a group like this, picked out simply by date of birth, is how
much more rapidly the working classes age. They don't, however,
live less long, or only a few years less long, than the middle class. But
they have an enormous middle age, stretching from thirty to sixty.

*14 April*
The news today is appalling. The Germans are at the Egyptian
frontier and a British force in Tobruk has the appearance of being
cut off, though this is denied from Cairo. Opinion is divided as to
whether the Germans really have an overwhelming army in Libya, or
whether they have only a comparatively small force while we have
practically nothing, most of the troops and fighting vehicles having
been withdrawn to other fronts as soon as we had taken Benghazi. In
my opinion the latter is the likelier, and also the probability is that
we sent only European troops to Greece and have chiefly Indians
and Negroes in Egypt. D, speaking from a knowledge of South
Africa, thinks that after Benghazi was taken the army was removed
not so much for use in Greece as to polish off the Abyssinian campaign, and that the motive for this was political, to give the South
Africans, who are more or less hostile to us, a victory to keep them
in a good temper. If we can hang on to Egypt the whole thing will
have been worth while for the sake of clearing the Red Sea and opening that route to American ships. But the necessary complement to
this is the French West African ports, which we could have seized a
year ago almost without fighting.

Non-aggression pact between Russia and Japan, the published terms
of which are vague in the extreme. But there must presumably be

a secret clause by which Russia agrees to abandon China, no doubt gradually and without admitting what is happening, as in the case of Spain. Otherwise it is difficult to see what meaning the pact can have.

From Greece no real news whatever. One silly story about a British armoured-car patrol surprising a party of Germans has now been repeated three days running.

*15 April*

Last night went to the pub to listen to the 9 o'clock news, and arriving there a few minutes late, asked the landlady what the news had been. "Oh, we never turn it on. Nobody listens to it, you see. And they've got the piano playing in the other bar, and they won't turn it off just for the news." This at a moment when there is a most deadly threat to the Suez canal. Cf during the worst moment of the Dunkirk campaign, when the barmaid would not have turned on the news unless I had asked her. . . . . Cf also the time in 1936 when the Germans reoccupied the Rhineland. I was in Barnsley at the time. I went into a pub just after the news had come through and remarked at random, "The German army has crossed the Rhine." With a vague air of remembering something, someone murmured "Parley-voo." No more response than that. . . . . So also at every moment of crisis from 1931 onwards. You have all the time the sensation of kicking against an impenetrable wall of stupidity. But of course at times their stupidity has stood them in good stead. Any European nation situated as we are would have been squealing for peace long ago.

*17 April*

Very heavy raid last night, probably the heaviest in many months, so far as London is concerned. . . . . Bomb in Lord's cricket ground (schoolboys having their exercise at the nets as usual this morning, a few yards from the crater) and another in St John's Wood church-yard. This one luckily didn't land among the graves, a thing I have been dreading will happen. . . . . Passed this morning a side-street somewhere in Hampstead with one house in it reduced to a pile of rubbish by a bomb—a sight so usual that one hardly notices it. The street is cordoned off, however, digging squads at work, and a line of ambulances waiting. Underneath that huge pile of bricks there are mangled bodies, some of them perhaps alive.

The guns kept up their racket nearly all night. . . . . Today I can find no one who admits to having slept last night, and E says the same. The formula is: "I never closed my eyes for an instant". I believe this is all nonsense. Certainly it is hard to sleep in such a din, but E and I must have slept quite half the night.

*22 April*

Have been 2 or 3 days at Wallington. Saturday night's blitz could easily be heard there—45 miles distant.

Sowed while at Wallington 40 or 50 lb of potatoes, which might give 200 to 600 lb according to the season, etc. It would be queer —I hope it won't be so, but it quite well may—if, when this autumn comes, those potatoes seem a more important achievement than all the articles, broadcasts, etc I shall have done this year.

The Greek-British line seems to have swung south, hinging on Janina, to a position not far north of Athens. If the newspaper reports are truthful, they got across the plain of Thessaly without being too much damaged. The thing that disturbs everyone and is evidently going to raise a storm in Australia, is the lack of real news. Churchill in his speech said that even the Government had difficulty in getting news from Greece. The thing that most disturbs *me* is the repeated statement that we are inflicting enormous casualties, the Germans advance in close formation and are mown down in swathes, etc etc. Just the same as was said during the battle of France. . . . . Attack on Gibraltar, or at any rate some adverse move in Spain, evidently timed to happen soon. Churchill's speeches begin to sound like Chamberlain's—evading questions, etc etc.

British troops entered Iraq a couple of days ago. No news yet as to whether they are doing the proper thing, wiping up German agents, etc. People on all sides saying, "Mosul will be no good to Hitler even if he gets there. The British will blow up the wells long before." Will they, I wonder? Did they blow up the Rumanian wells when the opportunity existed? The most depressing thing in this war is not the disasters we are bound to suffer at this stage, but the knowledge that we are being led by weaklings. . . . . It is as though your life depended on a game of chess, and you had to sit watching it, seeing the most idiotic moves being made and being powerless to prevent them.

*23 April*

The Greeks appear to be packing up. Evidently there is going to be hell to pay in Australia. So long as it merely leads to an inquest on the

Greek campaign, and a general row in which the position of Australia in the Empire will be defined and perhaps the conduct of the war democratised somewhat, this is all to the good.

## 24 April

No definite news from Greece. All one knows is that a Greek army, or part of a Greek army, or possibly the whole Greek army, has capitulated. No indication as to how many men we have there, what sort of position they are left in, whether it will be possible to hang on, and if so, where, etc etc. Hints thrown out in the *Daily Express* suggest that we have practically no aeroplanes there. Armistice terms drawn up by the Italians evidently aim at later using Greek prisoners as hostages, with a view to blackmailing the British into giving up Crete and other islands.

No indication of the Russian attitude. The Germans are now close to the Dardanelles and attack on Turkey evidently imminent. The Russians will then have to decide definitely whether to make a stand against Germany, put pressure on Turkey not to resist and perhaps get Iran as the price of this, or sit still and watch the whole southern shore of the Black Sea pass into German hands. In my opinion they will do the second, or less probably the third, in either case with public orgies of self-righteousness.

## 25 April

C, of my section of the Home Guard, a poulterer by trade but at present dealing in meat of all kinds, yesterday bought 20 zebras which are being sold off by the Zoo. Only for dog meat, presumably, not human consumption. It seems rather a waste. . . . . There are said to be still 2,000 race-horses in England, each of which will be eating 10–15 lb of grain a day, i.e. these brutes are devouring *every day* the equivalent of the bread ration of a division of troops.

## 28 April

Churchill's speech last night very good, as a speech. But impossible to dig any information out of it. The sole solid fact I could extract was that at the time of his offensive in Libya Wavell could never concentrate more than 2 divisions, say 30,000 men. Heard the speech at the Home Guard post. The men impressed by it, in fact moved. But I think only two of the ones there were men below the £5 a week level. Churchill's oratory is really good, in an old-fashioned way, though I don't like his delivery. What a pity that he either can't, or doesn't want, or isn't allowed, ever to say anything definite!

*2 May*

A man came from ——'s yesterday morning to cut out the cover for our armchair. The usual draper type, smallish, neat, with something feminine about him and nests of pins all over his person. He informed me that this was the only domestic job he was doing today. Nearly all the time he is cutting out covers for guns, which it seems have to be made in the same way as chair covers. ——'s are keeping going largely on this, he said.

*3 May*

The number evacuated from Greece is now estimated at 41–43,000, but it is stated that we had less men there than had been supposed, probably about 55,000. Casualties supposed to be 3,000, and prisoners presumably 7 or 8 thousand, which would tally with the German figures. 8,000 vehicles said to have been lost, I suppose vehicles of all kinds. No mention of ships lost, though they must have lost some. Spender, one of the Australian ministers, states publicly that "rifles are as useless against tanks as bows and arrows." That at any rate is a step forward.

Apparently there is what amounts to war in Iraq. At the very best this is a disaster. . . . . In all probability we shan't even deal properly with the so-called army of Iraq, which could no doubt be bombed to pieces in a few hours. Either some sort of agreement will be signed in which we shall give away everything and leave the stage set for the same thing to happen again; or you will hear that the Iraq Government is in control of the oil wells, but this doesn't matter, as they have agreed to give us all necessary facilities, etc etc, and then presently you will hear that German experts are arriving by plane or via Turkey; or we shall stand on the defensive and do nothing until the Germans have managed to transport an army by air, when we shall fight at a disadvantage. Whenever you contemplate the British Government's policy, and this has been true without a single break since 1931, you have the same feeling as when pressing on the accelerator of a car that is only firing on one cylinder, a feeling of deadly weakness. One doesn't know in advance exactly what they will do, but one does know that in no case can they possibly succeed, or possibly act before it is too late. . . . . It is curious how comparatively confident one feels when it is a question of mere *fighting*, and how helpless when it is a question of strategy or diplomacy. One knows in advance that the strategy of a British Conservative Government *must* fail, because the will to make it succeed is not there. Their scruples about attacking neutrals—and that is the chief strategic difference between us and Germany in the present war—are merely the sign of a subconscious desire to fail. People don't have scruples when they are fighting for a cause they believe in.

*6 May*
The Turks have offered to mediate in Iraq, probably a bad sign. Mobilisation in Iran. The American Government stops shipments of war materials to the USSR, a good thing in itself but probably another bad sign.

Astonishing sights in the Tube stations when one goes through late at night. What is most striking is the cleanly, normal, domesticated air that everything now has. Especially the young married couples, the sort of homely cautious types that would probably be buying their houses from a building society, tucked up together under pink counterpanes. And the large families one sees here and there, father, mother and several children all laid out in a row like rabbits on the slab. They all seem so peacefully asleep in the bright lamplight. The children lying on their backs, with their little pink cheeks like wax dolls, and all fast asleep.

*11 May*
The most important news of the last few days, which was tucked away on a back page of the newspapers, was the Russian announcement that they could not any longer recognise the governments of Norway and Belgium. Ditto with Jugoslavia, according to yesterday's papers. This is the first diplomatic move since Stalin made himself premier, and amounts to an announcement that Russia will now acquiesce in any act of aggression whatever. It must have been done under German pressure, and coming together with Molotov's removal must indicate a definite orientation of Russian policy on the German side, which needs Stalin's personal authority to enforce it. Before long they must make some hostile move against Turkey or Iran, or both.

Heavy air raid last night. A bomb slightly damaged this building, the first time this has happened to any house I have been in. About 2 am, in the middle of the usual gunfire and distant bombs, a devastating crash, which woke us up but did not break the windows or noticeably shake the room. E got up and went to the window, where she heard someone shouting that it was this house that had been hit. A little later we went out into the passage and found much smoke and a smell of burning rubber. Going up on the roof, saw enormous fires at most points of the compass, one over to the west, several miles away, with huge leaping flames, which must have been a warehouse full of some inflammable material. Smoke was drifting over the roof, but we finally decided that it was not this block of flats that had been hit. Going downstairs again we were told that it *was* this block, but that everyone was to stay in his flat. By this time the smoke was thick enough to make it difficult to see down the passage. Presently we heard shouts of "Yes! Yes! There's still someone in Number 111!" and the wardens shouting to us to get out. We slipped on some clothes, grabbed up a few things and went out, at this time imagining that the house might be seriously on fire and it might be impossible to get back. At such times one takes what one feels to be important, and I noticed afterwards that what I had taken was not my typewriter or any documents but my firearms and a haversack containing food etc, which was always kept ready. Actually all that had happened was that the bomb had set fire to the garage and burned out the cars that were in it. We went in to the Ds, who gave us tea, and ate a slab of chocolate we had been saving for months. Later I remarked on E's blackened face, and she said "What do you think your own is like?" I looked in the glass and saw that my face was quite black. It had not occurred to me till then that this would be so.

### 13 May

I have absolutely no theory about the reason for Hess's[1] arrival. It is completely mysterious. The one thing I know is that if a possibility exists of missing this propaganda opportunity, the British government will find it.

### 18 May

Iraq, Syria, Morocco, Spain, Darlan, Stalin, Raschid Ali, Franco —sensation of utter helplessness. If there is a wrong thing to do, it

---

[1] Rudolf Hess (1894–   ), German Nazi, second to Goering as Hitler's successor, flew to Scotland on 10 May 1941, allegedly bearing peace proposals to be delivered to the Duke of Hamilton. He was interned in Britain and sentenced to life imprisonment by the international war crimes tribunal at Nuremberg in 1946.

will be done, infallibly. One has come to believe in that as if it were a law of nature.

Yesterday or the day before on the newspaper placards, "Nazis using Syrian air bases", and reports in the paper that when this fact was announced in Parliament there were cries of "Shame!" Apparently there are people capable of being surprised when the armistice terms are broken and the French empire made use of by the Nazis. And yet any mere outsider like myself could see on the day France went out of the war that this would happen.

Evidently all chance of winning the war in any decent way is lost. The plan of Churchill and Co is apparently to give everything away and then win it all back with American aeroplanes and rivers of blood. Of course they can't succeed. The whole world would swing against them, America probably included. Within two years we shall either be conquered or we shall be a Socialist republic fighting for its life, with a secret police force and half the population starving. The British ruling class condemned themselves to death when they failed to walk into Dakar, the Canaries, Tangier and Syria while the opportunity existed.

*21 May*

All eyes on Crete. Everyone saying the same thing—that this will demonstrate one way or the other the possibility of invading England. This might be so if we were told the one relevant fact, i.e. how many men we have there, and how equipped. If we have only 10–20,000 men, and those infantry, the Germans may overwhelm them with mere numbers, even if unable to land tanks etc. On balance, the circumstances in Crete are much more favourable to the Germans than they could be in England. In so far as the attack on Crete is a try-out, it is much more likely to be a try-out for the attack on Gibraltar.

*24 May*

News from Crete ostensibly fairly good, but a note of pessimism visible everywhere under the surface. No news at all from Syria or Iraq, and that is the worst indication. Darlan announces that he is not going to hand over the French fleet. More punches will be pulled, no doubt, on the strength of this palpable lie.

*25 May*

I hear privately that we have lost three cruisers in the operations off Crete. Much excuse-making in the papers about our having no fighter planes there. No explanation of why such landing grounds as exist in Crete had not been previously been made impossible for the German troop-carriers, nor of why we failed to arm the Cretan population until it was too late.

*31 May*

Still not quite happy about Abyssinia. Saw today the news reel of the South African troops marching into Addis Ababa. At the Emperor's palace (or whatever the building was) the Union Jack was hauled up first and only afterwards the Abyssinian flag.

*1 June*

We are clearing out of Crete. Mention of 13,000 men being evacuated. No mention yet of the total number involved. The most frightful impression will be created if we remove the British troops and leave the Greeks behind, though from a cold-blooded military point of view it might be the right thing to do.

The British are in Bagdad. It would be even better to hear they were in Damascus. One knows in advance that we shall not make sufficiently harsh terms with the Iraqis, i.e. shall not make possession of the oil wells a condition of granting them an armistice. Hess has simply dropped out of the news for some days past. The evasive answers to questions about him in Parliament, denial that the Duke of Hamilton had ever received a letter from him, statement that the MOI had been "misinformed" when it issued this piece of news, failure apparently by the whole House to ask who had misinformed the MOI, and why, were so disgraceful that I am tempted to look the debate up in Hansard and find out whether it was not censored in the newspaper reports.

The sirens have just sounded, after a period of 3 weeks in which there has not been a single air raid.

*3 June*

Now that the evacuation of Crete is completed, there is talk of 20,000 men having been removed. Obviously, therefore, they must have begun clearing out long before this was admitted in the press, and the ships sunk were probably lost in that operation. Total losses will presumably be about 10,000 men, 7 warships (3 cruisers, 4 destroyers), probably some merchant ships as well, a good many AA guns, and a few tanks and aeroplanes. And all this for absolutely nothing. . . . . The newspapers criticise more boldly than they have ever done hitherto. One of the Australian papers says openly that it is no use trying to defend Cyprus unless we are taking action against Syria. No sign of this, apparently. Reports this morning that the Germans have already landed armoured units at Latakia. Together with this, vague hints that the British "may" invade Syria. Within a few days it may be too late, if it is not six months too late already.

*8 June*
The British entered Syria this morning.

*14 June*
Complete mystery, about which no one has any real news, surrounds the state of affairs between Russia and Germany. Cannot yet make contact with anyone who has seen Cripps since his return. One can only judge by general probabilities, and it seems to me that the two governing facts are (i) Stalin will not go to war with Germany if there is any way short of suicide of avoiding it, and (ii) it is not to Hitler's advantage to make Stalin lose face at this stage, as he is all the while using him against the working class of the world. Much likelier than any direct attack on Russia, therefore, or any agreement that is manifestly to Russia's disadvantage, is a concession masked as an alliance, perhaps covered up by an attack on Iran or Turkey. Then you will hear that there has been an "exchange of technicians" etc etc, and that there seem to be rather a lot of German engineers at Baku. But the possibility that the whole seeming manoeuvre is simply a bluff to cover some approaching move elsewhere, possibly the invasion of England, has to be kept sight of.

*19 June*
Non-aggression pact between Germany and Turkey. This is our reward for not mopping up Syria quickly. From now on the Turkish press will be turned against us, and this will have its effect on the Arab peoples.

The Derby was run yesterday, at Newmarket, and apparently attended by enormous crowds. Even the *Daily Express* was derisive about this. The *Evening Standard* has been declaring that Hitler must invade Britain within 80 days and suggesting that the manoeuvres in Eastern Europe are probably a mask for this— but this, I think, with the idea of frightening people into working harder.

The British Government has ceased issuing navicerts to Petsamo and stopped three Finnish ships, on the ground that Finland is now for all purposes enemy-occupied territory. This is the most definite indication yet that something is really happening between Russia and Germany.

*20 June*

We have all been in a semi-melting condition for some days past. It struck me that one minor benefit of this war is that it has broken the newspapers of their idiotic habit of making headline news out of yesterday's weather.

*22 June*

The Germans invaded the USSR this morning. Everyone greatly excited. It is universally assumed that this development is to our advantage. It is only so, however, if the Russians actually intend to fight back and can put up a serious resistance, if not enough to halt the Germans, at any rate enough to wear down their air force and navy. Evidently the immediate German objective is not either territory or oil, but simply to wipe out the Russian air force and thus remove a danger from their rear while they deal finally with England. Impossible to guess what kind of show the Russians can put up. The worst omen is that the Germans would probably not have attempted this unless certain that they can bring it off, and quite rapidly at that.

*23 June*

Churchill's speech in my opinion very good. It will not please the Left, but they forget that he has to speak to the whole world e.g. to Middle-Western Americans, airmen and naval officers, disgruntled shopkeepers and farmers, and also the Russians themselves, as well as to the left-wing political parties. His hostile references to Communism were entirely right, and simply emphasised the fact that this offer of help was sincere. One can imagine the squeal that will be raised over these by correspondents in the *New Statesman* etc. What sort of impression do they think it would make if Stalin stood up and announced "I have always been a convinced supporter of capital-ism?"

Impossible to guess what impression this move of Hitler's will make in the USA. The idea that it will promptly bring into being a strong pro-Nazi party in England is a complete error. There are no doubt wealthy people who would like to see Hitler destroy the Soviet régime, but they will be a small minority. The Catholics will certainly be among them, but will probably be too acute to show their hands until Russian resistance begins to break down. Talking to people in the Home Guard, including Blimps and quite wealthy business men, I find everyone completely pro-Russian, though much divided in opinion about the Russian capacity to resist. Typical conversation, recorded as well as I can remember it:

*Wholesale poulterer:* "Well, I hope the Russians give them a bloody good hiding."

*Clothing manufacturer (Jewish):* "They won't. They'll go to pieces, just like last time. You'll see."

*Doctor (some kind of foreigner, perhaps refugee):* "You're abso-lutely wrong. Everyone's underrated the strength of Russia. They'll wipe the floor with the Nazis."

*Wholesale grocer:* "Damn it, there's two hundred bloody millions of them."

*Clothing manufacturer:* "Yes, but they're not organised" etc etc etc.

All spoken in ignorance, but showing what people's sentiments are. Three years ago the great majority of people with above £1000 a year, or even about £6 a week, would have sided with the Germans as against the Russians. By this time, however, hatred of Germany has made them forget everything else.

All really depends on whether Russia and Britain are ready really to co-operate, with no *arrière-pensée* and no attempt to shove the brunt of the fighting on to one another. No doubt a strong pro-Nazi party exists in Russia, and I dare say Stalin is at the head of it. If Russia changes sides again and Stalin plays the part of Pétain, no doubt the Communists here will follow him and go pro-Nazi again. If the Soviet régime is simply wiped out and Stalin killed or taken prisoner, many Communists would in my opinion transfer their loyalty to Hitler. At present the British Communists have issued some kind of manifesto calling for a "People's Government" etc etc. They will change their tune as soon as the hand-out from Moscow comes. If the Russians are really resisting, it is not in their interest to have a weak government in Britain, or subversive influences at work here. The Communists will no doubt be super-patriotic within ten days—the slogan will probably be "All power to Churchill"—and completely disregarded. But if the alliance between the two countries is genuine, with a certain amount of give-and-take, the internal political effects on both sides must be all for the best. The special circumstances which made the Russian military assistance a bad influence in Spain don't exist here.

Everyone is remarking in anticipation what a bore the Free Russians will be. It is forecast that they will be just like the White Russians. People have visions of Stalin in a little shop in Putney, selling samovars and doing Caucasian dances etc etc.

*30 June*

No real news of the Russo-German campaign. Extravagant claims by both sides, all through the week, about the number of enemy tanks etc destroyed. All one can really believe in is captures of towns etc and the German claims so far are not large. They have taken Lemberg and appear to have occupied Lithuania, and claim also to have by-passed Minsk, though the Russians claim that their advance has been stopped. At any rate there has been no breakthrough. Everyone already over-optimistic. "The Germans have bitten off more than they can chew. If Hitler doesn't break through in the next week he is finished" etc etc. Few people reflect that the Germans are good soldiers and would not have undertaken this campaign without weighing the chances beforehand. More sober estimates put it thus: "If by October there is still a Russian army in being and fighting against Hitler, he is done for, probably this winter." Uncertain what to make of the Russian government's action in confiscating all private wirelesses. It is capable of several explanations.

Nothing definite about the nature of our alliance with the USSR. Last night everyone waited with much amusement to hear whether the Internationale was played after the national anthems of the other allies. No such thing, of course. However, it was a long time before the Abyssinian national anthem was added to the others. They will ultimately have to play some tune to represent the USSR, but to choose it will be a delicate business.

*3 July*

Stalin's broadcast speech is a direct return to the Popular Front, defence of democracy line, and in effect a complete contradiction of all that he and his followers have been saying for the past two years. It was nevertheless a magnificent fighting speech, just the right counterpart to Churchill's, and made it clear that no compromise is intended, at any rate at this moment. Passages in it seemed to imply that a big retreat is contemplated, however. Britain and the USA referred to in friendly terms and more or less as allies, though apparently no formal alliance exists as yet. Ribbentrop and Co spoken of as "cannibals", which *Pravda* has also been calling them. Apparently one reason for the queer phraseology that translated Russian speeches often have is that Russian contains so large a vocabulary of abusive words that English equivalents do not exist.

One could not have a better example of the moral and emotional shallowness of our time, than the fact that we are now all more or less pro-Stalin. This disgusting murderer is temporarily on our side, and so the purges etc are suddenly forgotten. So also with Franco, Mussolini etc should they ultimately come over to us. The most one can truly say for Stalin is that probably he is individually sincere, as his followers cannot be, for his endless changes of front are at any rate his own decision. It is a case of "when Father turns we all turn", and Father presumably turns because the spirit moves him.

*6 July*

Several of the papers are growing very restive because we are not doing more to help the USSR. I do not know whether any action, other than air raids, is really intended, but if nothing is attempted, quite apart from the military and political consequences this may have, it is a disquieting symptom. For if we can't make a land offensive now, when the Germans have 150 divisions busy in Russia, when the devil shall we be able to? I hear no rumours whatever about movements of troops, so apparently no expedition is being prepared at any rate from England. The only new development is the beginning of Beaverbrook's big drive for tanks, similar to his drive for planes last year. But this can't bear fruit for some months, and where these tanks are to be used there is no hint. I can't believe they want them for use against a German invasion. If the Germans were in a position to bring large numbers of armoured units here, i.e. if they had complete command of the sea and air, we should have lost the war already.

No talk of any formal alliance with Russia, nor indeed anything clarifying our relationship, in spite of more or less friendly utterances on either side. We can't, of course, take any big risk until it is certain that they are in firm alliance with us, i.e. will go on fighting even if they have succeeded in beating back the invasion.

No reliable news from the fronts. The Germans are across the Pruth, but it seems to be disputed whether they are across the Beresina. The destruction claimed by both sides is obviously untruthful. The Russians claim that German casualties are already 700,000, i.e. about 10 per cent of Hitler's whole army.

Examined a number of Catholic papers, also several copies of *Truth*,[1] to see what their attitude is to our quasi-alliance with the USSR. The Catholic papers have not gone pro-Nazi, and perhaps will not do so. The "line" apparently is that Russia is objectively on our side and must be supported, but that there must be no definite alliance. *Truth*, which hates Churchill, takes much the same line but is a shade more anti-Russian, perhaps. Some of the Irish Catholic papers have now gone frankly pro-Nazi, it appears. If that is so, there will have been similar repercussions in the USA. It will be interesting to see whether the "neutrality" that has been imposed on the Irish press, forbidding it to make any comment on any belligerent, will be enforced in the case of Russia, now that Russia is in the war.

The People's Convention have voted full support for the government and demand "vigorous prosecution of the war"—this only a fortnight after they were demanding a "people's peace". The story is going round that, when the news of Hitler's invasion of Russia reached a New York café where some Communists were talking, one of them who had gone out to the lavatory returned to find that the "party line" had changed in his absence.

*28 August*

I am now definitely an employee of the BBC.

The line on the Eastern front, in so far as there is a line, now runs roughly: Tallinn, Gomel, Smolensk, Kiev, Dnepropetrovsk, Kherson. The Germans have occupied an area which must be larger than Germany, but have not destroyed the Russian armies. The British and Russians invaded Iran 3 days ago and the Iranians have

[1] A journal of the extreme Right.

already packed up. No rumours that one can take hold of about movements of troops in this country. They have only about a month now in which to start something on the continent, and I don't believe they intend anything of the kind. Beneath the terms of the Churchill-Roosevelt declaration one can read that American anti-Hitler feeling has cooled off as a result of the invasion of the USSR. On the other hand, there is no sign that willingness to endure sacrifices, etc in this country has increased because of it. There are still popular complaints because we are not doing enough to help the USSR, but their whole volume is tiny. I think the Russian campaign can be taken as settled in the sense that Hitler cannot break through to the Caucasus and the Middle East this winter, but that he is not going to collapse and that he has inflicted more damage than he has received. There is no victory in sight at present. We are in for a long, dreary, exhausting war, with everyone growing poorer all the time. The new phase which I foresaw earlier has now started, and the quasi-revolutionary period which began with Dunkirk is finished. I therefore bring this diary to an end, as I intended to do when the new phase started.

## 58. War-time Diary: *14 March 1942–15 November 1942*

### *14 March 1942*

I reopen this diary after an interval of about 6 months, the war being once again in a new phase.

The actual date of Cripps's departure for India was not given out, but presumably he has gone by this time.[1] Ordinary public opinion here seems gloomy about his departure. A frequent comment— "They've done it to get him out of the way" (which is also one of the reasons alleged by the German wireless). This very silly and reflects the provincialism of English people who can't grasp that India is of any importance. Better-informed people are pessimistic because the non-publication of the Government's terms to India indicates almost certainly that they are not good terms. Impossible to discover what powers Cripps has got. Those who may know something will disclose nothing and one can draw hints out of them only by indirect means. E.g. I propose in my newsletters,[2] having been instructed to give Cripps a build-up, to build him up as a political extremist. This draws the warning, "don't go too far in that direction", which raises the presumption that the higher-ups haven't much hope of full independence being offered to India.

Rumours of all descriptions flying round. Many people appear to suspect that Russia and Germany will conclude a separate peace this year. From studying the German and Russian wireless I have long come to the conclusion that the reports of Russian victories are largely phony, though, of course, the campaign has not gone according to the German plan. I think the Russians have merely won

---

[1] Sir Stafford Cripps flew to India on 22 March in an attempt to arrange a compromise settlement with the Indian Congress Party, the party of Indian independence, to ensure Indian co-operation during the war and allow for a very gradual transition to independence when it was over. Nehru and the Congress Party would accept nothing less than complete independence and, as Cripps was not authorised to offer this, the talks broke down on 10 April and he returned to England.

[2] For broadcasting to India on the BBC Eastern Service.

the kind of victory that we did in the Battle of Britain—i.e. staving off defeat for the time being but deciding nothing. I don't believe in a separate peace unless Russia is definitely knocked out, because I don't see how either Russia or Germany can agree to relinquish the Ukraine. On the other hand some people think (I had this, e.g. from Abrams, a Baltic Russian of strong Stalinist sympathies though probably not a CP member) that if the Russians could get the Germans off their soil they would make a sort of undeclared peace and thereafter only keep up a sham fight.

Rumours about Beaverbrook's departure:[1]

a. Cripps insisted on this as a condition of entering the government.

b. Beaverbrook was got rid of because he is known to be in contact with Goering with a view to a compromise peace.

c. The army insisted on Beaverbrook's removal because he was sending all the aeroplanes etc to Russia instead of to Libya and the Far East.

I have now been in the BBC about 6 months. Shall remain in it if the political changes I foresee come off, otherwise probably not. Its atmosphere is something halfway between a girls' school and a lunatic asylum, and all we are doing at present is useless, or slightly worse than useless. Our radio strategy is even more hopeless than our military strategy. Nevertheless one rapidly becomes propaganda-minded and develops a cunning one did not previously have. E.g. I am regularly alleging in all my newsletters that the Japanese are plotting to attack Russia. I don't believe this to be so, but the calculation is:

If the Japanese do attack Russia, we can then say "I told you so".

If the Russians attack first, we can, having built up the picture of a Japanese plot beforehand, pretend that it was the Japanese who started it.

If no war breaks out after all, we can claim that it is because the Japanese are too frightened of Russia.

All propaganda is lies, even when one is telling the truth. I don't think this matters so long as one knows what one is doing, and why. . . .

[1] On the pretext of physical illness Lord Beaverbrook had resigned from his post as Minister for War Production and left the Government. The real political reasons behind this move are still matters of speculation.

On 11 March 1942 I started the rumour that beer is to be rationed, and told it to 3 different people. I shall be interested to see at what date this rumour comes back to me. (30 May 1942. Never came back. So this casts no light on the way in which rumours come into being.)

Talked for a little while the other day to William Hickey,[1] just back from the USA. He says morale there is appalling. Production is not getting under way and anti-British feeling of all kinds is rampant, also anti-Russian feeling stimulated by the Catholics.

### 15 March

Short air-raid alert about 11.30 this morning. No bombs or guns. The first time in 10 months that I had heard this sound. Inwardly rather frightened, and everyone else evidently the same, though studiously taking no notice and indeed not referring to the fact of there being a raid on until the All Clear had sounded.

### 22 March

Empson[2] tells me that there is a strict ban by the Foreign Office on any suggestion that Japan is going to attack the USSR. So this subject is being studiously avoided in the Far Eastern broadcasts while being pushed all the time in the India broadcasts. They haven't yet got onto the fact that we are saying this, we haven't been warned and don't officially know about the ban, and are making the best of our opportunity while it lasts. The same chaos everywhere on the propaganda front. E.g. *Horizon* was nearly stopped from getting its extra paper to print copies for export on the strength of my article on Kipling (all well at the last moment because Harold Nicolson and Duff Cooper intervened), at the same time as the BBC asked me to write a "Feature" based on the article.

German propaganda is inconsistent in quite a different way—i.e. deliberately so, with an utter unscrupulousness in offering everything to everybody, freedom for India and a colonial empire for Spain, emancipation to the Kaffirs and stricter race laws to the Boers, etc etc. All quite sound from a propaganda point of view in my opinion,

---

[1] "William Hickey", a social diary which has appeared in the *Daily Express* for the last thirty-five years, edited by various people. At this time it was edited by its originator, Tom Driberg, a left-wing politician who later became a Labour MP.

[2] William Empson (1906–    ), the poet and critic. At this time working in the Eastern Service of the BBC broadcasting to China.

seeing how politically ignorant the majority of people are, how un-interested in anything outside their immediate affairs, and how little impressed by inconsistency. A few weeks back the NBBS[1] was actually attacking the Workers' Challenge Station,[2] warning people not to listen to it as it was "financed from Moscow".

The Communists in Mexico are again chasing Victor Serge[3] and other Trotskyist refugees who got there from France, urging their expulsion etc etc. Just the same tactics as in Spain. Horribly depressed to see these ancient intrigues coming up again, not so much because they are morally disgusting as from this reflection: for twenty years the Comintern has used these methods and the Comintern has always and everywhere been defeated by the Fascists; therefore, we, being tied to them by a species of alliance, shall be defeated with them.

Suspicion that Russia intends making a separate peace now seems widespread. Of the two, it would be easier for Russia to surrender the Ukraine, both on geographical and psychological grounds, but they obviously couldn't give up the Caucasus oilfields without a fight. One possible development is a secret agreement between Hitler and Stalin, Hitler to keep what Russian territory he has overrun, or parts of it, but thereafter to make no further attacks but to direct his offensive southward towards the oilfields of Iraq and Iran, Russia and Germany keeping up a sham war meanwhile. It appears to me that a separate peace is distinctly likelier if we do make a continental invasion this year, because if we succeed in embarrassing the Germans and drawing off a great part of their army, Russia is immediately in a much better position both to win back the occupied territories, and to bargain. I nevertheless think that we ought to invade Europe if the shipping will run to it. The one thing that might prevent this kind of filthy double-crossing is a firm alliance between ourselves and the USSR, with war aims declared in detail. Impossible while this government rules us, and probably also while Stalin remains in power: at least only possible if we could get a different kind of government and then find some way of speaking over Stalin's head to the Russian people.

[1] New British Broadcasting Station, broadcasting propaganda in English from Germany.

[2] Another station broadcasting propaganda in English from Germany.

[3] Victor Serge (1890–1947), Russian by parentage, French by adoption, one of the most literary of the early Communists and author of innumerable books, friendly with the POUM during the Spanish civil war. He became a Trotskyist and in 1941 settled in Mexico.

The same feeling as one had during the Battle of France—that there is no news. This arises principally from endless newspaper reading. In connection with my newsletters I now read four or five morning newspapers every day and several editions of the evening ones, besides the daily monitoring report. The amount of new matter in each piece of print one reads is so small that one gets a general impression that nothing is happening. Besides, when things are going badly one can foresee everything. The only event that has surprised me for weeks past was Cripps's mission to India.

*27 March*

News of the terms Cripps took to India supposed to be bursting tomorrow. Meanwhile only rumours, all plausible but completely incompatible with one another. The best-supported—that India is to be offered a treaty similar to the Egyptian one. K.S. Shelvankar,[1] who is our fairly embittered enemy, considers this would be accepted if Indians were given the ministries of Defence, Finance and Internal Affairs. All the Indians here, after a week or two of gloom, much more optimistic, seeming to have smelt out somehow (perhaps by studying long faces in the India Office) that the terms are not so bad after all.

Terrific debate in the House over the "affaire" *Daily Mirror*.[2] A. Bevan reading numerous extracts from Morrison's own articles in the *DM*, written since war started, to the amusement of Conservatives who are anti-*DM* but can never resist the spectacle of two Socialists slamming one another. Cassandra[3] announces he is resigning to join the army. Prophesy he will be back in journalism within 3 months. But where shall we all be within 3 months anyway?

Government candidate defeated (very small majority) in the Grantham by-election. The first time since the war started that this has happened, I think.

Surprise call-out of our company of Home Guard a week or two back. It took $4\frac{1}{2}$ hours to assemble the company and dish out

[1] K.S. Shelvankar, Indian writer and journalist, in England during the war as a correspondent for Indian newspapers.

[2] The *Daily Mirror*, a popular, leftist, daily newspaper had been called to order by Churchill for taking what he called a defeatist line i.e. critical of the Government's handling of the war. After a famous debate in the House the affair fizzled out.

[3] Pseudonym of William Connor (1909–67), Kt. 1966, well-known radical journalist who wrote a personal column in the *Daily Mirror*.

ammunition, and would have taken another hour to get them into their battle positions. This mainly due to the bottleneck caused by refusing to distribute ammunition but making each man come to HQ and be issued with it there. Sent a memo on this to Dr Tom Jones, who has forwarded it direct to Sir Jas. Grigg.[1] In my own unit I could not get such a memo even as far as the Company Commander—or at least, could not get it attended to.

Crocuses now full out. One seems to catch glimpses of them dimly through a haze of war news.

Abusive letter from H.G. Wells, who addresses me as "you shit", among other things.

The Vatican is exchanging diplomatic representatives with Tokyo. The Vatican now has diplomatic relations with all the Axis powers and —I think—with none of the Allies. A bad sign and yet in a sense a good one, in that this last step means that they have now definitely decided that the Axis and not we stands for the more reactionary policy.

*1 April*

Greatly depressed by the apparent failure of the Cripps mission. Most of the Indians seem down in the mouth about it too. Even the ones who hate England want a solution, I think. I believe, however, that in spite of the "take it or leave it" with which our government started off, the terms will actually be modified, perhaps in response to pressure at this end. Some think that the Russians are behind the plan and that this accounts for Cripps's confidence in putting forward something so apparently uninviting. Since they are not in the war against Japan the Russians cannot have any official attitude about the Indian affair, but may serve out a directive to their followers, from whom it will get round to other pro-Russians. But then not many Indians are reliably pro-Russian. No sign yet from the English Communist Party, whose behaviour might give a clue to the Russian attitude. It is on this kind of guesswork that we have to frame our propaganda, no clear or useful directive ever being handed out from above.

Connolly yesterday wanted to quote a passage from *Homage to Catalonia* in his broadcast. I opened the book and came on these sentences:

---

[1] Sir James Grigg, KCB (1890–1964), Permanent Under-Secretary of State for War 1939–42; Secretary of State for War 1942–45.

"One of the most horrible features of war is that all war propaganda, all the screaming and lies and hatred, comes invariably from people who are not fighting. . . . It is the same in all wars; the soldiers do the fighting, the journalists do the shouting, and no true patriot ever gets near a front-line trench, except on the briefest of propaganda tours. Sometimes it is a comfort to me to think that the aeroplane is altering the conditions of war. Perhaps when the next great war comes we may see that sight unprecedented in all history, a jingo with a bullet-hole in him."

Here I am in the BBC, less than 5 years after writing that. I suppose sooner or later we all write our own epitaphs.

*3 April*

Cripps's decision to stay an extra week in India is taken as a good omen. Otherwise not much to be hopeful about. Gandhi is deliberately making trouble, sending telegrams of condolence to Bose's[1] family on the report of his death, then telegrams of congratulation when it turned out that the report was untrue. Also urging Indians not to adopt the scorched earth policy if India is invaded. Impossible to be quite sure what his game is. Those who are anti-Gandhi allege that he has the worst kind of (Indian) capitalist interests behind him, and it is a fact that he usually seems to be staying at the mansion of some kind of millionaire or other. This is not necessarily incompatible with his alleged saintliness. His pacifism may be genuine, however. In the bad period of 1940 he also urged non-resistance in England, should England be invaded. I do not know whether Gandhi or Buchman is the nearest equivalent to Rasputin in our time.

Anand[2] says the morale among the exiled Indians here is very low. They are still inclined to think that Japan has no evil designs on India and are all talking of a separate peace with Japan. So much for their declarations of loyalty towards Russia and China. I said to him that the basic fact about nearly all Indian intellectuals is that they don't expect independence, can't imagine it and at heart don't want it. They want to be permanently in opposition, suffering a

[1] Subhas Chandra Bose (1897–?1945), Indian nationalist leader and left-wing member of Congress. He was so violently anti-British that when the Japanese attacked the Americans he offered his services to Japan, organised an Indian Revolutionary Army and led a military campaign against India. His death remains mysterious and unconfirmed.

[2] Mulk Raj Anand.

painless martyrdom, and are foolish enough to imagine that they could play the same schoolboy games with Japan or Germany as they can with Britain. Somewhat to my surprise he agreed. He says that "opposition mentality" is general among them, especially among the Communists, and that Krishna Menon[1] is "longing for the moment when negotiations will break down". At the same moment as they are coolly talking of betraying China by making a separate peace, they are shouting that the Chinese troops in Burma are not getting proper air support. I remarked that this was childish. A: "You cannot overestimate their childishness, George. It is fathomless." The question is how far the Indians here reflect the viewpoint of intellectuals in India. They are further from the danger and have probably, like the rest of us, been infected by the peaceful atmosphere of the last 10 months, but on the other hand nearly all who remain here long become tinged with a western Socialist outlook, so that the Indian intellectuals proper are probably far worse. A himself has not got these vices. He is genuinely anti-Fascist, and has done violence to his feelings, and probably to his reputation, by backing Britain up because he recognises that Britain is objectively on the anti-Fascist side.

*6 April*
Yesterday had a look at the bit of the by-pass road which is being built between Uxbridge & Denham. Amazed at the enormous scale of the undertaking. West of Uxbridge is the valley of the Colne, and over this the road runs on a viaduct of brick and concrete pillars, the viaduct being I suppose $\frac{1}{4}$ mile long. After that it runs on a raised embankment. Each of these pillars is 20 feet high or thereabouts, about 15 feet by 10 feet thick, and there are two of them every fifteen yards or so. I should say *each pillar* would use 40,000 bricks, exclusive of foundations, and exclusive of the concrete runway above, which must use up tons of steel and concrete for every yard of road. Stupendous quantities of steel (for reinforcing) lying about, also huge slabs of granite. Building this viaduct alone must be a job comparable, in the amount of labour it uses up, to building a good-

---

[1] V. K. Krishna Menon (1897– ), Indian statesman, lawyer, author and journalist. At this time he was living in England and was active in left-wing English politics. He was also the spokesman of the Indian Congress Party in England during the period of the struggle to achieve independence. In 1947 when India had been granted independence he was appointed High Commissioner for India. Represented India at UNO 1952–61.

sized warship. And the by-pass is very unlikely to be of any use till after the war, even if finished by that time. Meanwhile there is a labour shortage everywhere. Apparently the people who sell bricks are all-powerful. (Cf the useless surface shelters, which even when they were being put up were pronounced to be useless by everyone who knew anything about building, and the unnecessary repairs to uninhabited private houses which are going on all over London.) Evidently when a scandal passes a certain magnitude it becomes invisible.

Saw in Denham someone driving a dog-cart, in quite good trim.

### 10 April
British naval losses in the last 3 or 4 days, 2 cruisers and an aircraft carrier sunk, 1 destroyer wrecked. Axis losses, 1 cruiser sunk.

From Nehru's speech today: "Who dies if India live?" How impressed the pinks will be—and how they would snigger at "Who dies if England live?"

### 11 April
It[1] has flopped after all. I don't regard this as final, however.

Listened-in to Cripps's speech coming from Delhi, which we were re-broadcasting for England etc. These transmissions which we occasionally listen-in to from Delhi are our only clue as to how our own broadcasts sound in India. Always very bad quality and a great deal of background noise which it is impossible to take out in recordings. The speech good in the earlier part and plain-speaking enough to cause, I should think, a lot of offence. In the later part it rather moved off into the breezy uplands vein. It is a curious fact that in the more exalted passages in his speeches Cripps seems to have caught certain inflexions of voice from Churchill. This may point to the fact—which would explain his having undertaken this mission when only having such bad terms to offer—that he is at present much under Churchill's personal influence.

### 18 April
No question that Cripps's speeches etc have caused a lot of offence, i.e. in India. Outside India I doubt whether many people blame the British Government for the breakdown. One trouble at the moment is the tactless utterances of Americans who for years have been

_____
[1] Cripps's mission to India.

blahing about "Indian freedom" and British imperialism, and have suddenly had their eyes opened to the fact that the Indian intelligentsia don't want independence, i.e. responsibility. Nehru is making provocative speeches to the effect that all the English are the same, of whatever party etc etc, also trying to make trouble between Britain and the USA by alleging that the USA has done all the real fighting. At the same time he reiterates at intervals that he is not pro-Japanese and Congress will defend India to the last. The BBC thereupon picks out these passages from his speeches and broadcasts them without mentioning the anti-British passages, whereat Nehru complains (quite justly) that he has been misrepresented. A recent directive tells us that when one of his speeches contains both anti-British and anti-Japanese passages, we had better ignore it altogether. What a mess it all is. But I think on balance the Cripps mission has done good, because without discrediting Cripps in this country (as it so easily might have done) it has clarified the issue. Whatever is said officially, the inference the whole world will draw is that (a) the British ruling class doesn't intend to abdicate and (b) India doesn't want independence and therefore won't get it, whatever the outcome of the war.

Talking to Wintringham[1] about the possible Russian attitude towards the Cripps negotiations (of course, not being in the war against Japan, they can't have an official attitude) I said it might make things easier if as many as possible of the military instructors etc who will later have to be sent to India were Russians. One possible outcome is that India will ultimately be taken over by the USSR, and though I have never believed that the Russians would behave better in India than ourselves, they might behave differently, owing to the different economic set-up. Wintringham said that even in Spain some of the Russian delegates tended to treat the Spaniards as "natives", and would no doubt do likewise in India. It's very hard not to, seeing that in practice the majority of Indians *are* inferior to Europeans and one can't help feeling this and, after a little while, acting accordingly.

American opinion will soon swing back and begin putting all the

---

[1] Thomas Henry (Tom) Wintringham (1898–1949), writer and soldier. Served in France 1916–18 with the Air Force. Went to Spain in 1936 as war correspondent; in 1937 became commander of the British Battalion of the International Brigade. Founded Osterley Park training centre for the Home Guard. Publications include *New Ways of War*, *Politics of Victory* and *People's War*.

blame for the Indian situation on the British, as before. It is clear from what American papers one can get hold of that anti-British feeling is in full cry and that all the Isolationists, after a momentary retirement, have re-emerged with the same programme and slogans as before. Father Coughlin's[1] paper, however, has just been excluded from the mails. What always horrifies me about American anti-British sentiment is its appalling ignorance. Ditto presumably with anti-American feeling in England.

*19 April*
Tokyo bombed, or supposed to have been bombed, yesterday. Hitherto this comes only from Japanese and German sources. Nowadays one takes it so much for granted that everyone is lying that a report of this kind is never believed until confirmed by both sides. Even an admission by the enemy that his capital has been bombed might for some reason or other be a lie.

E[2] says that Anand remarked to her yesterday, as though it were a matter of course, that Britain would make a separate peace this year, and seemed surprised when she demurred. Of course Indians have to say this, and have been saying it ever since 1940, because it furnishes them if necessary with an excuse for being anti-war, and also because if they could allow themselves to think any good of Britain whatever their mental framework would be destroyed. Fyvel told me how in 1940, at the time when Chamberlain was still in the Government, he was at a meeting at which Pritt and various Indians were present. The Indians were remarking in their pseudo-Marxist way "Of course the Churchill-Chamberlain Government is about to make a compromise peace," whereat Pritt told them that Churchill would never make peace and that the only difference (then) existing in Britain was the difference between Churchill and Chamberlain.

More and more talk about an invasion of Europe—so much so as to make one think something of the kind must be afoot, otherwise the newspapers would not risk causing disappointment by talking so much about it. Amazed by the unrealism of much of this talk. Nearly everyone appears still to think that gratitude is a factor in power politics. Two assumptions which are habitually made

[1] Father Coughlin, American priest and demagogue of distinctly Fascist leanings, discredited by his ecclesiastical superiors in 1942.
[2] Eileen, Orwell's wife.

throughout the Left press are (a) that opening up a Second Front is the way to stop Russia making a separate peace, (b) that the more fighting we do the more say we shall have in the final peace settlement. Few people seem to reflect that if an invasion of Europe succeeded to the point of drawing the German armies away from Russia, Stalin would have no strong motive for going on fighting, and that a sell-out of this kind would be quite in line with the Russo-German Pact and the agreement which the USSR has evidently entered into with Japan. As to the other assumption, many people talk as though the power to decide policy when a war has been won were a sort of reward for having fought well in it. Of course the people actually able to dominate affairs are those who have the most military power, cf America at the end of the last war.

Meanwhile the two steps which could right the situation, (a) a clear agreement with the USSR, with a joint (and fairly detailed) declaration of war aims, and (b) an invasion of Spain, are politically quite impossible under the present Government.

*25 April*

US airmen making forced landing on Russian soil after bombing Tokyo have been interned. According to the Japanese wireless the Russians are expediting the movement of Japanese agents across Russia from Sweden (and hence from Germany) to Japan. If true, this is a new development, this traffic having been stopped at the time when Germany attacked the USSR.

The mystery of Subhas Chandra Bose's whereabouts remains impenetrable. The leading facts are:—

1. At the time of his disappearance, the British Government declared that he had gone to Berlin.

2. A voice, identified as his, broadcasts on the Free India radio (Germany).

3. The Italian radio has claimed at least once that Bose is in Japanese territory.

4. Indians here seem on the whole to think that he is in Japanese territory.

5. Escape to Japanese territory would have been physically easier than escape in the other direction, though the latter would not be impossible.

6. The Vichy report of his death in a plane accident between Bangkok and Tokyo, though almost certainly mistaken, seemed to

suggest that Vichy quarters took it for granted that he was in Japanese territory.

7. According to engineers it would not be impossible to broadcast his voice scrambled from Tokyo to Berlin and there unscramble and rebroadcast it.

There are innumerable other considerations and endless rumours. The two questions hardest to answer are: if Bose *is* in Japanese territory, why this elaborate effort to make it appear that he is in Berlin, where he is comparatively ineffectual? If Bose is in German territory, how did he get there? Of course it is quite reasonably likely that he got there with Russian connivance. Then the question arises, if the Russians had previously passed Bose through, did they afterwards tip us off when they came into the war on our side? To know the answer to that would give one a useful clue to their attitude towards ourselves. Of course one can get no information about questions of that type here. One has to do one's propaganda in the dark, discreetly sabotaging the policy directives when they seem more than usually silly.

To judge from their wireless, the Germans believe in a forthcoming invasion, either of France or Norway. What a chance to have a go at Spain! As, however, they have fixed a date for it (May 1st) they may merely be discussing the possibility of invasion in order to jeer when it does not come off. No sign here of any invasion preparations—no rumours about assembly of troops or boats, re-arrangement of railway schedules etc. The most positive sign is Beaverbrook's pro-invasion speech in the USA.

There seems to be no news whatever. It must be months since the papers were so empty.

Struck by the mediocre physique and poor general appearance of the American soldiers one sees from time to time in the street. The officers usually better than the men, however.


*27 April*

Much speculation about the meaning of Hitler's speech yesterday. In general it gives an impression of pessimism. Beaverbrook's invasion speech is variously interpreted, at its face value, as a pep talk for the Americans, as something to persuade the Russians that we are not leaving them in the lurch, and as the beginning of an attack on Churchill (who may be forced into opposing offensive action).

Nowadays, whatever is said or done, one looks instantly for hidden motives and assumes that words mean anything except what they appear to mean. . . .

We are all drowning in filth. When I talk to anyone or read the writings of anyone who has any axe to grind, I feel that intellectual honesty and balanced judgement have simply disappeared from the face of the earth. Everyone's thought is forensic, everyone is simply putting a "case" with deliberate suppression of his opponent's point of view, and, what is more, with complete insensitiveness to any sufferings except those of himself and his friends. The Indian nationalist is sunken in self pity and hatred of Britain and utterly indifferent to the miseries of China, the English pacifist works himself up into frenzies about concentration camps in the Isle of Man and forgets about those in Germany etc etc. One notices this in the case of people one disagrees with, such as Fascists or pacifists, but in fact everyone is the same, at least everyone who has definite opinions. Everyone is dishonest, and everyone is utterly heartless towards people who are outside the immediate range of his own interests and sympathies. What is most striking of all is the way sympathy can be turned on or off like a tap according to political expediency. All the pinks, or most of them, who flung themselves to and fro in their rage against Nazi atrocities before the war, forgot all about these atrocities and obviously lost their sympathy with the Jews etc as soon as the war began to bore them. Ditto with people who hated Russia like poison up to 22 June 1941 and then suddenly forgot about the purges, the GPU etc the moment Russia came into the war. I am not thinking of lying for political ends, but of actual changes in subjective feeling. But is there no one who has both firm opinions and a balanced outlook? Actually there are plenty, but they are powerless. All power is in the hands of paranoiacs.

### 29 April

Yesterday to the House to hear the India debate. A poor show, except for Cripps's speech. They are now sitting in the House of Lords. During C's speech one had the impression that the house was full, but on counting I found only about 200–250 members, which is enough to fill most of the seats. Everything had a somewhat mangy look. Red rexine cushions on the benches—I could swear they used to be red plush at one time. The ushers' shirt-fronts were very dingy. When I see this dreary rubbish going on, or when I read about the later days of the League of Nations or the antics of Indian politicians with their endless changes of front, line-ups, *démarches*, denunciations, protests and gestures generally, I always remember that the Roman senate still existed under the later Empire. This is the twilight of Parliamentary democracy and these creatures are simply ghosts gibbering in some corner while the real events happen elsewhere.

*6 May*

People do not seem pleased about Madagascar[1] as they did about Syria,[2] perhaps not grasping equally well its strategical significance, but more, I think, for want of a suitable propaganda build-up beforehand. In the case of Syria the obviousness of the danger, the continual stories about German infiltration, and the long uncertainty as to whether the Government would act, gave people the impression that it was public opinion which had forced the decision. For all I know it may even have done so, to some extent. No similar preparation in this case. As soon as it became clear that Singapore was in danger I pointed out that we might have to seize Madagascar and had better begin the build-up in our Indian newsletters. I was somewhat choked off even then, and some weeks back a directive came, I suppose from the Foreign Office, that Madagascar was not to be mentioned. Reason given (after the British troops had landed), "So as not to give the show away". Result, the seizure of Madagascar can be represented all over Asia as a piece of imperialist grabbing.

Saw two women driving in an old-fashioned governess-cart today. A week or two back saw two men in a carriage-and-pair, and one of the men actually wearing a grey bowler hat. . . .

*8 May*

According to Warburg[3] a real Anglo-Russian alliance is to be signed up and the Russian delegates are already in London. I don't believe this.

The Turkish radio (for some time past I think this has been one of the most reliable sources of information) alleges that both Germans

[1] The Allies had invaded and taken over the island of Madagascar, a French colony of strategic importance which supported Pétain.

[2] In 1941 the Germans seemed on the point of taking over Syria as an air force base. Allied forces recaptured it from the Vichy French and successfully held it for the rest of the war.

[3] F. J. Warburg, managing director of Secker & Warburg.

and Russians are preparing to use poison gas in the forthcoming battle.

Great naval battle in progress in the Coral Sea. Sinkings claimed by both sides so vast that one does not know what to believe. But from the willingness of the Japanese radio to talk about the battle (they have already named it the Battle of the Coral Sea) the presumption is that they count on making their objective. . . .

*11 May*
Another gas warning (in Churchill's speech) last night. I suppose we shall be using it before many weeks are over.

From a Japanese broadcast: "In order to do justice to the patriotic spirit of the Koreans, the Japanese Government have decided to introduce compulsory military service in Korea."

Rumoured date for the German invasion of Britain: May 25th.

*15 May*
I saw Cripps on Wednesday, the first time I had actually spoken to him. Rather well impressed. He was more approachable and easy-going than I had expected, and quite ready to answer questions. Though aged 53 some of his movements are almost boyish. On the other hand he has decidedly a red nose. I saw him in one of the reception rooms, or whatever they are called, off the House of Lords. Some interesting old prints on the walls, coronets on the chairs and on the ashtrays, but everything with the vaguely decayed look that all Parliamentary institutions now have. A string of nondescript people waiting to see Cripps. As I waited trying to talk to his secretary, a phrase I always remember on these occasions came into my mind— "shivering in ante-rooms". In eighteenth-century biographies you always read about people waiting on their patrons and "shivering in ante-rooms". It is one of those ready-made phrases like "leave no stone unturned", and yet how true it is as soon as you get anywhere near politics, or even the more expensive kinds of journalism.

Cripps considers that Bose is in German territory. He says it is known that he got out through Afghanistan. I asked him what he thought of Bose (whom he used to know well), and he described him as "a thoroughly bad egg". I said there seemed little doubt that he is subjectively pro-Fascist. Cripps: "He's pro-Subhas. That is all he really cares about. He will do anything he thinks will help his own career along."

I am not certain, on the evidence of B[ose]'s broadcasts, that this
is so. I said I thought very few Indians were reliably anti-Fascist.
Cripps disagreed so far as the younger generation go. He said the
young Communists and left-wing Socialists are wholeheartedly anti-
Fascist and have a western conception of Socialism and internationalism. Let's hope it's so.

*19 May*
Attlee reminds me of nothing so much as a recently dead fish, before
it has had time to stiffen.

*21 May*
Molotov is said to be in London. I don't believe this.

*22 May*
It is said that Molotov is not only in London but that the new
Anglo-Russian treaty is already signed. This however comes from
Warburg who is alternately over-optimistic and over-pessimistic—
at any rate, always believes in the imminence of enormous and
dramatic changes. If true, it would be a godsend for the filling-up of
my newsletters. It is getting harder and harder to find anything to put
into these, with nothing happening except on the Russian front, and
the news from there, whether from Russian or German sources,
growing more and more phony. I wish I could spare a week to go
through the Russian and German broadcasts of the past year and tot
up their various claims. I should say the Germans would have killed
10 million men and the Russians must have advanced to somewhere
well out in the Atlantic Ocean. . . .

*27 May*
More rumours that Molotov is in London. Also cryptic paras in the
papers suggesting that this may be so (no mention of names, of
course).

*30 May*
Almost every day in the neighbourhood of Upper Regent Street
one can see a tiny, elderly, very yellow Japanese, with a face like
a suffering monkey's, walking slowly along with an enormous
policeman walking beside him. On some days they are holding a
solemn conversation. I suppose he is one of the Embassy staff. But

whether the policeman is there to prevent him committing acts of sabotage, or to protect him from the infuriated mob, there is no knowing.

The Molotov rumour seems to have faded out. Warburg, who accepted the Molotov story without question, has now forgotten it and is full of the inner story of why Garvin[1] was sacked from the *Observer*. It was because he refused to attack Churchill. The Astors are determined to get rid of Churchill because he is pro-Russian and the transformation of the *Observer* is part of this manoeuvre. The *Observer* is to lead the attack on Churchill and at the same time canalise the gifted young journalists who are liable to give the war a revolutionary meaning, making them use their energy on futilities until they can be dispensed with. All inherently probable. On the other hand I don't believe that David Astor, who acts as the decoy elephant, is consciously taking part in any such thing. It is amusing to see not only the Beaverbrook press, which is now *plus royaliste que le roi* so far as Russia is concerned, but the T[rade] U[nion] weekly *Labour's Northern Voice*, suddenly discovering Garvin as a well-known anti-Fascist who has been sacked for his radical opinions. One thing that strikes one about nearly everyone nowadays is the shortness of their memories. Desmond Hawkins[2] told me a little while back that he recently bought some fried fish, wrapped up in a sheet of newspaper dating from 1940. On one side was an article proving that the Red army was no good, on the other a write-up of that gallant sailor and well-known anglophile, Admiral Darlan[3]. . . .

[1] J.L. Garvin (1868–1947), right-wing journalist, editor of the *Observer* 1908–42. At the beginning of the war, when he was of advanced age, he disagreed with Viscount Astor, the proprietor of the paper, about the suitability of Churchill being at the same time Prime Minister and Minister of Defence—Lord Astor querying the advisability of this. Lord Astor had made his second son, the Hon. David Astor (1912–  ), a minority shareholder in the paper and, although David Astor spent the war in the Marines, he had a voice in the paper's affairs. At the end of the war the Astors made the *Observer* into a trust. In 1946 David Astor became its foreign editor and from 1948 he has been its editor. He met Orwell at the beginning of the war and they remained friends until Orwell's death.

[2] Desmond Hawkins (1908–  ), novelist, literary critic and broadcaster, who did much free-lance work with the Indian Service of the BBC during the war.

[3] Admiral Darlan (1881–1942), French naval officer and politician. He commanded all the French naval forces until the Fall of France in May 1940. He became Naval Minister in Pétain's Government and was regarded as being next in succession to him. He was in North Africa at the time of the invasion in

*4 June*

Very hot weather. Struck by the normality of everything—lack of hurry, fewness of uniforms, general unwarlike appearance of the crowds who drift slowly through the streets, pushing prams or loitering in the squares to look at the hawthorn bushes. It is already noticeable that there are much fewer cars, however. Here and there a car with a fuel converter at the back, having slightly the appearance of an old-fashioned milk cart. Evidently there is not so much bootleg petrol about after all.

*6 June*

The Molotov rumour still persists. He was here to negotiate the treaty, and has gone back, so it is said. No hint about this in any newspaper, however.

There is said to be much disagreement on the staff of the *New Statesman* over the question of the Second Front. Having squealed for a year that we must open a Second Front immediately, Kingsley Martin[1] now has cold feet. He says that the army cannot be trusted, the soldiers will shoot their officers in the back etc—this after endeavouring throughout the war to make the soldiers mistrust their officers. Meanwhile I think now that a Second Front is definitely projected, at any rate if enough shipping can be scraped together.

*7 June*

The *Sunday Express* has also gone cold on the Second Front. The official line now appears to be that our air raids *are* a Second Front. Obviously there has been some kind of government hand-out telling the papers to pipe down on this subject. If the government merely wishes to stop them spreading misleading rumours, the puzzle is why they weren't silenced earlier. It is just possible that the invasion has now been definitely decided on and the papers have been told to go anti-Second Front in order to throw the enemy off the scent. In this labyrinth of lies in which we are living the one explanation one never believes is the obvious one. Cf David Astor's story about the two German Jews meeting in the train:

---

November 1942 and his transfer of support to the Allied side and his appointment as Chief of State in North Africa caused wide controversy. He was assassinated by a young French anti-Fascist in Algiers in November 1942.

[1] Kingsley Martin (1897–    ), left-wing journalist, editor of the *New Statesman* 1931–60.

*First Jew:* "Where are you going to?"
*Second Jew:* "Berlin."
*First Jew*: "Liar! You just say that to deceive me. You know that if you say you are going to Berlin I shall think you are going to Leipzig, and all the time, you dirty crook, you really *are* going to Berlin!"

Last Tuesday spent a long evening with Cripps (who had expressed a desire to meet some literary people) together with Empson, Jack Common, David Owen, Norman Cameron, Guy Burgess[1] and another man (an official) whose name I didn't get. About 2½ hours of it, with nothing to drink. The usual inconclusive discussion. Cripps, however, very human and willing to listen. The person who stood up to him most successfully was Jack Common. Cripps said several things that amazed and slightly horrified me. One was that many people whose opinion was worth considering believed that the war would be over by October—i.e. that Germany would be flat out by that time. When I said that I should look on that as a disaster pure and simple (because if the war were won as easily as that there would have been no real upheaval here and the American millionaires would still be *in situ*) he appeared not to understand. He said that once the war was won the surviving great powers would in any case have to administer the world as a unit, and seemed not to feel that it made much difference whether the great powers were capitalist or Socialist. Both David Owen and the man whose name I don't know supported him. I saw that I was up against the official mind, which sees everything as a problem in administration and does not grasp that at a certain point, i.e. when certain economic interests are threatened, public spirit ceases to function. The basic assumption of such people is that everyone wants the world to function properly and will do his best to keep the wheels running. They don't realise that most of those who have the power don't care a damn about the world as a whole and are only intent on feathering their own nests.

I can't help feeling a strong impression that Cripps has already

[1] William Empson, the poet and critic; Jack Common, a working-class writer, editor, and friend of Orwell's; David Owen, Cripps's secretary; Norman Cameron (1905–53), a poet whose works include *The Winter House*, a friend and disciple of Robert Graves; Guy Burgess (1911–63), educated at Eton and Trinity College, Cambridge, an unsuspected Communist, of considerable intellectual gifts, wit and charm. After working for the British Security Services and the BBC in liaison with the Foreign Office, he joined the Foreign Office. His pro-Soviet activities went undetected until, in May 1951, he suddenly left for Moscow with Donald Maclean and remained there until his death.

been got at. Not with money or anything of that kind of course, nor
even by flattery and the sense of power, which in all probability he
genuinely doesn't care about: but simply by responsibility, which
automatically makes a man timid. Besides, as soon as you are in
power your perspectives are foreshortened. Perhaps a bird's eye
view is as distorted as a worm's eye view. . . .

*10 June*

The only time when one hears people singing in the BBC is in the
early morning, between 6 and 8. That is the time when the char-
women are at work. A huge army of them arrives all at the same
time. They sit in the reception hall waiting for their brooms to be
issued to them and making as much noise as a parrot house, and then
they have wonderful choruses, all singing together as they sweep the
passages. The place has a quite different atmosphere at this time
from what it has later in the day.

*11 June*

The Germans announce over the wireless that as the inhabitants of a
Czech village called Lidice (about 1200 inhabitants) were guilty of
harbouring the assassins of Heydrich, they have shot all the males in
the village, sent all the women to concentration camps, sent all the
children to be "re-educated", razed the whole village to the ground
and changed its name. I am keeping a copy of the announcement, as
recorded in the BBC monitoring report.

It does not particularly surprise me that people do this kind of
thing, nor even that they announce that they are doing them. What
does impress me, however, is that other people's reaction to such
happenings is governed solely by the political fashion of the moment.
Thus before the war the pinks believed any and every horror story
that came out of Germany or China. Now the pinks no longer believe
in German or Japanese atrocities and automatically write off all
horror stories as "propaganda". In a little while you will be jeered at
if you suggest that the story of Lidice could possibly [be] true. And
yet there the facts are, announced by the Germans themselves
and recorded on gramophone discs which no doubt will still be
available. Cf the long list of atrocities from 1914 onwards, German
atrocities in Belgium, Bolshevik atrocities, Turkish atrocities, British
atrocities in India, American atrocities in Nicaragua, Nazi atrocities,
Italian atrocities in Abyssinia and Cyrenaica, red and white atrocities

in Spain, Japanese atrocities in China—in every case believed in or disbelieved in according to political predilection, with utter non-interest in the facts and with complete willingness to alter one's beliefs as soon as the political scene alters.

| Date | Atrocities (post 1918) Believed in by the Right | Believed in by the Left |
|---|---|---|
| *c.* 1920 | Turkish atrocities (Smyrna) Sinn Fein atrocities Bolshevik atrocities | Turkish atrocities (Smyrna) Black & Tan atrocities British atrocities in India (Amritsar) |
| 1923 | | French atrocities (the Ruhr) |
| 1928 | | American atrocities (Nicaragua) (?) |
| 1933 | Bolshevik atrocities (Ukraine famine) | |
| 1934–9 | | Nazi atrocities |
| 1935 | | Italian atrocities (Abyssinia and Cyrenaica) |
| 1936–9 | Red atrocities in Spain | Fascist atrocities in Spain |
| 1937 | Bolshevik atrocities (the purges) | Japanese atrocities (Nanking) |
| 1939 *et seq.* | German atrocities | British atrocities (the ss *Dunera* etc) |
| 1941 *et seq.* | Japanese atrocities | |

*13 June*

The most impressive fact about the Molotov visit is that the Germans knew nothing about it. Not a word on the radio about Molotov's presence in London till the signature of the treaty was officially announced, although all the while the German radio was shouting about the Bolshevisation of Britain. Obviously they would have spilt the beans if they had really known. Taken in conjunction with certain other things (e.g. the capture last year of two very amateurish spies dropped by parachute, with portable wireless transmitters and actually with chunks of German sausage in their suitcases) this suggests that the German spy system in this country cannot be up to much. . . .

*15 June*
From BBC monitoring report.

Prague (Czech Home Stations) in German for Protectorate.
10.6.42. *Heydrich Revenge: Village Wiped Out: All Men Shot:*
ANNOUNCEMENT
It is officially announced: The search and investigation for the murderers of SS *Obergruppenführer* Gen. Heydrich has established unimpeachable indications (sic) that the population of the locality of Lidice, near Kladno, supported and gave assistance to the circle (sic) of perpetrators in question. In spite of the interrogation of the local inhabitants, the pertinent means of evidence were secured without the help of the population. The attitude of the inhabitants to the outrage thus manifested, is emphasised also by other acts hostile to the Reich, by the discoveries of printed matter hostile to the Reich, of dumps of arms and ammunition, of an illegal wireless transmitter, and of huge quantities of controlled goods, as well as by the fact that inhabitants of the locality are in active enemy service abroad. Since the inhabitants of this village (sic) have flagrantly violated the laws which have been issued, by their activity and by the support given to the murderers of SS *Obergruppenführer* Heydrich, the male adults have been shot, the women have been sent to a concentration camp and the children have been handed over to appropriate educational authorities. The buildings of the locality have been levelled to the ground, and the name of the community has been obliterated.
(Note: This is an identical repetition, in German, of an announcement made in Czech from Prague at 1900, when reception was very bad.) . . .

No question now that the Second Front has been decided on. All the papers talk of it as a certainty and Moscow is publicising it widely. Whether it is really feasible remains to be seen, of course.

*21 June*
The thing that strikes one in the BBC—and it is evidently the same in various of the other departments—is not so much the moral squalor and the ultimate futility of what we are doing, as the feeling of frustration, the impossibility of getting *anything* done, even any successful piece of scoundrelism. Our policy is so ill-defined, the

disorganisation is so great, there are so many changes of plan and the fear and hatred of intelligence are so all-pervading, that one cannot plan any sort of wireless campaign whatever. When one plans some series of talks, with some more or less definite propaganda line behind it, one is first told to go ahead, then choked off on the ground that this or that is "injudicious" or "premature", then told again to go ahead, then told to water everything down and cut out any plain statements that may have crept in here and there, then told to "modify" the series in some way that removes its original meaning; and then at the last moment the whole thing is suddenly cancelled by some mysterious edict from above and one is told to improvise some different series which one feels no interest in and which in any case has no definite idea behind it. One is constantly putting sheer rubbish on the air because of having talks which sound too intelligent cancelled at the last moment. In addition the organisation is so over-staffed that numbers of people have almost literally nothing to do. But even when one manages to get something fairly good on the air one is weighed down by the knowledge that hardly anybody is listening. Except, I suppose, in Europe, the BBC simply isn't listened to overseas, a fact known to everyone concerned with overseas broadcasting. Some listener research has been done in America and it is known that in the whole of the USA about 300,000 people listen to the BBC. In India or Australia the number would not be anywhere near that. It has come out recently that (two years after the Empire service was started) plenty of Indians with shortwave sets don't even know that the BBC broadcasts to India.

It is the same with the only other public activity I take part in, the Home Guard. After two years no real training has been done, no specialised tactics worked out, no battle positions fixed upon, no fortifications built—all this owing to endless changes of plan and complete vagueness as to what we are supposed to be aiming at. Details of organisation, battle positions, etc have been changed so frequently that hardly anyone knows at any given moment what the current arrangements are supposed to be. To give just one example, for well over a year our company has been trying to dig a system of trenches in Regents Park, in case airborne troops should land there. Though dug over and over again these trenches have never once been in a completed state, because when they are half done there is always a change of plan and fresh orders. Ditto with everything. Whatever one undertakes, one starts out with the knowledge that presently there will come a sudden change of orders, and then another change, and so on indefinitely. Nothing ever happens except continuous dithering, resulting in progressive disillusionment all round. The best one can hope is that it is much the same on the other side.

### 24 June

Listened in last night to Lord Haw-Haw—not Joyce, who apparently has been off the air for some time, but a man who sounded to me like a South African, followed by another with more of a cockney voice. There was a good deal about the Congress of the Free India movement in Bangkok. Was amazed to notice that all the Indian names were mispronounced, and grossly mispronounced—e.g. Ras Behari Bose rendered as "Rash Beery Bose".[1] Yet after all the Indians who are broadcasting from Germany are available for advice on these points. They probably go in and out of the same building as Lord Haw-Haw every day. It is rather encouraging to see this kind of slovenliness happening on the other side as well.

### 26 June

Everyone very defeatist after the Libya business.[2] Some of the papers going cold on the Second Front again. Tom Driberg ("William Hickey") wins the Malden by-election, scoring twice as many votes as the Conservative candidate. That makes 4 out of the last 6 elections that the Government has lost.

### 1 July

At Callow End, Worcs (staying on a farm). No noise except aeroplanes, birds, and the mowers cutting the hay. No mention of the war, except with reference to Italian prisoners, who are working on some of the farms. They seem to be considered good workers, and for fruit-picking are preferred to the town people who come out from Worcester and are described as "artful". In spite of the feeding difficulties, plenty of pigs, poultry, geese and turkeys about. Cream for every meal at this place.

[1] Ras Behari Bose, an Indian nationalist who had worked for his country's independence since 1911. He was held responsible for the organisation of certain terrorist movements and in 1915 went to Japan to try to mobilise Asian support for the Indian Independence League which organised the Indian International Army. In 1943 the leadership of this army passed to Subhas Chandra Bose.

[2] On 20 June Tobruk had fallen to the Germans, marking a bad set-back in the North African campaign.

Huge bombers flying overhead all day. Also aeroplanes doing extraordinary things, e.g. towing other planes by a wire (perhaps gliders?) or carrying smaller planes perched on their backs.

### 3 July

Vote of censure defeated 475–25. This figure means that there were very few abstentions. The same trick as usual—the debate twisted into a demand for a vote of confidence in Churchill himself, which has to be given, since there is no one to take Churchill's place. Things are made much easier for the Government by the obvious bad motives of some of its chief attackers, e.g. Hore-Belisha.[1] I don't know how much longer this comedy can go on, but not much longer.

No reference to the Second Front in Churchill's speech.

The Japanese are evidently going to attack Russia fairly soon. They appear to be firmly lodged in the outer Aleutians, which can't have any meaning except as a move to cut communications between Russia and the USA.

The pinks are panicking to an extent they haven't equalled since Dunkirk. The *NS*'s leading article is headed "Facing the Spectre". They take the loss of Egypt for granted. Heaven knows whether this will actually happen, but these people have prophesied the loss of Egypt so often before that their doing so again is almost enough to persuade one that it won't happen. It is curious how they always do what the Germans want them to do—e.g. for some time past, demanding that we stop the raids on Germany and send our bombers to Egypt. A little earlier we were to send our bombers to India. In each case the same move as was being demanded by the German "freedom" stations. A thing that strikes me also is the airy disdain with which all the pinks talk of our air raids on Germany—air raids make very little impression etc etc. And these are the people who squealed loudest during the blitz on London. . . .

### 10 July

A day or two ago a couple of lorries belonging to the navy arrived with a party of Wrens[2] and sailors who put in several hours work

---

[1] Leslie Hore-Belisha (1898–1957), MP (National Liberal 1923–42, Independent 1942–45). He became Secretary for War in 1937, and was dismissed by Chamberlain in 1940. Churchill did not give him a place in his government and throughout the war Hore-Belisha remained out of office.

[2] Women's Royal Naval Service.

weeding out the turnips in Mr Phillips's field. All the village women
delighted by the appearance of the sailors in their blue tousers and
white singlets. "Don't they look clean, like! I like sailors. They
always look so clean." The sailors and Wrens also seemed to enjoy
their outing and drinks in the pub afterwards. It appeared that they
belonged to some volunteer organisation which sends workers out
as they are needed. Mrs Phillips explains it: "It's the voluntary
organisation from Malvern. Sometimes it's ATS[1] they send and
sometimes it's sailors. Of course we like having them. Well, it makes
you a bit independent of your own work-people, you see. The
work-people, they're awful nowadays. Just do so much and no
more. They know you can't do without them, you see. And you
can't get a woman to do a bit indoors nowadays. The girls won't
stay here, with no picture-house in the village. I do have a
woman who comes in, but I can't get any work out of her. It
helps a bit when you get a few voluntary workers. Makes you more
independent, like."

How right and proper it all is, when you consider how necessary
it is that agricultural work should not be neglected, and how right
and proper also that town people should get a bit of contact with the
soil. Yet these voluntary organisations, plus the work done by
soldiers in haymaking etc and Italian prisoners, are simply blackleg
labour. . . .

The "Blue Bell" again shut for lack of beer. Quite serious boozing
for 4 or 5 days of the week, then drought. Sometimes, however, when
they are shut the local officers are to be seen drinking in a private
room, the common soldiers as well as the labourers being shut out.
The "Red Lion" in the next village goes on a different system which
the proprietor explains to me: "I don't hold with giving it all to the
summer visitors. If beer's short, let the locals come first, I say. A lot
of days I keep the front door shut, and then only the locals know the
way in at the back. A man that's working in the fields needs his beer,
'specially with the food they got to eat nowadays. But I rations 'em. I
says to 'em, 'Now look here, you want your beer regular, don't you?
Wouldn't you rather have a pint with your dinner every day than four
pints one day and three the next.' Same with the soldiers. I don't like
to refuse beer to a soldier, but I only lets 'em have a pint their first
drink. After that it's 'Half pints only, boys.' Like that it gets shared
out a bit."

[1] Auxiliary Territorial Service, the women's branch of the army.

*22 July*

From Ahmed Ali's last letter from India:

"Here is a little bit of old Delhi which might interest you.

In a busy street a newsboy was shouting in Urdu: 'Pandit Jaw-aharlal saying his rosary the other way round.' What he meant was that he had changed his attitude towards the Government. Questioned he said: 'You can never be sure of him; today he says side with the Government and help in the war effort, tomorrow just the opposite.' He turned away from me and began shouting his cry, adding: 'Jawaharlal has given a challenge to the Government.' I could not find this 'challenge' in the papers.

Other newsboys selling Urdu papers: 'Germany has smashed Russia in the very first attack.' Needless to say I read just the opposite in my English papers the next morning. Obviously the Urdu papers had reported what Berlin had said. No one stops the newsboys from shouting what they like.

One day going in a 'tonga' I heard the driver shout to his horse as he shied: 'Why do you get back like our Sarkar! Go forward like Hitler,' and he swore.

Its rather fun going out to the bazaars and markets and listening to the loud gossip—provided, of course, it is not unbearably hot. I shall tell you more from time to time, if you are interested."

*23 July*

I now make entries in this diary much more seldom than I used to, for the reason that I literally have not any spare time. And yet I am doing nothing that is not futility and have less and less to show for the time I waste. It seems to be the same with everyone—the most fearful feeling of frustration, of just footling round doing imbecile things, not imbecile because they are a part of the war and war is inherently foolish, but things which in fact *don't* help or in any way affect the war effort, but are considered necessary by the huge bureaucratic machine in which we are all caught up. Much of the stuff that goes out from the BBC is just shot into the stratosphere, not listened to by anybody, and *known* to those responsible for it to be not listened to by anybody. And round this futile stuff hundreds of skilled workers are grouped, costing the country tens of thousands per annum, and tagging on to them are thousands of others who in effect have no real job but have found themselves a quiet niche and are sitting in it pretending to work. The same everywhere, especially in the Ministries.

However, the bread one casts on the waters sometimes fetches up
in strange places. We did a series of 6 talks on modern English
literature, very highbrow and I believe, completely un-listened-to in
India. Hsiao Chi'en, a Chinese student, reads the talks in the
*Listener* and is so impressed that he begins writing a book in Chinese
on modern western literature, drawing largely on our talks. So the
propaganda aimed at India misses India and accidentally hits China.
Perhaps the best way to influence India would be by broadcasting
to China.

The Indian Communist Party, and its press, legalised again. I
should say after this they will have to take the ban off the *Daily
Worker*; otherwise the position is too absurd.

This reminds me of the story David Owen told me and which I
believe I didn't enter in this diary. Cripps on his arrival in India asked
the Viceroy to release the interned Communists. The Viceroy
consented (I believe most of them have been released since), but at
the last moment got cold feet and said nervously: "But how can you
be sure they're really Communists?"

We are going to have to increase our consumption of potatoes by
20 per cent, so it is said. Partly to save bread, and partly to dispose of
this year's potato crop, which is enormous.

*26 July*
Yesterday and today, on the Home Guard manoeuvres, passing
various small camps of soldiers in the woods, radiolocation stations
etc. Struck by the appearance of the soldiers, their magnificent health
and the brutalised look in their faces. All young and fresh, with
round fat limbs and rosy faces with beautiful clear skins. But sullen
brutish expressions—not fierce or wicked in any way, but simply
stupefied by boredom, loneliness, discontent, endless tiredness and
mere physical health.

*27 July*
Talking today with Sultana, one of the Maltese broadcasters. He
says he is able to keep in fairly good touch with Malta and conditions
are very bad there. "The last letter I get this morning was like a—
how you say?—(much gesticulation) like a sieve. All the pieces what
the censor cut out, you understand. But I make something out of it,
all the same." He went on to tell me, among other things, that 5 lb
of potatoes now cost the equivalent of 8 shillings. He considers that

of the two convoys which recently endeavoured to reach Malta the one from England, which succeeded in getting there, carried munitions, and the one from Egypt, which failed to get there, carried food. I said, "Why can't they send dehydrated food by plane?" He shrugged his shoulders, seeming to feel instinctively that the British government would never go to that much trouble over Malta. Yet it seems that the Maltese are solidly pro-British, thanks to Mussolini, no doubt.

The German broadcasts are claiming that Voroshilov is in London, which is not very likely and has not been rumoured here. Probably a shot in the dark, to offset their recent failure over Molotov, and made on the calculation that *some* high-up Russian military delegate is likely to be here at this moment. If the story should turn out to be true, I shall have to revise my ideas about the German secret service in this country.

The crowd at the Second Front meeting in Trafalgar Square yesterday estimated at 40,000 in the right-wing papers and 60,000 in the left-wing. Perhaps 50,000 in reality. My spy reports that in spite of the present Communist line of "all power to Churchill", the Communist speakers in fact attacked the Government very violently.

*28 July*
Today I have read less newspapers than usual, but the ones I have seen have gone cold on the Second Front, except for the *News Chronicle*. The *Evening News* published an anti-Second Front article by General Brownrigg on its front page. I remarked on this to Herbert Read who said gloomily "The Government has told them to shut up about it." It is true of course that if they are intending to start something they must still seem to deny it. Read said he thought the position in Russia was desperate and seemed very upset about it, though in the past he has been even more anti-Stalin than I. I said to him, "Don't you feel quite differently towards the Russians now they are in a jam?" and he agreed. For that matter I felt quite differently towards England when I saw that England was in a jam. Looking back, I see that I was anti-Russian (or more exactly anti-Stalin) during the years when Russia appeared to be powerful, militarily and politically, i.e. 1933 to 1941. Before and after those dates I was pro-Russian. One could interpret this in several different ways.

A small raid on the outskirts of London last night. The new rocket guns, some of which are now manned by Home Guards, were in action and are said to have brought down some planes (8 planes down altogether). This is the first time the Home Guard can properly be said to have been in action, a little over two years after its formation.

The Germans never admit damage to military objectives, but they acknowledge civilian casualties after our bigger raids. After the Hamburg raid of 2 nights ago they described the casualties as heavy. The papers here reproduce this with pride. Two years ago we would all have been aghast at the idea of killing civilians. I remember saying to someone during the blitz, when the RAF were hitting back as best they could, "In a year's time you'll see headlines in the *Daily Express*: 'Successful Raid on Berlin Orphanage. Babies Set on Fire'." It hasn't come to that yet, but that is the direction we are going in.

*1 August*

If my figures given are correct, the Germans have lost about 10 per cent of their strength in each of the last raids. According to Peter Masefield[1] this isn't anything to do with the new guns but has all been done by the night fighters. He also told me off the record that the new FW 190 fighter is much better than any fighter we now have in actual service. An aircraft construction man named Bowyer who was broadcasting together with him agreed with this. Oliver Stewart[2] considers that the recent German raids are reconnaissance raids and that they intend starting the big blitz again soon, at any rate if they can get their hands free in Russia.

Not much to do over the bank holiday week-end. Busy at every odd moment making a hen-house. This kind of thing now needs great ingenuity owing to the extreme difficulty of getting hold of timber. No sense of guilt or time-wasting when I do anything of this type— on the contrary, a vague feeling that any *sane* occupation must be useful, or at any rate justifiable.

*3 August*

David Astor says Churchill is in Moscow. He also says that there isn't going to be any Second Front. However, if a Second Front is

---

[1] Peter Masefield (1914–   ), air correspondent of the *Sunday Times* 1940–3, personal adviser to Lord Beaverbrook 1943–5; now Chairman of the British Airports Authority.

[2] Major Oliver Stewart, MC, AFC, expert on aeronautics, journalist and broadcaster, and air correspondent of the *Manchester Guardian*, 1941–58.

intended, the Government must do all it can to spread the contrary impression beforehand, and D.A might be one of the people used to plant the rumour.

D.A says that when the commandos land the Germans never fight but always clear out immediately. No doubt they have orders to do so. This fact is not allowed to be published—presumable reason, to prevent the public from becoming over-confident.

According to David Astor, Cripps *does* intend to resign from the Government and has his alternative policy ready. He can't, of course, speak of this in public but will do so in private. However, I hear that [John] Macmurray when staying with Cripps recently could get nothing whatever out of him as to his political intentions.

### 4 August
The Turkish radio (among others) also says Churchill is in Moscow.

### 5 August
General dismay over the Government of India's rash act in publishing the documents seized in their police raid on Congress headquarters.[1] As usual the crucial document is capable of more than one interpretation and the resulting squabble will simply turn wavering elements in Congress more anti-British. The anti-Indian feeling which the publication has aroused in America, and perhaps Russia and China, is not in the long run any good to us.

The Russian Government announces discovery of a Tsarist plot, quite in the old style. I can't help a vague feeling that this is somehow linked up with the simultaneous discovery of Gandhi's plot with the Japanese.

### 7 August
Hugh Slater is very despondent about the war. He says that at the rate at which the Russians have been retreating it is not possible that Timoshenko[2] has really got his army away intact, as reported. He

---

[1] After the failure of Cripps's mission to India, Congress had become increasingly intransigent and at the beginning of August Gandhi had inaugurated a campaign of civil disobedience. As part of its attempts to ensure order, the Government of India raided Congress headquarters and seized the text of the original draft of the Resolution on Indian Independence submitted to the Congress Working Committee, which it then published.

[2] Marshal Timoshenko was succesfully withdrawing across the Don to defend the Volga near Stalingrad.

also says that the tone of the Moscow press and wireless shows that morale in Russia must be very bad. Like almost everyone I know, except Warburg, he considers that there isn't going to be any Second Front. This is the inference everyone draws from Churchill's visit to Moscow. People say, "Why should he go to Moscow to tell them we're going to open a Second Front? He must have gone there to tell them we can't do it." Everyone agrees with my suggestion that it would be a good job if Churchill were sunk on his way home, like Kitchener. Of course the possibility remains that Churchill isn't in Moscow.

Last night for the first time took a Sten gun to pieces. There is almost nothing to learn in it. No spare parts. If the gun goes seriously wrong you simply chuck it away and get another. Weight of the gun without magazine is $5\frac{1}{2}$ lb—weight of the tommy gun would be 12–15 lb. Estimated price is not 50/- as I had imagined, but 18/-. I can see a million or two million of these things, each with 500 cartridges and a book of instructions, floating down all over Europe on little parachutes. If the Government had the guts to do that they would really have burned their boats.

*9 August*
Fired the Sten gun for the first time today. No kick, no vibration, very little noise, and reasonable accuracy. Out of about 2500 rounds fired, 2 stoppages, in each case due to a dud cartridge—treatment, simply to work the bolt by hand.

*10 August*
Nehru, Gandhi, Azad[1] and many others in jail. Rioting over most of India, a number of deaths, countless arrests. Ghastly speech of Amery,[2] speaking of Nehru and Co as "wicked men", "saboteurs" etc. This of course broadcast on the Empire Service and re-broadcast by AIR.[3] The best joke of all was that the Germans did their best to jam it, unfortunately without success.

Terrible feeling of depression among the Indians and everyone sympathetic to India. Even Bokhari,[4] a Moslem League man,

[1] Abul Kalam Azad, Indian Nationalist Moslem Leader, spokesman for Congress in the 1945 negotiations for Independence.
[2] Leo Amery (1873–1955), a Conservative politician and MP, Secretary of State for India 1940–45.
[3] All India Radio.
[4] Zulfaqar Ali Bokhari, organiser of the Indian Programmes in the BBC Eastern Service.

almost in tears and talking about resigning from the BBC. It is strange, but quite truly the way the British Government is now behaving in India upsets me more than a military defeat.

*12 August*

Appalling policy hand-out this morning about affairs in India. The riots are of no significance—situation is well in hand—after all the numbers of deaths is not large etc etc. As to the participation of students in the riots, this is explained along "boys will be boys" lines. "We all know that students everywhere are only too glad to join in any kind of rag" etc etc. Almost everyone utterly disgusted. Some of the Indians when they hear this kind of stuff turn quite pale, a strange sight.

Most of the press taking a tough line, the Rothermere press disgustingly so. If these repressive measures in India are seemingly successful for the time being, the effects in this country will be very bad. All seems set for a big come-back by the reactionaries, and it almost begins to appear as though leaving Russia in the lurch were part of the manoeuvre. . . .

*14 August*

Horrabin[1] was broadcasting today, and as always we introduced him as the man who drew the maps for Wells's *Outline of History* and Nehru's *Glimpses of World History*. This had been extensively trailed and advertised beforehand, Horrabin's connection with Nehru naturally being a draw with Indian listeners. Today the reference to Nehru was cut out from the announcement—Nehru being in prison and therefore having become bad.

*18 August*

From Georges Kopp's[2] last letter from Marseilles after some rigmarole about the engineering work he has been doing. . . . "I am

---

[1] J.F. Horrabin (1884–1962), journalist and illustrator; on the left wing of the Labour Party; Labour MP 1929–31; achieved a considerable reputation for his educational maps and atlases, combining geography with historical fact to present a broad survey of world economic problems.

[2] Georges Kopp had been the commander of the POUM unit with which Orwell served in Spain. They remained close friends until Kopp's death in 1951. He had joined the French Foreign Legion in September 1939, was captured by the Germans in June 1940, had escaped and worked in France as an engineer and British agent until 1943 when he was flown to Britain by the Allies.

about to start production on an industrial scale. But I am not
at all certain that I shall actually go on, because I have definite
contracts with my firm, which has, I am afraid, developed lately
connections which reduce considerably its independence and it is
possible that another firm would eventually profit by my work,
which I should hate since I have no arrangements at all with the
latter and will not, for the time being, be prepared to sign any. If
I am compelled to stop, I really don't know what I am going to
do; I wish some of my very dear friends to whom I have written
repeatedly would not be as slow and as passive as they seem to be.
If no prospects open in this field, I contemplate to make use of
another process of mine, related to bridge-building, which, you may
remember, I have put into successful operation at San Mateo
before the war."

Translated: "I am afraid France is going into full alliance with
Germany. If the Second Front is not opened soon I shall do my
best to escape to England."

### 19 August

Big Commando raid on Dieppe today. Raid was still continuing
this evening. Just conceivably the first step in an invasion, or a
try-out for the first step, though I don't think so. The warning that
was broadcast to the French people that this was only a raid and
they were not to join in would in that case be a bluff.

### 22 August

David Astor very damping about the Dieppe raid, which he saw
at more or less close quarters and which he says was an almost
complete failure except for the very heavy destruction of German
fighter planes, which was not part of the plan. He says that the
affair was definitely misrepresented in the press and is now being
misrepresented in the reports to the PM and that the main facts
were:—Something over 5000 men were engaged, of whom at least
2000 were killed or prisoners. It was not intended to stay on shore
longer than was actually done (i.e. dawn till about 4 pm), but the
idea was to destroy all the defences of Dieppe, and the attempt to do
this was an utter failure. In fact only comparatively trivial damage
was done, a few batteries of guns knocked out etc and only one of
the 3 main parties really made its objective. The others did not get
far and many were massacred on the beach by artillery fire. The

defences were formidable and would have been difficult to deal with even if there had been artillery support, as the guns were sunk in the face of the cliff or under enormous concrete coverings. More tank-landing craft were sunk than got ashore. About 20 or 30 tanks were landed but none were got off again. The newspaper photos which showed tanks apparently being brought back to England were intentionally misleading. The general impression was that the Germans knew of the raid beforehand. Almost as soon as it was begun they had a man broadcasting a spurious "eye-witness" account from somewhere further up the coast, and another man broadcasting false orders in English. On the other hand the Germans were evidently surprised by the strength of the air support. Whereas normally they have kept their fighters on the ground so as to conserve their strength, they sent them into the air as soon as they heard that tanks were landing, and lost a number of planes variously estimated, but considered by some RAF officers to have been as high as 270. Owing to the British strength in the air the destroyers were able to lie outside Dieppe all day. One was sunk, but this was by a shore battery. When a request came to attack some objective on shore, the destroyers formed in line and raced inshore firing their forward guns while the fighter planes supported them overhead.

David Astor considers that this definitely proves that an invasion of Europe is impossible. Of course we can't feel sure that he hasn't been planted to say this, considering who his parents are. I can't help feeling that to get ashore at all at such a strongly defended spot, without either bomber support, artillery support except for the guns of the destroyers (4·9 guns I suppose), or airborne troops, was a considerable achievement.

### 25 August

One of the many rumours circulating among Indians here is that Nehru, Gandhi and others have been deported to South Africa. This is the kind of thing that results from press censorship and suppressing newspapers.

### 27 August

Ban on the *Daily Worker* lifted. It is to reappear on Sept 7th (same day as Churchill makes his statement to Parliament).

German radio again alleging S.C. Bose is in Penang. But the indications are that this was a slip of the tongue for R.B. Bose.

*29 August*
Advert in pub for pick-me-up tablets—phenacetin or something of
the kind:

BLITZ

Thoroughly recommended by the
Medical Profession
The
"LIGHTNING"
Marvellous discovery
Millions take this Remedy for
for
Hangover
War Nerves
Influenza
Headache
Toothache
Neuralgia
Sleeplessness
Rheumatism
Depression etc etc
Contains no Aspirin

Another rumour among the Indians about Nehru—this time that
he has escaped.

*7 September*
There is evidently trouble in Syria. Hand-out this morning to the
effect that—most unfortunately and much against HM Government's will—General de Gaulle is insisting that Syria is still under
a French Mandate and it is impossible yet to make a treaty, as in
the case of Iraq. General de Gaulle's attitude is considered most
deplorable, but as he *is*, after all, the accredited leader of the Free
French and the whole legal position is very obscure (the matter
should be decided upon by the League of Nations which unfortunately no longer exists), HM Government is unable etc etc etc.
In other words the Syrians will get no treaty, the blame for this is
placed on our puppet de Gaulle, and if possible we shall swipe Syria
for ourselves. When I heard this hollow rubbish trotted out by
Rushbrook-Williams[1] this morning, and we all had to listen and

[1] L.F. Rushbrook-Williams, at this time Eastern Service Director of the BBC.

keep straight faces, there came into my head, I don't quite know why, the lines from Hardy's *Dynasts* about the crowning of Napoleon in Rome:

> Do not the prelate's accents falter thin,
> His lips with inheld laughter grow deformed,
> In blessing one whose aim is but to win
> The golden seat that other bums have warmed?

The *Daily Worker* reappeared today—very mild, but they are urging *a.* a Second Front, *b.* all help to Russia in the way of arms etc, and *c.* a demagogic programme of higher wages all round which would be utterly incompatible with *a.* and *b.*

## 10 September

Lecturing last night at Morley College, Lambeth. Small hall, about 100 people, working-class intelligentsia (same sort of audience as Left Book Club[1] branch). During the questions afterwards, no less than 6 people asked, "Does not the lecturer think that it was a great mistake to lift the ban from the *Daily Worker*"—reasons given, that the *DW*'s loyalty is not reliable and it is a waste of paper. Only one woman stood up for the *DW*, evidently a Communist at whom one or two of the others expressed impatience ("Oh, she's always saying that!"). This after a year during which there has been a ceaseless clamour from Left organisations for the lifting of the ban. One is constantly being thrown out in one's judgements because one listens to the articulate minority and forgets the other 99 per cent. Cf Munich, when the mass of the people were almost certainly behind Chamberlain's policy, though to read the *New Statesman* etc you wouldn't have thought so.

## 15 September

Ghastly feeling of impotence over the India business, Churchill's speeches, the evident intention of the Blimps to have one more try at being what they consider tough, and the impudent way in which the newspapers can misrepresent the whole issue, well knowing that the public will never know enough or take enough interest to

[1] The Left Book Club had been founded and published by Victor Gollancz in 1936. It still continued to publish a book a month on anti-Fascist or Socialist topics and the practice of holding local group meetings had been revived in the middle of 1942 and some fifty branches formed.

verify the facts. This last is the worst symptom of all—though actually our own apathy about India is not worse than the non-interest of Indian intellectuals in the struggle against Fascism in Europe.

*21 September*

Yesterday met Liddell Hart for the first time . . . . In a great stew about the barbarism of bombing Lübeck. Considered that during the wars of recent centuries the British have the worst record of all for atrocities and destructiveness. Although, of course, strongly opposed to the Second Front, also anxious for us to call off the bombing. There is no point in doing it, as it can achieve nothing and does not weaken Germany. On the other hand we ought not to have started the bombing in the first place (he stuck to it that it was we who started it), as it merely brought heavier reprisals on ourselves.

Osbert Sitwell was also there. . . . Both of them professed to be disgusted by our seizure of Vichy colonies. Sitwell said that our motto was, "When things look bad, retake Madagascar". He said that in Cornwall in case of invasion the Home Guard have orders to shoot all artists. I said that in Cornwall this might be all for the best. Sitwell: "Some instinct would lead them to the good ones."

*22 September*

Most of the ammunition for our Sten guns is Italian, or rather made in Germany for Italy. I fancy this must be the first weapon the British army has had whose bore was measured in millimetres instead of inches. They were going to make a new cheap automatic weapon, and having the vast stocks of ammunition captured in Abyssinia handy, manufactured the guns to fit the cartridges instead of the other way about. The advantage is that the ammunition of almost any continental sub-machine-gun will fit it. It will be interesting to see whether the Germans or Japanese come out with a ·303 weapon to fit captured British ammunition.

*28 September*

Open-air church parade in Regents Park yesterday. How touching the scene ought to be—the battalion in hollow square, band of the Coldstream Guards, the men standing bareheaded (beautiful autumn day, faint mist and not a leaf stirring, dogs gambolling round) and singing the hymns as best they could. But unfortunately there was a sermon with the jingoistic muck which is usual on these occasions and which makes me go pro-German for as long as I listen to it. Also a special prayer "for the people of Stalingrad"—the Judas kiss. A detail that gets me down on these occasions is the clergyman's white surplice, which looks all wrong against a background of military uniforms. Struck by the professionalism of the band, especially the bandmaster (an officer in the black peaked cap of the Guards). As each prayer drew towards its close, a stirring in the band, the trombones come out of their leather suitcases, the bandmaster's baton comes up, and they are ready to snap into the Amen just as the priest reaches "through Jesus Christ our Lord".

*5 October*

New Viceroy of India to be appointed shortly. No clue as to who he will be. Some say General Auchinleck—who, it is said, gets on well with left-wing Indians.

Long talk with Brander,[1] who is back after his 6 months tour in India. His conclusions so depressing that I can hardly bring myself to write them down. Briefly—affairs are much worse in India than anyone here is allowed to realise, the situation is in fact retrievable but won't be retrieved because the Government is determined to make no real concessions, hell will break loose when and if there is a Japanese invasion, and our broadcasts are utterly useless because nobody listens to them. Brander did say, however, that the Indians listen to the BBC *news*, because they regard it as more truthful than that given out by Tokyo or Berlin. He considers that we should broadcast news and music and nothing else. This is what I have been saying for some time past.

*10 October*

Today in honour of the anniversary of the Chinese Revolution, the Chinese flag was hoisted over Broadcasting House. Unfortunately it was upside down.

According to David Astor, Cripps is going to resign shortly— pretext, that the War Cabinet is a sham, Churchill being in reality the sole power in it.

[1] Laurence Brander, author, had lectured on English literature in India for twelve years before the war. From 1941–4 he was employed by the BBC as Intelligence Officer, Eastern Service.

*11 October*
The authorities in Canada have now chained up a number of
German prisoners equal to the number of British prisoners chained
up in Germany. What the devil are we coming to?...[1]

*17 October*
Heard a "Jew joke" on the stage at the Players' theatre last night—
a mild one, and told by a Jew, but still slightly anti-Jew in tendency.

More Second Front rumours. The date this time is given as October 20th, an unlikely date, being a Tuesday. It seems pretty clear
that something is going to happen in West or North-West Africa,
however.

*15 November*
Church bells rung this morning—in celebration for the victory in
Egypt. The first time that I have heard them in over two years.

[1] See also 37.

# Appendix I

BOOKS BY OR CONTAINING CONTRIBUTIONS BY GEORGE ORWELL

*Down and Out in Paris and London*, London, 1933; New York, 1933.
*Burmese Days*, New York, 1934; London, 1935.
*A Clergyman's Daughter*, London, 1935; New York, 1936.
*Keep the Aspidistra Flying*, London, 1936; New York, 1956.
*The Road to Wigan Pier*, London, 1937; New York, 1958.
*Homage to Catalonia*, London, 1938; New York, 1952.
*Coming Up for Air*, London, 1939; New York, 1950.
*Inside the Whale*, London, 1940.
*The Lion and the Unicorn*, London, 1941.
*The Betrayal of the Left*, by Victor Gollancz, George Orwell, John Strachey and others, London, 1941.
*Victory Or Vested Interest?* by G.D.H. Cole, George Orwell and others, London, 1942.
*Talking to India*, edited with an introduction by George Orwell, London, 1943.
*Animal Farm*, London, 1945; New York, 1946.
*Critical Essays*, London, 1946; (American title) *Dickens, Dali and Others*, New York, 1946.
*James Burnham and the Managerial Revolution*, London, 1946 (Pamphlet).
*Love of Life and Other Stories*, by Jack London. Introduction by George Orwell, London, 1946.
*The English People*, London, 1947.
*British Pamphleteers*, Vol. 1, edited by George Orwell and Reginald Reynolds. Introduction by George Orwell, London, 1948.
*Nineteen Eighty-Four*, London, 1949; New York, 1949.

POSTHUMOUS COLLECTIONS

*Shooting an Elephant*, London, 1950; New York, 1950.
*Such, Such Were the Joys*, New York, 1953.
*England Your England*, London, 1953.
*The Orwell Reader*, edited by Richard H. Rovere, New York, 1956.
*Collected Essays*, London, 1961.

# Appendix II

## Chronology

### 1940

On 11 March *Inside the Whale* was published by Victor Gollancz.

On 13 March Orwell returned home to The Stores, Wallington, after spending six weeks, part of the time ill with influenza, at Crooms Hill, Greenwich. His wife, Eileen, had been living since September 1939 at this address, the home of her brother Laurence O'Shaughnessy, partly to be company for his wife, Gwen, when he went into the army, but principally to take a job in the Censorship Department in order to supplement Orwell's meagre earnings.

His first contribution to *Tribune*, a review of *The Memoirs of Sergeant Bourgogne*, appeared in the issue of 29 March 1940. In the spring of this year he was projecting a long novel in three parts which he had had in his mind since the late autumn of 1938. Financial worries, his disappointment at being rejected as medically unfit by the army or to find any job in which he could serve his country, and the distraction of the war situation prevented his settling down to the writing of it.

During May Orwell left Wallington, still keeping on, however, The Stores as a country cottage till 1947, and he and his wife moved into 18 Dorset Chambers, Chagford Street, near Regent's Park. On 18 May Orwell's first piece of theatre criticism for *Time and Tide* appeared. He joined the Local Defence Volunteers, formed on 10 May, and became a sergeant in "C" Company of the 5th County of London Home Guard Battalion in St John's Wood. At the beginning of June Laurence O'Shaughnessy was killed at Dunkirk.

From August to October Orwell was writing *The Lion and the Unicorn*, which was to be the first of the Searchlight Books. This was a series of booklets focusing attention on war-time problems and offering solutions to them, which was edited by T.R. Fyvel and Orwell for Secker & Warburg. Out of the projected seventeen titles only ten were published over the next two years.

### 1941

On 3 January Orwell wrote the first of the fifteen "London Letters" he contributed to *Partisan Review* over the next five and a half years.

On 19 February *The Lion and the Unicorn* was published. On 3 March Victor Gollancz published *The Betrayal of the Left* which contained two chapters by Orwell, "Fascism and Democracy" and "Patriots and Revolutionaries". By the beginning of April Orwell and his wife, who about this time gave up working in the Censorship Department, had moved to a flat at 111 Langford Court, Abbey Road, St John's Wood. On 18 August Orwell joined the British Broadcasting Corporation at a salary of £640 a year, as a Talks Assistant, later becoming Talks Producer, in the Indian section of its Eastern Service.

## 1942–43

During these two years, in addition to his full-time work at the BBC, Orwell contributed to *Horizon, Partisan Review, Tribune,* the *New Statesman and Nation,* and the *Nation* (New York) and wrote for *Poetry London* and *New Road.* He also carried out Home Guard and firewatching duties. In April 1942 Eileen Blair began working for the Ministry of Food organising the "Kitchen Front" broadcast talks.

On 8 March 1942 Orwell contributed an unsigned political comment, "Mood of the Moment", to the *Observer* and on 10 May there appeared his review of Edmund Wilson's *The Wound and the Bow,* the first of the many articles and reviews Orwell wrote for the *Observer* until February 1949. On 15 May Routledge published *Victory or Vested Interest?* which included the lecture "Culture and Democracy" Orwell had given to the Fabian Society on 22 November 1941.

By the summer of 1942 Orwell and his wife had moved to a flat at 10a Mortimer Crescent, Maida Vale. At the end of June Orwell spent a fortnight's fishing holiday at Callow End, Worcestershire. In 1942 Orwell's mother and his sister, Avril Blair, came to live in Alexandra Road, which adjoined Mortimer Crescent. Ida Blair worked at Selfridges and Avril Blair worked in a sheet metal factory at King's Cross. On 19 March 1943 Ida Blair, aged 67, died of a heart attack.

On 18 November 1943 Allen & Unwin published *Talking to India: A Selection of English Language Broadcasts to India,* edited with an introduction by George Orwell. On 23 November Orwell left the Home Guard on medical grounds. He resigned from the BBC on 24 November and before the end of the month he had become literary editor of *Tribune.* In November he started writing *Animal Farm.*

Ian Angus

# INDEX

## Compiled by Oliver Stallybrass

All numbers refer to pages, not items. Footnotes are indicated by "n" or "(n)" after the page-number; "n" refers *only* to the footnote, "(n)" to text *and* footnote. The *first* footnote to any individual person usually includes a brief biographical outline.

Subheadings are arranged in order of first page reference, except where chronological order (e.g. Orwell: *chronology*) or alphabetical order (e.g. Orwell: *writings*: individual titles) is clearly more appropriate.

George Orwell is abbreviated to GO throughout.

*Books by George Orwell*

available in paperback editions from
Harcourt Brace Jovanovich, Inc.

DOWN AND OUT IN PARIS AND LONDON

BURMESE DAYS

A CLERGYMAN'S DAUGHTER

KEEP THE ASPIDISTRA FLYING

THE ROAD TO WIGAN PIER

HOMAGE TO CATALONIA

COMING UP FOR AIR

DICKENS, DALI & OTHERS

A COLLECTION OF ESSAYS

THE ORWELL READER: FICTION, ESSAYS AND REPORTAGE

THE COLLECTED ESSAYS, JOURNALISM AND LETTERS
OF GEORGE ORWELL:

I. An Age Like This, 1920–1940

II. My Country Right or Left, 1940–1943

III. As I Please, 1943–1945

IV. In Front of Your Nose, 1945–1950

*Four volumes, boxed set*